W9-ANO-128

Amsterdam

Rob van Driesum
Nikki Hall

LONELY PLANET PUBLICATIONS
Melbourne • Oakland • London • Paris

Amsterdam
2nd edition – June 2000
First published – July 1997

Published by
Lonely Planet Publications Pty Ltd A.C.N. 005 607 983
192 Burwood Rd, Hawthorn, Victoria 3122, Australia

Lonely Planet Offices
Australia PO Box 617, Hawthorn, Victoria 3122
USA 150 Linden St, Oakland, CA 94607
UK 10a Spring Place, London NW5 3BH
France 1 rue du Dahomey, 75011 Paris

Photographs
Many of the images in this guide are available for licensing from
Lonely Planet Images.
email: lpi@lonelyplanet.com.au

Front cover photograph
Architecture along the Rokin, Amsterdam (Richard Nebesky; image
digitally modified by Lonely Planet)

ISBN 0 86442 789 1

text & maps © Lonely Planet 2000
photos © photographers as indicated 2000

Printed by The Bookmaker Pty Ltd
Printed in China

All rights reserved. No part of this publication may be reproduced,
stored in a retrieval system or transmitted in any form by any means,
electronic, mechanical, photocopying, recording or otherwise, except
brief extracts for the purpose of review, without the written permission
of the publisher and copyright owner.

LONELY PLANET and the Lonely Planet logo are trademarks of Lonely
Planet Publications Pty Ltd.

**Although the authors
and Lonely Planet try
to make the informa-
tion as accurate as
possible, we accept
no responsibility for
any loss, injury or
inconvenience sus-
tained by anyone
using this book.**

Contents – Text

2 Contents – Text

Contents – Maps

The Authors

Rob van Driesum

Rob wrote the 1st edition and coordinated this update. He grew up in several Asian and African countries before moving to the Netherlands, where he finished school in The Hague and studied modern history at the University of Amsterdam. He lived in a canal house on Reguliersgracht for 11 years, studying and working as a history teacher, bartender and freelance journalist to finance his motorcycle travels. A motorcycle journey around the world was cut short in Australia, where he worked as a labourer, flower salesman, truck driver and motorcycle magazine editor before joining Lonely Planet to help set up its range of Europe titles. He is now Lonely Planet's Associate Publisher in charge of guidebooks. Though firmly ensconced in Mt Macedon outside of Melbourne, which he considers an ideal place to live, he still thinks of Amsterdam as 'home' and an ideal place to visit.

Nikki Hall

Nikki updated the Places to Eat, Entertainment and Shopping chapters. The gift of a Barbie doll from Hong Kong at the age of six left Melbourne-born Nikki in no doubt that there was a whole world of shopping beyond Australia's shores. Under the guise of homewares buyer and merchandiser she has since travelled the world searching for the perfect handbag, lipstick and vodka martini. Nikki has co-authored Lonely Planet's *Sydney Condensed* and *Amsterdam Condensed* guides and contributed to the Melbourne and Sydney *Out to Eat* restaurant guides. She also turns her hand to article writing for magazines and visual merchandising.

This Book

From the Publisher

This 2nd edition of *Amsterdam* was edited in Lonely Planet's Melbourne office by Shelley Muir with assistance from Kalya Ryan. Design and mapping were coordinated by Ann Jeffree with assistance from Chris Lee Ack, and Paul Dawson laid the book out. David Kemp and Maria Vallianos designed the cover, and Quentin Frayne compiled the Language chapter. Photographs were provided by Lonely Planet Images. Thanks to the Amsterdams Historisch Museum for kind permission to use historical illustrations.

From the Authors

Rob van Driesum It's difficult to research this sort of book while holding down a full-time job – help from others is invaluable. Many thanks to Jeremy Gray for last-minute checking; Doekes Lulofs, Reinier van den Hout and Wendy Bloemheuvel for tips and advice; Jules Marshall for information on digital Amsterdam; Marleen Slob, editor of the COC magazine, *XL*, for information on gay & lesbian Amsterdam; Peter van Brummelen, music critic of *Het Parool*, for information about the Amsterdam music scene; Els Wamsteeker from the Amsterdam Tourist Board; the good folk at Unica; Gerard Pieters from Amsterdam's Economic Development Department; and Imogen Franks, Jen Loy and Leonie Mugavin from LP's London, Oakland and Melbourne offices for transport details.

Much of the Excursions chapter was adapted from the Netherlands chapter in LP's *Western Europe*, written by Leanne Logan & Geert Cole.

I'm also indebted to my colleagues at Lonely Planet's Melbourne office who covered for me in my absence, and in particular to my editor, Shelley Muir, and cartographer, Ann Jeffree. Warm thanks also to my co-author, Nikki, who added panache to the book. Last but certainly not least, a heartfelt thanks to Liesbeth Blomberg for putting up with it all.

Nikki Hall Thanks to Alan Lazer, Neil Finaughty and Kelly McConville for assistance on gay listings, and Heleen d'Oliveira, Dia Roozemond, Anita and Daan Smeelen for their invaluable tips about Amsterdam's lesbian scene. A special thank you to Roel de Boer for incisive information on the city's club scene.

THANKS
Many thanks to the travellers who used the last edition and wrote to us with helpful hints, advice and interesting anecdotes. Your names appear in the back of this book.

5

Foreword

ABOUT LONELY PLANET GUIDEBOOKS

The story begins with a classic travel adventure: Tony and Maureen Wheeler's 1972 journey across Europe and Asia to Australia. Useful information about the overland trail did not exist at that time, so Tony and Maureen published the first Lonely Planet guidebook to meet a growing need.

From a kitchen table, then from a tiny office in Melbourne (Australia), Lonely Planet has become the largest independent travel publisher in the world, an international company with offices in Melbourne, Oakland (USA), London (UK) and Paris (France).

Today Lonely Planet guidebooks cover the globe. There is an ever-growing list of books and there's information in a variety of forms and media. Some things haven't changed. The main aim is still to help make it possible for adventurous travellers to get out there – to explore and better understand the world.

At Lonely Planet we believe travellers can make a positive contribution to the countries they visit – if they respect their host communities and spend their money wisely. Since 1986 a percentage of the income from each book has been donated to aid projects and human rights campaigns.

Updates Lonely Planet thoroughly updates each guidebook as often as possible. This usually means there are around two years between editions, although for more unusual or more stable destinations the gap can be longer. Check the imprint page (following the colour map at the beginning of the book) for publication dates.

Between editions up-to-date information is available in two free newsletters – the paper *Planet Talk* and email *Comet* (to subscribe, contact any Lonely Planet office) – and on our Web site at www.lonelyplanet.com. The *Upgrades* section of the Web site covers a number of important and volatile destinations and is regularly updated by Lonely Planet authors. *Scoop* covers news and current affairs relevant to travellers. And, lastly, the *Thorn Tree* bulletin board and *Postcards* section of the site carry unverified, but fascinating, reports from travellers.

Correspondence The process of creating new editions begins with the letters, postcards and emails received from travellers. This correspondence often includes suggestions, criticisms and comments about the current editions. Interesting excerpts are immediately passed on via newsletters and the Web site, and everything goes to our authors to be verified when they're researching on the road. We're keen to get more feedback from organisations or individuals who represent communities visited by travellers.

Lonely Planet gathers information for everyone who's curious about the planet – and especially for those who explore it first-hand. Through guidebooks, phrasebooks, activity guides, maps, literature, newsletters, image library, TV series and Web site we act as an information exchange for a worldwide community of travellers.

Research Authors aim to gather sufficient practical information to enable travellers to make informed choices and to make the mechanics of a journey run smoothly. They also research historical and cultural background to help enrich the travel experience and allow travellers to understand and respond appropriately to cultural and environmental issues.

Authors don't stay in every hotel because that would mean spending a couple of months in each medium-sized city and, no, they don't eat at every restaurant because that would mean stretching belts beyond capacity. They do visit hotels and restaurants to check standards and prices, but feedback based on readers' direct experiences can be very helpful.

Many of our authors work undercover, others aren't so secretive. None of them accept freebies in exchange for positive write-ups. And none of our guidebooks contain any advertising.

Production Authors submit their raw manuscripts and maps to offices in Australia, USA, UK or France. Editors and cartographers – all experienced travellers themselves – then begin the process of assembling the pieces. When the book finally hits the shops, some things are already out of date, we start getting feedback from readers and the process begins again ...

WARNING & REQUEST

Things change – prices go up, schedules change, good places go bad and bad places go bankrupt – nothing stays the same. So, if you find things better or worse, recently opened or long since closed, please tell us and help make the next edition even more accurate and useful. We genuinely value all the feedback we receive. Julie Young coordinates a well travelled team that reads and acknowledges every letter, postcard and email and ensures that every morsel of information finds its way to the appropriate authors, editors and cartographers for verification.

Everyone who writes to us will find their name in the next edition of the appropriate guidebook. They will also receive the latest issue of *Planet Talk*, our quarterly printed newsletter, or *Comet*, our monthly email newsletter. Subscriptions to both newsletters are free. The very best contributions will be rewarded with a free guidebook.

Excerpts from your correspondence may appear in new editions of Lonely Planet guidebooks, the Lonely Planet Web site, *Planet Talk* or *Comet*, so please let us know if you *don't* want your letter published or your name acknowledged.

Send all correspondence to the Lonely Planet office closest to you:

Australia: PO Box 617, Hawthorn, Victoria 3122
USA: 150 Linden St, Oakland, CA 94607
UK: 10A Spring Place, London NW5 3BH
France: 1 rue du Dahomey, 75011 Paris

Or email us at: talk2us@lonelyplanet.com.au

For news, views and updates see our Web site: www.lonelyplanet.com

HOW TO USE A LONELY PLANET GUIDEBOOK

The best way to use a Lonely Planet guidebook is any way you choose. At Lonely Planet we believe the most memorable travel experiences are often those that are unexpected, and the finest discoveries are those you make yourself. Guidebooks are not intended to be used as if they provide a detailed set of infallible instructions!

Contents All Lonely Planet guidebooks follow roughly the same format. The Facts about the Destination chapters or sections give background information ranging from history to weather. Facts for the Visitor gives practical information on issues like visas and health. Getting There & Away gives a brief starting point for researching travel to and from the destination. Getting Around gives an overview of the transport options when you arrive.

The peculiar demands of each destination determine how subsequent chapters are broken up, but some things remain constant. We always start with background, then proceed to sights, places to stay, places to eat, entertainment, getting there and away, and getting around information – in that order.

Heading Hierarchy Lonely Planet headings are used in a strict hierarchical structure that can be visualised as a set of Russian dolls. Each heading (and its following text) is encompassed by any preceding heading that is higher on the hierarchical ladder.

Entry Points We do not assume guidebooks will be read from beginning to end, but that people will dip into them. The traditional entry points are the list of contents and the index. In addition, however, some books have a complete list of maps and an index map illustrating map coverage.

There may also be a colour map that shows highlights. These highlights are dealt with in greater detail in the Facts for the Visitor chapter, along with planning questions and suggested itineraries. Each chapter covering a geographical region usually begins with a locator map and another list of highlights. Once you find something of interest in a list of highlights, turn to the index.

Maps Maps play a crucial role in Lonely Planet guidebooks and include a huge amount of information. A legend is printed on the back page. We seek to have complete consistency between maps and text, and to have every important place in the text captured on a map. Map key numbers usually start in the top left corner.

Although inclusion in a guidebook usually implies a recommendation we cannot list every good place. Exclusion does not necessarily imply criticism. In fact there are a number of reasons why we might exclude a place – sometimes it is simply inappropriate to encourage an influx of travellers.

Introduction

Amsterdam is a work of art, a living monument with some of Europe's finest 17th and 18th-century architecture. It's also at the cutting edge of social, cultural and economic developments thanks to its famed tolerance, which brings together people, ideas and products and allows them to flourish.

There's a lively arts scene, fantastic pubs and unrivalled nightlife. Gays and lesbians find the city a breath of fresh air. Affordable restaurants serve food from all corners of the globe and mix them successfully. Street artists – musicians, acrobats, fire-eaters – provide ready entertainment. Open-air markets sell anything from food and flowers to funky clothes, disused furniture and 78rpm records, and myriad shops full of quirky items line side streets and alleyways.

Despite the ready availability of sex and drugs there's surprisingly little violent crime. Whoever made this whole affair work has done a great job.

Amsterdam has often been called the Venice of the north, and in many respects the comparison is apt. Venice occupies a lagoon, Amsterdam a marshland where river meets sea, and both have had to struggle with water in order to survive (Venice has 117 islands, 150 canals and 400 bridges; Amsterdam has 90 islands, 160 canals and 1281 bridges). Both were city-states that built far-flung maritime trading empires. Both had a ruling class with strongly republican sentiments, whose wealth rested on money created through commerce and finance, not on inherited property. Both left a world-class legacy in visual arts.

But there are marked differences: Venice has no road traffic – only pedestrians and a large fleet of busy water craft; Amsterdam has 550,000 bicycles, fortunately not much road traffic any more, and little water transport apart from tourist boats. Venice is an architectural marvel full of tourists, but in the off season the place seems dead; Amsterdam is equally attractive and full of tourists, but in the off season it keeps powering along. In short, Amsterdam is a thriving city that's alive in all respects; Venice is a

Herengracht on the corner with Leidsegracht, painted in 1783 by Isaak Ouwater

museum with relatively little to sustain itself in the modern age.

The phrase 'cosmopolitan melting pot' is often used carelessly for cities around the world but it is appropriate for Amsterdam, which has always enticed migrants and non-conformists. Despite (or because of) this transient mix, people accept each other as they are and strive to be *gezellig*, a nigh-untranslatable term that means something like 'chummy' or 'convivial', a mood often experienced by people warmly chatting over a drink or two in a cosy 'brown' café.

The whole city is *gezellig* – buildings are attractive, intimate, very rarely imposing, and pleasantly balanced by tree-lined canals and scattered parks (Amsterdam is Europe's greenest capital city). Everything seems designed on a human scale. It is also compact and easily explored on foot, with frequent and efficient public transport to and from the central canal belt.

The rest of the country is compact too, and is serviced by an efficient train network.

Within an hour you can walk along the beach and through magnificent dunes; explore old fishing villages along the IJsselmeer; visit small but proud cities such as Haarlem, Leiden or Delft; admire Europe's most beautiful sculpture garden in the forested Hoge Veluwe national park; shop along the refined streets of The Hague; tour the busiest harbour in the world at Rotterdam; or cycle through endless, brightly coloured fields of blossoming bulbs.

On these sorts of trips you'll realise that Amsterdam is unique even within the Netherlands, with a mix of old and new, moral rectitude and sleaze, and traditional and alternative cultures that visitors both Dutch and foreign find baffling and delightful.

This book provides background reading, advice and tips, but a lot of things happen in Amsterdam that guidebook researchers can't always know about. Go out and discover the place for yourself: few cities are more rewarding.

Facts about Amsterdam

HISTORY
Birth of the City

The oldest archaeological finds in Amsterdam date from Roman times, when the IJ (pronounced as the 'ey' in 'they'), an arm of the shallow Zuiderzee or 'Southern Sea', formed part of the northern borders of the Roman Empire. Coins and a few artefacts betray human presence but there is no evidence of settlement.

This is not surprising because most of the region that later became known as Holland (in the west of the present-day Netherlands) was a soggy land of constantly shifting lakes, swamps and spongy peat lying at or below sea level. Its contours kept changing with fierce autumn storms and floods. This was certainly the case where the Amstel River emptied into the IJ – the site of what was to become Amsterdam.

Isolated farming communities gradually tamed the marshlands with ditches and dykes. Between 1150 and 1300 the south bank of the IJ was dyked all the way to the north of Haarlem. Dams were built across the rivers flowing into the IJ, with locks to let water out and boats in. Around 1200 there was a fishing community known as 'Aemstelredamme' – the dam built across the Amstel, at what is now Dam Square.

The distant feudal authorities (the bishop of Utrecht and later the Holy Roman Emperor) cared little for these massive water-engineering feats and the ever-present threat of dyke-bursts. So the local inhabitants, under the tutelage of the count of Holland, set up a network of work-and-maintenance groups and pooled their resources against the common foe. This tradition of local democracy and pioneering self-help fostered notions of local autonomy, and no doubt instilled a regard for individual opinions and contributions.

On 27 October 1275 the count of Holland granted toll freedom to those who lived around the Amstel dam, which meant they didn't have to pay tolls to sail through the locks and bridges of Holland. This event stands as the official founding of Amsterdam. The town had obviously become important in the count's power struggle with the bishop of Utrecht, and soon it received city rights – the right to self-government and taxation. Shortly after 1300, the count incorporated the surrounding areas into Holland, severing Amsterdam's ties with the bishopric of Utrecht for good.

Early Trade

The city grew rapidly. Agriculture in this marshland was difficult at the best of times so fishing remained important, but trade provided new opportunities for growth. Powerful cities of the day, such as Dordrecht, Utrecht, Haarlem, Delft and Leiden, concentrated on overland trade to and from the burgeoning economies of Flanders and northern Italy. Amsterdam, however, focused on maritime trade in the North and Baltic Seas, which was dominated by the Hanseatic League.

Using cheap timber from Germany and the Baltic regions, Amsterdam's wharves churned out cogs – broad-beamed merchant ships with a capacity of 100 tonnes, five times that of their predecessors. They revolutionised maritime trade and enabled the city to play a key role in the transit trade between Hanseatic cities and southern Europe. The toll freedom helped, too.

Instead of joining the League, Amsterdam's freebooters (from the Dutch word *vrijbuiters*, 'those chasing booty') bypassed prominent Hanseatic cities such as Hamburg and Lübeck and sailed straight to the Baltic themselves, with cargoes of cloth and salt in return for grain and timber. Their efficient transport and acute business sense outclassed the intricate contracts and transport agreements of the Hanseatic merchants.

The Amsterdammers cooperated as their forebears had done when they built dykes, pooling resources into firms that financed ships and spread risk by dividing large and

St Andrew's Crosses & the Cog

Amsterdam's coat of arms consists of three St Andrew's crosses arranged vertically – a wonderfully simple design that is found on anything from VVV tourist brochures to the thousands of brown bollards or 'penises' (so-called *Amsterdammertjes*) that keep cars from parking on pavements. Its origins are unclear, though the St Andrew's Cross itself was a popular symbol in this part of the world before Amsterdam existed.

According to legend, a Norwegian prince on the run with a Frisian fisherman and his dog drifted around for days in their damaged boat before being blown into the reeds along the IJ, where they founded Amsterdam. When the city began to engage in Baltic trade it did so with cogs, ships of a late-medieval design known around Europe. The clinker-built (or lapstrake) vessels had a single mast, a rounded bow and stern, fore and after castles and were very broad in the beam. They reduced the cost of transport to a fraction of what it had been with the

St Andrew's crosses, topped by the crown of Holy Roman Emperor Maximilian I

smaller and less seaworthy ships used previously.

The city authorities gave thanks to the cog by promot-

ing a coat of arms (see left) that consisted of a cog with two men (a soldier and a merchant) and a dog (symbolising loyalty). This survived for several centuries, often depicted together with the St Andrew's crosses, but the crosses proved more durable.

valuable cargoes among several ships, thus enabling them to undertake audacious ventures without fear of losing everything in a single shipwreck. This novel form of cooperation was spectacularly successful: by the late 1400s, 60% of ships sailing to and from the Baltic Sea were from Holland, and the vast majority of these had Amsterdam as their base.

The original harbour in the Damrak and Rokin had been extended into the IJ along what is now Centraal Station. Canals were cut to cater for growing numbers of merchant warehouses – in the 1380s the Oudezijds Voorburgwal and Oudezijds Achterburgwal, as well as the Nieuwezijds Voorburgwal and Nieuwezijds Achterburgwal (the present Spuistraat), then the Geldersekade and Kloveniersburgwal, and around 1500 the Singel (the 'girdle canal' or moat). By then the population numbered 10,000. A great fire in 1452 destroyed three-quarters of the city, including most of the

wooden buildings, but it was soon rebuilt, with regulations stipulating the use of brick.

Amsterdam started life as a 'modern' city, a place where skippers, sailors, merchants, artisans and opportunists from the Low Countries (roughly the present-day Netherlands, Belgium and Luxembourg) gained their livelihood through contacts with the outside world. There was no tradition of stable feudal relationships sanctioned by the Church, no distinction between nobility and serfs, and little if any taxation by some far-away monarch. In time, of course, class distinctions did develop based on wealth, with the so-called patricians at the top of the pyramid, but it's fair to say that Amsterdam society was more individualistic and proto-capitalist than others in Europe – even the Italian city-states.

Ironically, Amsterdam was also a city of religious pilgrimage, a 'Canterbury of the Low Countries' thanks to a banal but profitable religious miracle: in 1345 a dying man regurgitated the Host, which was thrown in the fire where it refused to burn. A miracle was proclaimed and soon the city crammed no less than 20 monasteries into its confined space, and Holy Roman Emperors such as Maximilian I and Charles V visited to pay their religious respects. In 1489 Maximilian recovered from an illness here and showed his gratitude by allowing the city to use the imperial crown on its documents, buildings and ships.

The Reformation put an end to all this but Amsterdam never became as staunchly Protestant as the other cities of Holland – after all, diversity and tolerance were good for trade.

The Independent Republic

The northern European Protestant reform movement known as the Reformation was more than just a religious affair: it was a struggle for power between the emerging class of merchants and artisans in the cities on the one hand, and the aristocratic order sanctioned by the established – the 'universal', or 'Catholic' – Church on the other; between 'new money' earned through trade and manufacturing, and 'old money' rooted in land ownership.

The form of Protestantism that took hold in the Low Countries was Calvinism, the most radically moralistic stream. It stressed the might of God as revealed in the Bible and treated humans as sinful creatures whose duty in life was sobriety and hard

The Anabaptists

The city authorities promoted tolerance and diversity in the name of trade but ruthlessly persecuted the Anabaptists, a revolutionary Protestant sect of the early 16th century that was strong in Germany and the Low Countries. Anabaptists, influenced by the teachings of Ulrich Zwingli in Zürich, believed that people shouldn't be baptised until they knew the difference between right and wrong; they also believed in a form of communism that included polygamy, and sometimes walked around naked because everyone was equal that way. Martin Luther was appalled and advised his followers to join even with Catholics to suppress the movement.

Many Anabaptists fled from Germany to Amsterdam, where their ideas appealed to the city's artisans in a time of rising prices and stagnating incomes. Their political agenda – a communist state, ruled by the faithful – was fleetingly carried out in the German town of Münster in 1534–35 under the dictatorship of a Dutch tailor, John of Leyden, but the expected world revolution failed to materialise. In Amsterdam a group of Anabaptists occu-

John of Leyden

pied the city hall but were defeated by the city watch. The survivors had their hearts ripped out and thrown in their faces – uncharacteristically harsh treatment in a city that punished other heretics, such as Lutherans, by making them take part in Catholic processions. Anabaptists advocated the abolition of property and called for the overthrow of the state, and this was too much even for the tolerant Amsterdam authorities.

An Anabaptist was last burned at the stake on Dam Square in 1576, the symbolic end of Protestantism's radical fringe. The more moderate Baptists retained the principle of mature baptism but not the Anabaptists' revolutionary politics.

work. It scorned Church hierarchy and based religious experience on local communities led by lay elders, similar to Presbyterianism in Scotland.

Calvinism was integral to the struggle for independence from the fanatically Catholic Philip II of Spain, who, thanks to the inheritance politics of the day, had acquired the 17 provinces that made up the Low Countries and ruled them as if they were a South American colony. The trouble began in 1566 when a coalition of Catholic and Calvinist nobles petitioned Philip not to introduce the Spanish Inquisition in the Low Countries. Philip refused and the resulting war of independence lasted more than 80 years.

Fanatical Calvinist brigands, who wore the disparaging nickname *geuzen* ('beggars') as a badge of honour, roamed from city to city, murdering priests, nuns and Catholic sympathisers and smashing 'papist idolatry' in the churches. Some took to the water as *watergeuzen* and harassed Spanish and other Catholic ships. Amsterdam was caught in the middle: its ruling merchants were pragmatic Catholics, but the merchants who weren't in power adopted Calvinism along with most of the population, who resented the heavy Spanish taxation imposed from Brussels. In 1578 the geuzen captured Amsterdam in a bloodless coup, the so-called Alteration.

With mighty Amsterdam now on their side, the seven northern provinces, led by Holland and Zeeland, formed the Union of Utrecht the following year and declared themselves an independent republic. The union was led by a stadholder (chief magistrate), a role played by William the Silent of the House of Orange, the forefather of today's royal family (dubbed 'the Silent' because he refused to enter into religious debate). The provinces were represented in a parliament, the Estates General, that sat in The Hague. The Seven United Provinces (the republic's official name) became known to the outside world as the Dutch Republic – or simply 'Holland' because of that province's dominance. Within Holland, Amsterdam towered over the other cities put together.

The Golden Age (1580–1700)

Amsterdam's fortunes continued to rise when its major trading rival in the Low Countries, the Protestant city of Antwerp, was retaken by the Spaniards. In retaliation, watergeuzen from Zeeland closed off the Scheldt River, which was Antwerp's access to the sea and its trade lifeline. Half the population fled, including the merchants, skippers and artisans who flocked to Amsterdam with trade contacts and silk and printing industries – the world's first regular newspaper, full of trade news from around Europe, was printed in Amsterdam in 1618.

Amsterdam also welcomed persecuted Jews from Portugal and Spain (some via

Merchants & Burgomasters

The city government during Amsterdam's Golden Age was headed by four burgomasters, or mayors, who were elected for a one-year period. Their power was almost unlimited, although judicial matters were handled by a *schout* (sheriff) and nine *schepenen* (magistrates) who were also elected for one-year periods. The electing was done by a *vroedschap* (council) of 36 *burgers* (citizens) who had to be consulted on important matters.

These officials and 'citizens' almost always came from the wealthiest merchant families, the so-called patrician class, who made sure they stayed in control through co-optation and nepotism and so cultivated a new aristocracy in all but name. Nevertheless, the division of power and the annual elections meant that a lot of politicking went on, with constantly shifting coalitions and factions, and government was probably as democratic as it could get in those days. It was also remarkably efficient and competent, at least until about 1700 when self-serving lethargy took over.

Order was upheld by several *schutterijen* (citizen militias) that were also dominated by patricians. Rembrandt's famous *Nightwatch* (a name later given to the painting because it had become so dirty) shows one of these militias in full regalia.

Antwerp) who knew about trade routes to the West and East Indies. They also introduced the diamond industry (fed by Brazilian diamonds) and made Amsterdam a tobacco centre. In later years came Germans who provided a ready source of sailors and labourers; a new wave of Jews from Central and Eastern Europe; and many persecuted Calvinists from France, the enterprising Huguenots. Amsterdam had become a cosmopolitan city where money and pragmatism combined to pioneer new developments in the world economy.

Money reigned supreme and Amsterdam was not averse to trading with the enemy. Spanish armies were paid with money borrowed from Amsterdam banks and fed on Baltic grain imported through Amsterdam; wrecked Spanish fleets including the Armada were rebuilt with timber supplied by Amsterdam merchants. Amsterdam shrewdly avoided land battles and was never raided by Spanish troops like so many other Dutch cities.

Meanwhile the city kept growing – in 1600 the population numbered 50,000, by 1650 it was 150,000 and from 1700 it stabilised at around 220,000. In the 1580s land was reclaimed from the IJ and Amstel to the east (the current Nieuwmarkt neighbourhood). Two decades later, work began on the famous canal belt that more than tripled the area of the city.

By 1600, Dutch ships dominated seaborne trade between (and often along) England, France, Spain and the Baltic, and had a virtual monopoly on North Sea fishing and Arctic whaling.

Meanwhile, Portugal and Spain built trading empires beyond Europe. Some of this trade flowed to Amsterdam through the port of Lisbon until Spain conquered Portugal in 1580 and closed Lisbon to Dutch ships. Thanks to Jewish refugees, however, Dutch mariners learned something about distant trade routes and soon they plied the world's oceans, acquiring navigational intelligence of their own.

They searched in vain for an Arctic route to the Pacific and rounded the tip of South

The Bank of Amsterdam

European money in the 16th century was in a mess. There were hundreds of different coins minted by states, cities and even individuals who sometimes tampered with the silver or gold content. Having founded the world's first stock exchange in 1602 to trade in East India Company shares, the Amsterdam authorities realised a stable, reliable currency was vital if trade was to flourish, and founded the Bank of Amsterdam in the cellars of the city hall in 1609.

The bank accepted coins in any currency from anyone, assessed their gold or silver content, and allowed the depositor to withdraw the equivalent amount in gold florins minted by the bank. A *gulden florijn* – hence *gulden*, or guilder, and the abbreviation f or *fl* – was of fixed weight and purity, and was soon sought as 'real' money throughout Europe and parts of Asia, Africa and the Americas.

Depositors could also draw cheques against their accounts, which were guaranteed by the government, and take out loans at regulated interest rates. Amsterdam thus attracted capital far and wide, and remained the financial centre of Europe until Napoleon ruined the show and London took over.

TAMSIN WILSON

The stable *gulden florijn*, or gold florin, became a currency of choice throughout Europe and beyond

America instead, naming it Cape Horn after the city of Hoorn north of Amsterdam. In 1619, Dutch traders expelled the Portuguese from the Moluccas (the so-called Spice Islands) in what is now Indonesia, and established the town of Batavia (Latin for Holland, now Jakarta) as administrative centre for what was to become the Dutch East Indies. Five years later they founded a trading post on Manhattan Island called New Amsterdam, the future New York. They set up posts along the west coast of Africa, established plantations in South America and the Caribbean, and took a keen interest in the slave trade.

The Dutch competed with the Spaniards for control of Formosa (Taiwan) and gained the upper hand there in 1641. That year Japan expelled all foreigners except the Dutch, who received sole trading rights on an island at Nagasaki because their aims were more clearly mercantile than territorial or religious. In 1652 they captured the Cape of Good Hope from the Portuguese, a crucial staging post in trade with the East Indies. There they established one of the few colonies to attract Dutch settlers in significant numbers (the East Indies overtook it in later years), and the only colony apart from Suriname and the Antilles where Dutch language and culture persist to this day. They booted the Portuguese out of Ceylon (Sri Lanka) soon

after. They also explored the coastlines of New Zealand (named after the province of Zeeland) and New Holland (known as Australia since the 1850s) but found nothing of value there and focused their resources elsewhere.

The Dutch were traders first and foremost and didn't have the population reserves for the settler-type colonisation pursued by other European powers. Their arrival was often welcomed by local rulers who had suffered the missionary and imperial zeal of earlier colonists. Dutch traders consolidated their settlements with divide-and-rule tactics, bribery, gunship diplomacy and, where necessary, local mercenary forces. They also engaged in piracy, especially against the Spaniards, with whom they were theoretically at war until the Peace of Münster, one of the treaties comprising the Peace of Westphalia in 1648.

These overseas ventures were financed by merchants and other investors who pooled their resources in trading companies: the United East India Company (Vereenigde Oostindische Compagnie, or VOC) founded

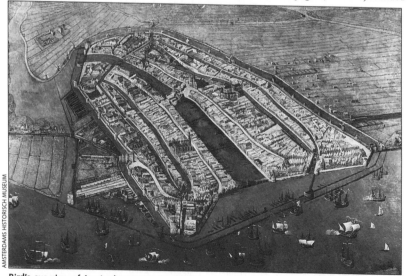

AMSTERDAMS HISTORISCH MUSEUM

Bird's-eye view of Amsterdam, painted in 1538 by Cornelis Anthonisz, looking southwards. This is the oldest surviving 'map' of the city.

The First Multinationals

The United East India Company (VOC) and West India Company (WIC) were the world's first multinationals. Their trading posts around the globe operated with a great degree of autonomy. They were authorised to negotiate with local rulers on behalf of the Dutch Republic, to pursue trade opportunities as they saw fit, to build forts and to raise local militias. More than 1000 shareholders back home – not only merchants but also artisans, clergy, shopkeepers and even servants – contributed capital for ships and trade ventures, thus spreading risk and reaping rewards through generous annual dividends when risks paid off.

Logo of the Amsterdam chamber of
the United East India Company

The VOC was founded to coordinate the often competing trade efforts of cities in Holland and Zeeland. It consisted of six 'chambers' representing Amsterdam, Middelburg, Delft, Rotterdam, Hoorn and Enkhuizen, and was supervised by 17 directors (the Heeren XVII, or '17 Gentlemen') on behalf of the shareholders. Because of the high degree of risk and long turnaround times in trade with the East, the VOC's shareholders tended to be people with money to spare – usually wealthy merchants based in Amsterdam, who owned more than half the VOC's capital.

The WIC consisted of five 'chambers' supervised by 19 directors. Trade in the Atlantic was less risky and had shorter turnaround times but offered a lower rate of return. The WIC attracted small investors, particularly in Zeeland. Competition from Spain and Portugal (and later Britain and France) was fierce, and the WIC's expenditures often outstripped income. The company relied on state subsidies to conquer and defend its sugar plantations and slave ports, and was thus more truly colonial than the VOC. As with the VOC, more than half the WIC's capital was owned in Amsterdam, but there was more internal bickering and jealousy between Holland and Zeeland.

Wealthy merchants preferred the comforts of home to the dangers of tropical trading posts, so VOC and WIC employees came mainly from the poorer strata of society and were almost always underpaid. Not that salaries made much difference one way or the other: employees were left to their own devices and supervision was minimal (there was no colonial ministry to oversee and coordinate them), so they were easily tempted to pursue personal gain. Penalties were harsh but rarely enforced, and shrewd operators amassed great personal wealth in the course of glittering careers.

---

in 1602, which pursued trade in India and the Far East; and the West India Company (WIC, 1621), which ran plantations in the Americas and soon controlled half the world's slave trade.

Despite the glamour of these expeditions and the exotic products that became commodities back home (coffee, tea, spices, tobacco, cotton, silk, porcelain), most of Amsterdam's wealth was still generated by the mundane fishing industry and European trade. In the 1590s Amsterdam's shipwrights introduced the flûte (from the Dutch *fluyt*), a small supply vessel that could be sailed by 10 people instead of the 30 required for ships of similar size – perfect for coastal freight. Around 1650 the Dutch had more seagoing merchant vessels than England and France combined, and half of all ships sailing between Europe and Asia were Dutch.

It still seems a bit of a mystery why tiny Amsterdam played such a prominent role on the world stage (Venice at the height of its power was an overture by comparison) but several factors helped. Both England and France were beset by internal troubles, and Spain was far too busy managing its

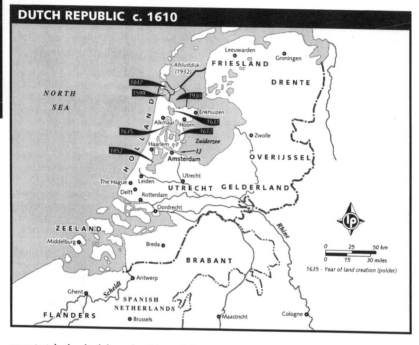

DUTCH REPUBLIC c. 1610

overstretched colonial empire. Meanwhile, Dutch freight was unrivalled in terms of cost and efficiency thanks to a combination of cheap Baltic hemp and timber, Europe's largest shipbuilding industry, abundant investment capital supplied by thousands of shareholders, and low wages for sailors, many of whom had small farming plots north of Amsterdam.

England, however, began to flex its muscle and in 1651 passed the first of several Navigation Acts: goods shipped to England and its colonies had to be carried in English ships, or ships of the country where the goods originated. This posed a serious threat to the Dutch transit trade, and the two countries fought several naval wars that were generally inconclusive, though the Dutch lost New Amsterdam. Louis XIV of France took the opportunity to march into the Low Countries, where he occupied the Spanish provinces in the south and three of

the seven republican provinces in the north during what was known as the 'Disaster Year' of 1672.

The Dutch rallied behind their stadholder, William III of Orange, who repelled the French with the help of Austria, Spain and Brandenburg (Prussia). A consummate politician, William then supported the Protestant factions in England against their Catholic King James II, who was to all intents and purposes in Louis XIV's employ. In 1688 William invaded England, where he and his wife, Mary Stuart (James II's Protestant daughter – the plot thickens), were proclaimed king and queen.

After this, England played a key role in checking France's expansion on the Continent. It is ironic that the military leader of the Dutch Republic, denied a throne at home because of Amsterdam's opposition, became king of a foreign country and thus ensured the Republic's survival.

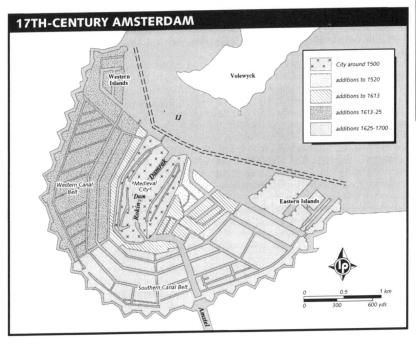

17TH-CENTURY AMSTERDAM

Western Islands

Volewyck

IJ

Western Canal Belt

Medieval City

Damrak

Rokin

Dam

Eastern Islands

Southern Canal Belt

Amstel

	City around 1500
	additions to 1520
	additions to 1613
	additions 1613-25
	additions 1625-1700

0   0.5   1 km
0   300   600 yds

Wealthy Decline (1700–1814)

The dramatic events in the second half of the 17th century stretched the Republic's resources to the limit, and its naval heroism made way for peace at all costs – a combination of neutrality and bribery. The Republic didn't have the human resources to keep meeting France and England head-on but at least it had Amsterdam's money to hold them off and ensure freedom of the seas. Money became more important than trade as merchants began to invest their fortunes more securely, often in the form of loans to foreign governments.

The result in the 18th century was stagnation. Gone were the heady days of daring sea voyages to unknown lands, of new trading posts and naval expeditions against the Spaniards, of monumental achievements in art, science and technology, of pioneering forms of government and finance. The cosmopolitan melting pot of Amsterdam, where everything was possible if it turned a profit, became a lethargic place where wealth creation was a matter of interest rates. It was still the wealthiest city in Europe and Dutch freight was still the cheapest, but the 17th-century ambition to conquer the world was gone. Harbours such as London and Hamburg became powerful rivals.

The decline in trade brought poverty to those without money in the bank, among them many Jews who had escaped pogroms in Germany and Poland – between 1700 and 1800, the proportion of Jews in Amsterdam's population increased from 3% to 10%. To compound matters, the 18th century brought a mini ice age over Europe, with exceptionally cold winters that made for colourful paintings of skating scenes but also hampered transport and led to serious food shortages. The winters of 1740 and 1763 were so severe that some Amsterdam residents froze to death and many suffered thirst – the canals doubled as sewers and clean water supplies from elsewhere had come to a halt.

The ruling patrician class became ever more corrupt and self-centred, and there was intense political bickering between patricians, Orangists (monarchists) and a new-generation middle class with enlightened ideals, the so-called Patriots.

Amsterdam's rulers naively supported the American War of Independence, resulting in a British blockade of the Dutch coast followed by British conquests of Dutch trading posts around the world. The West India Company folded in 1791, and the mighty East India Company, which once controlled European trade with Asia, went bankrupt in 1800.

Amsterdam's patricians eventually allied themselves with Orangists against the Patriots, who had become emboldened by the American example and were ever more vocal in their democratic demands. A Patriot coup in Amsterdam in 1787 was put down by Prussian troops who had come to the aid of William V of Orange. By now, Amsterdam's leadership of the Dutch Republic was over.

In 1794, French revolutionary troops invaded the Low Countries and marched straight across the frozen rivers that should have formed a natural barrier. They were accompanied by exiled Patriots who helped the French install a Batavian Republic, transforming the fragmented 'united provinces' into a centralised state with Amsterdam as its capital.

In 1806 this republic became a monarchy when Napoleon nominated his brother Louis Napoleon as king. In 1808, the city prostrated itself by offering the grand city hall on Dam Square, symbol of the wealth and power of the merchant Republic, as a palace to the new king. Two years later Napoleon dismissed his uncooperative brother and annexed the Netherlands into the French Empire.

Britain responded to Napoleon's conquests by blockading the Continent and occupying the Dutch colonies on behalf of William V. Napoleon in turn prohibited all trade with Britain and tried to make the Continent self-sufficient with France as its hub – the so-called Continental System. Amsterdam's trade, already in decline, came to a complete halt along with its important fishing industry. Dutch society turned to agriculture and Amsterdam became a local market town.

After Napoleon's defeat at Leipzig in 1813, the French troops left Amsterdam peacefully. William V had died in exile, but his son returned to Holland and was crowned King of the Netherlands in the Nieuwe Kerk in 1814. The city hall became the new king's palace and has remained with the House of Orange ever since. The Britons returned the Dutch East Indies but kept the Cape of Good Hope and Ceylon. Amsterdam's seaborne economy recovered only slowly from Napoleon's disastrous Continental System and Britain now dominated the seas.

New Infrastructure (1814–1918)

The new kingdom included present-day Belgium which fought for its independence in 1831. Apart from this incident, Amsterdam in the first half of the 19th century was a sleepy place. Its harbour had been neglected, and the sand banks in the IJ, which were always an obstacle in the past, proved too great a barrier for modern ships. Rotterdam was set to become the country's premier port.

Things began to look up again as the rail system took shape – the country's first railway, between Amsterdam and Haarlem, opened in 1839. Major infrastructure projects were funded by the notorious 'culture system' in the East Indies – forced, large-scale production of tropical crops for export, overseen by the VOC and WIC's successor, the Netherlands Trading Society. Trade with the East Indies was now the backbone of Amsterdam's economy. The North Sea Canal between Amsterdam and IJmuiden, built between 1865 and 1876, and later the Merwede Canal to the Rhine (expanded into the Amsterdam-Rhine Canal after WWII) also allowed the city to benefit from the industrial revolution at home and in Germany.

The harbour was expanded to the east. The diamond industry boomed after the discovery of diamonds in South Africa. Amsterdam again attracted immigrants and its population, which had declined in the Napoleonic era, doubled in the second half

Republicans & Monarchists

Contrary to the European trend, the Netherlands began life as a republic and regressed to a monarchy. The Dutch Republic was a loose federation of autonomous provinces dominated by cities, with almighty Amsterdam determining foreign policy and influencing most other things the weak central government did.

Amsterdam's role was similar to that played by Athens among the ancient Greek city-states, except that there was no Sparta to act as a counterweight. There was, however, the stadholder, the chief magistrate of the Republic and the military leader of the revolt against Spain. After William the Silent's assassination the mantle passed to his son, who in turn passed it on to his, thus laying the foundations for a monarchy under the House of Orange. This was not to the liking of the patricians of Amsterdam who had established their own oligarchy based on trade wealth and were not about to have this taxed by some monarch.

TAMSIN WILSON
William the Silent

Dutch politics between 1580 and 1800 seesawed between the republican (and 'pacifist', pro-business) sentiments of Amsterdam's ruling elite and the monarchistic, 'militaristic' aspirations of the House of Orange. The latter faction was often supported by the poorest classes of society and the many cities who were keen to keep 'arrogant' Amsterdam in its place. In 1673, in the midst of war against France, the provinces (with the sole exception of Holland) voted to make the office of stadholder hereditary in the House of Orange, but Amsterdam's influence was strong enough to keep the state a republic until Napoleon installed his brother as king in 1806.

Under French occupation the provinces became a unitary state with Amsterdam as its capital. In 1813 the French left, and in 1814 William VI of Orange was proclaimed King William I of the Netherlands in Amsterdam's Nieuwe Kerk.

of the 19th century, passing the half-million mark by 1900. Speculators hastily erected new housing estates beyond the canal belt – dreary tenement blocks, shoddily built and with minimal facilities.

In 1889 the city was literally cut off from its harbour by the massive Centraal Station, built on a series of artificial islands in the IJ. Commentators at the time saw this as the symbolic severing of Amsterdam's ties with the sea. An open waterfront was no longer considered vital to the city's survival, and in the closing years of the 19th century some of its major waterways (Damrak, Rokin, Nieuwezijds Voorburgwal) and smaller canals were filled in, both for hygienic reasons (after several cholera epidemics) and to

allow for increased road traffic. Plans to fill in more canals were shelved amid mounting criticism of 'ostentatious boulevards'.

The Netherlands remained neutral in WWI but Amsterdam's trade with the East Indies suffered from naval blockades. There were riots over food shortages, exacerbated by refugees from Belgium, but on the whole things could have been worse. There was even an attempt to extend the socialist revolutions in Russia and Germany to the Netherlands but this was quickly put down by loyalist troops.

Boom & Depression (1918–40)

After the war Amsterdam remained the country's industrial centre, with a wide range of enterprises that fed each other. Its shipbuilding industry was no longer the world leader, but the Dutch Shipbuilding Company still operated the world's second-largest wharf and helped carry an extensive steel and diesel-motor industry.

The harbour handled tropical produce that was finished locally (tobacco into cigars, copra into margarine, cocoa into chocolate – Amsterdam is still the world's main distribution centre for cocoa).

In 1920 the KLM (Koninklijke Luchtvaart Maatschappij – Royal Aviation Company) began the world's first regular air service, between Amsterdam and London, from an airstrip south of the city and bought many of its planes from Anthony Fokker's aircraft factory north of the IJ. There were two huge breweries, a sizeable clothing industry, and even a local car factory that produced the venerable Spijker. The 1920s were boom years for Amsterdam, crowned by the Olympic Games hosted in 1928.

The population kept growing until it reached 700,000 in the mid-1920s, still the figure today. The city had already begun expanding north of the IJ, with housing projects for harbour workers and dockers in the new suburb of Amsterdam North. Then it expanded southwards, filling in the area between the Amstel and what was to become the Olympic Stadium.

Unfortunately the world depression in the 1930s hit Amsterdam hard. Unemployment rose to 25% and would have risen further if the East Indies hadn't borne the brunt of the misery. Labour party members, who dominated the city council, resigned in protest at public-service salary cuts, and the conservative, spend-nothing national government of Hendrik Colijn (the Herbert Hoover of the Netherlands) had free reign.

Public-works projects such as the Amsterdamse Bos (a recreational area southwest of the city) did little to defuse mounting tensions between socialists, communists and the small but vocal party of Dutch fascists. The fascists' influence on national politics was negligible, but they gained a few seats in the Amsterdam council elections of 1939 and had strong support

among colonists in the East Indies. Amsterdam received some 25,000 Jewish refugees from Germany, although a shamefully large number were turned back at the border because of the Netherlands' neutrality policy.

WWII (1940–45)

The Netherlands tried to stay neutral in WWII but Germany had other plans and invaded in May 1940. For the first time in almost 400 years the population of Amsterdam experienced the grim realities of war first-hand. Few wanted to believe that things would turn nasty, and when the German occupiers began to introduce anti-Jewish measures they did so in a series of carefully staged small steps. Local police and public servants cooperated. In February 1941 Amsterdam's working class finally came out in force to support their Jewish compatriots in a general strike led by dockworkers, but the strike was soon put down and by then it was already too late.

Only one in seven Jews in the country survived the war, and in Amsterdam only one in 16. It was the highest proportion of Jews murdered anywhere in Western Europe. This sad fact was effectively whitewashed after the war by Anne Frank's diary which created the impression that Amsterdam hid its Jews.

Anti-Semitic feeling was not particularly strong among the Dutch and they didn't care much for fascism; but the ingrained – some would say 'Calvinist' – ethos of order and propriety told them to shun the futile grand gesture, to retreat within the privacy of their homes and mind their own business in order to survive.

The Germans cultivated such compliance by treating the country relatively leniently at first, strengthening people's hopes that things would be all right if they avoided trouble – and if they ignored the plight of the Jews. The resistance movement, set up by an unlikely alliance of Calvinists and Communists, only became large-scale when the increasingly desperate Germans began to round up able-bodied men to work in Germany and shattered the sanctity of home and family.

The severe winter of 1944–45 was the Winter of Hunger. The Allies had liberated the south of the country but were checked at Arnhem and decided to concentrate on their push into Germany, thus isolating the north-west and Amsterdam. Coal shipments from the south ceased, men aged between 17 and 50 had gone into hiding or worked in Germany if they had no dispensation, public utilities ground to a halt, and the Germans began to plunder anything that could help their war effort. Dark, freezing Amsterdam suffered severe famine and thousands died. In May 1945, at the very end of the war in Europe, Canadian troops finally liberated the city.

Postwar Growth (1945–62)

The city's growth resumed after the war, with US aid (through the Marshall Plan) and newly discovered fields of natural gas compensating for the loss of the East Indies, which became independent Indonesia after a four-year fight. The focus of the harbour moved westwards, towards the widened North Sea Canal that had provided access to the sea since the 1932 completion of the Afsluitdijk – the 30km-long barrier dam between North Holland and Friesland that closed off the Zuiderzee and turned it into the IJsselmeer (IJssel Lake). The long-awaited Amsterdam-Rhine Canal opened in 1952.

Massive apartment blocks arose in areas annexed to the west of the city – Bos en Lommer, Osdorp, Geuzenveld, Slotermeer and Slotervaart – to meet the continued demand for housing, made ever more acute by the demographic shift away from extended families. The massive Bijlmermeer housing project (now called the Bijlmer) to the south-east of the city, begun in the mid-1960s and finished in the early 1970s, was built in a similar vein.

The Cultural Revolution (1962–82)

In the early 1960s Amsterdam began to undergo a cultural revolution that lasted 20 years and was at the cutting edge of similar developments abroad. It was fuelled by the interaction between a conservative established order and tolerance (but not necessarily love) of alternative views, and the tradition of incorporating such views into the structure of society.

Over the previous 80 years Dutch society had become characterised by *verzuiling* ('pillarisation'), a social order sanctioned by the 1917 'Pacification' compromise in which each religion and/or political persuasion achieved the right to do its own thing, with its own schools, political parties, trade unions, cultural institutions, sports clubs etc. Each persuasion represented a pillar that supported the status quo in a general 'agreement to disagree'. This elegant solution for a divided society in the 19th and early 20th centuries, however, had to make way for a society where the old divisions were increasingly irrelevant. In the 1960s people began to question the status quo and the pillars came tumbling down.

Provos & the 'Magic Centre' The first group to rattle the structure were the Provos, successors to the beatniks, whose core consisted of a small group of anarchic individuals. They staged playful 'happenings', or creative, playful provocations (hence the name), which elicited senseless and disproportionately harsh police reprisals. These polarised public opinion and led even the older generation to wonder whether this was what they had stood for during the war. See the following boxed text for further details on them.

The Provos won a seat in the municipal elections of 1966, much to the horror of some of the creative anarchists at the heart of the movement. In the summer of 1967, they buried Provo in the Vondelpark with a ceremony involving a coffin. However, their representative in the city council, Roel van Duijn, kept alive their concerns about urban congestion and pollution.

As society broke out of its prewar framework, Amsterdam became the 'Magic Centre' of Europe, an exciting place where anything was possible. The late 1960s saw an influx of hippies smoking dope at the Nationaal Monument on Dam Square, unrolling sleeping bags in the

The Protesting Provos

The Provos awoke Dutch society from its slumber in the 1960s with their street 'happenings'. In 1962 a self-professed window cleaner and sorcerer, Robert Jasper Grootveld, began to deface cigarette billboards with a huge letter 'K' (for *kanker*, cancer) in order to expose the role of advertising in addictive consumerism by the *klootjesvolk* ('narrow-minded populace'). He held get-togethers in his garage – dressed as a medicine man and chanting antismoking mantras under the influence of pot – which attracted other bizarre types, such as the poet Johnny van Doorn, a.k.a. Johnny the Selfkicker, who bombarded his audience with frenzied, stream-of-consciousness recitals; Bart Huges, who drilled a hole in his forehead – a so-called 'third eye' – to relieve pressure on his brain and attain permanently expanded consciousness; and Rob Stolk, a rebellious, working-class printer, whose streetwise tactics came to the fore when the get-togethers moved to the streets.

In the summer of 1965 the venue of choice was the rather appropriate *Lieverdje* ('Little Darling') on Spui Square, the endearing statuette of an Amsterdam street-brat donated to the city by a cigarette company. The police, unsure of how to deal with 'public obstructions' by excited youngsters chanting unintelligible (and indeed often meaningless) slogans around 'medicine man' Grootveld, responded the only way they knew: with the baton and arbitrary arrests.

The pub terraces lining the square were a favourite haunt of journalists, resulting in eyewitness accounts of senseless police brutality against kids having fun. Soon it seemed the whole country was engaged in heated debate for and against the authorities. The generation gap was only part of it: many of the older generation, uneasy about how little had changed after the war, came out in favour of the Provos and could not understand why the authorities had so completely lost the plot.

TAMSIN WILSON

The *Lieverdje* (Little Darling) on Spui Square, an appropriate focus for campaigns by the Provos against addictive consumerism

Throughout 1965 and 1966 the Provos maintained the initiative with a series of White Plans to protect the environment, including the famous White Bicycle Plan to tackle the city's traffic congestion with a fleet of free white bicycles. They symbolically donated a white bicycle that was promptly confiscated by the police.

Provos were at the centre of public protests against the wedding on 10 March 1966 of Princess Beatrix and the congenial German diplomat Claus von Amsberg, who had served in Hitler's army. The princess insisted on getting married in Amsterdam, against the advice of the mayor. In spite of massive security precautions a live chicken was hurled at the royal coach, smoke bombs ignited as the procession made its way along Raadhuisstraat, and bystanders chanted 'my bicycle back' – a reference to the many bikes commandeered by German soldiers in the final months of the war. Scuffles and police charges were beamed out live on TV.

The following June, Provos supported construction workers in a violent strike in which one of the workers died of a heart attack. The resulting political fallout led to the dismissal by the national government in The Hague of Amsterdam's chief of police and later the mayor himself.

Vondelpark, and tripping in the nightlife hot spots of Paradiso, Fantasia and the Melkweg.

It was also a time of upheaval in the universities, with students demanding a greater say and, in 1969, occupying the Maagdenhuis on Spui Square, the administrative centre of the University of Amsterdam. The women's movement took hold: the Dolle Minas ('Mad Minas', after the radical late-19th-century Dutch feminist Wilhelmina Drucker) began a *Baas in eigen Buik* ('Boss in own Belly') campaign that fuelled the abortion debate throughout the 1970s.

Kabouters The Provos' successors called themselves kabouters (gnomes), after the helpful, bearded gnomes of Dutch folklore. In 1970 they proclaimed an Orange Free State on Dam Square, an alternative city populated by caring people preoccupied with the environment. In the elections that year they won five seats in the Amsterdam city council and several more in other cities. Kabouter idealism soon fell victim to the grim realities of urban politics, but many of their ideals – such as banning cars from the city centre to foster an inner city where people could live, work and shop – became widely accepted.

In the early 1970s, while city planners were still preoccupied with vast apartment blocks in the suburbs populated by commuters who worked in offices and banks in the city centre, the public mood was shifting. A projected motorway from the south-east to the IJ-Tunnel and Centraal Station – the wide Weesperstraat and Wibautstraat are ugly reminders – was stopped by public protests from intruding any further into the city.

Metro & Nieuwmarkt The fiercest conflict between arrogant planners and disaffected Amsterdammers involved the metro line through the Nieuwmarkt neighbourhood. The original plans for the huge Bijlmermeer housing project south-east of the city called for a four-line metro network, though this was eventually whittled down to a single line between the Bijlmermeer and

Centraal Station. The available technology did not yet allow tunnelling through swampy ground, and a large portion of the derelict Nieuwmarkt had to be razed so caissons could be lowered. The inhabitants, many of them former Provos and kabouters who had settled there as krakers (squatters), refused to leave and turned the area into a fortress. The Nieuwmarkt was eventually cleared with much violence on 'Blue Monday', 24 March 1975. Some 30 people were injured, most of them policemen, and it was surprising that no-one was killed.

The Nieuwmarkt episode was a watershed: in the following years the council set about renovating inner-city neighbourhoods and providing new housing there. Nieuwmarkt itself was rebuilt, not with the planned office complexes and luxury apartments but with affordable council houses. The metro opened in 1980, with wall paintings in Nieuwmarkt station commemorating the events five years earlier.

Squatters Meanwhile families still deserted the city and the demographic balance continued to shift towards the elderly and the young – small households with modest incomes whose housing needs outstripped the council's efforts to meet them. The housing shortage fuelled a speculative trend, particularly within the desirable canal belt, which pushed free-market rents – let alone the cost of buying a house – out of reach of the average citizen. The waiting period for a council apartment was anything up to five years.

Many young people saw squatting as the only solution, and buildings left empty by speculators (or assumed speculators) provided an appropriate target. Existing legislation made eviction difficult, giving rise to the phenomenon of *knokploegen*, or 'fighting groups' of tracksuited heavies sent by owners to evict squatters by force. The squatters of the late 1970s, however, were of a new generation, less ideologically or politically motivated than their predecessors and more prepared to defend personal needs with barricades and a well-organised support network.

In February 1980 police evicted squatters from an empty office at Vondelstraat 72. Hundreds of squatters retook the building and erected street barricades that were eventually cleared by tanks fitted with bulldozer blades. A few months later, on 30 April, Queen Beatrix was crowned in the Nieuwe Kerk and the squatting movement vented its anger with a large demonstration that soon got out of hand. Literally everyone who was out on the streets that day had tears in their eyes – not for joy over the coronation but from tear gas that hung thick in the air. The term 'proletarian shopping', a euphemism for looting, entered the national lexicon. Never before or since has Amsterdam experienced rioting on such a scale.

In the following months and years several famous squats made world headlines, but the movement was weakened by internal power struggles and became more and more isolated. 'Ordinary' Amsterdammers, initially sympathetic towards exposure of the housing shortage, became fed up with violent riots, such as the three-day rampage (complete with burning tram) that followed the clearing of the 'Lucky Luyk' villa in the Jan Luyckenstraat in October 1982.

Law-abiding citizens who waited years for council accommodation watched squatters jump the queue and grab choice living space. Squatters often reached rental agreements with the owners or were bribed to leave peacefully. Sometimes the council bought the building so the squatters could stay with subsidised rents. By the mid-1980s the movement had little or no outside support and was all but dead. Squatting still takes place now, but the rules of the game are clear and the mood is far less confrontational.

New Consensus

Twenty years after the first Provo 'happenings' on Spui Square, Amsterdam's cultural revolution had run its course. Gone were the days of unbridled growth for growth's sake, of autocratic government, of arrogant planners and grandiose housing schemes in distant suburbs, of motorways and parking garages in the heart of the city, of demolition of old neighbourhoods. A new consensus had arrived, epitomised by the labour party mayor, Ed van Thijn. The ideals were decentralised government through neighbourhood councils; a livable city with work, schools and shops within walking distance; a city no longer strangled by cars; renovation rather than demolition; friendly neighbourhood police on hybrid bikes; a practical, non-moralistic approach towards drugs; and legal recognition of homosexual couples.

Thanks to this new consensus, the opening of the combined city hall and opera house in 1986 passed relatively peacefully, although opposition had been anything but peaceful when it was planned and built. This monstrosity, dominating the Amstel waterfront at what used to be the heart of the Jewish quarter on Waterlooplein, had attracted much criticism for its size and hybrid design. Opponents dubbed it the Stopera – pronounced 'stowpera', a contraction of *stadhuis* (city hall) and opera, and of 'Stop the Opera' – and the name has stuck.

As the city entered the calm 1990s it had changed beyond recognition. Families and small manufacturing industries, which dominated inner-city neighbourhoods in the early 1960s, had been replaced by tertiary-sector professionals and a service industry of pubs, 'coffeeshops', restaurants and hotels. The ethnic make-up had changed too: Surinamese, Moroccans, Turks and Antillians, once a small minority, now comprise 25% of the population, and including other nationalities it's 45%.

The harbour, fifth-largest in Europe, has a new lease of life with petrochemical industries and container transshipment and is moving ever farther westwards. Schiphol airport is booming and running out of space to expand. The same applies to Amsterdam in general and the new catch phrase is *inbreiding*, 'inspansion': turning old industrial complexes and docklands into (often very expensive) housing estates. The eastern harbour areas are rapidly being transformed in this way, and the same is beginning to happen in the old western harbour districts, for instance the grain silo area north of Prinseneiland.

New office towers are arising to the southeast, south and west of the city around the completed ring freeway, including the largest office complex in the country, the new ABN-AMRO head office in the southern section which defies architectural logic by being wider at the upper floors than at ground level. Amsterdam's first baby skyscraper, the Rembrandttoren (Rembrandt Tower), owned by the Nedlloyd insurance company and (temporarily) housing the Philips head office, arose along the Amstel next to Amstelstation in the late 1990s. Its 'lighthouse' spire topped by a bright light bulb can be seen from almost anywhere and no-one seems to mind its presence – quite astonishing, considering what public attitudes would have been like if this had been tried 15 years ago.

Even the metro network is back on the agenda, with new technology allowing tunnelling through swampy ground. A line from Amsterdam North straight through the city to the World Trade Centre in the south should be complete in 2006.

Tourists keep flocking to the city – only London, Paris and Rome attract more of them in Europe. But the lack of affordable tourist accommodation shows that Amsterdam's most pressing problem remains its housing shortage.

GEOGRAPHY

Much of the land around Amsterdam is *polder*, land that used to be at the bottom of lakes or the sea. It was reclaimed by building dykes across sea inlets or across rivers feeding lakes, and pumping the water out with windmills, and later with steam and diesel pumps. Polders were created on a massive scale: in this century for instance, huge portions of the former Zuiderzee (now the IJsselmeer, a lake closed off from the sea by the Afsluitdijk) were surrounded by dykes and the water was pumped out to create vast swathes of flat and fertile agricultural land – the complete province of Flevoland, north-east of Amsterdam, was reclaimed from the sea.

For more on water management, see Cleaning the Canals in the following Ecology & Environment section.

Sea Level & NAP

It is said that most of Amsterdam (and indeed more than half the country) lies a couple of metres below sea level, but what is sea level? This varies around the globe, and even the average level of the former Zuiderzee, in the lee of Holland, was slightly lower than that of the North Sea along Holland's exposed west coast. A display in the Stopera, in the arcade between the Muziektheater and City Hall (near the Waterlooplein metro exit), shows the ins and outs of NAP (Normaal Amsterdams Peil – 'Normal Amsterdam Level' or Amsterdam Ordnance Datum), established in the 17th century as the average high-water mark of the Zuiderzee. This still forms the zero reference for elevation anywhere in the country and is also used in Germany and several other European countries.

Water in the canals is kept at 40cm below NAP and many parts of the city lie lower still. Touch the bronze knob as you walk down the stairs and you'll realise the importance of all those dykes. Three water columns represent the sea levels at IJmuiden and Flushing (Vlissingen), and the highest level reached in the disastrous floods in 1953 (4.55m above NAP) that led to the extensive Delta Works in the province of Zeeland. Pamphlets in Dutch, English, French, German, Italian and Spanish explain the details.

The water in the canals is about 3m deep but residents reckon you can deduct 1m for sludge and another metre for discarded bicycles. People have indeed received nasty cuts from falling into the water.

Peat & Piles

Amsterdam, that big city, is built on piles/And if that city were to fall over, who would pay for it?

Dutch nursery rhyme

Amsterdam sits on a mixture of spongy peat and clay resting on a stable layer of sand more than 12m down. The first wooden houses were simply placed on top of the peat and occasionally had to be raised as they sank. When heavier brick and stone replaced wood, engineers perfected the art of driving wooden piles down to the sand layer, sawing off the protruding ends to equal height and erecting buildings on top of the stable foundation – there are 13,659 piles under the palace on Dam Square alone!

So long as the piles were completely submerged in ground water and air couldn't get to them, they wouldn't rot, but ground-water levels varied a bit and problems were unavoidable. Also, less scrupulous builders didn't always use enough piles, drive them deeply enough or worry about piles that snapped in the process, and many old buildings show signs of unequal subsidence – very expensive to fix. Since WWII, concrete piles have been used: they cannot rot and can be driven deeper – 20m, into the second sand layer, or even 60m, into the third.

CLIMATE

Amsterdam has a temperate maritime climate with cool winters and mild summers. Precipitation is spread rather evenly over the year, often in the form of endless drizzle, though in the spring months of March to May it tends to fall in short, sharp bursts. May is a pleasant time to visit: the elms along the canals are in bloom and everything is nice and fresh.

The sunniest months are May to August and the warmest are June to September. Summer can be humid and uncomfortable for some people. Indian summers are common in September and into early October, which is usually an excellent time to visit. Blustery autumn storms occur in October and November.

December to February are the coldest months with occasional slushy snow and temperatures around freezing point. Frosts usually aren't severe enough to allow skating on the canals, but when they are, the city comes alive with colourfully clad skaters. When snow adds a serene white setting, you couldn't wish for better photo material.

ECOLOGY & ENVIRONMENT

Foreign visitors in the past commented on residents obsessively scrubbing stoops and cleaning windows. The spotless houses stood in stark contrast to smelly, filthy canal water and foul air thick with smoke from coal and peat fires.

Today's young residents are less obsessed with cleaning their houses than with sorting their rubbish – the environment is cherished in a country with so little of it. The canals are cleaner than they've ever been (see the following section) and environmentally friendly natural gas has cleared the air. Industrial pollution is kept firmly in check with some of the strictest regulations in the world. Even the visual pollution of thousands of TV antennas disappeared in the 1980s when everyone got hooked up to cable TV.

The inner city has become a much more pleasant place for pedestrians since the mid-1980s thanks to the council's *autoluw* ('car-abatement') policies. The number of parking spaces is strongly curtailed and cars are actively discouraged. Amsterdam is very much a residential city, and cars and highways have a very limited place.

One environmental problem persists, however: Amsterdam is still the dog-shit capital of the world, even though owners are compelled to steer pooch to the gutter and have to carry a spade and bag on their daily walk. Amsterdammers love dogs, which is nothing new: Japanese artists used to depict Dutchmen with dogs. They keep them in great numbers, cooped up in 3rd-floor apartments, and will stand up for their mutt's right to do whatever it damn well likes on its daily sniff around the block.

Greenpeace supporters will be interested to know that the international head office (☎ 523 62 22) is at Keizersgracht 176; the Dutch branch (☎ 626 18 77, information on ☎ 422 33 44) is in the same complex at Keizersgracht 174.

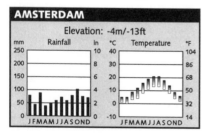

AMSTERDAM			
Elevation: -4m/-13ft			

Cleaning the Canals

Until the 1980s the canals doubled as sewers and had to be flushed daily. Before the 17th century this was relatively straightforward: the water level in the canals was regulated by locks leading into the IJ, and sea water was allowed into the canals at rising tide and back out again as the tide dropped. This made the canal water brackish and led to a backup of filth in the Amstel. From 1674 the Amstelsluizen in front of today's Carré Theatre allowed flushing to occur with fresh water from the Amstel, a vast improvement. Maids protested that they would lose their jobs because they wouldn't have to clean windows and stoops as often.

With the opening of the North Sea Canal in the 19th century and the completion of locks at Schellingwoude at the mouth of the IJ, the IJ was cut off from tidal influences. The solution, used to this day, was to pump water from the Zuiderzee (later IJsselmeer) into the canals, since WWII by means of a huge pumping station on the artificial island of Zeeburg opposite Schellingwoude. Locks on the west side of the city were left open so water could flow out into the North Sea Canal, taking canal filth with it. This was released into the North Sea at low tide (or pumped out if necessary), completing the hydraulic system.

Until the mid-1980s the Zeeburg station pumped 600,000 cubic metres of water each night, the equivalent of 300 swimming pools. Now that all households are connected to sewerage pipes (except for 2500 houseboats), the pumps are turned on twice a week in winter and four times a week in summer. When the Amstel is in flood, or westerly storms increase water levels in the North Sea Canal, the pumps at Zeeburg are reversed and water is pumped out of the canals into the IJsselmeer.

The canal water is relatively clean these days, despite its dirty appearance and occasional algal blooms. Oxygen levels are healthy and many fish species have returned, though you still wouldn't want to drink it.

The council employs seven boats to collect flotsam – anything from old fridges, dolls, handbags and bits of driftwood to discarded bicycles (about 10,000 a year). Three dredges slowly work their way around the 100km of canals, completing the circuit every 10 years. The polluted sludge they dredge up is processed in special facilities in the Jan van Riebeeckhaven.

FLORA

An aerial photo of Amsterdam creates the impression of a huge park because it includes the many gardens rarely visible from the street. The centre of Amsterdam has more trees per square kilometre than any other capital city in Europe. The canals used to be lined with linden trees but these were replaced with elms in the 18th century, chosen for their light leaf cover that allows daylight to filter into the houses. Dutch elm disease is so named because local arborists did much research into this beetle-induced fungus that first entered the country in the 1920s.

The city has many pleasant parks with an amazing variety of species. The Hortus Botanicus at Plantage Middenlaan is justly famous, but the Vondelpark, Artis zoo and the Amsterdamse Bos also hold much of interest, as do smaller local parks such as the Sarphatipark and Oosterpark. And when it comes to flowers, where do you start? Try March or April, when bulbs (tulips, hyacinths and daffodils) burst into bloom everywhere.

FAUNA

There are some 35 mammal species in the city, including the mole and the wood mouse, found in parks, along with rabbits and hares a bit farther out; bats, especially the dwarf bat; rats, including the water vole and brown rat; and the house mouse. The black rat and otter, once common in and around Amsterdam, now seem to have disappeared from the city.

Sparrows, thrushes, swifts and crows are common birds here as elsewhere in Europe, and in some parts of the city you might wonder whether any other birds exist besides feral pigeons. The canals are favoured by mallards, coots and the occasional heron, swan or grebe, and in water areas around the city you'll see herons, cormorants and coots.

Black-headed gulls (with white heads in winter) seem to be everywhere, supremely adapted to this windswept, coastal habitat.

Reptiles include the harmless grass snake, which is becoming rare, and the sand lizard, which is on the verge of extinction. You might spot an occasional red-cheeked turtle but it will always be a released pet – the North American import can't reproduce in this climate. The common toad and both brown and green frogs are prevalent.

About 60 fish species exist in Amsterdam waters. The habitat varies from fresh (the canals) to salt (the deeper parts of the North Sea Canal, the western harbour area and parts of the IJ), with transitional, brackish zones. Many sea fish enter the North Sea Canal through the huge sluices at IJmuiden. The eel, which survives in both fresh and salt water (and hails from the Sargasso Sea off Bermuda!), is common in the city's canals, as is bream – outnumbered only by the roach. White bream, rudd, pike, perch, stickleback and carp also enjoy the canal environment.

There are 12 crustacean species in the waters in and around Amsterdam, of which the common shrimp and the epidemic import, the Chinese mitten crab, are the most common.

GOVERNMENT & POLITICS

The Greater Amsterdam area (population 1.3 million) consists of the City of Amsterdam (population 731,000), Almere, Amstelveen, Haarlemmermeer (Schiphol), Purmerend and Zaanstad. These municipalities established formal administrative cooperation in 1992 and are in the process of full integration under a single council.

In the meantime, the City of Amsterdam's city council and municipal executive (consisting of the mayor and aldermen) oversee the city's 16 districts – each with their own district council and executive committee – and run the central city within the canal belt and the western harbour area. The 45 members of the council are elected every four years by all residents over 18 years of age, including foreigners who have been resident for at least five years. Council members elect the aldermen (currently seven) from

their midst, but the mayor is appointed by the Crown (the queen plus the national government) for a period of six years.

District councils serve residents in their daily lives, within guidelines laid down by the city council and municipal executive. Electricity, gas, water, sewerage, water management, health and public transport are handled by the central city administration.

Amsterdam has been a left-wing city ever since its residents achieved the vote. At the last council elections in 1998 the labour party (PvdA) won 15 seats, followed by the conservative liberals (VVD) with nine, environmental socialists (Green Left) with seven, progressive liberals (D66) with four, the Christian Democrats, radical socialists (SP) and Greens with three each, and Mokum Mobiel 99 (pro-car lobbyists) with one. The current municipal executive, which includes the appointed mayor (traditionally labour), is a coalition of four labour, two conservative liberal, two environmental socialists and one progressive liberal.

City politics are lively, with plenty of media coverage. Amsterdammers have strong opinions about their city and aren't afraid to voice them. Burning issues include IJburg, a scheme that would see 15,000 residences on artificial islands in the shallows of the eastern IJ, which would wipe out wildlife in this ecologically sensitive area; and, concurrently, the persistent housing shortage with 50,000 house-hunters.

Land & Housing Policies

About 80% of land in the city is government-owned and is leased to private owners under 50-year leasehold arrangements (also 100-year leaseholds since 1991). Most land within the canal belt, however, is freehold (ie, owned privately in perpetuity), though any freehold land acquired by the government is converted to leasehold. A leasehold is only granted when a property developer has an end user lined up, which keeps speculation in check and ensures that supply meets demand.

A whopping 40% of city real estate is government-owned, and is either rented out or used for government purposes; of the remaining 60% in private hands, only one-tenth is owner-occupied and the rest is rented out. Rents are strictly controlled, unless the property is so upmarket that it jumps the hurdle into the free-market category. There are also strict controls on the number of rooms a household may occupy, regardless of whether the dwelling is rented or owner-occupied.

There are about 2500 houseboats, accommodating 6000 people, moored along the canals. These converted barges began proliferating with the first acute housing shortage in the 1950s, but rules have been tightened and the only way you can live on a boat these days is to rent or buy an existing one. An average boat in the older parts of Amsterdam costs up to f300,000, which includes f50,000 for the spot (a similar two-bedroom apartment costs f350,000-plus). Owners pay f500 to f1000 a year in tax, for which they receive garbage service and connections to gas, electricity and water. It might seem romantic to live on a boat, but it can get cold and damp in winter and maintenance bills are high.

ECONOMY

Until about 25 years ago Amsterdam was the industrial centre of the Netherlands, a role it had played since the industrial revolution of the mid-19th century. In the 1960s and 1970s, however, the city's worsening congestion and environmental constraints forced many industries to move to parts of the country where industrial conditions were more relaxed. This caused great hardship among employees who were too old to reskill or relocate, but the city bounced back as it reinvented its historical role as a centre of trade, finance and services.

The main economic activities in the Greater Amsterdam area can now be divided into four categories employing roughly equal numbers of people: manufacturing and crafts; commerce, tourism and finance; administration; and science and arts. Tourism generates a turnover of f2 billion a year and employs 6% of the workforce.

The harbour is still the fifth-largest in Europe and Schiphol airport is the fastest

growing – the third-largest in terms of freight and fourth-largest in terms of passengers. Less well known is the fact that the Dutch control about 45% of European road freight and many of these trucking companies are based in Amsterdam. The government has devoted massive subsidies to office complexes to the west, south and south-east of the city. This, coupled with a highly skilled, multilingual workforce and easy-going tax laws, has prompted many multinationals to establish their European headquarters here to take advantage of the single European market.

The city remains the undisputed financial capital of the country and a major money centre in Europe. It holds the headquarters of the mighty ABN-AMRO banking group, the ING (Postbank) and the Nederlandsche Bank (the central bank), along with several other private banks and the offices of some 60 foreign banks. The European Options Exchange and the national stock exchange, merged into Amsterdam Exchanges, add to the city's financial clout – 15% of the working population is employed in finance and related sectors.

Industry remains important in the corridor between Amsterdam and IJmuiden, particularly chemicals, petrochemicals, food and steel. Other important industries include cars and trucks, engine-building, clothing, paper and of course diamonds (industrial-grade). The country's major printers, including the national newspapers, are based south-east and north-west of the city. Amsterdam is also one of the world centres for the development of electronic media.

In spite of a strong base in the service economies of the future and a rock-solid currency, Amsterdam's economy is under continual strain from generous social security provisions. These include the blanket public pension scheme in a greying population, and welfare cheques of just over f1000 a month (after tax) guaranteed to every resident of working age who cannot find employment (a sum, by the way, that hasn't changed in 15 years). This problem exists in the national economy too, but Amsterdam is particularly hard hit because so much of its population is either young or old. The proportion of welfare recipients is around 10%, down from 20% in the mid-1980s but still twice the national average.

The official unemployment rate in Amsterdam is 12.8%, more than twice the national average. Some people claim that the real rate is more like 30% but is masked by the high proportion of part-time jobs – and part-time workers aren't considered unemployed. A survey by *The Economist* newspaper found that only 11% of Dutch men and less than 5% of women work more than 40 hours a week, the lowest percentage in the developed world; in the USA, those figures are 80% for men and 60% for women, and in the Czech Republic they're over 90% for men and 80% for women.

POPULATION & PEOPLE

Amsterdam has an official population of 731,000 plus an estimated 20,000 unregistered ('illegal') residents. About 30% of the population is aged between 20 and 35; the proportion of elderly (60 years-plus) inhabitants is also relatively high. Children and middle-aged people are underrepresented compared with other Dutch cities. All in all, 54% of households are single and that figure is rising. Couples without children far outnumber those with.

Ethnic minorities make up about 45% of the population, and the majority of primary school kids now have a non-Dutch background. In the mid-1970s, the granting of independence to the Dutch colony of Suriname in South America saw a large influx of Surinamese, who now number 72,000 and form the vast majority of the city's 10% black population. In the 1960s, 'guest labourers' from Morocco and Turkey performed jobs spurned by the Dutch; they and their descendants now number 54,000 and 34,000 respectively. There are about 24,000 people from Indonesia, 19,000 Germans and 11,000 migrants from the Netherlands Antilles. Next in line are the Brits, with 7500. About 3700 Americans and 1000 Aussies also call Amsterdam home – officially, that is.

ARTS

Amsterdam has always been an international centre of the arts thanks to its tolerant and cosmopolitan spirit. It lacked a powerful court and wealthy Church – the usual art patrons elsewhere in Europe – but more than compensated for this with a large middle class that didn't mind spending a bit of money on art. Amsterdam achieved international renown in painting and architecture, and the current music scene is second to none. Unfortunately the city's impressive literary and theatrical traditions are less accessible to foreigners.

Painting

The distinction between Dutch and Flemish painting dates from the late 16th century, when the newly Protestant northern provinces of the Low Countries kicked out the Spaniards but couldn't dislodge them from the provinces in the south. Until then, most paintings in the Low Countries originated in the southern, 'Flemish' centres of Ghent, Bruges and Antwerp, and dealt with the biblical and allegorical subject matter popular with patrons of the day – the Church, the court and to a lesser extent the nobility.

Famous names include **Jan van Eyck** (died 1441), the founder of the Flemish School who perfected the technique of oil painting; **Rogier van der Weyden** (1400–64), whose religious portraits showed the personalities of his subjects; **Hieronymus (Jeroen) Bosch** (1450–1516), with macabre allegorical paintings full of religious topics; and **Pieter Breugel the Elder** (1525–69), who used Flemish landscapes and peasant life in his allegorical scenes.

In the northern Low Countries, meanwhile, artists began to develop a style of their own. In Haarlem, painters were using freer, more dynamic arrangements in which people came to life. **Jan Mostaert** (1475–1555), **Lucas van Leyden** (1494–1533) and **Jan van Scorel** (1494–1562) brought realism into their works, modifying the mannerist ideal of exaggerated beauty. Around 1600 the art teacher Karel van Mander proclaimed that Haarlem was creating a distinctively Dutch style of painting.

Many of Amsterdam's former warehouses have become houses or offices.

The Tattoo Museum will make an indelible impression.

ELLIOT DANIEL

A short black and a long joint

RICHARD NEBESKY

JEREMY GRAY

Sign above the Spanish Cultural Centre

Tuschinskitheater, a sumptuous Art-Deco cinema

KIM GRANT

'That's enough museums for today, OK?'

RICHARD NEBESKY

Groovy, baby

ELLIOT DANIEL

Nightclub poster

ZAW MIN YU

Street performer in Dam Square

LEANNE LOGAN

Resident with traditional scarf

Souvenirs at Waterlooplein flea market

Bust of the famous Dutch writer & freethinker

Street musician

Heraldic shield of Amsterdam City

In Utrecht, however, followers of the Italian master Caravaggio, such as **Hendrick ter Bruggen** (1588–1629) and **Gerrit van Honthorst** (1590–1656), made a much more fundamental break with mannerism. They opted for realism altogether and played with light and shadow, with night scenes where a single source of light created dramatic contrasts – the *chiaroscuro* ('clear-obscure') approach used to such dramatic effect by Caravaggio in Rome.

Golden Age (17th Century) Both these schools influenced the Golden Age of Dutch painting in the 17th century with its stars like Rembrandt, Vermeer and Frans Hals. Unlike earlier painters or some contemporaries, none of this trio made the almost obligatory pilgrimage to Italy to study the masters. Their work showed that they no longer followed but led – much like the young Republic that seemed to burst out of nowhere.

Artists suddenly had to survive in a free market. Gone was the patronage of Church and court. In its place was a new, bourgeois society of merchants, artisans and shopkeepers who didn't mind spending 'reasonable' money to brighten up their houses and workplaces with pictures they could understand. Painters rose to the occasion by becoming entrepreneurs themselves, churning out banal works, copies and masterpieces in studios run like factories. Paintings became mass products that were sold at markets among the furniture and chickens. Soon the wealthiest households were covered in paintings from top to bottom like wallpaper. Foreign visitors commented that everyone seemed to have a painting or two on the wall, even bakeries and butcher shops.

Artists specialised in different categories. There was still a market for religious art but it had to be 'historically correct' rather than mannerist, in line with the Calvinist emphasis on 'true' events as described in the Bible. Greek or Roman historical scenes were an extension of this category. Portraiture, in which Flemish and Dutch painters had already begun to excel, was a smash hit in this society of middle-class upstarts

brimming with confidence, though group portraits cost less per head and suited a republic run by committees and clubs. Maritime scenes and cityscapes sold well to the government, and landscapes, winter scenes and still lifes (especially of priceless, exotic flowers and delicious meals) were found in many living rooms. Another favourite in households was genre painting, which depicted domestic life or daily life outside.

These different categories may help visitors to the Rijksmuseum understand what they're looking at, but some painters defy such easy classification. **Rembrandt van Rijn** (1606–69), the greatest and most versatile of 17th-century artists, excelled in all these categories and pioneered new directions in each. Sometimes he was centuries ahead of his time, as with the emotive brush strokes of his later works. See the following boxed text for further details of his life.

Another great painter of this period, **Frans Hals** (1581/85–1666), was born in Antwerp but lived in Haarlem. He devoted most of his career to portraits, dabbling in occasional genre scenes with dramatic chiaroscuro. His ability to render the expressions of his subjects was equal to that of Rembrandt though he didn't explore their characters as much. Both masters used the same expressive, unpolished brush strokes, and seemed to develop from a bright exuberance in their early careers to a darker, more solemn approach later on.

A good example of Hals' 'unpolished' technique is *The Merry Drinker* (1630) in the Rijksmuseum, which could almost have been painted by one of the 19th-century impressionists who so admired his work. His children's portraits are similar. Hals was also an expert of beautiful group portraits in which the groups almost looked natural, unlike the rigid lineups produced by lesser contemporaries – though he wasn't as cavalier as Rembrandt in subordinating faces to the composition. A particularly good example is the pair of paintings known collectively as *The Regents & the Regentesses of the Old Men's Alms House* (1664) in the Frans Hals Museum in Haarlem, which he painted near the end of his long life.

Rembrandt: From Wealth to Bankruptcy

MARTIN MOOS

**See how the master lived and worked
in the Rembrandthuis Museum**

The 17th century's greatest artist, Rembrandt van Rijn, grew up in Leiden as the son of a miller and was already an accomplished chiaroscuro painter when he came to Amsterdam in 1631 to run Hendrick van Uylenburgh's painting studio. Portraits were the most profitable line and Rembrandt and his staff (or 'pupils') churned out scores of them, including group portraits such as *The Anatomy Lesson of Dr Tulp* (1632). In 1634 he married Van Uylenburgh's Frisian niece Saskia, who often modelled for him.

Rembrandt fell out with his boss, but his wife's capital helped him buy the sumptuous house next door (the current Rembrandthuis) where he set up his own studio, with staff who worked in a warehouse in the Jordaan. These were happy years: his paintings were a success and his studio became the largest in Holland, though his gruff manners and open agnosticism didn't win him dinner-party invitations from the elite.

Rembrandt became one of the city's main art collectors and often sketched and painted for himself, urging staff to do likewise. Residents of the surrounding Jewish quarter provided perfect material for his dramatic biblical scenes.

In 1642, a year after the birth of their son Titus, Saskia died and business went downhill. Rembrandt's majestic group portrait, *The Nightwatch* (1642), was considered innovative by the art critics of the day (it's now the Rijksmuseum's prize exhibit), but the people in the painting had each paid f100 and some were unhappy that they were pushed to the background. Rembrandt told them where to push the painting and suddenly he received far fewer orders. He began an affair with his son's governess but kicked her out a few years later when he fell for the new maid, Hendrickje Stoffels, who bore him a daughter, Cornelia. The public didn't take kindly to the man's lifestyle and his spiralling debts, and in 1656 he went bankrupt. His house and rich art collection were sold and he moved to the Rozengracht in the Jordaan.

No longer the darling of the wealthy, he continued to paint, draw and etch – his etchings on display in the Rembrandthuis are some of the finest ever produced in this medium – and received the occasional commission. His pupil Govert Flinck was asked to decorate the new city hall, and when Flinck died Rembrandt scored part of the job and painted the monumental *Conspiracy of Claudius Civilis* (1661). The authorities disliked it and soon had it removed. In 1662 he completed the *Staalmeesters* (the 'Syndics') for the drapers' guild and ensured that everybody remained clearly visible, but it was the last group portrait he did.

The works of his later period show that Rembrandt lost none of his touch. No longer constrained by the wishes of wealthy clients, he enjoyed a new-found freedom and his works became more unconventional while showing an even stronger empathy with their subject matter, for instance in *A Couple: The Jewish Bride* (1665). The many portraits of Titus and Hendrickje, and his ever gloomier self-portraits, are among the most stirring in the history of art.

A pest epidemic in 1663–64 killed one in seven Amsterdammers, among them his faithful companion Hendrickje. Titus died in 1668, aged 27 and just married, and Rembrandt died a year later, a broken man.

The grand trio of 17th-century masters is completed by **Jan Vermeer** (1632–75) of Delft. He produced only 35 meticulously crafted paintings in his career and died a poor man with 10 children – his baker accepted two paintings from his wife as payment for a debt of more than f600. His work is devoted mainly to genre painting, which he mastered like no other. Other paintings include a few historical/biblical scenes in his earlier career, his famous *View of Delft* (1661) in the Mauritshuis in The Hague, and some tender portraits of unknown women, such as the stunningly beautiful *Girl with a Pearl Earring* (1666), also in the Mauritshuis. His Catholicism and lingering mannerism help explain the emphasis on beauty rather than the personalities of the people he portrayed.

The Little Street (1658) in the Rijksmuseum is Vermeer's only street scene; the others are set indoors, bathed in serene light pouring through tall windows. The calm, spiritual effect is enhanced by dark blues, deep reds and warm yellows, and by supremely balanced compositions that adhere to the rules of perspective. Good examples include the Rijksmuseum's *The Kitchen Maid* (also known as *The Milkmaid*, 1658) and *Woman in Blue Reading a Letter* (1664), or, for his use of perspective, *The Love Letter* (1670). In Woman in Blue, note the map on the wall, a backdrop he used in several other works, as did many other artists of the period. Maps were appreciated as valuable works of art in 17th-century Dutch society just like paintings, which might say something about Dutch appreciation for spatial relationships (something to do with the flat country and ongoing land reclamation perhaps?).

Around the middle of the century the atmospheric unity in Dutch paintings, with their stern focus on mood and the subtle play of light, began to make way for the splendour of the baroque. **Jacob van Ruysdael** went for dramatic skies and **Albert Cuyp** for Italianate landscapes, while Ruysdael's pupil **Meindert Hobbema** preferred less heroic and more playful bucolic scenes full of pretty detail.

This almost frivolous aspect of baroque also announces itself in the genre paintings of **Jan Steen** (1626–79), the tavern-keeper whose depictions of domestic chaos led to the Dutch expression 'a Jan Steen household' for a disorderly household. A good example is the animated revelry of *The Merry Family* (1668) in the Rijksmuseum. It shows adults having a good time around the dinner table, oblivious to the children in the foreground pouring themselves a drink. There's a lot going on in this painting, and it's very busy as baroque art so often is, but it all comes together well.

18th & 19th Centuries The Golden Age of Dutch painting ended almost as suddenly as it began, when the French invaded the Low Countries in the 'Disaster Year' of 1672. The economy collapsed and with it the market for paintings. A mood of caution replaced the carefree optimism of the years when the world lay at the Republic's feet. Painters who stayed in business did so with 'safe' works that repeated earlier successes, and in the 18th century they copied French styles, pandering to the awe for anything French.

They produced many competent works but nothing ground-breaking. **Cornelis Troost** (1697–1750) was one of the best genre painters, sometimes compared to Hogarth for introducing quite un-Calvinistic humour into his pastels of domestic revelry reminiscent of Jan Steen.

Gerard de Lairesse (1640–1711) and **Jacob de Wit** (1695–1754) specialised in decorating the walls and ceilings of buildings – De Wit's *trompe l'oeil* decorations in the current Theatermuseum and Bijbels Museum are worth seeing.

The late 18th century and most of the 19th century produced little of note, though the landscapes and seascapes of **Johan Barthold Jongkind** (1819–91) and the gritty, almost photographic Amsterdam scenes of **George Hendrik Breitner** (1857–1923) were a bit of an exception. They appear to have inspired French impressionists, many of whom visited Amsterdam at the time.

The work of these two painters also reinvented 17th-century realism and influenced the Hague School in the last decades of the 19th century, with painters such as **Hendrik Mesdag** (1831–1915), **Jozef Israels** (1824–1911) and the three **Maris brothers** (Jacob, Matthijs and Willem). The landscapes, seascapes and genre works of this school are on display in the Mesdag Museum in The Hague, where the star attraction is the *Panorama Mesdag* (1881), a gigantic, 360° painting by the artist of the seaside town of Scheveningen viewed from a dune. It's quite impressive.

Without a doubt the greatest 19th century Dutch painter was **Vincent van Gogh** (1853–90), whose convulsive patterns and furious colours were in a world of their own and still defy comfortable categorisation. A post-impressionist? A forerunner of expressionism? For more about his life and works, see the description of the Van Gogh Museum in the Things to See & Do chapter.

20th Century In his early career, **Piet Mondriaan** (1872–1944) – he dropped the second 'a' in his name when he moved to Paris in 1910 – painted in the Hague School tradition, but after discovering theosophy he began reducing form to its horizontal (female) and vertical (male) essentials. After flirting with Cubism he began painting in bold rectangular patterns, using only the three primary colours of yellow, blue and red set against the three neutrals (white, grey and black), a style known as 'neo-plasticism' – an undistorted expression of reality in pure form and pure colour. His Composition in Red, Black, Blue, Yellow & Grey (1920) in the Stedelijk Museum is an elaborate example of this. His later works were more stark (or 'pure') and became dynamic again when he moved to New York in 1940. The world's largest collection of his paintings resides in the Gemeentemuseum (Municipal Museum) of his native The Hague.

Mondriaan was one of the leading exponents of De Stijl (The Style), a Dutch design movement that aimed to harmonise all the arts by bringing artistic expressions back to their essence. Its advocate was the magazine of the same name, first published in 1917 by **Theo van Doesburg** (1883–1931).

Van Doesburg produced works similar to Mondriaan's, though he dispensed with the thick, black lines and later tilted his rectangles at 45°, departures serious enough for Mondriaan to call off the friendship.

Throughout the 1920s and 1930s, De Stijl attracted not just painters but also sculptors, poets, architects and designers. One of these was **Gerrit Rietveld** (1888–1964), designer of the Van Gogh Museum and several other buildings but best known internationally for his furniture, such as the Mondriaanesque *Red Blue Chair* (1918) on display in the Stedelijk Museum, and his range of uncomfortable zigzag chairs that, viewed side-on, are simply a 'Z' with a backrest.

Other schools of the prewar period included the Bergen School, with the expressive realism of **Annie 'Charley' Toorop** (1891–1955), daughter of the symbolist painter Jan Toorop; and De Ploeg (The Plough), headed by **Jan Wiegers** (1893–1959) in Groningen, who were influenced by the works of Van Gogh and German expressionism. In her later works Charley Toorop also became one of the exponents of Dutch surrealism, more correctly known as Magic Realism, which expressed the magical interaction between humans and their environment. Leading Magic Realists included Carel Willink (1900–83) and the almost naive autodidact Pyke Koch (1901–91).

One of the most remarkable graphic artists of this century was **Maurits Cornelis Escher** (1902–72). His drawings, lithos and woodcuts of blatantly impossible images continue to fascinate mathematicians. Strange loops defy the laws of Euclidean geometry: a waterfall feeds itself, people go up and down a staircase that ends where it starts, a pair of hands draw each other. He also possessed an uncanny knack for tessellation, or 'tiling' – the art of making complex, preferably 'organic' shapes fit into one another in recurring but subtly changing patterns. Though sometimes dismissed as novelties that belong in poster shops, Escher's meticulously crafted works betray a highly talented artist who deserves credit for challenging our view of reality.

After WWII, artists rebelled against artistic conventions and vented their rage in abstract expressionism, the more furious the better. In Amsterdam, **Karel Appel** (1921–) and **Constant** (Constant Nieuwenhuis, 1920–) drew on styles pioneered by Paul Klee and Joan Miró, and exploited bright colours and 'uncorrupted' children's art to produce incredibly lively works that leapt off the canvas. In Paris in 1945, they met up with the Dane Asger Jorn (1914–73) and the Belgian Corneille (Cornelis van Beverloo, 1922–), and together with several other artists and writers formed a group known as CoBrA (Copenhagen, Brussels, Amsterdam).

Their first major exhibition, in the Stedelijk Museum in 1949, aroused a storm of protest with predictable comments along the lines of 'My child paints like that too'. Still, the CoBrA artists exerted a strong influence in their respective countries even after they disbanded in 1951. The Stedelijk Museum has a good collection of their works but the CoBrA Museum in Amstelveen displays the more complete range, including the most colourful ceramics you're ever likely to see.

It is probably too early to say much about the significance of Dutch art from the 1960s onwards – form your own opinions in the Stedelijk Museum. Works include the op art of Jan Schoonhoven, influenced by the Zero movement in Germany; the abstracts of Ad Dekkers and Edgar Fernhout; and the photographic collages of Jan Dibbets.

Architecture

Amsterdam is an architectural marvel, though there are no grand monuments and only a few buildings that impress with size. Its beauty, especially within the canal belt, lies in the countless private buildings with distinguishing features that make each one stand out in its own particular way. No other city in Europe has such a wealth of residential architecture. Amsterdam was built by citizens and businesses, not by government.

Middle Ages The oldest surviving building is the Gothic Oude Kerk (Old Church), which dates from the early 14th century. The second-oldest is the late-Gothic Nieuwe Kerk from the early 15th century. In both these churches, note the timber vaulting (the marshy ground precluded the use of heavy stone) and the use of brick rather than stone in the walls. Stone was not only heavy but also scarce; there was plenty of clay and sand to produce bricks. Also note how the interior focus has shifted from the (Catholic) choir and altar to the (Protestant) pulpit. The pulpit takes centre stage in churches built after the Protestant takeover in 1578; a good example is the Noorderkerk in the Jordaan.

The earliest houses were made of timber and clay with thatched roofs. In the 15th century, timber side walls made way for brick in a process of natural selection brought about by fires, and in the 16th century the thatched roofs were replaced by tiles. Timber was still used for facades and gables into the 17th century but eventually brick and sandstone triumphed here too. Only two houses have survived with timber facades: Begijnhof 34 (mid-15th century) and Zeedijk 1 (mid-16th century). Timber, however, remained an essential building material for floor beams and roof frames.

Dutch Renaissance From about the middle of the 16th century the Italian Renaissance began to filter through to the Netherlands, where architects developed a unique style with rich ornamentation that merged classical and traditional elements. In the facades they used mock columns, so-called pilasters, and they replaced the traditional spout gables with step gables richly decorated with sculptures, columns and obelisks. The playful interaction of red (or rather, orange) brick and horizontal bands of white or yellow sandstone was based on strict mathematical formulas that pleased the eye.

The city carpenter Hendrick Staets (who planned the canal belt), the city bricklayer Cornelis Danckerts and the city sculptor **Hendrick de Keyser** (1565–1621) were jointly responsible for municipal buildings. Utrecht-born De Keyser's artistic contributions were the most visible and it was he who perfected Dutch-Renaissance architecture. His Bartolotti House at Herengracht

170–172 is one of the finest examples of his work. He also designed the Zuiderkerk and the Westerkerk in which he retained Gothic elements, but he set a new direction in Dutch Protestant church-building with the Noorderkerk, laid out like a Greek cross with the pulpit in the centre.

Dutch Classicism During the Golden Age of the 17th century, architects such as Jacob van Campen (1595–1657) and Philips Vingboons (1607–78) and his brother Justus adhered more strictly to Greek and Roman classical design and dropped many of De Keyser's playful decorations. Influenced by Italian architects such as Palladio and Scamozzi, they made facades resemble temples. The pilasters looked more like columns, with pedestals and pediments. In order to accentuate the vertical lines, the step gable changed to a neck gable with decorative scrolls, topped by a triangular or rounded fronton to imitate a temple roof. Soft red brick was made more durable with brown paint. Van Campen's city hall (now Royal Palace) on Dam Square is the most impressive example of this style.

The Vingboons brothers specialised in residential architecture and their work can be found throughout the western canal belt, such as the current Bijbels Museum at Herengracht 364–370 and the White House (now Theatermuseum) next to the Bartolotti House, or the fine example at Keizersgracht 319.

Classical elements became more restrained later in the 17th century. Make-believe columns became less ornamental or disappeared altogether as external decorations made way for sumptuous interiors. This was the period of the southern canal belt, when wealthy Amsterdammers often bought two adjoining plots and built houses five windows wide instead of the usual three. Justus Vingboons' Trippenhuis at Kloveniersburgwal 29 is a good example.

This austere classicism is best seen, however, in the works of **Adriaan Dortsman** (1625–82), whose designs include the Round Lutheran Church and the current Museum Van Loon at Keizersgracht 672–674. A mathematician by training, he favoured a stark, geometrical simplicity – preferably with flat, sandstone facades – that enhanced the grandeur of his buildings.

18th-Century 'Louis Styles' The wealthy class now began to enjoy the fortunes amassed by their predecessors. Many turned to banking and finance and conducted their business from the comfort of opulent homes. Those who still engaged actively in trade no longer stored goods in the attic but in warehouses elsewhere.

The preoccupation with all things French provided fertile ground for Huguenot refugees, such as **Daniel Marot** (1661–1752) and his assistants **Jean and Anthony Coulon**, who introduced French interior design with matching exteriors. Interiors were bathed in light thanks to stuccoed ceilings and tall sash windows (a French innovation), and everything from staircases to furniture was designed in harmony. Elegant bell gables, introduced around 1660, became commonplace, though many architects did away with gables altogether in favour of richly decorated horizontal cornices.

The Louis XIV style dominated until about 1750, with its dignified symmetry and facades decorated with statuary and leaves. Around 1740 the Louis XV style brought asymmetrical rococo shapes resembling rocks and waves. Pilasters or pillars made a comeback around 1770 with Louis XVI designs that showed a renewed interest in classical motifs. An extreme example of this is the Felix Meritis building at Keizersgracht 324 designed by **Jacob Otten Husly** (1738–97), with enormous Corinthian half-columns that seem to carry the structure. The Maagdenhuis on Spui Square, designed by city architect **Abraham van der Hart** (1747–1820), is a much more sober interpretation of the new classicism.

19th-Century Neo-Styles Architecture stagnated in the first half of the 19th century as Amsterdam struggled to recover from the economic disasters of the Napoleonic era. Safe neoclassicism held sway until the 1860s when architects here and elsewhere

Gables & Hoists

A gable not only hid the roof from public view but also helped to identify the house until the French-led government introduced house numbers in 1795 (the current system of odd and even numbers dates from 1875). The more ornate the gable, the easier it was to recognise. Other distinguishing features included facade decorations, signs or wall tablets (cartouches).

There are four main types of gables. The simple **spout gable** with semicircular windows or shutters, a copy of the earliest wooden gables, was used mainly for warehouses from the 1580s to the early 1700s. The **step gable** was a late-Gothic design favoured by Dutch-Renaissance architects from 1580 to 1660. The **neck gable**, also known as the bottle gable, was introduced in the 1640s and proved most durable, featuring occasionally in designs of the early 19th century. Some neck gables incorporated a step. The **bell gable** first appeared in the 1660s and became popular in the 18th century.

Many houses built from the 18th century onwards no longer had gables but straight, horizontal cornices that were richly decorated, often with pseudo-balustrades.

Many canal houses have a slight forward lean. This has nothing to do with subsidence but everything to do with hoisting goods into the attic and furniture into the (removable) windows without them bumping into the house. A few houses have huge hoist-wheels in the attic with a rope and hook that run through the hoist beam. Almost all others, even those built today, have a beam with a hook for a hoist block. The forward lean also allows the facade and gable to be admired from the street – a fortunate coincidence.

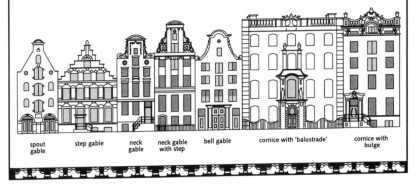

| spout gable | step gable | neck gable | neck gable with step | bell gable | cornice with 'balustrade' | cornice with bulge |

in Europe began to rediscover other styles of the past.

The main Amsterdam styles in the latter half of the century were neo-Gothic, harking back to the grand Gothic cathedrals in which no design element was superfluous; and neo-Renaissance, which brought De Keyser's Dutch-Renaissance architecture back into the limelight. The former suited the boom in Catholic church-building now that Catholics were free to build new churches in Protestant parts of the country; the latter appealed to local architects because

houses in this style were being demolished at a rapid rate.

One of the leading architects of this period was **Pierre Cuypers** (1827–1921), who built several neo-Gothic churches but often merged the two styles, as can be seen in his Centraal Station and Rijksmuseum which have Gothic structures and Dutch-Renaissance brickwork. Another fine example of this mixture is CH Peters' general post office (now Magna Plaza) at Nieuwezijds Voorburgwal 182. Alfred Tepe's Krijtberg church at Singel 448 is more clearly Gothic (but note the use of brick), while the milk factory at Prinsengracht 739–741 designed by Eduard Cuypers (Pierre's nephew) sits firmly in the Dutch-Renaissance tradition.

Other architects were more eclectic and also incorporated medieval Dutch and German designs in a very personal way. Good examples are Isaac Gosschalk's houses at Reguliersgracht 57–59 and 63, and AC Bleijs' PC Hooft store on the corner of Keizersgracht and Leidsestraat. AL van Gendt's Concertgebouw is obviously neo-classical but its interplay of red brick and white sandstone is Dutch Renaissance.

A popular European style around the turn of the century was Art Nouveau. In Amsterdam, Art Nouveau's abundant use of steel and glass with curvilinear designs resembling plants showed up mainly in shop fronts but in little else. There are, however, a handful of fine examples, such as the current Greenpeace headquarters at Keizersgracht 174–176, the American Hotel at Leidseplein, and the riotous Tuschinskitheater at Reguliersbreestraat 26–28.

Berlage & the Amsterdam School The neo-styles and their reliance on the past were strongly criticised by Hendrik Petrus Berlage (1856–1934), the father of modern Dutch architecture. Instead of expensive construction and excessive decoration, he favoured simplicity and a rational use of materials. His Beurs (Bourse, or Stock Exchange) on Damrak displayed his ideals to the full. He cooperated with sculptors, painters and tilers to ensure that ornamentation was integrated into the overall design in a supportive role, rather than being tacked on as an embellishment to hide the structure.

Berlage's residential architecture approached a block of buildings as a whole, not as a collection of individual houses. In this he influenced the young architects of what became known as the Amsterdam School, though they rejected his stark rationalism and preferred more creative designs. Leading exponents were **Michel de Klerk** (1884–1923), **Piet Kramer** (1881–1961) and **Johan van der Mey** (1878–1949). The latter

heralded the Amsterdam School in his Scheepvaarthuis at Prins Hendrikkade.

These architects built in brick and treated housing blocks as sculptures, with curved corners, oddly placed windows and ornamental, rocket-shaped towers. Their housing estates, such as De Klerk's 'Ship' in the Oostzaanstraat and Kramer's Cooperatiehof in the Pijp neighbourhood, have been described as fairy-tale fortresses rendered in a Dutch version of Art Deco. Their preference for form over function meant that their designs were interesting to look at but not always fantastic to live in, with small windows and inefficient use of space.

Many architects of this school worked for the city council and designed the buildings of the ambitious 'Plan South'. This was a large-scale expansion of good-quality housing, wide boulevards and cosy squares between the Amstel and what was to become the Olympic Stadium. It was mapped out by Berlage and instigated by the labour party alderman FM Wibaut, though Berlage didn't get much of a chance to design the buildings, with council architects pushing their own designs. Subsidised housing corporations provided the funding here and elsewhere in the 1920s, a period of frantic residential building activity beyond the canal belt.

Functionalism While Amsterdam School-type buildings were being erected all over the city, a new generation of architects began to rebel against the school's impractical (not to mention expensive) structures. Influenced by the Bauhaus School in Germany, Frank Lloyd Wright in the USA and Le Corbusier in France, they formed a group called de 8 (the 8) in 1927.

Architects such as B Merkelbach and Gerrit Rietveld believed that form should follow function and sang the praises of steel, glass and concrete. Buildings should be spacious, practical structures with plenty of sunlight, not masses of brick treated as works of art to glorify architects.

The all-important Committee of Aesthetics Control didn't agree with this, however, and kept the functionalists out of the canal belt, relegating them to the new housing estates on the outskirts of the city – although Rietveld did build his glass gallery on top of the Metz department store at Keizersgracht 455.

Functionalism finally came to the fore after WWII and put its stamp on new suburbs west and south of the city, thanks to the General Extension Plan that had been adopted in 1935 but interrupted by the war. The acute housing shortage meant that these high-rise suburbs were built on a larger scale than originally planned, yet they still weren't sufficient and the Bijlmermeer south-east of the city was added in the 1960s. By this time, however, there was increasing resistance to such high-rise monstrosities.

Suburbs have been built on a more human scale since the 1960s, with low and medium-rise apartments integrated with shops, schools and offices. The eastern docklands in the harbour are a good example of current developments. Strict functionalism has also made way for more imaginative designs, such as A Alberts and M van Huut's ING Bank (1987) in the Bijlmermeer: built on anthroposophical principles, this S-shaped complex of linked towers has few right angles.

In the inner city, the emphasis has been on urban renewal with innovative designs on a scale appropriate to their surroundings. Architects follow examples set by Aldo van Eyck (1918–) and his student Theo Bosch (1940–). Van Eyck's designs include the Moederhuis at Plantage Middenlaan 33; Bosch's include the Pentagon housing complex on the corner of St Anthoniesbreestraat and Zwanenburgwal. Opinions are mixed, however, with critics dismissing such designs as 'parasite architecture' – modern housing projects that look a bit out of place, with huge windows so residents can stare out of their aquarium onto wonderful 17th and 18th-century surroundings.

Many aspects of urban planning are on permanent display in the Zuiderkerk (see Zuiderkerk in the Things to See & Do chapter). The Architectuur Centrum Amsterdam (ARCAM, ☎ 620 48 78), Waterlooplein 213, organises temporary displays about architectural themes.

Music

The dour church elders of the past dismissed music as frivolous but began to allow organ music in churches in the 17th century because it kept people out of pubs. Amsterdam therefore contributed relatively little to the world's music heritage, which makes its vivid music scene today all the more remarkable.

The world's top acts are billed matter-of-factly, and local musicians excel in (modern) classical music, jazz and techno/dance. In July and August, free jazz, classical and world-music performances are staged in the Vondelpark, and free lunch-time concerts are held at various venues throughout the year. The Uitmarkt festival at the end of August (see Public Holidays & Special Events in the Facts for the Visitor chapter) also provides lots of free music. For more about music venues, see the Music section in the Entertainment chapter, and check the free entertainment paper *Uitkrant* for details.

Classical The country's best symphony orchestras and classical musicians perform in the Concertgebouw. You can't go wrong with tickets for the world-renowned, Riccardo Chailly-conducted Concertgebouw Orkest, which plays music by 'big' composers but also highlights modern and unknown works.

If the pianist Ronald Brautigam is on the bill you'll be guaranteed a top-flight performance. He often collaborates with violinist Isabelle van Keulen. Cellists of note (so to speak) are Quirine Viersen and Pieter Wispelwey. The pianist Wibi Soerjadi is one of the most successful classical musicians in the country. He specialises in romantic works, and elderly ladies swoon over this handsome youngster who looks like a Javanese prince. Soprano Charlotte Margiono and mezzo-soprano Jard van Nes are worth catching too.

In 'old music', you can't go past the Combattimento Consort Amsterdam (Bach, Vivaldi and Händel), or the Amsterdam Baroque Orchestra conducted by Ton Koopman. He also heads the Radio Chamber Orchestra, along with Frans Brüggen, best known for his work with The 18th Century Orchestra. Performances by the Radio Philharmonic Orchestra, conducted by the Sydney Symphony Orchestra's Edo de Waart (usually in the Concertgebouw), are often recorded for radio and TV.

The Nederlandse Opera is based in the Stopera (officially called the Muziektheater), where it stages world-class performances though not everyone will appreciate the sometimes experimental approach.

Modern Classical & Experimental The IJsbreker is the usual venue for this type of music, which seems to thrive in Amsterdam. Dutch modern composers include Louis Andriessen, Theo Loevendie, Klaas de Vries and the late Ton de Leeuw. Worthwhile performers include The Trio, Asko Ensemble, Nieuw Ensemble and last but not least the Reinbert de Leeuw-conducted Schönberg Ensemble.

Jazz The distinction between modern classical and improvised music can be vague. Jazz band leaders such as Willem Breuker and Willem van Manen of the Contraband have a decades-long reputation for straddling the two genres.

More recently, the Dutch jazz scene has become more mainstream with gifted young chanteuses such as Fleurine and especially Suriname-born Denise Jannah, widely recognised as the country's best jazz singer. The latter is the first singer from Suriname to be signed to the legendary Blue Note label where she recently released her third CD. Her repertory consists of American standards but she adds elements of Surinamese music on stage.

Astrid Seriese and Carmen Gomez operate in the crossover field, where jazz verges on, or blends with, pop. Father and daughter Hans and Candy Dulfer, tenor and alto saxophonists respectively, are a bit more daring. Dad in particular constantly extends his musical boundaries by experimenting with sampling techniques drawn from the hip-hop genre. Daughter is better known internationally, thanks to her performances with Prince, Van Morrison,

Dave Stewart, Pink Floyd and Maceo Parker, among others.

Trumpeter Saskia Laroo mixes jazz with dance but is also respected in more traditional circles. In instrumental jazz, you can't go past pianist and Thelonius Monk Award-winning Michiel Borstlap and his soul and label-mate, bass player Hein van de Geyn.

The city's most important jazz venue is the Bimhuis on Oude Schans – others come and go but the Bimhuis remains an institution. It will move to a new venue in the Eastern Islands (near the ship passenger terminal) in 2002.

Pop & Dance Amsterdam may have been a 'Magic Centre' in the 1960s but its pop scene was slow to develop (the country's pop centre in those days was The Hague, with bands like Shocking Blue and Golden Earring who both hit No 1 in the USA). Famous Amsterdam bands in the '60s were the Outsiders – a wild band whose lead singer, Wally Tax, was reputed to be the man with the longest hair in the country – and the Hunters, an instrumental guitar group that included Jan Akkerman, who later achieved international fame in the progressive rock band Focus and was proclaimed the best guitarist in the world in a readers' poll by English magazine *Melody Maker* in 1973.

In the late 1970s the squatter movement provided fertile ground for a lively punk music scene, followed by synthesizer-dominated New Wave. In the mid-1980s Amsterdam was a centre for guitar-driven rock bands, such as the still active garage rockers Claw Boys Claw.

Since then it has evolved into a capital of the dance genre, from house to techno to R&B, centred on the dance club Roxy which spectacularly burned down in 1999. Perhaps the best known Dutch dance variant internationally is the so-called 'gabber', a style in which the number of beats per minute and the noise of buzzing synthesizers goes beyond belief. Amsterdam also boasts a vital hip-hop scene, spearheaded by the Osdorp Posse who rap in their mother tongue.

Rave parties are organised in the Amsterdam dance clubs, such as Mazzo, Seymour Likely and iT, and especially Escape with its Saturday Chemistry evenings. The Westergasfabriek hosts Speedfreax evenings, where fashionable hipsters sip champagne while undergoing mostly English speed garage.

Worthwhile DJs who do the club rounds include the Belgian grandmaster and Amsterdam resident Eddy de Clerq, as well as Dimitri, Marcello and 100% Isis. Quazar is an excellent dance project set up by Gert van Veen, music critic with the newspaper *De Volkskrant*.

Alternative rockers Claw Boys Claw, 1960s pop legend Wally Tax and the Dutch-language rockers The Scene, De Dijk and Trockener Kecks have survived everything new, but rock bands are making a comeback and promising new bands are surfacing – check the bills at Paradiso, Melkweg and Arena, or mingle with Amsterdam's rock musicians at music café De Koe. The Excelsior Records label is home to Daryll Ann and upstarts such as Caesar, Johan, Benjamin B and Scram C Baby.

Experimental pop's heyday is over and it seems to have gone underground again. However, with the music of Det Whiel being used by top international choreographers for modern dance performances in the Muziektheater, the future for 'difficult music' could be looking brighter. New Age music is gaining territory – Coen Bais is one of the household names – while Human Alert represents the reborn punk movement.

World Music Cosmopolitan Amsterdam offers a wealth of world music. Suriname-born Ronald Snijders, a top jazz flautist, often participates in world-music projects. Another jazz flautist heading towards 'world' is the eternal Chris Hinze, for instance with his album Tibet Impressions, though most of his repertoire falls in the New Age category.

Fra-Fra-Sound plays 'paramaribop', a unique mixture of traditional Surinamese kaseko and jazz (the moniker is a contraction of Paramaribo, the capital of Suriname, and bebop), but the bulk of world repertoire

from Amsterdam is Latin, ranging from Cuban salsa to Dominican merengue and Argentinian tango. Try the following bands to get a taste of the local world scene: Nueva Manteca (salsa), Sexteto Canyengue (tango) and Eric Vaarzon Morel (flamenco).

For more information about these artists and gigs at Melkweg (especially), Paradiso, Akhnaton and Latin bars, see the excellent monthly salsa magazine *Oye Listen*. It's published in Dutch and Spanish, costs f5, and is available in specialist world-music shops such as South Miami Plaza (☎ 662 28 17), Albert Cuypstraat 182, or Concerto (☎ 623 52 28), Utrechtsestraat 52-60. Look for CDs by the above-mentioned bands on the Lucho, Munich and M&W labels.

The Roots Music Festival of world music is organised at different locations every year in June – check with the Uitburo or the VVV. The theatre of the Tropenmuseum (museum for the tropics) often hosts non-Western music concerts – ring ☎ 568 85 00 for details.

Literature

Dutch literature has been neglected by the English-speaking world, which is a shame. The lack of English translations is partly to blame. Interestingly, Flemish authorities are happy to subsidise translations of their authors but Dutch authorities are less inclined to do so.

The Dutch Shakespeare, Joost van den Vondel, is heavy going in his tragedy *Gijsbrecht van Aemstel* (1637), which is available in translation. It recounts the agony of the local count who had to go into exile after losing out to the count of Holland and his toll privileges. Vondel's best tragedy, *Lucifer* (1654), which describes the rebellion of the archangel against God, has also been translated. Other big authors of this period, Bredero (comedies) and Hooft (poems, plays, history, philosophy), have yet to appear in English.

The most interesting 19th-century author was Eduard Douwes Dekker, a colonial administrator and Amsterdam native who wrote under the pseudonym Multatuli (Latin for 'I have suffered greatly'). His *Max Havelaar:*

or the Coffee Auctions of the Dutch Trading Company (1860) exposed colonial narrow-mindedness in the dealings of a self-righteous coffee merchant. It shocked Dutch society and led to a review of the 'culture system' in the East Indies (the forced production of tropical crops for export). The Hague author Louis Couperus (*The Hidden Force*, 1900) explored the mystery of the East Indies from the colonialist's perspective.

The WWII occupation was a traumatic period that spawned many insightful works. *The Diary of Anne Frank* is a moving account of a Jewish girl's thoughts and yearnings while hiding in an annexe to avoid deportation by the Germans. The poignancy is enhanced by the knowledge that she was killed in the end. Etty Hillesum's *Etty: An Interrupted Life* is in a similar vein but more mature. Marga Minco *(The Fall, An Empty House, Bitter Herbs)* explores the war years from the perspective of a Jewish woman who survived.

Amsterdam author Harry Mulisch focuses on Dutch apathy during WWII *(The Last Call* and *The Assault*, which was made into an Oscar-winning film), but he has written much else that doesn't involve the war. His works have their ups and downs but he is one of the Great Authors of Dutch literature.

Jan Wolkers shocked Dutch readers in the 1960s with his provocatively misogynist but powerful *Turkish Delight*, which was made into a (Dutch) film by Paul Verhoeven starring Rutger Hauer. Xaviera Hollander (Vera de Vries) shocked the USA with an account of her call-girl experiences in *The Happy Hooker*.

Simon Carmiggelt *(A Dutchman's Slight Adventures, I'm Just Kidding)* wrote amusing vignettes of Pijp neighbourhood life in his column in the newspaper *Het Parool*. Nicolas Freeling *(A Long Silence, Love in Amsterdam, Because of the Cats)* created the BBC's Van der Valk detective series. Jan-Willem van der Wetering *(Hard Rain)* is another author of off-beat detective stories.

Cees Nooteboom *(A Song of Truth and Semblance, In the Dutch Mountains)* is accessible and amusing. Lieve Joris, a Flemish author who lives in Amsterdam, writes about cultures in transition in Africa, the Middle East and Eastern Europe. Her *Gates of Damascus*, about daily life in Syria, has been published in the Lonely Planet Journeys series, as has *Mali Blues*, an account of her quest to get to know a Mali musician. Another books in this series is *The Rainbird: A Central African Journey* by Jan Brokken, a highly regarded novelist, travel narrator and literary journalist. It's a fascinating account of white explorers, missionaries, slavers and adventurers who traipsed through the jungles of Gabon.

For more about books and where to buy them, see the Bookshops and Markets sections in the Shopping chapter. The third week in March is the national Boekenweek, when buyers who spend more than a certain amount in a bookshop receive a free (Dutch) book.

Cinema

Dutch films haven't exactly set the world on fire, though this has more to do with the language barrier and funding problems in a modest distribution area than with lack of talent.

One of the most important Dutch directors of all time was Joris Ivens (1898–1989), who was influenced by Russian film-makers but added his own impressionistic lyricism. He made award-winning documentaries about social and political issues – the Spanish Civil War, impoverished Belgian miners, Vietnam – but was also an accomplished visual artist in his own right; for instance in *Rain* (1929), a 15-minute impression of a rain shower in Amsterdam that took four months to shoot.

Directors, actors and camera operators who made the jump to English have done quite well for themselves. Paul Verhoeven *(Robocop, Total Recall, Basic Instinct, Starship Troopers)* is perhaps the best known director abroad, though his reputation has suffered from his disastrous *Showgirls*. George Sluizer *(The Vanishing)*, Dick Maas *(Flodder in Amerika, Amsterdamned)*, Fons Rademakers *(The Assault)* and Marleen Gorris *(Antonia's Line*, which won the

Oscar for best foreign film in 1996) have also made a name internationally, if not always among the general public. Ms Gorris' follow-up is an English-language film adaptation of Virginia Woolf's *Mrs Dalloway* starring Vanessa Redgrave. Jan de Bont, who won accolades for his camera work in *Jewel of the Nile* and *Black Rain*, directed the box-office hits *Speed* and *Twister*.

Rutger Hauer began his acting career at home as the lead in Paul Verhoeven's *Turks Fruit* (Turkish Delight, an Oscar nominee for best foreign film in the early 1970s), but has since gained glory in Hollywood with convincing bad-guy performances in disturbing films such as *The Hitcher* and *Blade Runner*. Jeroen Krabbé also became a well-paid Hollywood actor *(The Fugitive, The Living Daylights, Prince of Tides)* and has now turned to directing, with *Left Luggage* starring Isabella Rosselini.

The Filmmuseum in the Vondelpark is the national museum on this subject – it's not a museum with regular displays but screens interesting films from its huge archive. See Cinemas in the Entertainment chapter for more about films.

Theatre

The city has a rich theatrical tradition dating back to medieval times. In the Golden Age, when Dutch was the language of trade, local companies toured the theatres of Europe with Vondel's tragedies, Bredero's comedies and Hooft's verses. They're still performed locally in more modern renditions.

Theatre was immensely popular with all levels of society, perhaps because the city lacked a decent theatre building and plays were often performed outdoors. Gradually, however, the patrician class and their preoccupation with French culture turned theatre into a more elitist affair, and towards the end of the 19th century it had become snobbish, with little room for development.

This attitude persisted until the late 1960s, when disgruntled actors began to throw tomatoes at their older colleagues and engaged the audience in discussion about the essence of theatre. Avant-garde theatre companies such as Mickery and Shaffy

made Amsterdam a centre for experimental theatre, and many smaller companies sprang up in the 1970s and 1980s.

Most of these have now merged or disappeared as a result of cutbacks in government subsidies, while musicals and cabaret are enjoying a revival. But survivors and newcomers are still forging ahead with excellent productions – visual feasts with striking sets, lighting and creative costumes. The language barrier is of course an issue with Dutch productions, though with some of them it's hardly relevant.

English-language companies often visit Amsterdam, especially in summer – check the *Uitkrant* or ask at the AUB Uitburo. For more about theatre venues, see Theatre in the Entertainment chapter. The Holland Festival in June and the Uitmarkt on the last weekend in August are big theatre events (see Public Holidays & Special Events in the Facts for the Visitor chapter). Also worth catching is the International Theatre School Festival at the end of June, held in the theatres around Nes (Frascati, Brakke Grond etc).

SOCIETY & CONDUCT
Stereotypes

The Netherlands in general and Amsterdam in particular can be 15 years ahead of the rest of the world on some moral and social issues (drugs, abortion, euthanasia, homosexuality). On others they're 15 years behind, for instance with media policy, where every religious and ideological affiliation can broadcast but commercial motivation is still more or less frowned upon. Sometimes they step 15 years sideways, for instance in preaching to the rest of the world about right and wrong – perhaps the only other preachers with similar drive are the Americans.

Critics attribute this to the 'minister's mentality' of moral rectitude epitomised by the Calvinist minister scowling from the pulpit. Indeed, an acute sense of moral right and wrong comes through in the earnest insistence that it hardly matters *how* you say something, it's *what* you say that counts, which gives the Dutch a bit of a reputation for bluntness. And they do get carried away, hence the English term 'Dutch uncle' for someone who criticises frankly and severely.

It also gives them a reputation for lack of humour, yet they have an unusual ability to laugh at themselves and will cut down people who take themselves too seriously. 'Act normal, that's crazy enough', goes the saying.

Amsterdammers have little nationalist pride except on the soccer field. They love to complain about their city and their 'irrelevant' country, and are keen to learn new things foreign. English words in daily speech and print almost betray a national inferiority complex.

The city has few monumental buildings or projects. Most attempts at grandeur have traditionally been criticised, ridiculed and sabotaged, though Calvinist frugality has played a role too. Every separate house or building shines in its own individual way; grandeur is considered gross. It's almost as if people are proud of not being proud, except in their opinions.

It is said that the Calvinist Dutch, like the Presbyterian Scots, are careful with money, and they certainly have proven to be astute traders. It's worth remembering that the Netherlands and especially Amsterdam have always had a money culture: there was little or no traditional aristocracy with large landholdings. The people who dominated society built their own wealth and did so entirely on money – if they squandered it, they had nothing to fall back on. It determined prosperity and thus virtue.

The earlier History section discussed the phenomenon of 'pillarisation' (verzuiling), which allowed different ideologies their place in society so long as they maintained the status quo by compromise – important in an overpopulated country where opinions are taken so seriously. Verzuiling's social and cultural segmentation is considered outdated now, but it has left a strong legacy in a culture of tolerance and willing acceptance of an endless string of petty rules and regulations to make things work fairly. The Dutch will deliberate endlessly before they issue a planning permit or form a government. Everyone is expected to have an opinion and to voice it, but meddling in

others' affairs is 'not done' – at least not without following the proper procedures.

For instance, many foreigners have commented that thick cigarette smoke not just in pubs seems at odds with the high level of ecological concern. But it flows out of the Dutch commandment to be 'reasonable', to let everyone have their place and live their own life even if this puts some burdens on society. Public smoking is slowly being pushed back but these things take time. Can't get more Dutch than that.

Do's & Don'ts

The accepted greeting is a handshake – make it firm but not bone-crushing. Cheek-kissing (two or three pecks) is common between men and women (and between women) who know one another socially.

The typically pragmatic convention for queuing is to take a numbered ticket from a dispenser and await your turn. Always check whether there's a dispenser if you're in a post office, government office, bakery, at a delicatessen counter in a supermarket etc.

If you're invited home for dinner, bring something for the host: a bunch of flowers or a plant, a bottle of wine, or some good cake or pastries. It's polite to arrive five to 15 minutes late (never early) but business meetings start on time.

Dress standards are casual (most concerts, most restaurants) or smart casual (theatre, opera, upmarket restaurants and some business dealings); and slightly formal (most business dealings) or quite formal (bankers).

A special note for drug tourists: it is 'not done' to smoke dope in public. At 'coffeeshops' it's OK and in some other situations too, but even the hippest locals detest foreigners who think they can just toke anywhere. The same applies to drinking out on the street: the fact that you can do it doesn't mean it's accepted.

RELIGION

Amsterdam began as a Catholic city without being fervently anti-Protestant – after all, the money machine dictated tolerance. Even after the Alteration of 1578, when Amsterdam went over to the Protestant camp and

Calvinism became the leading faith in the northern Netherlands, the city authorities still promoted religious tolerance (though not freedom), even towards those who didn't belong to any church. Civil marriages (sanctioned by public officials rather than clergy) were legally recognised as early as the 17th century, a first in Europe.

The Protestant Hervormde Kerk (Dutch Reformed Church) was also fairly tolerant of dissenting views among its members, but in the late 19th century a growing minority of low-income strugglers disagreed with such tolerance and broke off to form the Gereformeerde Kerk ('Re-reformed' Church) in pursuit of orthodox-Calvinist doctrine. The schism persists to this day though it affects an ever smaller number of people.

Agnosticism and atheism reign supreme: almost 60% of Amsterdammers say they have no religious affiliation. Catholics are the largest religious grouping with 19% of the population against a national average of 32% – the term 'Catholic' should be used in preference to 'Roman Catholic' because many Catholics locally and nationally disagree with the pope on church hierarchy, contraception and abortion. The next largest religious grouping is Muslim at 8.3% (the national average is 3.7%), followed by Hervormd at 5.5% (15%), Gereformeerd at 3% (7%) and other religions (mainly Hindu and Buddhist) at 5.2% (3%).

LANGUAGE

Almost every Amsterdammer from age eight onwards seems to speak English, often very well and better than you're ever likely to learn Dutch. So why bother trying to communicate in the local language? That's a good question because you'll rarely get the opportunity to practise – your Dutch acquaintances will launch into English, maybe to show off but also because they're probably avid travellers, interested in foreigners, and know what it's like to struggle in situations like these. Nevertheless, a few words in Dutch are always appreciated – especially the phrase *Spreekt u Engels?* (Do you speak English?) before launching into English – and you might even begin to understand a bit more of what's going on around you.

For a brief guide to Dutch and some useful words and phrases, see the language chapter at the back of this book. For more extensive coverage of the language, pick up Lonely Planet's *Western Europe phrasebook*.

Facts for the Visitor

WHEN TO GO

Any time can be the best time to visit. The summer months are wonderful as the whole city seems to live outdoors and things happen everywhere. It's also the peak tourist season: accommodation is hard to find and prices are high. Many Amsterdammers go on holidays in summer and some businesses close down or adapt their activities (eg, museums, orchestras).

From mid-October to mid-March the climate is miserable but there are fewer tourists. Accommodation is relatively cheap (except around New Year) though some hotels might be closed. You'll mingle with 'real' Amsterdammers in cosy pubs and be able to enjoy the city's cultural life at its most authentic. The shoulder seasons, roughly from mid-March to late May and late August to mid-October, can offer the best of both worlds, though you might want to avoid Easter with its hordes of tourists and expensive hotels.

A festival or special event can enhance your visit – see Public Holidays & Special Events later in this chapter – but it won't be a secret and you might have trouble finding accommodation. If weather is your main concern, see Climate in the previous chapter.

ORIENTATION

Most of Amsterdam lies south of the IJ, an arm of what was once the Zuiderzee (an extension of the North Sea) but is now a vast lake, the IJsselmeer. The modern city sprawls in all directions and is several times larger than it was 50 years ago.

The old city is contained within the ring of concentric canals *(grachten)*, dating from the 17th century, that form the crescent-shaped canal belt *(grachtengordel)* bordered by the Singelgracht. Most areas beyond this tidy structure have been added since the second half of the 19th century.

The Amstel River cuts through the old city, which arose around Dam Square. East of this is the Old Side (Oude Zijde) and west is the New Side (Nieuwe Zijde). This medieval *binnenstad* (inner city) is enclosed by the Singel ('moat', not to be confused with the Singelgracht) to the west and south, and by the Kloveniersburgwal/Geldersekade to the east.

Centraal Station – the central train and bus station – lies on the south bank of the IJ at what used to be the mouth of the Amstel River, but the 'centre of town' is Dam Square a little to the south. It's the city's largest square and major road arteries radiate out from it, though there are several other 'centres' where everything seems to happen: Leidseplein, with much of the city's cultural life and nightlife, Rembrandtplein (nightlife), Spui ('intellectual' life), Muntplein (the city's busiest intersection), Stationsplein in front of Centraal Station (the main transport hub), Nieuwmarkt Square (daily life in general), Waterlooplein with the Stopera (market life behind a landmark on the Amstel), the large Museumplein (culture), and other, smaller focal points that make the city such a joy to explore.

Finding your way around the canal belt can be confusing, though it's a breeze compared with Venice. Think of it as the bottom half of a bicycle wheel: the medieval city is the hub, and several main roads and minor canals (and the Amstel itself) function as spokes. Orientation becomes easier once you know the sequence of the main canals (from the centre outwards: Singel, Herengracht, Keizersgracht, Prinsengracht and Singelgracht) and the names of some of the major 'spokes' (anticlockwise: Haarlemmerstraat/ Haarlemmerdijk, Brouwersgracht, Raadhuisstraat/Rozengracht, Leidsestraat, Vijzelstraat, Utrechtsestraat, Amstel, Weesperstraat and Plantage Middenlaan).

House numbers along the main canals start at the north-western end, at Brouwersgracht, with odd numbers along the inner quays (the 'city-centre' sides). Elsewhere, numbers start at the end of the street closest to the city centre.

MAPS

The maps in this book will probably suffice in most cases. Lonely Planet's handy *Amsterdam City Map* has a street index that covers the more popular parts of town in detail – and is plastic-coated to make it rainproof. The VVV tourist offices also have a map but it's not free.

If you need something that shows every street in the whole city including the outer suburbs, then newsagencies and many other outlets sell the Dutch-produced Cito Plan or the German Falkplan. They're both good but the Cito is probably the clearest, in either the ring-bound booklet or large sheet version, though it has to be tilted clockwise a bit to get true north facing up. The Swiss Hallwag sheet map is also good and very clear but the smallest streets aren't labelled. Michelin has finally brought out a proper map of Amsterdam, a large sheet map with all the meticulous linework one has come to expect from this renowned map maker. Unfortunately it's already out of date and doesn't show as much detail in the new parts of the city as the Cito does.

A beautiful souvenir map to hang on the wall when you get home is the lovingly drawn bird's-eye view produced by Bollmann, a German map publisher specialising in this type of product. The map shows the city centre in 1971 and every house is recognisable. It can be hard to find, but geographical bookshop Jacob van Wijngaarden (Map 6; ☎ 612 19 01) at Overtoom 97 should have it.

TOURIST OFFICES
Local Tourist Offices

Within the Netherlands, tourist information is supplied by the VVV (Vereniging voor Vreemdelingenverkeer – Society for Foreigner Traffic), which has four offices in Amsterdam and a fifth, called Holland Tourist Information, at the airport. All its publications cost money and it charges high commissions for services (f6 per person to find a room, f2.50 to f5 on theatre tickets etc). The offices are often very busy but it's worth queuing to get an Amsterdam Culture & Leisure Pass (see Other

Documents & Cards in the following Documents section).

The GWK office (official exchange bureau, see Exchanging Money in the later Money section) inside Centraal Station also books rooms for a f5 commission (plus 10% of the hotel fee) at a separate counter that's usually quieter than the VVV counters.

The VVV information number (☎ 0900-400 40 40) operates Monday to Friday from 9 am to 5 pm and costs a hefty f1 a minute. The VVV fax number is 625 28 69 and the mailing address is Postbus 3901, 1001 AS Amsterdam. Office details are as follows:

VVV (Map 2) Stationsplein 10 in front of Centraal Station. The main VVV office, open seven days a week from 9 am to 5 pm; expect long queues and variable service

VVV, inside Centraal Station, along track 2 ('spoor 2'). Open Monday to Saturday from 8 am to 7.45 pm, Sunday from 9 am to 5 pm; often busy but often not (luck of the draw)

VVV (Map 4) Leidseplein 1 on the corner of Leidsestraat. Open Monday to Friday from 9 am to 7 pm, weekends to 5 pm; shares premises with a GWK-affiliated exchange office that offers reasonable rates

VVV (Map 1) Van Tuyll van Serooskerkenweg 125 at Stadionplein. Open seven days a week from 9 am to 5 pm; useful if you're arriving by car from the south and usually much quieter than the other offices

Holland Tourist Information (VVV), Schiphol Plaza in the airport. Open seven days a week from 7 am to 10 pm

Tourist Offices Abroad

The Nederlands Bureau voor Toerisme (NBT) handles tourism inquiries outside the country:

Belgium & Luxembourg (☎ 02-543 08 00) NBT, Louizalaan 89, Postbus 136, 1050 Brussels

Canada (☎ 416-363 15 77) Netherlands Board of Tourism, 25 Adelaide St East, Suite 710, Toronto, Ont, M5C 1Y2

France (☎ 1 43 12 34 20) Office Néerlandais du Tourisme, 9 rue Scribe, 75009 Paris

Germany (☎ 0221-9257 1727) Niederländisches Büro für Tourismus, Friesplatz 1, Postfach 270580, 50511 Cologne

euro currency converter f1 = €0.45

Japan (☎ 03-32 22 11 15) Netherlands Board of Tourism, NK Shinwa Building 5f 5-1, Koij-machi, Chiyoda-ku, Tokyo 102

Sweden, Denmark, Norway & Finland (☎ 08-5560 0750) Holländska Turistbyrån, Högbergsgatan 50-1tr, 1118 26 Stockholm

UK & Ireland (☎ 020-7828 7900) Netherlands Board of Tourism, 18 Buckingham Gate, PO Box 523, London SW1E 6NT

USA (☎ 312-819 17 40) Netherlands Board of Tourism, 225 N Michigan Ave, Suite 1854, Chicago, IL 60601

The NBT office in Sydney, Australia, has closed down – the embassy in Canberra, consulates in the major cities or the KLM office in Sydney might be able to help.

Other Information Sources

The VVV is all right for mainstream tourist information but other places might serve you better. If you're interested in the arts (theatres, concerts, films, museums etc) the Amsterdam Uitburo, or AUB (Map 6; ☎ 0900-01 91, f0.75 per minute), Leidseplein 26, has lots of free magazines and brochures, and sells tickets for a f3 markup. The staff are friendlier and more helpful than at the VVV. The office is open daily from 10 am to 6 pm, Thursday to 9 pm. The telephone number operates seven days a week from 9 am to 9 pm for information and ticket reservations. You can email specific queries to ✉ aub@aub.nl.

The Dutch automobile association ANWB (Map 6; ☎ 673 08 44), Museum-plein 5, has free or discounted maps and brochures and provides a wide range of useful information and assistance if you're travelling with any type of vehicle (car, bicycle, motorcycle, yacht etc). The material on Amsterdam itself is limited but there's more than enough about the Netherlands and Europe. You'll probably have to show proof of membership of your automobile club (see Other Documents & Cards in the following section).

If you plan to stay in Amsterdam for a while, the city hall information centre (Map 4; ☎ 624 11 11), Amstel 1 (Waterlooplein entrance), has pamphlets and booklets on almost every aspect of living in the city,

some of them in English. It's open Monday to Friday from 8.30 am to 5 pm. The staff are quite helpful and, as almost everywhere else, speak good English. They use their computerised database to track down addresses and phone numbers of relevant organisations, or you can have a go yourself.

See also the Internet Resources section later in this chapter for useful Web sites on Amsterdam.

DOCUMENTS
Visas

Tourists from Australia, Canada, Israel, Japan, Korea (south), New Zealand, Singapore, the USA and most of Europe need only a valid passport – no visa – for a stay of up to three months. EU nationals can enter for three months with just their national identity card or a passport expired less than five years.

Nationals of most other countries need a so-called Schengen Visa valid for 90 days, named after the Schengen Agreement that abolished passport controls between the EU member states (except the UK and Ireland) plus Norway and Iceland. A visa for any of these countries should, in theory, be valid throughout the area, but it pays to double-check with the embassy or consulate of each country you intend to visit because the agreement is not yet fully implemented – some countries may impose additional restrictions on some nationalities. Residency status in any of the Schengen countries negates the need for a visa, regardless of your nationality.

Schengen visas are issued by Dutch embassies or consulates and can take a while to process (up to three months, if you're unlucky), so don't leave it till the last moment. You'll need a valid passport (valid till at least three months after your visit) and 'sufficient' funds to finance your stay. Fees vary depending on your nationality – the embassy or consulate can tell you more.

Visas for study purposes are complicated – check with the Dutch embassy or consulate. For work visas, see Work later in this chapter.

Visa Extensions The Netherlands is the most densely populated country in Europe and voters seem to support the government crackdown on people who don't 'belong'. Tourist visas can be extended for another three months maximum, but you'll need a good reason and the extension will only be valid for the Netherlands, not the Schengen area.

Visa extensions and residence permits are handled by the Vreemdelingenpolitie (Aliens' Police; Map 1; ☎ 559 63 00), Johan Huizingalaan 757 out in the southwestern suburbs, Monday to Friday from 8 am to 5 pm. A visa extension shouldn't take long if you make an appointment – if you just turn up you may have to wait a couple of hours. Residence permits are handled by appointment only.

Travel Insurance
Medical or dental costs might already be covered through reciprocal health-care arrangements (see Health later in this chapter) but you'll still need cover for theft or loss, and for unexpected changes to travel arrangements (ticket cancellation etc). Check what's already covered by your local insurance policies or credit card: you might not need separate travel insurance. In most cases, though, this secondary type of cover is very limited with lots of tricky small print. For peace of mind, nothing beats straight travel insurance at the highest level you can afford.

Driving Licence & Permits
Naturally you'll need to show a valid driving licence when hiring a car. Visitors from outside the EU should also consider an international driving permit (IDP). Car-rental firms will rarely ask for one but the police might do so if they pull you up. An IDP can be obtained for a small fee from your local automobile association – bring along a valid licence and a passport photo – and is only valid (for a year) together with your original licence.

Automobile Association If you're travelling with any type of vehicle, the Dutch automobile association ANWB (see Other Information Sources in the previous section) will provide a wide range of services free of charge if you can show proof of membership of the equivalent association at home, preferably in the form of a letter of introduction such as the yellow Entraide Touring Internationale document. Your automobile club should be able to provide this; if the staff have never heard of it, ask for someone who knows their stuff.

Hostel Cards
A Hostelling International card is useful at the official youth hostels – nonmembers are welcome but pay f5 more per night. Other hostels may give small discounts. If you don't pick up a HI card before leaving home you can buy one at youth hostels in the Netherlands.

Student & Youth Cards
An International Student Identity Card (ISIC) won't give admission discounts but it might pay for itself through discounted air and ferry tickets, and the GWK exchange offices will charge 25% less commission when exchanging cash. The same applies to hostel cards, as well as the GO 25 card for people aged under 26 who aren't students, issued by the Federation of International Youth Travel Organisations (FIYTO), through student unions or student travel agencies.

The Cultureel Jongeren Paspoort (CJP, Cultural Youth Passport) is a national institution that gives people aged under 27 whopping discounts to museums and cultural events around the country – any young person with a particular interest in the arts is well advised to get one. It costs f22.50 a year and is available at VVV offices or the Amsterdam Uitburo (see Other Information Sources earlier in this chapter). You don't have to be Dutch but you do need decent ID.

Other Documents & Cards
If you plan to visit several of Amsterdam's excellent but expensive museums, invest in a Museumjaarkaart (Museum Year Card), which gives free admission to most of the city's museums – see the boxed text

'A Medley of Museums' in the Things to See & Do chapter.

Teachers, professional artists, museum conservators and certain categories of students may get discounts at a few museums or even be admitted free – it sometimes depends on the person behind the counter. Bring proof of affiliation, eg, an International Teacher Identity Card (ITIC).

The VVV offices and some large hotels sell the Amsterdam Culture & Leisure Pass. This contains 31 vouchers that give free entry or substantial discounts to the most important museums, a free canal cruise, and discounts on land and water transport and some restaurants. The pass represents a total value of f170 and sells for f39.50, which could be a good investment depending on your interests.

Seniors get discounts on a wide range of services (see Senior Travellers later in this chapter).

Copies

All important documents (passport data page and visa page, credit cards, travel insurance policy, air/bus/train ticket, driving licence etc) should be photocopied before you leave home. Leave one copy with someone at home and keep another one with you, separate from the originals.

It's also a good idea to store details of your vital travel documents in Lonely Planet's free online Travel Vault in case you lose the photocopies. Your password-protected Travel Vault is accessible online anywhere in the world – create it at www.ekno.lonelyplanet.com.

EMBASSIES & CONSULATES
Dutch Embassies & Consulates

Dutch embassies abroad include the following:

Australia (☎ 02-6273 3111) 120 Empire Circuit, Yarralumla, ACT 2600
Belgium (☎ 02-679 17 11) Herrmann Debroux-laan 48, 1160 Brussels
Canada (☎ 613-237 5030) Suite 2020, 350 Albert St, Ottawa, Ont K1R 1A4
France (☎ 01 40 62 33 00) 7–9 Rue Eblé, 75007 Paris

Germany (☎ 030-20 95 60) 20th & 21st Floor, Friedrichstrasse 95, 10117 Berlin
Ireland (☎ 01-269 3444) 160 Merrion Rd, Dublin 4
Luxembourg (☎ 22 75 70) 5 rue CM Spoo, L-2546 Luxembourg
New Zealand (☎ 04-471 6390) Investment House, Cnr Featherston & Ballance Sts, Wellington
UK (☎ 020-7590 3200) 38 Hyde Park Gate, London SW7 5DP
USA (☎ 202-244 5300) 4200 Linnean Ave, NW Washington, DC 20008

Consulates in Amsterdam

Amsterdam is the country's capital but the government and ministries are based in The Hague, so that's where all the embassies are (a 45-minute train ride away, f16.75). There are, however, 37 consulates in Amsterdam, listed under 'Consulaat' in the phone book. These include:

Denmark (☎ 682 99 91) Radarweg 503
France (Map 6; ☎ 530 69 69) Vijzelgracht 2 – open weekdays from 9 to 11 am
Germany (Map 1; ☎ 673 62 45) De Lairesse-straat 172
Italy (Map 4; ☎ 624 00 43) Herengracht 609
Japan (Map 6; ☎ 691 69 21) Vijzelgracht 50
Luxembourg (☎ 301 56 22) Reimersbeek 2
Norway (Map 4; ☎ 624 23 31) Keizersgracht 534-I
Spain (Map 6; ☎ 620 38 11) Frederiksplein 34 – open weekdays from 9 to 11 am
Thailand (☎ 679 99 16) Emmastraat 40
UK (Map 1; ☎ 676-43 43) Koningslaan 44 near the Vondelpark – open weekdays from 9 am to noon and 2 to 3.30 pm
USA (Map 6; ☎ 575 53 09) Museumplein 19 near the Concertgebouw – open weekdays from 8.30 am to noon and 1.30 to 3.30 pm

Embassies in The Hague

Australia (☎ 070-310 82 00) Carnegielaan 4
Belgium (☎ 070-312 34 56) Lange Vijverberg 12
Canada (☎ 070-311 16 00) Sophialaan 7
Finland (☎ 070-363 85 75) Groot Hertoginne-laan 16
Ireland (☎ 070-363 09 93) Dr Kuijperstraat 9
Korea (south) (☎ 070-358 60 76) Verlengde Tolweg 8
New Zealand (☎ 070-346 93 24) Carnegielaan 10-IV

South Africa (☎ 070-392 45 01)
Wassenaarseweg 40
Sweden (☎ 070-412 02 00) Van Karnebeeklaan
6A

Your Own Embassy

It's important to realise what your own embassy – the embassy of the country of which you are a citizen – can and can't do to help you if you get into trouble. Generally speaking, it won't be much help in emergencies if the trouble you're in is remotely your own fault. Remember that you are bound by the laws of the country you are in. Your embassy will not be sympathetic if you end up in jail after committing a crime locally, even if such actions are legal in your own country.

In genuine emergencies you might get some assistance, but only if other channels have been exhausted. For example, if you need to get home urgently, a free ticket home is exceedingly unlikely – the embassy would expect you to have insurance. If you have all your money and documents stolen, it might assist with getting a new passport, but a loan for onward travel is out of the question.

Some embassies used to keep letters for travellers or have a small reading room with home newspapers, but these days the mail holding service has usually been stopped and even newspapers tend to be out of date.

CUSTOMS

Visitors from EU countries can bring virtually anything they like, provided it's for personal use and they bought it in an EU country where the appropriate local tax was levied. Duty-free allowances on cigarettes and alcohol have been abolished within the EU, though allowances on others products (perfume etc) remain in place. The staff at duty-free shops will ask to see your ticket and will tell you in no uncertain terms how much (or rather, little) they're willing to sell you – though you're welcome to buy your whisky at the local, taxed price.

Visitors from a European country outside the EU and not resident in the EU can import goods and gifts valued up to f125 (bought tax-free) as well as 200 cigarettes (or 50 cigars or 250g of tobacco), 1L of liquor more than 22% by volume or 2L less than 22% by volume, plus 2L of wine and 8L of nonsparkling Luxembourg wine, 60g of perfume and 0.25L of eau de toilette.

Visitors from outside Europe and resident outside Europe can bring in 400 cigarettes (or 100 cigars or 500g of tobacco) plus other goods, spirits, wines and perfumes as for non-EU Europeans.

Tobacco and alcohol may only be brought in by people aged 17 and over.

MONEY
Currency

The unit of currency is the guilder (*gulden*, abbreviated f, fl, Hfl or Dfl), divided into 100 cents. There are f1000, f250, f100, f50, f25 and f10 bank notes, and f5, f2.50, f1, f0.25, f0.10 and f0.05 coins. One-cent coins no longer exist – prices in supermarkets are still indicated in cents (eg, f5.99) but the bill is rounded off to the nearest five cents when paid in cash.

The Dutch flair for graphic design shows in the eye-catching bank notes (the bland coins are widely considered a flop), in particular the f100 note with its Escher-type 'building blocks', or the stunning f10 bill. If you're on the sort of budget where you would receive a f1000 note from the bank, ask to have it broken down into f250 and preferably f100 and f50 notes because many places refuse the largest denominations.

The Netherlands is participating in the euro, the European single currency. See the following boxed text 'Introducing the Euro' for an explanation of this process and what it means for the visitor.

Exchange Rates

Exchange rates at the time of going to press were:

Australia	A$1	=	f1.41
Belgium	Bf10	=	f0.55
Canada	C$1	=	f1.54
Denmark	Dkr1	=	f0.30
euro	€1	=	f2.20
France	1FF	=	f0.34
Germany	DM1	=	f1.13
Italy	L1000	=	f1.14
Japan	¥100	=	f2.02

euro currency converter f1 = €0.45

Introducing the Euro

On 1 January 1999 a new currency, the euro, was introduced in Europe and on that date the exchange rates of the participating countries were irrevocably fixed to the euro – in the case of the Netherlands, at f2.20371 to the euro. Denmark, Greece, Sweden and the UK refused to participate (for the time being), but the other EU members including the Netherlands are gradually phasing out their local currencies in favour of the euro. One of the main benefits will be that you can easily compare prices in the participating countries without all those tedious calculations.

At the time of writing, the euro is used for 'paper' accounting and prices are often displayed in guilders as well as euros, though cash payments are still entirely in guilders. On 1 January 2002 euro banknotes and coins will usher in a period of dual use as guilders are withdrawn from circulation. By July 2002 only euro notes and coins will remain.

The €5 note in the Netherlands is the same €5 note you will use in Italy and Portugal. Notes will come in denominations of 500, 200, 100, 50, 20, 10 and five euros. Coins will come in denominations of two and one euros, then 50, 20, 10, five, two and one cents. On the reverse side of the coins each participating state will be able to use their own designs, but all euro coins can be used anywhere that accepts euros.

It is uncertain exactly what practices will be adopted until the euro takes over completely. The Dutch in general are happy to adopt the euro but some shops might be more ready to do so than others. For the time being, it's wise to check euro bills and coins carefully to make sure that any conversion from guilders has been calculated correctly. The most confusing period will probably be between January 2002 and July 2002 when there will be two sets of notes and coins.

After that date, you won't need to change money at all when travelling to other single-currency members. Banks may still charge a handling fee (yet to be decided) for travellers cheques but they won't be able to profit by buying the currency from you at one rate and selling it back to you at another.

The Lonely Planet Web site at www.lonelyplanet.com has a link to a currency converter and up-to-date news on the euro integration process.

Australia	A$1	=	€0.64	Canada	C$1	=	€0.70
France	1FF	=	€0.15	Germany	DM1	=	€0.51
Japan	¥100	=	€0.92	Netherlands	f1	=	€0.45
New Zealand	NZ$1	=	€0.50	Spain	100 pta	=	€0.60
UK	UK£1	=	€1.63	USA	US$1	=	€1.02

Switzerland	Sfr1	=	f1.37
UK	UK£	=	f3.59
USA	US$1	=	f2.24

Exchanging Money

Avoid the private exchange booths dotted around the tourist areas: they're convenient and open late hours but rates and/or commissions are lousy, though competition is fierce and you may do reasonably well if you hunt around. Banks and post offices (every post office is an agent for the Postbank) stick to official exchange rates and charge a commission of f5 to f6, as do the Grenswisselkantoren (GWK, Border Exchange Offices; ☎ 0800-566, free informa-

tion service). Keep in mind that exchange rates between euro currencies are fixed and it all comes down to commissions these days. Reliable exchange centres include:

GWK (☎ 627 27 31) Centraal Station at the west end of the station hall. Open 24 hours; charges various commissions on cash and travellers cheques (with a student card there's 25% less commission on cash). Usually very busy (though its separate hotel-booking counter for bookings only, open from 7.45 am to 10 pm seven days a week, is usually quieter than the VVV ones). There's a GWK-affiliated office with slightly worse rates for non-euro currencies next to the VVV office in Leidsestraat, on the corner of Leidseplein

GWK (☎ 653 51 21) Schiphol airport. Open 24 hours

American Express (Map 4; ☎ 504 87 77) Damrak 66. Open Monday to Friday from 9 am to 5 pm, Saturday to noon; no commission on AmEx cheques

Thomas Cook (Map 4; ☎ 625 09 22), Dam 23–25, with other offices at the beginning of Damrak opposite Centraal Station (Map 4) and at Leidseplein 31A (Map 6). Open weekdays from 9 am to 7 pm, Saturday to 6 pm, Sunday from 10 am to 4.30 pm; no commission on Thomas Cook cheques; report lost or stolen cheques to ☎ 0800-022 86 30

VSB Bank (Map 4; ☎ 624 93 40) Singel 548 at the Flower Market near Vijzelstraat. Just one of several branches of this bank, where you can withdraw money over the counter with a credit card; 24-hour exchange machine (and of course the usual ATMs) outside

Cash This is still very much a cash-based society and nothing beats cash for convenience – or risk of theft/loss. Plan to pay cash for most daily expenses, though staff at upmarket hotels might cast a furtive glance if you pay a huge bill with small-denomination notes rather than a credit card, and car-rental agencies will probably refuse to do business if you only have cash. Keep the equivalent of about US$50 separate from the rest of your money as an emergency stash.

Travellers Cheques & Eurocheques

Banks charge a commission to cash travellers cheques (with ID such as a passport). American Express and Thomas Cook don't charge commission on their own cheques but their rates might be less favourable. Shops, restaurants and hotels always prefer cash; a few might accept travellers cheques but their rates will be anybody's guess.

Eurocheques (with guarantee card) – not to be confused with the new currency (though you can of course write them in euros) – are much more widely accepted, and because you write the amount in guilders there's no confusion about exchange rates; they get charged to your account at the more favourable interbank rate.

ATMs Automatic teller machines can be found outside most banks, though in some cases you might have to swipe your card through a slot to gain entry to a secure area. There are ATMs around the airport halls as well, and a couple with long queues in the main hall of Centraal Station (diagonally to the left as you enter through the main entrance). Visa and MasterCard/Eurocard are widely accepted, as well as cash cards that access the Cirrus network. Logos on ATMs show what they accept. Beware that if you're limited to a maximum withdrawal per day, the 'day' will coincide with that in your home country.

Credit Cards All the major international cards are recognised, but Amsterdam is still strongly cash-based and many restaurants and hotels (even some of the more upmarket ones) may refuse payment by card. Check first. Shops often levy a cheeky 5% surcharge (sometimes more) on credit cards to offset the commissions charged by card providers.

To withdraw money at a bank counter instead of through an ATM, go to a VSB Bank or GWK branch. You'll need to show your passport.

Report lost or stolen cards to the following 24-hour numbers:

American Express – ☎ 504 80 00 (Monday to Friday from 9 am to 6 pm), ☎ 504 86 66 (other times)

Diners Club – ☎ 557 34 07

Eurocard and **MasterCard** have a number in Utrecht (☎ 030-283 55 55) but foreigners are advised to ring the emergency number in their home country to speed things up.

Visa – ☎ 660 06 11

International Transfers Transferring money from your home bank will be easier if you've authorised somebody back home to access your account. In Amsterdam, find a large bank and ask for the international division. A commission is charged on telegraphic transfers, which can take up to a week but usually less if you're well prepared; by mail, allow two weeks.

The GWK is an agent for Western Union and money is transferred within 15 minutes of lodgment at the other end. The person lodging the transfer pays a commission that

euro currency converter f1 = €0.45

varies from country to country. Money can also be transferred via American Express and Thomas Cook.

Costs

The sky's the limit in Amsterdam: you can easily throw hundreds of guilders down the drain each day with little to show for it. At rock-bottom, if you stay at a camp site or hostel and eat cheaply, you might get away with f50 a day. A (very) cheap hotel, pub meals and the occasional beer and sundries will set you back f100. Things become a bit more comfortable on f150 a day.

Tipping & Bargaining

Tipping is not compulsory, but if you're pleased with the service by all means 'round up' the bill by 5% to 10% – many people do so in taxis and restaurants. A tip of 10% is considered quite generous. In pubs with pavement or table service it's common practice (but not compulsory) to leave the small change. Service is usually efficient but hardly ever formal and sometimes quite indifferent; shouting or 'talking down' to staff will ensure they ignore you. Toilet attendants should be tipped f0.25 to f0.50, though in some clubs they demand f1.

Ironically for a city with such a rich trading history, there's very little bargaining – it's definitely not done in shops. People do bargain at flea markets, though you'll have to be pretty good at this if your Dutch isn't fluent. Prices at food markets are generally set but become more negotiable later in the day.

The so-called Dutch auction, where the auctioneer keeps lowering the price until somebody takes the item, is still practised at flower and plant auctions such as the huge flower market in Aalsmeer and the Monday plant market on Amstelveld.

Taxes & Refunds

Value-added tax (Belasting Toegevoegde Waarde, or BTW) is calculated at 19% for most goods except consumer items like food and books, which attract 6%. The usual high excise *(accijns)* is levied on petrol, cigarettes and alcohol – petrol here is among the most expensive in Europe. The price for a packet of cigarettes is indicated on an excise sticker, and it will cost the same whether you buy it in the Amstel Hotel or the corner tobacco shop, separately or by the carton.

Hotel accommodation is subject to a 5% 'city hotel tax' that is usually included in the quoted price except at the more expensive hotels.

Travellers from non-EU countries can have the BTW refunded on goods over f300 if they're bought from one shop on one day and are exported out of the EU within three months. To claim the tax back, ask the shop owner to provide an export certificate when you make the purchase. When you leave for a non-EU country, get the form endorsed by a Dutch customs official, who will send the certificate to the supplier, who in turn refunds you the tax by cheque or money order. If you want the tax as you leave the country, it's best to buy from shops displaying a 'Tax Free for Tourists' sign, though you'll lose about 5% of the refund in commissions. In this case the shopkeeper gives you a stamped cheque that can be cashed when you leave.

Buying with a credit card is the best system as you won't pay tax so long as you get customs to stamp the receipt the shop owner gave you and you send the receipt back to the shop.

POST & COMMUNICATIONS
Post

Post offices are open weekdays from 9 am to 5 pm, more or less. The main post office at Singel 250 (Map 4) is open weekdays from 9 am to 7 pm and Saturday to noon. The poste restante section is to the left of the main entrance as you face the building, downstairs in the postbox area. The district post office at Centraal Station, Oosterdokskade 3 (Map 5; a few hundred metres east of the station, alongside the huge boat hotel), is open weekdays from 9 am to 9 pm and Saturday to noon. The large post office in the Stopera (the city hall/opera complex at Waterlooplein; Map 4) is open weekdays from 9 am to 6 pm, and Saturday from 10 am to 1.30 pm.

For queries about postal services, ring ☎ 0800-04 17 (free) – wait for the messages to finish and you'll eventually be helped by a human.

Mail is delivered locally six days a week. Unless you're sending mail within the Amsterdam region, the slot to use in the rectangular, red letterboxes is *Overige Post-codes* (Other Postal Codes).

Rates Letters within Europe (only air mail, known as 'priority') cost fl up to 20g; beyond Europe they cost fl.60 (priority) or fl.25 (standard). Postcards (only priority) cost fl to anywhere outside the country. An aerogram *(priorityblad)* costs fl.30. Within the country, letters (up to 20g) or postcards cost f0.80.

Standard mail (also available within Europe for parcels and printed matter) is not much cheaper than priority and takes about twice as long to reach the destination. For instance, a priority parcel to the UK takes two to three days, whereas standard takes four to five; to the USA, it's four to six days as opposed to eight to 12.

Addresses The postal code (four numbers followed by two letters) comes in front of the city or town name, eg, 1017 LS Amsterdam. The codes are complicated and there's little apparent logic to them, but they pinpoint an address to within 100m. The telephone book provides the appropriate postal code for each address, or you can pick up a free booklet at a post office (not always in stock). Amsterdam postal codes start with 10. No two streets in the city have the same name, so if you don't know the code but you've got the address right your mail should still arrive with a few days' delay.

There are a few peculiarities with street numbers. Sometimes they're followed by a letter or number (often in Roman numerals). Letters (eg, No 34A or 34a) usually indicate the appropriate front door when two or more share the same number, whereas numbers (34-2, 34² or 34-II) indicate the appropriate floor. In modern dwellings, letters often indicate the appropriate apartment irrespective of the floor. The suffix 'hs' (34hs)

stands for *huis* (house) and means the dwelling is on the ground floor, which may be half a floor above street level (in which case it's sometimes called *beletage*, the floor behind the door bell). The suffix 'bg' (34bg) stands for *begane grond* (ground floor). The suffix 'sous' (34sous) stands for *souterrain* and means the dwelling is in the basement (or rather, a basement that's half under street level; it can't be much deeper because of groundwater).

Telephone

This used to be one of the more expensive European countries for phone calls but prices keep coming down with the new phenomenon of competition, and the network has become even more efficient. Unfortunately there's no longer an official telephone centre but there are plenty of public telephones and you can always call from a post office. There are a few Primafoon phone centres run by the privatised KPN-Telecom company but they seem more interested in selling mobile phones and answering machines. 'International call centres' aren't as ubiquitous as they used to be, which is probably a good thing because some seem to be run by shady-looking characters who charge funny rates. As always, using a hotel phone is much more expensive than any other type of phone.

For local directory information, call ☎ 0900-80 08 (f0.95 for up to three numbers, free from a phone box). International directory inquiries can be reached on ☎ 0900-84 18 (fl.05 for up to two numbers). To place a collect call *(collect gesprek)*, ring ☎ 0800-01 01 (free call). For other operator-assisted calls, ring ☎ 0800-04 10 (free call, though you'll be charged a f7.70 service fee if you could have rung the country direct).

Dialling Tones Tones are similar to those used throughout most of Continental Europe: an even dialling tone at fairly lengthy intervals means the number is ringing; a similar tone at shorter intervals means the number is engaged; a three-step tone means the number isn't in use or has been disconnected.

euro currency converter f1 = €0.45

Costs Calls within the metropolitan area are time-based, and the official, KPN-Telecom public phone boxes cost a flat f0.20 a minute regardless of when you ring (public phones in cafés, supermarkets and hotel lobbies can charge anything up to f0.50 a minute). The minimum charge from a public phone is f0.25. Private phones cost f0.06 a minute weekdays from 8 am to 8 pm, f0.03 a minute in the evenings, and f0.02 a minute from 8 pm Friday to 8 am Monday. For calls outside the metropolitan area, KPN's public phones charge f0.30 a minute regardless of when you ring, whereas private phones cost f0.125 a minute between 8 am and 8 pm weekdays and half that at other times.

The cost of international calls varies with the destination and changes frequently due to competition. At the time of writing, Britain cost f0.21 a minute, the USA f0.19, and Australia f0.80 to f0.90 – but don't forget to add f0.20 a minute to these rates when ringing from a KPN phone box.

Phonecards There's a wide range of local and international phonecards. Lonely Planet's eKno Communication Card (see the insert at the back of this book) works from private as well as public phones and is aimed specifically at independent travellers. It provides budget international calls (for local calls you're better off with a local card), a range of messaging services, free email and travel information. You can join online at www.ekno.lonelyplanet.com, or by phone from Amsterdam by dialling ☎ 0800-022 35 16 (free call). Once you have joined, to use eKno from the Netherlands, dial ☎ 0800-022 36 05.

Most public telephones in Amsterdam are cardphones and there may be queues at the few remaining coin phones. KPN-Telecom cards are available at post offices, train station counters, VVV and GWK offices and tobacco shops for f5, f10 and f25, and calls cost the same regardless of the value of the card (ie, you get no discount). Note that railway stations have Telfort phone booths that require a Telfort card, though there should be KPN booths outside.

0800, 0900 & 06 Numbers Many information services, either recorded or live, use phone numbers beginning with ☎ 0800 (free) or ☎ 0900 (which cost between f0.22 and f1.05 a minute depending on the number). To avoid running up big phone bills, care should be taken whenever dialling ☎ 0900. Businesses that quote an 0900 number are required by law to state what it costs, but costs can vary depending on where you ring from so this isn't always clear.

Numbers beginning with ☎ 06-5 or ☎ 06-6 are mobile and pager numbers. Numbers beginning with ☎ 0909 are for paid amusement (radio and TV games, for instance); ☎ 0906 numbers are for sex and chat lines.

Using Phone Books Similar surnames are listed alphabetically by address and not by initials, because local research has shown that people recall an address more readily than someone's initials. Confusingly, Dutch dictionaries and most other listings put the contracted vowel 'ij' after the 'i' but phone books treat it as a 'y'. Note that surnames beginning with 'van', 'de' etc are listed under the root name, eg, 'V van Gogh' would be listed as 'Gogh, .V van'. For married women and widows who use their husbands' names, the maiden name traditionally comes after the name of the husband.

The phone book lists postal codes for each entry and fax numbers where relevant. The pink pages at the front are business pages but business names are copied in the white pages as well.

Phone Codes To ring abroad, dial ☎ 00 followed by the country code for your target country, the area code (drop the leading 0 if there is one) and the subscriber number. The country code for the Netherlands is ☎ 31 and the area code for Greater Amsterdam is ☎ 020 (drop the leading 0 if ringing from another country). Other area codes include:

Alkmaar	☎ 072
Delft	☎ 015
Haarlem	☎ 023
IJmuiden	☎ 0255

Leiden	☎ 071
Rotterdam	☎ 010
The Hague	☎ 070
Utrecht	☎ 030
Zaandam	☎ 075

The area code for Schiphol is the same as for Amsterdam but numbers are listed separately at the end of the phone book, just before the 0800/0900 listings. The southern suburb of Amstelveen is not included in the Amsterdam phone book, nor is the eastern suburb of Diemen, though they have the same 020 area code.

Home Country Direct Instead of placing a collect call through the local operator you could dial directly to your home country operator and then reverse charges, charge the call to a phone company credit card or perform other credit feats. This is possible to many (not all) countries and costs a fair bit – check with your home phone company before you leave though you might not get the full cost story. The following is a selection (with the relevant country codes in brackets for reference; ring international directory inquiries if your country isn't listed or the number appears to have changed:

(61) Australia	☎ 0800-022 00 61 (Telstra)
	☎ 0800-022 55 61 (Optus)
(32) Belgium	☎ 0800-022 11 32
(1) Canada	☎ 0800-022 91 16
(358) Finland	☎ 0800-022 03 58
(33) France	☎ 0800-022 20 33
(49) Germany	☎ 0800-022 00 49
(852) Hong Kong	☎ 0800-022 08 52
(353) Ireland	☎ 0800-022 03 53
(39) Italy	☎ 0800-022 60 39
(81) Japan	☎ 0800-022 00 81
(82) Korea (south)	☎ 0800-022 00 82
(352) Luxembourg	☎ 0800-022 03 52
(64) New Zealand	☎ 0800-022 44 64
(47) Norway	☎ 0800-022 00 47
(65) Singapore	☎ 0800-022 88 65
(27) South Africa	☎ 0800-022 02 27
(34) Spain	☎ 0800-022 00 34
(46) Sweden	☎ 0800-022 00 46
(886) Taiwan	☎ 0800-022 08 86
(66) Thailand	☎ 0800-022 01 66
(44) UK	☎ 0800-022 99 44
(1) USA	☎ 0800-022 91 11 (AT&T)
	☎ 0800-022 91 22 (MCI)
	☎ 0800-022 91 19 (Sprint)

Mobile Phones The Netherlands uses GSM 900/1800, which is compatible with the rest of Europe and Australia but not with the North American GSM 1900 or the totally different system in Japan (though some North Americans have GSM 1900/900 phones that do work here). Check with your service provider about using your phone in the Netherlands, and beware of calls being routed internationally (very expensive for a 'local' call). You can also rent one at the KPN-Telecom Rent Centre (☎ 653 09 99) at Schiphol airport (to the left of the central exit at Schiphol Plaza) for around f150 a week. In this case you can't use your existing number, however.

Fax & Telegraph

It's difficult to send or receive faxes as a visitor. Some of the more upmarket hotels are happy to help if you announce your requirements in advance, and most hotels with fax (some of the cheaper hotels don't have one) will at least let you receive the occasional message. (Business travellers take note: this might convince the boss that you need to stay at something a bit more upmarket.) Copy shops and call centres send faxes, but in order to receive one you have to be on good terms with the proprietor. Kinko's (Map 6; ☎ 589 09 10, fax 589 09 20), Overtoom 62 near Leidseplein, offers 24-hour office support and will send faxes for f3.50/4.50 a page within/outside Europe and receive them for f1 a page.

You can send (but not receive) faxes from large post offices but it's not cheap. If you're sending to a private machine, the basic charge is f25 plus f3/5 a page within/outside Europe – it's probably cheaper to use a copy shop or telecommunication centre. If the fax is going to a post office and has to be hand delivered, the costs per page are the same but the basic charge is f37.50.

Telegrams can be sent from post offices or lodged by phone for a basic charge of

euro currency converter f1 = €0.45

FACTS FOR THE VISITOR

FACTS FOR THE VISITOR

f23.50 plus f0.99/1.45 per word (maximum 10 characters, otherwise it's two words) within/outside Europe, including address and signature. It doesn't take much for a telegram to cost considerably more than a hand-delivered fax. The only advantage of a telegram is that it might be quicker because it's delivered immediately, whereas a hand-delivered fax goes by regular mail delivery (though telegrams to the USA have been known to take seven days!). For more information, including lodgment by telephone (billed to the phone account), ring ☎ 0800-04 09.

Email & Internet Access

If you packed your laptop, note that Holland uses a four-pin phone plug that accommodates a US, French or Australian-style jack but not a six-pin UK one. Otherwise adapters are cheaply picked up at the airport and the usual retail outlets.

There are a number of public Net terminals around town that use phonecards (eg, outside De Balie and Artis Zoo, in the Vondelpark youth hostel, just to the left of Centraal Station, and in all post offices and libraries), but you don't want to rely on them. Though a neat idea, they've been prone to crashing, plus you can't save or print mail.

Internet Cafés The number of bars and coffeeshops offering cheap Internet access has been growing almost by the month – and indeed, for travellers from prohibitionist countries, there's a bit of a frisson in sitting down and beginning your emails: 'Hi, I'm sitting here with a fat joint in my mouth.' Unless stated otherwise, they charge f2.50 to f3.50 per 20 minutes.

ASCI, a very cool, free squatters' Net café, was located on the Herengracht but slated for eviction. It may move to the underground bookshop,

Silicon Polder

A line – albeit a rather wiggly one – can be drawn from Amsterdam's Golden Age right through to its cyber-present. As the *Financial Times* put it: 'The Netherlands knows its place in the world, and it has changed remarkably little over the centuries.' The city and country rose to power as an economy dependent on international trade, with an outward-looking culture that has been constant from the 17th century to today's era of 'value-added logistics' and e-commerce. Amsterdam's 'Silicon Polder', as it has inevitably been dubbed, is more than just a clever marketing phrase: the city has ambitions to be a global cyber-city player, and its 'Amsterdam-ness' is one of its unique selling propositions.

Around the beginning of the 1990s, an influential and talented group of hackers based around the Hacktic club were tolerated, even celebrated, and as the market changed and the hackers grew up, so a ready pool of techno-talent was in place. And as the bolshie squatters movement of the 1980s matured, it provided ideological, technical and organisational expertise, with venues such as Paradiso, De Balie and the Society for Old and New Media all organising ground-breaking conferences, shows and exhibitions to give Amsterdam a unique take on the new global economy.

Morphing into the country's first commercial Internet access providers, xs4all ('access for all'), Hacktic combined with these organisations and the city government in 1994 to establish Europe's first Digital City, a 'virtual district' in which users can contact local councillors, arts and culture organisations and set up free home pages of their own. Strong traditions in graphic design, an instinctive feel for the emerging e-economy and an excellent infrastructure completed the picture.

In the early 1990s, the city was one of the most heavily cabled for TV in the world. The pipe carrying all Internet traffic between Europe and America disappears into the ground in the east of the city, and a thriving science park (in Watergraafsmeer) and cyber-complex (the Matrix buildings) grew up around this important telecoms node.

'Silicon Polder' currently boasts more than 1300 multimedia companies employing 10,000 people, mostly in the shiny new medium-rise blocks of the city's satellites. Continued success, though, will

Fort van Sjakoo, but check www.squat.net for the latest news about the movement.

Boek 'n Serve (☎ 664 34 46) Ferdinand Bolstraat 151–153. A charming (mostly Dutch) magazine and bookshop that also sells CD-ROMs, coffee and ice cream, making it an attractive place to check your email in the south of the city. While the relaxing music tinkles away downstairs, enjoy smokefree Web surfing upstairs on five PCs; open weekdays from 9.30 am to 7 pm (from noon Monday and to 9 pm Thursday), Saturday from 9 am to 6 pm, and tram No 25 will get you there.

Cyber C@fe (☎ 623 51 46) Nieuwendijk 191. A classy oasis in a grubby street offering three PCs and four Macs. There's a printer, networked gaming (Doom, Hexen etc) and free email accounts. The vibe is light and jazzy, the decor funky-aboriginal; open from 10 am to 1 am weekdays, to 3 am weekends.

EasyEverything may make all this information outdated when it opens. Charismatic cheapflights magnate Stelios Haji-Ioannou (of Easy-Jet fame), having established the biggest Net café in Europe at London's Victoria Station, is extending the chain into Europe, starting with one on Reguliersbreestraat (near Rembrandtplein) in April 2000. Expect around 7500 sq metres, open 24 hours a day and cheap access for up to 500 surfers. Check www.easyeverything.com for details.

Freeworld (☎ 620 09 02) Korte Nieuwendijkstraat 30, **Internet Coffeeshop Tops** (☎ 638 41 08) Prinsengracht 480, and **Get Down** (☎ 420 15 12) Korte Leidsedwarsstraat 77. All are fairly standard smoking venues with Net access, the latter being a dingy basement with a permanent heavy rock soundtrack, that offers emailing and printing from seven PCs.

Internet Café (☎ 627 10 52) Martelaarsgracht 11. Just 50m from Centraal Station; open from 9 am to 1 am every day (to 3 am Friday and Saturday) and offers a free email address and 18 PCs.

Mad Processor (☎ 421 14 82) Bloemgracht 82. Aims to be a sort of 'Kinko's for the masses' on two floors of a Jordaan canal house. It offers 14 buffed-for-graphics Pentium III PCs connected to the Net by fibre-optic cable (f2.50 for 10 minutes or f12.50 per hour), office facilities, dozens of popular games, laminating, DTP etc.

Silicon Polder

require some fancy footwork. The cable network that gave the population of 10 years ago the then unheard-of choice of more than a dozen TV channels is too old and creaky to be of use for the new broad-band, all-singing, all-dancing services of the next stage of the new-media economy.

Privatised five years ago, the network fell into the hands of media giant UPC, which is rushing to upgrade it with a glass-fibre network. Following a 2000-home test (many of them in the new Eastern Docklands development, where homes are built 'fully wired'), the privatised state phone company KPN-Telecom is on the verge of rolling out a new, super-fast ADSL network to compete.

A trickle of US-style venture capital is rapidly turning into a real gusher. The government is looking at establishing a new f650 million 'knowledge district', a testbed of 50,000 households and companies to be fitted with high-speed glass-fibre connections to see how business and social relations evolve in such a system. In the autumn of 1999, Dutch casinos were given permission to begin Net gambling operations. Free-Net-access fever broke out, with (at last count) six new services opening within weeks of each other, all trying to maximise their electronic land-grab. Plans were announced for a compulsory national ID chip-card, though exactly when is yet to be decided. It may build on the muted success of the two competing cash chip-card schemes launched a few years back.

Around the same time, a national cybercop unit was established with the announcement that 'Cybercity (the Dutch online community) now boasts around 2.5 million inhabitants; it's time they got their own police force'. The 15-strong squad will focus on surveillance (to counter child porn, subversive and racist statements, the offering of fake driver's licences or drugs for sale, and fraud), digital research (examining hard drives used in a crime), and research and development.

The city remains a popular venue for 'flesh meets' and has close ties with the San Francisco digerati. The late Tim Leary, JP Barlow, Howard Rheingold and RU Sirius have been frequent visitors. *Wired* magazine began life as an Amsterdam-based bimonthly called *Electric Word*.

On-Line coffeeshop (☎ 470 30 11) Daniël Stalpertsraat 106. Near Boek 'n Serve, it has two PCs at f5 per half-hour and f2.50 per 15 minutes after that; open from 10 am to 1 am every day.

Peter Stuyvesant Travel Store (☎ 530 49 49) Reguliersbreestraat 3. A convenient one-stop shop for Amsterdam nightlife tickets, travel bargains and Web surfing (two PCs inside plus two touch-screen kiosks outside); open from 10 am to 8 pm Monday to Saturday, Sunday from 1 to 6 pm.

Siberie (☎ 623 59 09) Brouwersgracht 11. Open daily from 11 am to 11 pm (to midnight Friday and Saturday); one of the liveliest coffeeshops in central Amsterdam, and though it has just one PC, it's free as long as you consume something (20 minutes max).

The Site (☎ 520 60 80) Nieuwezijds Voorburgwal 323. Open Tuesday to Sunday from noon to 8 pm; an 'info-theque' for Amsterdam youth (aged 15 to 20) with free Net access, advice, talks, workshops and even a job centre. Foreigners can use the facilities for the usual fee.

The Waag (☎ 557 98 98). Another tip for the cash-poor, this old weigh house in the middle of Nieuwmarkt Square houses the Society for Old and New Media. It offers free Net surfing in an atmospheric public reading room-cum-bar/restaurant so long as you consume something. There's no hard-and-fast rule how many cappuccinos you have to drink to stay online, but think of those waiting; open daily from 10 am to 1 am (Monday from 11 am).

INTERNET RESOURCES

The World Wide Web is a rich resource for travellers. You can research your trip, hunt down bargain air fares, book hotels, check on weather conditions or chat with locals and other travellers about the best places to visit (or avoid!).

There's no better place to start your Web explorations than the Lonely Planet Web site (www.lonelyplanet.com). Here you'll find succinct summaries on travelling to most places on earth, postcards from other travellers and the Thorn Tree bulletin board, where you can ask questions before you go or dispense advice when you get back. You can also find travel news and updates to many of our most popular guidebooks, and the subWWWay section links you to the most useful travel resources elsewhere on the Web.

The definitive Web reference for anything to do with Amsterdam is www.amsterdam .nl (click the 'english site' button), with more information and links than you'll ever need, plus a very useful map-finder function. You could also try www.visitamsterdam.nl, run by the Netherlands Board of Tourism (which actually supplies the tourist information for www.amsterdam.nl), or its parent site www.visitholland.com.

The Digital City site (www.dds.nl) remains an essential reference, with hundreds of information resources (many of which are in English), interaction opportunities, home pages and links.

The Amstel brewery operates a nice-looking, award-winning city guide at www.amstel.com, though how well it will be maintained remains to be seen.

Homesick Aussies who want to keep up to date with the footy or the latest furphies in Canberra should check www.firststep. com.au/gday (the authors of this book live in Australia after all!).

BOOKS
Guidebooks

There are more guidebooks to Amsterdam than you can shake a bicycle spoke at. Women might wish to consult Catherine Stebbings' *Amsterdam – The Woman's Travel Guide* published by Virago. The *Best Guide to Amsterdam & the Benelux* is the definitive gay guide.

If you plan to settle in Amsterdam for a while, get hold of *Live & Work in Belgium, The Netherlands and Luxembourg* from Vacation Work Publications, with detailed explanations of the necessary paperwork and more. *Living & Working in the Netherlands* by Pat Rush (How To Books) isn't bad either.

History

CR Boxer's *The Dutch Seaborne Empire 1600–1800*, first published in 1965, remains one of the most readable academic textbooks on how this small corner of Europe dominated world trade. Simon Schama's *The Embarrassment of Riches: An Interpretation of Dutch Culture in the Golden Age* (1987) deals with the tensions between vast wealth and Calvinist sobriety, and much more. Peter Burke's *Venice and Amsterdam* (1994) discusses the similarities and differences between these trading empires.

Amsterdam, A Short History (1994) by Dr Richter Roegholt provides a good, concise summary but few insights. Serious students should track down Pieter Geyl's *The Revolt of the Netherlands, 1555–1609* (1958) and *The Netherlands in the 17th Century, 1609–1648* (1961/64). Johan Huizinga's *The Waning of the Middle Ages: A Study of the Forms of Life, Thought, and Art in France and the Netherlands in the 14th and 15th Centuries* (1924) is famous, as much a literary work as a study.

If you read Dutch, Geert Mak's *Een Kleine Geschiedenis van Amsterdam* (1994) offers revelations and potted dramas, and a perceptive analysis of the cultural revolution that swept the city from the mid-1960s to mid-1980s – Mak calls it the '20-year city war'.

The famous *Diary of Anne Frank*, an autobiography written by a Jewish teenager, movingly describes life in hiding in Nazi-occupied Amsterdam.

General

For practical architecture and engineering, see *Building Amsterdam* by Herman Janse (De Brink, 1994), with clear drawings showing how it was done, from houses and churches to bridges and locks. The most beautifully produced book about canal-belt architecture is *Het Grachtenboek* (1993) by Paul Spies and others, which catalogues every building along the canals with a wealth of historical photos and illustrations. Part 1 deals with the major canals and Part 2 with the medieval city. Part 1 also used to be available in English but they're all out of print. A few bookshops may still have them if you hunt around – try Architectura & Natura (Map 4; ☎ 623 61 86), Leliegracht 22, which still had the Dutch set for f225 at the time of research.

Dutch Painting (1978) by RH Fuchs is a good introduction to the subject.

The UnDutchables (1989) by Colin White & Laurie Boucke takes a humorous look at Dutch life; sometimes it's spot-on and sometimes so wide of the mark it's slapstick. A more realistic appraisal of Dutch customs, attitudes and idiosyncrasies is Hunt Janin's very readable *Culture Shock! Netherlands* (1998), or the rather serious but knowledgeable *Dealing with the Dutch* by Jacob Vossestein who runs the Royal Tropical Institute's 'Understanding the Dutch' training programs for businesspeople and expatriates.

Henry James described the Amsterdam canals as 'perfect prose' and 'perfect bourgeois' in *Transatlantic Sketches* (1875).

For literature by Amsterdam authors, see the Arts section in the Facts about Amsterdam chapter.

Most books are published in different editions by different publishers in different countries. As a result, a book might be a hardcover rarity in one country while it's readily available in paperback in another. Fortunately, bookshops and libraries search by title or author, so your local bookshop or library is best placed to advise you on the availability of the above recommendations.

NEWSPAPERS & MAGAZINES

The European editions of *The Economist* and *Time* are printed here, and most of the major international newspapers and magazines (and many of the more obscure ones) are readily available. Newsagents at the airport and Centraal Station stock a wide selection, as do the Athenaeum newsagency on Spui Square and Waterstone's in the Kalverstraat.

By far the largest national newspaper is the Amsterdam-based *De Telegraaf*, a right-wing daily with sensationalist news but good coverage of finance. Its Wednesday edition is worth perusing for rental accommodation but you'll need help from a Dutch speaker. Also based in Amsterdam are *De Volkskrant*, a one-time Catholic daily with leftist leanings, and *Het Parool*, an evening paper full of Amsterdam politics and *the* paper to read if you want to know what's happening in the city (especially the daily supplement, *PS*, or better still, the weekly what's-on listing in the Saturday *PS*). The highly regarded *NRC Handelsblad*, a merger of two elitist papers

FACTS FOR THE VISITOR

from Rotterdam and Amsterdam, sets the country's journalistic standards. *Het Financieele Dagblad* focuses on business and finance, with an English-language section at the back.

Useful Publications

The free *Uitkrant* is the definitive publication for art and entertainment – if it's not listed here it's not happening. It's published 11 times a year, unfortunately all in Dutch but you can usually decipher enough to make a phone call to the relevant establishment for more information. Pick up a copy at the Amsterdam Uitburo or anywhere with free publications, such as Centraal Station, the Stopera, book and magazine outlets, shopping centres and many museums.

The VVV's English-language *What's On in Amsterdam* is published monthly and costs f4.50. It has entertainment schedules and an address listing but is far less comprehensive than *Uitkrant*. It's available from the VVV, large book and magazine outlets and many hotels.

Via Via, a paper with reams of classified ads, is published Tuesday and Thursday (in Dutch) and lists everything from apartments to starter motors.

RADIO & TV

The BBC broadcasts on 648kHz medium wave, loud and clear on any AM radio. Most of the programs are in English and the German broadcasts seldom last longer than 30 minutes.

Dutch TV sends insomniacs to sleep, though the large proportion of ad-free, English-language sitcoms and films with Dutch subtitles is a plus. Fortunately the Netherlands have the highest density cable TV network in the world, and in Amsterdam the percentage of households hooked up to cable is approaching 100%. Cable means access not just to Dutch and Belgian channels but many channels from Britain, France, Germany, Italy and Spain, and all sorts of other so-called Euro-channels with sport and music clips, as well as Turkish and Moroccan stuff and, of course, CNN. At the time of research, Eurosport was off the

cable in Amsterdam because it refused to pay a commission to the cable company.

Teletext, a wonderful information service that hides behind many TV channels, offers hundreds of pages of up-to-date information. English-language versions are available on BBC and CNN.

PHOTOGRAPHY & VIDEO

Film is widely available but fairly expensive by European standards – a Kodak 64 (36-exposure) slide film costs about f22 – so it's best to stock up tax-free on your way over. High-speed film (200 ASA or higher) is sensible because the sky is often overcast, and even if it's not, buildings and trees tend to cast shadows. If there's a blanket of snow with sunshine (a rare combination but a fantastic photo opportunity) you might want slower film. Film developing is quick and costs f5.50 plus f1 per print. Cassettes for video cameras cost about f7.50/24 for 30/90 minutes.

Home video cassette recorders here use the PAL image-registration system, the same as most of Europe and Australia, which is incompatible with the NTSC system used in North America and Japan or the SECAM system used in France. If you buy a pre-recorded video tape here check that it's compatible with your home unit. Shops might stock NTSC versions but very few have tapes in SECAM.

TIME

The Netherlands are on Central European time, GMT/UTC plus one hour. Noon in Amsterdam is 3 am in San Francisco, 6 am in New York and Toronto, 11 am in London, 9 pm in Sydney and 11 pm in Auckland, and then there's daylight-saving time. Clocks are put forward one hour at 2 am on the last Sunday in March and back again at 3 am on the last Sunday in October. They used to be put back in September which gave an even six months, but this was changed as an EU concession to the wayward Brits and Irish.

When telling the time, beware that Dutch uses *half* to indicate 'half before' the hour. If you say 'half eight' (8.30 in many forms of English), a Dutch person will take this to

Decorative neck gable

Sign above a coffee shop

Huge and hip, Café-Restaurant Amsterdam features industrial-style decor and 100-foot ceilings.

ELLIIOT DANIEL

Golden Fleece Condom Shop

JULIET COOMBE

Summertime window boxes add colour

DOEKES LULOFS

A corner of 'The Ship' housing estate, a prominent example of Amsterdam School architecture

People-watching at Nederlands Filmmuseum café

Magna Plaza, the former GPO

Westerkerk's crowning glory

Houseboats line Amsterdam's canals.

An afternoon stroll in the Vondelpark

Freewheeling art

mean 7.30. Dutch also uses constructions like *tien voor half acht* (7.20) and *tien over half acht* (7.40), and less surprisingly, *kwart voor acht* (7.45) and *kwart over acht* (8.15).

ELECTRICITY
Electricity is 220V, 50Hz and plugs are of the Continental two-round-pin variety. If you need an adapter, get it before you leave home because most of the ones available in the Netherlands are for locals going abroad.

WEIGHTS & MEASURES
Napoleon introduced the metric system which has been used ever since (before then it was a local version of feet, inches and pounds). In shops, 100g is an *ons* and 500g is a *pond* (sound familiar?). EU directives have prohibited the use of *ons* in pricing and labelling but the term is so ingrained it will take a while to disappear. Like other Continental Europeans, the Dutch indicate decimals with commas and thousands with points.

LAUNDRY
A self-service laundry is called a *wasserette* or a *wassalon* and Amsterdam could do with more of them. They normally cost about f8 to wash 5kg; add a few f1 coins for the dryer. You can also get the staff to wash, dry and fold a load (a full garbage bag) for around f15 – drop it off in the morning, pick it up in the afternoon. Upmarket hotels will of course do your laundry too, but at a price.

Happy Inn (Map 4; ☎ 624 84 64) Warmoesstraat 30 near Centraal Station. Costs f14.50 to wash, dry and fold up to 6kg; open Monday to Saturday from 9 am to 6 pm

Wasserette Van den Broek (Map 4; ☎ 624 17 00) Oude Doelenstraat 12, the eastern extension of Damstraat. Full service (f15 to wash, dry and fold up to 5kg) or self service, open Monday to Friday from 8.30 am to 7 pm, Saturday from 10 am to 4 pm

Wasserette (Map 2) Haarlemmerstraat 45. Open Monday to Saturday from 9 am to 7 pm, Sunday from 10 am to 5 pm

The Clean Brothers (Map 4; ☎ 622 02 73) Kerkstraat 56 off Leidsestraat. Costs f8 to wash up to 5kg plus f1.25 to dry, or leave it with them for f13.50; open daily from 7 am to 9 pm

TOILETS
Public toilets are scarce but there are plenty of bars or other establishments you can pop into. Their toilets aren't always the cleanest – public facilities in department stores are more hygienic. Toilet attendants (of which there are a lot) should be tipped f0.25 to f0.50, though some attendants in clubs will demand f1.

LEFT LUGGAGE
For details of left-luggage facilities at the airport, see the Airport section of the Getting Around chapter. Luggage lockers at Centraal Station cost f4 (small) or f6 (large) per 24 hours up to a maximum of 72 hours.

HEALTH
The Netherlands have reciprocal health arrangements with other EU countries and Australia – check with your public health insurer which form to include in your luggage (E111 for British and Irish residents, available at post offices). You still might have to pay on the spot but you'll be able to claim back home. Citizens of other countries are well advised to take out travel insurance – medical or dental treatment is less expensive than in North America but still costs enough.

There are no compulsory vaccinations but if you've just travelled through a yellow fever area you could be asked for proof that you're covered. Up-to-date tetanus, polio and diphtheria immunisations are always recommended whether you're visiting Amsterdam or not.

For minor health concerns, pop into a local *drogist* (chemist) or *apotheek* (pharmacy, to fill prescriptions). For more serious problems, go to the casualty ward of a *ziekenhuis* (hospital) or ring the Centrale Doktersdienst (☎ 0900-503 20 42), the 24-hour central medical service that will refer you to an appropriate doctor, dentist or pharmacy. In a life-threatening emergency, the national telephone number for ambulance, police and fire brigade is ☎ 112.

Forget about buying flu tablets and antacids at supermarkets: for anything more medicinal than toothpaste you'll have to go to a drogist or apotheek, of which there are far too few because it's a protected profession.

The following hospitals have 24-hour emergency facilities:

Onze Lieve Vrouwe Gasthuis (Map 7; ☎ 599 91 11) Eerste Oosterparkstraat 1 at Oosterpark near the Tropenmuseum. The closest public hospital to the centre of town

Sint Lucas Ziekenhuis (Map 1; ☎ 510 89 11) Jan Tooropstraat 164, in the western suburbs

Slotervaart Ziekenhuis (Map 1; ☎ 512 41 13) Louwesweg 6, in the south-western suburbs

Academisch Ziekenhuis der VU (Map 1; ☎ 444 44 44) De Boelelaan 1117, Amsterdam Buitenveldert. Traditionally the VU (Vrije Universiteit, Free University) was orthodox-Calvinist but its hospital has established a name for itself in sex-change operations

Academisch Medisch Centrum (☎ 566 91 11) Meibergdreef 9, Bijlmer. Hospital of the Universiteit van Amsterdam, famous for AIDS research

Boven-IJ Ziekenhuis (☎ 634 63 46) Statenjachtstraat 1, Amsterdam North; bus No 34 from Centraal Station

STDs & HIV/AIDS

Free testing for sexually transmitted diseases is available at the Municipal Medical & Health Service, GG&GD (Map 4; ☎ 555 58 22), Groenburgwal 44 in the old town. It's open weekdays from 8 to 10.30 am and 1.30 to 3.30 pm but you must arrive in the morning to be tested that day. Bring along a book or magazine as you'll probably have to wait a couple of hours. If a problem is diagnosed they'll provide free treatment immediately, but the results of blood tests are only available after a week (they'll give you the results over the phone if you aren't returning to Amsterdam). This excellent service is available to everyone and it's not necessary to give an address or show identification (English is spoken). There's also a gay STD and HIV clinic (tests etc) Friday from 7 to 9 pm, but you have to make an appointment weekdays between 9 am and 12.30 pm or 1.30 and 5.30 pm.

HIV/AIDS is a problem in the Netherlands but the spread has been contained to some extent by practical education campaigns and free needle-exchange programs. Telephone help lines include:

AIDS Information Line (☎ 0800-022 22 20, free call) – questions about HIV and AIDS answered weekdays from 2 to 10 pm; discretion guaranteed

AIDS-HIVpluslijn (☎ 685 00 55) – telephone support line for people with HIV, or for their friends and relatives; Monday, Wednesday and Friday from 1 to 4 pm, Tuesday and Thursday from 8 to 10.30 pm

WOMEN TRAVELLERS

Dutch women attained the right to vote in 1919, and in the late 1960s and 1970s the Dolle Minas ('Mad Minas' – see the History section) made sure that abortion on demand was more or less accepted and paid for by the national health service. There is some way to go before it can be said that women are fully emancipated (their participation rate in the labour force, for instance, is one of the lowest in Europe, with the highest proportion of part-time work), but Dutch women on the whole are a rather confident lot. On a social level, equality of the sexes is taken for granted and women are almost as likely as men to initiate contact with the opposite sex. There's little street harassment and Amsterdam is probably as safe as it gets in the major cities of Europe. Just take care in the red-light district, where it's best to walk with a friend to minimise unwelcome attention.

The feminist movement is less politicised than elsewhere, more laid-back and focused on practical solutions such as cultural centres and archives, bicycle repair shops run by and for women, or support systems to help women set up businesses. For more about feminism, or a full rundown of the many women's groups, contact the following organisations:

Het Vrouwenhuis (The Women's House; ☎ 625 20 66) Nieuwe Herengracht 95, near the Botanical Garden. A centre for several women's organisations and magazines, with workshops, exhibitions and parties; there's also a bar and a library

IIAV (International Information Centre & Archives of the Women's Movement; ☎ 665 08 20) Obiplein 4, east of Muiderpoortstation. Centre for feminist studies; extensive collection of clippings, magazines and books

Organisations

The following organisations may prove useful in times of crisis:

De Eerste Lijn (The First Line; ☎ 613 02 45). For victims of sexual violence

Aletta Jacobshuis (Map 1; ☎ 616 62 22) Overtoom 323. Clinic named after the country's first female doctor, a feminist and tireless campaigner for birth control; information and help with sexual problems and birth control, including morning-after pills

Vrouwengezondheidscentrum Isis (Women's Health Centre; ☎ 693 43 58) Obiplein 4. For advice, support and self-help groups

Rechtshulp voor Vrouwen (Legal Aid for Women; Map 2; ☎ 638 73 02) Willemsstraat 24B

GAY & LESBIAN TRAVELLERS

Partisan estimates put the proportion of gay and lesbian people in Amsterdam at 20% to 30%. This is probably an exaggeration, but there's no doubt that Amsterdam is the gay and lesbian capital of Europe – although the lesbian scene, as always, is less developed than the gay one. Mainstream attitudes have always been reasonably tolerant but it wasn't until the early 1970s that the age of consent for gay sex was lowered to 16, in line with hetero sex, and in 1993 it became illegal to discriminate against jobseekers on the basis of sexual orientation.

The fact that Christian parties are in opposition for the first time since 1917 has finally made it possible to tackle issues relating to family law. Same-sex marriage has finally been recognised, though the attendant right to adopt children could take a bit longer to be sorted out. The government has long subsidised the national organisation COC – one of the world's largest organisations for gay and lesbian rights – but now trade unions are busy researching the lot of homosexual employees, the police advertise in the gay media for new applicants, and the acceptance of homosexuality in the army is greater than ever.

One attractive feature of gay and lesbian venues in the city is their openness: no covered windows or locked doors, but an open, welcoming attitude to anyone who wants to come in (and 'out'). There's no lack of places to go to, with more than 60 bars and nightclubs, gay hotels, bookshops, sport clubs, choirs, archives etc, and a wide range of organisations that help gays and lesbians who have questions or problems. Almost all these places are within walking distance of the centre of town or are easily accessible by public transport. See the listings below and the Places to Stay, Shopping and Entertainment chapters for further details.

Amsterdam also has its Homomonument, the first such monument in the world, designed by Karin Daan and unveiled under the shadow of the Westerkerk in 1987. It consists of three triangles of pink granite: one points to the Amsterdam office of the COC, the second to the Anne Frankhuis and the third to the water. It commemorates those who were persecuted for their homosexuality by the Nazis. From mid-July to the end of August, gay and lesbian visitors can consult an information kiosk here from noon to 6 pm called the Pink Point of Presence, or PPP (a play on the official tourist information office, VVV).

Information

One of the best guidebooks is the *Best Guide to Amsterdam & the Benelux*, which, as the title indicates, focuses mainly on Amsterdam. Catherine Stebbings' *Amsterdam – The Woman's Travel Guide* published by Virago is aimed at women in general but lesbians may find it useful. The SAD-Schorerstichting (see the listing below) publishes *Gay Tourist Information*, covering Amsterdam and safe sex, and a *Gay Tourist Map*, both available free of charge at gay venues.

There's a host of free tabloids, partly in English, including *Gay News*, *Gay and Night* and *Culture & Camp*, also available at gay venues. Dutch-language publications include the gay tabloid *De GAY Krant*, the more upmarket COC magazine *XL* for men and women, and the glossy *sQueeze*. For those aged under 27 there's *Expreszo*, and for lesbians *Zij aan Zij*. Gay and lesbian bookshops (see the Shopping chapter) sell most of the major foreign publications, and many newsagencies also have extensive selections.

A good English-language Web site with information about gay and lesbian Amsterdam

FACTS FOR THE VISITOR

is www.dds.nl/~gaylinc. The home page of the Dutch gay and lesbian body is at www.coc.nl – it's in Dutch and deals with political issues but there's also an English section. Gay information on Teletext is available on TV3, page 447. The local gay radio station MVS broadcasts from 6 to 9 pm daily on 106.8 FM (cable 103.8 FM), with an English program on Sunday.

Organisations

The following organisations may prove useful:

Gay & Lesbian Switchboard (☎ 623 65 65). The best first source for gay and lesbian information, addresses, what's on etc, daily from 10 am to 10 pm

COC Amsterdam (Map 4; ☎ 623 40 79) Rozenstraat 14. Amsterdam branch of the national gay & lesbian organisation. There's a mixed nightclub Friday and women's nightclub Saturday, both from 10 pm to 4 am – the women's is the only one in Amsterdam to have survived for years. A coffee shop is open Saturday from 1 to 5 pm and from 8 pm. The COC head office (☎ 623 45 96) is next door at Rozenstraat 8, open weekdays from 9 am to 5 pm, but isn't equipped to deal with general inquiries from the public.

SAD-Schorerstichting (Map 6; ☎ 662 42 06) PC Hooftstraat 5. Gay counselling, HIV prevention and homo buddy project (HIV support), weekdays from 9 am to 5 pm; gay STD and HIV clinic (tests etc) at Groenburgwal 44, Friday from 7 to 9 pm (make a telephone appointment weekdays between 9 am and 12.30 pm or 1.30 and 5.30 pm)

HIV Vereniging (Map 6; ☎ 616 01 60) Eerste Helmersstraat 17. National organisation for those who are HIV positive; runs an Internet service at www.hivnet.org and provides personal assistance; also operates the AIDS-HIVpluslijn (see the earlier Health section).

AIDS Information Line – see Health

Homodok & Lesbisch Archief (Map 1; ☎ 606 07 12) Nieuwpoortkade 2A. Extensive documentation centre for gay and lesbian studies, open Monday to Friday from 10 am to 5 pm; telephone inquiries weekdays from 9 am; ✉ info@homodok.nl (gay) or ✉ laa@dds.nl (lesbian)

Safe Sex

The Dutch government and organisations such as the COC, SAD-Schorerstichting and HIV Vereniging all do their bit to prevent the spread of STDs and HIV. Virtually all bars, bookshops and saunas that cater for gays provide safe-sex leaflets. Many also sell condoms suitable for anal sex, eg, the Hot Rubber or DUO brands.

Special Events

A Canal Parade takes place on the first Saturday in August, the only water-borne gay-pride parade in the world. Sport and culture programs are organised in the week leading up to this, inspired by the 1998 Amsterdam Gay Games. The Gay & Lesbian Switchboard can tell you more.

The biggest party in Amsterdam each year is *Koninginnedag* (Queen's Day) which celebrates the Queen Mother's birthday on 30 April. Ex-queen Juliana and her daughter Queen Beatrix are very popular among the gay community and this day is celebrated with great enthusiasm, causing some confusion among foreign gays about the 'queen' everyone is so happy about. On this day a big gay and lesbian party called the *Roze Wester* (Pink Wester) is held at the Homo-monument, with bands and street dancing; the Reguliersdwarsstraat and Amstel also get very lively. It helps if you like beer because you can hardly get anything else.

Cruising

Popular cruising places in and around the city include the Vondelpark, the nude beach at Zandvoort and the dunes behind it, and Landschapspark De Oeverlanden by the Nieuwe Meer bordering the Amsterdamse Bos, though the latter can be outright dangerous. A joke among gays is that the best place for cruising is an Albert Heijn supermarket between 5 and 6 pm, particularly the one in Westerstraat in the Jordaan.

Dangers & Annoyances

Gays and lesbians can generally move freely in Amsterdam but violent crime is a distinct possibility when cruising – don't carry too much money and certainly no cards or passport; an emergency whistle is worth considering. Always report antigay or antilesbian violence to the police. Most police stations have staff members who are trained to treat your case with respect.

DISABLED TRAVELLERS

Travellers with a mobility problem will find Amsterdam fairly well equipped to meet their needs, certainly considering the natural limitations of some of the older buildings. A large number of government offices and museums have lifts and/or ramps. Many hotels, however, are in old buildings with steep stairs and no lifts; restaurants tend to be on ground floors, though 'ground' sometimes includes a few steps. The metro stations have lifts, many trains have wheelchair access, and most train stations and public buildings have toilets for the disabled. People with a disability get discounts on public transport and, with some limitations, can park in the city free of charge (see the sections on Public Transport and Car & Motorcycle in the Getting Around chapter). Train timetables are published in braille and bank notes have raised shapes on the corners for identification.

Residents can use the *stadsmobiel* ('citymobile'), a fabulous taxi service for people with mobility, sight or hearing impairments, but foreigners have to use the commercial wheelchair-taxi service, which can be reached on ☎ 633 39 43 between 7 am and midnight seven days a week. The vehicles are also used for school transport so it's best to ring a couple of days in advance to ensure a booking at a time that suits you. One-way trips within Amsterdam cost f35 to f90 depending on the destination.

See also Car Rental in the Getting Around chapter for information about a car offered by Budget that's specially adapted for wheelchairs.

Organisations

Many Dutch organisations work with and for people with disabilities but unfortunately there's no central information service. However, the helpful Nederlands Instituut voor Zorg & Welzijn NIZW (☎ 030-230 66 03, fax 231 96 41), Postbus 19152, 3501 DD Utrecht, has extensive information on accessible places to stay throughout the country and can refer you to other organisations if your request is more specific.

The Amsterdam Uitburo (see Other Information Sources under the earlier Tourist Offices section) has information about accessible entertainment venues.

In Britain, the Royal Association for Disability & Rehabilitation (RADAR; ☎ 020-7250 3222), 12 City Forum, 250 City Rd, London EC1V 8AF, may be able to help plan your trip. Its guide, *European Holidays & Travel Abroad – A Guide for Disabled People*, gives a good overview of facilities in Europe (published in even-numbered years). It has a Web site at www.radar.org.uk.

In the USA, the Society for the Advancement of Travelers with Handicaps (SATH; ☎ 212-447 7284), 347 Fifth Ave, Suite 610, New York, NY 10016, has information sheets on a wide range of destinations or will research your specific requirements. Check its Web site at www.sath.org. Membership is $45 a year ($30 for seniors and students); the information charge for nonmembers is $5, which covers costs. Mobility International (☎ 541-343 1284), PO Box 10767, Eugene, OR 97440, offers international educational exchanges but will also answer questions and help travellers with special needs. It's at www.mobility-international.org on the Web.

Finally, it's well worth checking some of the many links at www.access-able.com, a Web page for travellers with disabilities.

SENIOR TRAVELLERS

The minimum age for senior discounts is 65 (60 for the male or female partner) and they apply to public transport, museum entry fees, theatres, concerts and more. You could try flashing your home-country senior card but you might have to show your passport to be eligible.

Senior travellers who are concerned about personal safety can perhaps take heart from the fact that people up to 24 years of age are six times more likely to become a victim of crime here than those aged over 65.

Organisations

An organisation worth knowing about is Gilde Amsterdam (Map 4; ☎ 625 13 90), open Monday to Friday from 1 to 4 pm. This is a group of volunteers aged 50 and over who share their experience in a variety of ways. Gilde members with a keen knowledge of Amsterdam organise walks for small groups of locals and visitors (maximum of eight people) – a wonderful way to discover the city with mature-aged people and to see and learn things that professional tours ignore. It helps if you're reasonably mobile because the walks last an hour or two. It's all very informal; every guide does it differently and you might even take the tram. There are three walks to choose from – the city centre, the Jordaan and 'roving' – and the cost per person is a f5 contribution, which gets you 50% off entry fees to the Amsterdams Historisch Museum (city history) and the Museum Willet-Holthuysen ('classical' canal house), as well as a 25% discount on pancakes at the end of the walk. Recommended.

Stichting Wijzer (☎ 560 03 25) organises a range of activities – film nights, music programs, summer excursions etc – aimed at Amsterdammers aged over 50 but foreigners are welcome too.

AMSTERDAM FOR CHILDREN

Lonely Planet's *Travel with Children* by Maureen Wheeler is worth reading if you're unsure about travelling with kids. Much of her advice is valid in Amsterdam, where there is much to keep them occupied. Unfortunately the city also has a lot of open water (all Dutch children learn to swim at school).

Attitudes to children are very positive, apart from some hotels with a no-children policy – check when you book. Most restaurants have high chairs and children's menus. Facilities for changing nappies (diapers), however, are limited to the big department stores and Centraal Station and you'll pay f0.50 to use them.

Amsterdam's children are surprisingly spontaneous and confident, a reflection of the relaxed approach to parenting. They're allowed in pubs (but aren't supposed to buy beer till they're 16) and the age of consent

is 12, though parents can intervene if the partner is over 16. There's a Kindertelefoon (☎ 0800-04 32) where children can report cases of abuse daily between 2 and 8 pm, and a Kinderrechtswinkel (Children's Rights Shop; ☎ 626 00 67), Staalstraat 19, where youngsters aged under 18 can inquire about their rights towards teachers, parents and employers.

Some hotels offer a baby-sitting service and others may be able to advise. Babysitters charge between f5 and f12.50 an hour depending on the time of day, sometimes with weekend and/or hotel supplements, and you might have to pay for their taxi home if it gets late. Agencies use male and female students and you may not always be able to specify which sex; they get busy on weekends so book ahead. Try Oppas-Centrale Kriterion (☎ 624 58 48), Roetersstraat 170hs, which has been in business for a long time and seems to be consistently reliable. Call between 5.30 and 7 pm daily. Oppas-centrale De Peuterette (☎ 679 67 93), Hectorstraat 20, also gets good reports. Call between 3 and 4 pm Tuesday and Thursday. There are one or two other agencies (look in the phone book under *Oppascentrale*).

Many special events and activities aimed at children take place throughout the year. Check the *Uitkrant* (under 'Agenda Jeugd') or contact the Amsterdam Uitburo. Or try the following options, most of which are described in more detail elsewhere in this book:

- the Vondelpark (Maps 1 & 6) – for picnics, children's playground, ducks etc
- Amsterdamse Bos (Map 1) – huge recreational area with animal enclosure, children's farm etc
- Tram Museum Amsterdam (Map 1) – ride in a historic tram past the Amsterdamse Bos
- Tropenmuseum (Map 7) – separate children's section with activities focusing on exotic locations
- climb up a church tower – if that doesn't exhaust them, nothing will
- Artis zoo (Map 5)
- the beach at Zandvoort – only a short train ride away
- hire a canal bike
- harbour cruise

- swimming pool – especially the high-tech Mirandabad (Map 1)
- circus – in Theater Carré (Map 7; from mid-December to early January
- Koninginnedag (Queen's Day) on 30 April – a wonderful party for kids as much as grown-ups
- newMetropolis Science & Technology Center (Map 5)
- hire a bike for a day out in the country
- go ice skating at the Jaap Edenbaan (Map 1)

Kids love the **Madame Tussaud Scenerama** (Map 4; ☎ 522 10 10, recorded message), Dam 20 on the corner of Dam Square and Rokin, open from 10 am to 5.30 pm (in July and August from 9.30 am to 7.30 pm). Admission costs a hefty f19.50, children up to 14 years pay f16 (free for those aged under 5), and family and group rates are available. Some of the characters on display won't mean much to foreigners.

The national aviation museum, **Aviodome Schiphol** (☎ 406 80 00), at the airport (Westelijke Randweg 201; take the train to Station Schiphol, or bus No 68, 173 or 174), is also a hit with kids, who can play in old planes and sit in a cockpit. Adults will also enjoy the displays, which consist of 25 aeroplanes including the Wright Flyer (with which the Wright brothers made the first motorised flight in 1903), several Fokker aircraft including a 1911 Fokker Spin ('Spider') and Baron von Richthofen's WWI triplane, a Spitfire and of course a Dakota. A section is devoted to space flight. The museum is open daily from 10 am to 5 pm (from October to April it's open from noon on weekends and closed Monday) and costs f10 (children aged between four and 12 pay f7.50).

LIBRARIES

Many museums and institutes have private libraries, mentioned throughout this book. To borrow books from a public library *(openbare bibliotheek)* you need to be a resident, show ID and pay f38.50 a year (f23 for young adults and seniors, free for under-18s), but you're free to browse or read.

The main public library, the Centrale Bibliotheek (Map 4; ☎ 523 09 00), is at Prinsengracht 587 and is open Monday from 1 to 9 pm, Tuesday to Thursday from

10 am to 9 pm, Friday and Saturday from 10 am to 5 pm, and Sunday (only October to March) from 1 to 5 pm. It has a wide range of English-language newspapers and magazines, a coffee bar and a useful notice board. For other public libraries, look in the phone book under *Bibliotheken, Openbare*.

UNIVERSITIES

Amsterdam has two universities and over 40,000 students. About 27,000 attend the Universiteit van Amsterdam (UvA), which has existed in various guises since 1632. Its buildings are spread throughout the city. The biggest UvA faculties are Arts, Social Sciences, Law and Economics.

Another 13,500 students attend the Vrije Universiteit (VU, Free University) established by orthodox Calvinists in 1880. Initially its buildings were also spread throughout the city but in the 1960s almost the entire VU moved to a large campus along De Boelelaan in the southern suburb of Buitenveldert. Calvinism is no longer an issue but Philosophy is still a compulsory subject so students think about the role of science in society. The biggest VU faculties are Economics, 'Social Cultural' Sciences and Medicine.

For information about international education programs in English offered by the University of Amsterdam, contact Universiteit van Amsterdam, Service & Informatiecentrum (☎ 525 33 33, fax 525 29 21, ℮ uva-info@bdu.uva.nl), Binnengasthuisstraat 9, 1012 ZA Amsterdam. Tuition fees are approximately f10,000 per academic year; fees for regular study programs in Dutch are approximately f2300 per academic year.

The Free University (Map 1) can be contacted at Onderwijsvoorlichting Vrije Universiteit (☎ 444 50 00), De Boelelaan 1105, 1081 HV Amsterdam, on Monday to Friday from 8.30 am to 4.30 pm.

The Foreign Student Service (☎ 671 59 15), Oranje Nassaulaan 5, 1017 AH Amsterdam, is a support agency for foreign students. It provides information about study programs and intensive language courses, and helps with accommodation,

FACTS FOR THE VISITOR

insurance and personal problems. It's open weekdays from 9 am to 5.30 pm.

CULTURAL CENTRES

There are many cultural centres and institutes besides the city's museums and theatres. These include:

British Council (☎ 550 60 60) Keizersgracht 269. Educational and cultural exchanges, open Monday to Friday from 9.30 am to 5.30 pm; information centre open Tuesday and Wednesday from 1 to 5 pm, Thursday to 6 pm

Cedla (☎ 525 34 98, library ☎ 525 32 48) Keizersgracht 395–397. Centre for Latin American studies and documentation, open weekdays from 9 am to 4 pm

De Balie (☎ 553 51 51, recording in Dutch and English) Kleine Gartmanplantsoen 10 at Leidseplein. Café, restaurant, theatre, seminars, political debates, lectures etc; hangout of trendy intellectuals; open weekdays from 9 am to 5 pm

Goethe Institut (Map 4; ☎ 623 04 21) Herengracht 470. German cultural centre with lectures, films (some with English subtitles), plays and discussions, plus German language courses at all levels and Dutch courses for Germans; office hours 9 am to 6 pm weekdays (to 4.30 pm Friday); library open Tuesday to Thursday from 1 to 6 pm, Friday to 4 pm

Italian Cultural Institute (☎ 626 53 14) Keizersgracht 564. Open weekdays from 10 am to noon and 2 to 4 pm

Jewish Cultural Centre (☎ 646 00 46) Van der Boechorststraat 26. Open by appointment only

John Adams Institute (☎ 624 72 80, with recording of upcoming events in English) Herenmarkt 97 in the former West Indisch Huis. Dutch-US friendship society that organises lectures, readings and discussions on US culture and history led by heavyweights such as Saul Bellow, Gore Vidal, Annie Proulx, Alice Walker, Seamus Heaney and Bret Easton Ellis; the lectures (once a month or more frequently) are often interesting and surprisingly affordable, and provide a focus for the US and British expat community; definitely worth checking

Maison Descartes (☎ 622 49 36) attached to the French Consulate at Vijzelgracht 2A. French cultural centre named after the philosopher who in Amsterdam found the intellectual freedom denied him at home; office open weekdays from 9.30 am to 4 pm, library from 1 to 6 pm (Tuesday and Thursday to 8 pm); many activities are organised by the Alliance Française (☎ 625 65 06) around the corner at Keizersgracht 708

South Africa Institute (☎ 624 93 18) Keizersgracht 141. Information centre and library, open Tuesday to Friday from 10 am to 4 pm

Vlaams Cultureel Centrum de Brakke Grond (Map 4; ☎ 622 90 14) Nes 45. Flemish cultural centre; very active (readings, plays and lectures); includes a theatre, café and restaurant; open weekdays from 9.30 am to at least 6 pm (or until whatever's on is over)

DANGERS & ANNOYANCES

Amsterdam is a small city by world standards but requires big-city street sense, though it's positively tame if you're used to New York or Johannesburg. Violent crime is unusual but theft, especially pickpocketing, is a real problem. Don't carry more money around than you intend to spend – use a secondary wallet or purse and keep your main one safe. Don't walk around conspicuously with valuables, or give away that you're a tourist with map, camera or video. Walking purposefully helps.

A car with foreign registration is a popular target, and if it's parked along a canal it will probably get broken into. Don't leave things in the car: definitely remove registration and ID papers, and if possible the radio.

If something is stolen, by all means get a police report for insurance purposes but don't expect the police to retrieve your property or to apprehend the thief – put the matter down to experience. This might seem weak but it's not a police state and usually there's very little they can do.

The people you see walking around in blue jackets with mobile phones aren't police but members of the 630-strong Surveillance Team, a make-work project for long-term unemployed. They keep an eye on things, help if you're lost or have a problem, and call for assistance if the matter is serious. The operation is part of the overall City Surveillance *(Stadstoezicht)* operation that also includes parking policy and the sanitation police (who see to it that people don't put out garbage too early, and who try to minimise graffiti and dog shit). Only 'real' police carry guns.

If you have trouble on the train to Amsterdam or at Centraal Station itself, contact the railway police *(spoorwegpolitie)* at the west end of track 2A. You can report violence or missing/stolen property here, and the staff can put you in touch with your consulate or other relevant support agencies. They'll also put through a station announcement if you're only looking for someone. This office is more or less always open.

The red-light district is full of shady characters loitering on street corners. They seem harmless enough, but if you're accosted, simply say *Nee dank* (No thanks) and keep walking. Don't take photos of the prostitutes.

Mosquitoes can be another nuisance in summer. They breed in stagnant parts of the canals and in water under houses. In some parts of the city they're no problem, but the author of this book used to live in a canal house where the tenants would sleep under mosquito nets six months of the year (no kidding!).

Amsterdam is still the dog-shit capital of the world (see Ecology & Environment in the Facts about Amsterdam chapter) and you soon learn to look where you're walking. Also, North Americans and Australians should accept that nonsmokers have few rights here: tobacco smoke in pubs can be thick enough to deter all but the most committed smokers, and unfortunately the Dutch seem allergic to open windows.

EMERGENCIES

The national emergency number (police, ambulance, fire brigade) is ☎ 112; the Amsterdam police can also be contacted directly on ☎ 559 91 11 at the headquarters on Elandsgracht 117 (along Marnixstraat; Map 4). For 24-hour medical service, call the Centrale Doktersdienst (☎ 0900-503 20 42) to be referred to an appropriate doctor, dentist or pharmacy.

DRUGS

Contrary to what you may have heard, cannabis products are illegal. The confusion arises because the authorities have had the sense to distinguish between 'soft' drugs (cannabis) and addictive 'hard' drugs (heroin, crack, pills) when deciding where to focus their resources. Soft drugs for personal use (defined as up to 5g, down

from 30g after table-thumping from France) are unofficially tolerated, but larger amounts put you in the persecuted 'dealer' category.

The key phrase is *gedogen* (sometimes translated as 'tolerating'), a wonderful Dutch term that means official condemnation but looking the other way when common sense dictates it. Hard drugs (including LSD) are treated just as seriously as anywhere else and can land you in big trouble, although the authorities tend to treat genuine, registered addicts as medical cases rather than as serial killers – Amsterdam was an early adopter of methadone and needle exchange programs and of safe injecting houses.

Neighbouring countries take a dim view of such tolerance now that border controls have been abolished in theory, and the government is under EU pressure to clamp down – never mind that most hashish reaches the Netherlands through France and Belgium and most heroin through Germany. In typical Dutch fashion this has led to some tightening of rules and regulations without losing sight of the common-sense approach.

One of the positive results of this approach has been to move cannabis out of the criminal circuit and into registered 'coffeeshops', driving a wedge between cannabis users and predatory street dealers who would rather sell the more profitable hard stuff. Since the late 1980s the number of heroin addicts in the Netherlands has stabilised at around 1.6 per 1000 inhabitants, slightly more than in Germany, Norway, Austria or Ireland; but in hardline France the proportion is 2.6 per 1000, and in Greece, Spain and Italy it's higher still. Dutch addicts have the best average survival rate in Europe and the lowest incidence of HIV infection.

These tolerant policies attract many drug tourists: drugs are cheaper and more readily available here than elsewhere, and generally of better quality. The country has become a major exporter of high-grade marihuana (grown locally) and is the European centre for the production of ecstasy. Much of Europe's cocaine passes through Rotterdam harbour.

For more about (soft) drugs, see 'Coffee-shops' in the Entertainment chapter.

Warning

Never, *ever* buy drugs on the street: you'll get ripped off or mugged. And *don't* light up in view of the police, or in an establishment without checking that it's OK to do so. Locals detest drug tourists who think they can just smoke dope anywhere.

LEGAL MATTERS

The Amsterdam police *(politie)* are a pretty relaxed and helpful lot, which is quite remarkable considering their workload. If you do something wrong, they can hold you up to six hours for questioning (another six hours if they can't establish your identity, or 24 hours if they consider the matter serious) and do not have to grant a phone call, though they'll ring your consulate.

Since 1994 there's a 'limited' requirement for anyone over 12 years of age to carry ID (eg, in public transport without a valid ticket, at soccer stadiums, in the work place and when opening a bank account). Typically, theory doesn't always match practice and everyone is confused, but it seems that foreigners should carry their passport. Then again, a photocopy of the relevant data pages should be OK unless there's reason to suspect you're an illegal immigrant. Logical, isn't it? A driving licence is not OK because it doesn't show your nationality.

The Bureau voor Rechtshulp (Office for Legal Help; Map 4; ☎ 626 44 77), Spuistraat 10 and three other offices around the city, is a nonprofit organisation of law students and qualified lawyers who give free legal advice during business hours to those who can't afford it. They deal with a wide range of issues, including immigration and residency, and will refer you if they can't deal with the matter themselves or if they think you're wealthy enough.

BUSINESS HOURS

As a general rule, banks are open from 9 am to 4 pm Monday to Friday, offices from 8.30 am to 5 pm Monday to Friday, and shops from 9 am to 5.30 pm Monday to Saturday. Now for the exceptions.

On Monday many shops don't open till noon but they stay open until 8 or 9 pm on Thursday night. Department stores and supermarkets generally close around 6 pm weekdays and at 5 pm on Saturday but most supermarkets near the city centre stay open till 8 pm. Most regular nontourist shops outside the canal belt close at 5 or 6 pm weekdays and at midday Saturday, depending on their line of trade, and almost all are closed on Sunday. Within the canal belt, however, most shops are open from 9 am (noon on Monday) to 5 pm (9 pm on Thursday) throughout the week including Saturday, and many are open from noon to 5 pm on Sunday (especially the first Sunday of the month).

Government offices, private institutions, monuments and even museums follow erratic and sometimes very limited opening hours to suit themselves; they're mentioned in this book where possible. Many museums are closed Monday.

PUBLIC HOLIDAYS & SPECIAL EVENTS

Public holidays are New Year's Day *(Nieuwjaarsdag)*, Good Friday *(Goede Vrijdag)*, Easter Sunday and Easter Monday *(Eerste* and *Tweede Paasdag)*, Queen's Day *(Koninginnedag)* on 30 April, Ascension Day *(Hemelvaartsdag)*, Whit Sunday (Pentecost) and Monday *(Eerste* and *Tweede Pinksterdag)*, Christmas Day and Boxing Day *(Eerste* and *Tweede Kerstdag)*. People take public holidays seriously and you won't get much done.

There are many festivals and special events throughout the year. Summer is a time of open-air concerts, theatre and other events around the city, often free; favoured venues include the Vondelpark and the Amsterdamse Bos. The queen mother's birthday on 30 April is celebrated with the biggest street party in the country, an unforgettable experience. Culture-lovers might aim for the Holland Festival in June or the Uitmarkt at the end of August. A few of the following events aren't in Amsterdam but are worth a day trip:

January

Elfstedentocht (Eleven Cities' Journey) – in this 'dead', seemingly never-ending month, with cold, dull, dark days, skating on the canals (frost permitting) is the only excitement. If it has been freezing hard enough for long enough, this gruelling skating marathon through the countryside of Friesland takes place. It attracts thousands of participants and stops the nation, with people going into a frenzy as they prepare for it. It was last held early in 1997 but years may pass before conditions are right

February

Carnaval – a southern (Catholic) tradition best enjoyed in Breda, Den Bosch or (especially) Maastricht, but Amsterdammers also know how to don silly costumes and party; information: Stichting Carnaval in Mokum (☎ 623 25 68), Herengracht 513, 1017 BV Amsterdam

Commemoration of the February Strike – 25 February, in memory of the anti-Nazi general strike in 1941; wreath-laying at the Dockworker monument in the former Jewish quarter

March

Stille Omgang – Silent Procession, Sunday closest to 15 March; Catholics walk along the Holy Way (the current Heiligeweg is a remnant) to St Nicolaaskerk to commemorate the Miracle of Amsterdam

HISWA boat show – the latest pleasure craft in the RAI exhibition grounds (☎ 549 12 12, fax 646 44 69)

Blues Festival – at the Meervaart Theatre (☎ 610 74 98), Meer en Vaart 1, 1068 KV Amsterdam

April

Floriade 2002 – from 1 April to 15 October 2002; an international horticultural exhibition that takes place every 10 years and drew 3.3 million visitors last time; this will be the fifth Floriade, and it will take place in Hoofddorp just south-west of Amsterdam; information: Stichting Floriade 2002 (☎ 023-562 20 02, ✉ info@flori ade.nl), Postbus 2002, 2130 GE Hoofddorp

World Press Photo exhibition – from mid-April to the end of May in the Oude Kerk; information: Bureau World Press Photo (☎ 676 60 96), Jacob Obrechtstraat 26, 1017 KM Amsterdam Web site: www.worldpressphoto.nl

National Museum Weekend – usually the third weekend of April; free entry to all museums (extremely crowded); information at Amsterdam Uitburo or Stichting Museumjaarkaart (☎ 0900-404 09 10)

Koninginnedag – Queen's Day, 30 April, actually Queen Mother Juliana's birthday (Queen Beatrix's birthday is in January, far too cold for *the* party of the year). If you could visit Amsterdam at any time, this is it. There's a free market throughout the city (anyone can sell anything they like, kids love it), street parties, live music, dense crowds and lots of beer – a collective madhouse. The whole country under the age of 30 visits Amsterdam, while all of Amsterdam over the age of 30 escapes

May

Remembrance Day – 4 May, for the victims of WWII; Queen Beatrix lays a wreath at the Nationaal Monument on Dam Square and the city observes two minutes silence at 8 pm; making noise then is thoughtless in the extreme (Germans in particular should take care)

Liberation Day – 5 May, end of German occupation in 1945; street parties, free market, live music; the Vondelpark is a good place to be

Luilak – 'Lazy-Bones', Saturday before Whit Sunday; children go around in the early hours ringing door bells, making noise and waking people up; remnant of pre-Christian festival celebrating the awakening of spring

National Cycling Day – second Saturday; family cycling trips along special routes; information: VVV, ANWB or NBT

National Windmill Day – second Saturday; windmills unfurl their sails and are open to the public; information: Vereniging De Hollandsche Molen (☎ 623 87 03), Sarphatistraat 634, 1018 AV Amsterdam

Drum Rhythm Festival – mid-month; world music, jazz and blues in the Westergasfabriek; information: Amsterdam Uitburo

Open Garden Days – mid-month; see some of the beautiful private gardens behind canal houses; information: VVV

June

Over het IJ Festival – from June throughout the summer months; big performing-arts events (dance, theatre, music) around the former NDSM shipyards north of the IJ, often exciting and always interesting; information: Amsterdam Uitburo or VVV

RAI Arts Fair – first week; exhibition of all facets of contemporary art in RAI exhibition grounds (☎ 549 12 12, fax 646 44 69)

Holland Festival – all month; the country's biggest music, drama and dance extravaganza, mainly in Amsterdam and The Hague; world premieres etc, often highbrow and pretentious but also many fringe events; information: VVV, Amsterdam Uitburo, or Stichting Holland

FACTS FOR THE VISITOR

Festival (☎ 530 71 10), Kleine Gartmanplantsoen 21, 1017 RP Amsterdam

Canal Run – usually second weekend but dates
vary; marathon consisting of 5, 9 and 18km runs
along the canals, organised by *De Echo*, a local
weekly paper; information: VVV or Echo
Grachtenloop (☎ 585 92 22), Basisweg 30, 1043
AP Amsterdam

Dutch TT Assen – last Saturday; Dutch round of
the world series motorcycle grand prix, held
since 1925 near Assen in the north-east of the
country; many European championship events
during 'Speedweek' leading up to the main event
that attracts crowds in excess of 150,000; a
unique experience even if you're not particularly
interested in motorcycles; just turn up at the gate

International Theatre School Festival – end of
the month; Dutch and international theatre
schools strut their stuff; information: Amsterdam Uitburo or VVV

July

North Sea Jazz Festival – mid-month; world's
largest indoor jazz festival, in the Congresge-
bouw in The Hague; many musicians take the
opportunity to visit Amsterdam at this time;
information: Amsterdam Uitburo or VVV

August

Prinsengracht Concert – middle or end of the
month, the culmination of a longer festival, the
Grachtenfestival; free classical concert from
boats in front of the Pulitzer Hotel; information:
Amsterdam Uitburo, VVV or Pulitzer Hotel
(☎ 523 52 35), Prinsengracht 315–331, 1016
GZ Amsterdam

Sail 2000 – 24–28 August 2000, probably one of
the biggest events this year (book your accommodation now!); more than 1000 sailing ships
from around the world, including the biggest
ones that are still operational (navy training vessels etc), converge on Amsterdam and strut their
stuff up and down the IJ on the first day, a magnificent sight and one not to be missed; it's also
the finish of the Cutty Sark Tall Ships' Race;
Sail Amsterdam is held every five years; information: VVV or NBT

Uitmarkt – last weekend of the month; local
troupes and orchestras present their coming
repertoires free of charge throughout the city; a
bit like Koninginnedag but much more easy-
going; information: Amsterdam Uitburo or VVV

September

Bloemencorso – Flower Parade, first Saturday;
spectacular procession of floats wends its way
from Aalsmeer in the morning to Dam Square

and back again at night (illuminated); information: VVV

Jordaan Festival – second week; street festival
with much merriment and entertainment in a
'typically Amsterdam' neighbourhood; information: VVV

Monumentendag – second Saturday; listed
buildings and monuments have an open day;
information: VVV or Bureau Monumentenzorg
(☎ 626 39 47, fax 620 37 66), Keizersgracht
123, 1015 CJ Amsterdam

Prinsjesdag – third Tuesday; opening of parliament in The Hague; Queen Beatrix arrives in
Golden Coach and presents budget

October

Jumping Amsterdam – international indoor
show-jumping at RAI exhibition grounds
(☎ 549 12 12, fax 646 44 69)

Delta Lloyd Amsterdam Marathon – middle of
the month; 8000 runners and in-line skaters do
a 21km loop through the city twice, starting and
finishing at the Olympic Stadium; information:
☎ 663 07 81

Web site: www.amsterdammarathon.nl

November

Sinterklaas arrives – mid-month; the children's
saint arrives by ship 'from Spain' (see December); the mayor presents the city key on Dam
Square; information: VVV

Cannabis Cup – third week; marihuana festival
hosted by *High Times* magazine; the cup itself
goes to the best grass, other awards to the
biggest spliff etc; also hemp expo and fashion
show; information: any 'coffeeshop'

December

Sinterklaas – officially 6 December but the main
focus is gift-giving on the evening of the 5th, in
honour of St Nicholas

Christmas – 25 & 26 December, but religious
families traditionally celebrate Christmas Eve
on the 24th instead, with Bible-readings and
carols around the Christmas tree

New Year's Eve – wild parties everywhere;
drunken revelry with fireworks, sometimes
burning tyres or even overturned cars; hundreds
of injuries each year

DOING BUSINESS

Amsterdam's authorities make much of the
city's function as the gateway to Europe
with its busy airport and harbour, its multilingual, highly educated and productive
workforce, its easy-going tax laws, its

Sinterklaas, the Original Santa Claus

Every year on 6 December the Dutch celebrate Sinterklaas in honour of St Nicholas, historically the bishop of Myra in western Turkey around AD 345 and the patron saint of children, sailors, merchants and pawnbrokers (Klaas is a nickname for Nicholas).

A few weeks beforehand, the white-bearded saint, dressed as a bishop with mitre and staff, arrives in Amsterdam by ship 'from Spain' (a legacy of Spanish colonial rule over the Netherlands) and enters the city on a grey or white horse to receive the city keys from the mayor. He is accompanied by a host of mischievous black servants called Black Peters (Zwarte Pieten) – or politically correct Blue and Green Peters – who throw sweets around and carry sacks in which to take naughty children away. Well-behaved children get presents in a shoe that they've placed by the fireplace with a carrot for the saint's horse (he stays on the roof while a Black Peter climbs down the chimney).

On the evening of 5 December people give one another anonymous and creatively wrapped gifts (surprises) accompanied by funny/perceptive poems about the recipient written by Sinterklaas. The gift itself matters less than the wrapping and poetry.

The commercialisation of Christmas has weakened the impact of this charming festival. Ironically, the American Santa Claus who dominates the Christmas spirit these days evolved from the Sinterklaas celebrations at the Dutch settlement of New Amsterdam (New York).

FACTS FOR THE VISITOR

international outlook and 'neutral' image, and its expertise in trade, transport, finance and communication services that make it an appropriate centre for international business. IBM, Xerox, Sony, HP, Canon and Nissan are just a few of the growing number of companies who have set up their European headquarters in Amsterdam.

The trade office at the Dutch embassy in your home country can provide initial information and help establish the necessary contacts, as can your embassy's trade office in The Hague. Also in The Hague, the Netherlands Foreign Investment Agency (fax 070-379 63 22) offers similar support.

Once you've decided to establish a base in Amsterdam, get in touch with the Amsterdam Foreign Investment Office (Map 5; ☎ 552 35 36, fax 552 28 60, ✉ afio@ez .amsterdam.nl), PO Box 2133, 1000 CC Amsterdam (street address: Metropool Building, Weesperstraat 89), who can provide the know-how and know-who to get you started. If it's trade contacts you're after, try the Amsterdam Chamber of Commerce & Industry (Map 2; ☎ 531 40 00, fax 531 47 99), De Ruijterkade 5, 1013 AA Amsterdam.

Businesswomen might find the Women's International Network useful, an association that offers business contacts, advice and support for professional women aged over 25 and employed for at least five years. Membership (f150 a year) is open to foreign women working in the Netherlands and Dutch women working for international companies or with experience of working abroad. Contact the founder of WIN (☎ 662 00 84) at Postbus 15692, 1001 ND Amsterdam.

Business Services

The luxury hotels (and Schiphol airport) all offer business services. Some have fully serviced business centres but they can be quite expensive. A cheaper option might be the Mini Office (Map 4; ☎ 625 84 55, fax 638 78 94, ✉ moffice@xs4all.nl), Singel 417, with services for the short-term business visitor including hardware and software that can be rented by the hour (if you need to fix a document or two), bindings and mailings, email and fax service (send and receive), personal answering service, private office, and even an office address.

The first European branch of the US Kinko's chain (minus the helpful and knowledgeable staff) offers the same services as the Mini Office but is open 24 hours. It's at Overtoom 62 near Leidseplein

euro currency converter f1 = €0.45

(Map 6; ☎ 589 09 10, fax 589 09 20), and does video-conferencing too.

If you're a bit more committed and want to start operating straight away without the headaches of establishing a base from scratch, the Euro Business Center (Map 2; ☎ 520 75 00, fax 520 75 10), Keizersgracht 62–64, can help with the paperwork and will supply an office with furniture, phone, computer etc for f1250 to f5000 a month. Secretarial help and a range of other services are also available. Regus Business Centre (☎ 301 22 00), Strawinskylaan 3051, 1077 ZX Amsterdam (and two other locations) is similar and also does video-conferencing.

For difficult translations, contact Berlitz Translation Services (☎ 639 14 06, fax 620 39 59), Rokin 87, though they're not cheap.

Exhibitions & Conferences

Amsterdam is a popular place for trade fairs and conferences – it hosts more than 100 international and many hundreds of national conventions each year.

The major luxury hotels, such as Grand Hotel Krasnapolsky on Dam Square, the Barbizon Palace opposite Centraal Station, the Okura Hotel in the southern suburbs or the Radisson near the red-light district (see Places to Stay), are often used for modest meetings and shows, and have facilities to handle groups of 25 to 2000 people.

Amsterdam RAI (Map 1; ☎ 549 12 12, fax 646 44 69), Europaplein 8, is the largest exhibition centre in the country (see the New South section in the Things to See & Do chapter). It's also a conference centre with 21 conference rooms and a main auditorium that seats 1750. If necessary, one of the 11 exhibition halls can be converted for that spectacular gathering. Nearby is the World Trade Center (Map 1; ☎ 575 91 11, fax 662 72 55), Strawinskylaan 1, with conference rooms seating four to 200 people, and a full range of facilities and support services including a branch office of the Chamber of Commerce & Industry.

WORK

Nationals from EU countries (as well as Iceland, Norway and Liechtenstein) may work in the Netherlands but they need a renewable residence permit, a tedious formality. There are few legal openings for non-EU nationals and the government tries to keep immigrants out of this already over-populated country. You may be eligible if you are filling a job that no Dutch or EU national has the (trainable) skill to do, are aged between 18 and 45, and have suitable accommodation, but there will be a mound of red tape. (Forget about teaching English: there's very little demand.) All this has to be set in motion before you arrive (with the exception of US nationals, who may look for work within three months after they arrive as a tourist).

As a rule, you need to apply for temporary residence before an employer can apply for a work permit in your name. If all goes well, you will be issued a residence permit for work purposes. The whole rigmarole should take about five weeks. For more information, contact the Dutch embassy or consulate in your home country. Alternatively, for residence permits you can contact the Immigratie- en Naturalisatiedienst (☎ 070-370 31 24, fax 370 31 34), Postbus 30125, 2500 GC The Hague. For work permits and details of the Aliens Employment Act, contact the Landelijk Bureau Arbeidsvoorziening, Postbus 415, 2280 AK Rijswijk.

Au pair work is easier to organise, provided you are aged between 18 and 25, hold medical insurance and your host family earns at least f3000 a month after tax. The maximum period is one year. Nationals of the EU, Australia, Canada, Japan, Monaco, New Zealand, Switzerland and the USA can organise the necessary residence permit with the Vreemdelingenpolitie (Aliens' Police – see Visa Extensions in the earlier Documents section) after arrival in the Netherlands; others must organise this with the Dutch embassy or consulate in their home country.

Nationals of Australia, Canada, Japan, New Zealand and maybe the USA can apply for a one-year working holiday visa if they're aged between 18 and 25 (though this can be stretched to 30), but the whole scheme is under review. Contact the Dutch embassy or consulate in your home country for further details.

Illegal jobs (working 'black') are pretty rare these days, with increased crackdowns on illegal immigrants working in restaurants, pubs and bulb fields (traditional employers of 'black' labour). Some travellers' hotels in Amsterdam still employ touts to pounce on newly arrived backpackers; the pay isn't much but you may get free lodging.

If you're fortunate enough to find legal work, the minimum adult wage is about fl700 a month after tax.

Getting There & Away

Amsterdam is an easy city to get to, and many travellers pass through. If you're looking for cheap deals, advice, shared rides or whatever, you're likely to be successful.

AIR

Many of the world's airlines fly directly to/from Amsterdam's Schiphol airport. As always, it pays to shop around but keep in mind that the best quote might not always be the cheapest: a package deal that includes hotel accommodation, for instance, could save you a small fortune on Amsterdam's notoriously expensive hotels.

Also consider the option of flying to other airports in the region, such as Frankfurt, Luxembourg, Brussels, Paris or London, which is one of the cheapest destinations from outside Europe. It doesn't cost much to take a train or bus from there to Amsterdam. If you're flying from outside Europe, many

airlines offer a free return flight within Europe (KLM even offers two) – definitely worth including in your calculations.

Amsterdam is a major European centre for discounted tickets to many destinations – see Travel Agents later in this chapter. For special deals, also check the Saturday editions of the *Volkskrant*, *Parool*, *Trouw* or *Telegraaf* newspapers, in that order.

On weekdays there are five daily return flight connections between Schiphol and four other airports in the Netherlands (reduced services on weekends): Eindhoven (KLM Cityhopper), Enschede and Groningen (Fairlines), and Maastricht/Aachen (Air Excel Commuter).

For information about the airport itself and transport to/from the city, see The Airport in the Getting Around chapter.

Departure Tax
A small airport tax is included in your flight ticket.

The UK & Ireland
There isn't really a low or high season for flights to Amsterdam: prices depend more on special offers and availability of seats. By taking advantage of special offers (which usually involve booking in advance and staying a minimum number of nights), you should be able to fly London-Schiphol return for less than UK£100. A regular, fully flexible and fully refundable ticket could cost as much as UK£320. The flight takes just under an hour and then it's another 20 minutes by train into the centre of the city (by bus, train or car from London you'll spend five to 10 hours or more).

STA Travel (☎ 020-7361 6161) and usit Campus (☎ 020-7730 3402) have worthwhile deals (STA seems to be a couple of pounds cheaper) but these change all the time and the flights mentioned below are just an indication. Check their Web sites at www.statravel.co.uk and www.usitcampus .com. Also check the Sunday papers, or the

WARNING

The information in this chapter is particularly vulnerable to change: prices for international travel are volatile, routes are introduced and cancelled, schedules change, special deals come and go, and rules and visa requirements are amended. Airlines and governments seem to take a perverse pleasure in making price structures and regulations as complicated as possible. You should check directly with the airline or a travel agent to make sure you understand how a fare (and ticket you may buy) works. In addition, the travel industry is highly competitive and there are many packages and bonuses.

The upshot of this is that you should get opinions, quotes and advice from as many airlines and travel agents as possible before you part with your hard-earned cash. The details given in this chapter should be regarded as pointers and are not a substitute for your own careful, up-to-date research.

Air Travel Glossary

Cancellation Penalties If you have to cancel or change a discounted ticket, there are often heavy penalties involved; insurance can sometimes be taken out against these penalties. Some airlines impose penalties on regular tickets as well, particularly against 'no-show' passengers.

Courier Fares Businesses often need to send urgent documents or freight securely and quickly. Courier companies hire people to accompany the package through customs and, in return, offer a discount ticket which is sometimes a phenomenal bargain. However, you may have to surrender all your baggage allowance and take only carry-on luggage.

Full Fares Airlines traditionally offer 1st class (coded F), business class (coded J) and economy class (coded Y) tickets. These days there are so many promotional and discounted fares available that few passengers pay full economy fare.

Lost Tickets If you lose your airline ticket an airline will usually treat it like a travellers cheque and, after inquiries, issue you with another one. Legally, however, an airline is entitled to treat it like cash and if you lose it then it's gone forever. Take good care of your tickets.

Onward Tickets An entry requirement for many countries is that you have a ticket out of the country. If you're unsure of your next move, the easiest solution is to buy the cheapest onward ticket to a neighbouring country or a ticket from a reliable airline which can later be refunded if you do not use it.

Open-Jaw Tickets These are return tickets where you fly out to one place but return from another. If available, this can save you backtracking to your arrival point.

Overbooking Since every flight has some passengers who fail to show up, airlines often book more passengers than they have seats. Usually excess passengers make up for the no-shows, but occasionally somebody gets 'bumped' onto the next available flight. Guess who it is most likely to be? The passengers who check in late.

Promotional Fares These are officially discounted fares, available from travel agencies or direct from the airline.

Reconfirmation If you don't reconfirm your flight at least 72 hours prior to departure, the airline may delete your name from the passenger list. Ring to find out if your airline requires reconfirmation.

Restrictions Discounted tickets often have various restrictions on them – such as needing to be paid for in advance and incurring a penalty to be altered. Others are restrictions on the minimum and maximum period you must be away.

Round-the-World Tickets RTW tickets give you a limited period (usually a year) in which to circumnavigate the globe. You can go anywhere the carrying airlines go, as long as you don't backtrack. The number of stopovers or total number of separate flights is decided before you set off and they usually cost a bit more than a basic return flight.

Transferred Tickets Airline tickets cannot be transferred from one person to another. Travellers sometimes try to sell the return half of their ticket, but officials can ask you to prove that you are the person named on the ticket. On an international flight tickets are compared with passports.

Travel Periods Ticket prices vary with the time of year. There is a low (off-peak) season and a high (peak) season, and often a low-shoulder season and a high-shoulder season as well. Usually the fare depends on your outward flight – if you depart in the high season and return in the low season, you pay the high-season fare.

listings magazine *Time Out* or the *Evening Standard* for good-value benchmarks.

KLM (or rather, KLM-UK; ☎ 0990-074 074) flies Heathrow-Schiphol return from around UK£100 including airport taxes; from Edinburgh and Leeds-Bradford, fares start at about UK£130 and UK£140 respectively. Its Web site is at www.klm.com. Other airlines include BA and British Midland, and lively competition ensures that their prices are similar.

From Ireland, Aer Lingus (☎ 01-705 3333) offers returns from Dublin from IR£150, and from Cork from IR£200. Check the Web site at www.aerlingus.ie.

The USA

Tickets in the high season can cost almost twice as much as those in the low season. The high season lasts roughly from mid-June to mid or late September; low is roughly from October to March. The few months on either side are the shoulder seasons, with prices gradually rising or falling like a bell curve, with August at the peak.

Many US airlines fly direct to Amsterdam. United, Delta and Northwest offer decent fares but KLM offers the most frequent flights in conjunction with its partner, Northwest. Approximate fares are US$545/1005 return in the low/high season from San Francisco or US$430/775 from New York. Many flights from the west coast stop in one other US city along the way. Check with a travel agent or in your local Sunday newspaper for the best deals.

Travellers aged under 27 may get a 15% discount on these fares from Council Travel (☎ 800-226 8624) or STA Travel (☎ 800-777 0112). These agencies specialise in cheap travel, even for those who are older, with occasional rock-bottom deals during the low season. They have offices in most major cities.

Airhitch (☎ 800-326 2009 or ☎ 212-864 2000, ✉ airhitch@netcom.com), 2641 Broadway, 3rd Floor, New York, NY 10025, offers flights on a stand-by basis. You must be able to leave any time within a set period (usually five to seven days). You may have to wait a bit longer to get a direct

flight to Amsterdam, or less if you are willing to fly to another major city nearby. A one-way flight costs US$169 from New York, and US$269 from San Francisco or Los Angeles.

Icelandair operates a flight between JFK (New York) and Amsterdam for US$510/718 return in the low/high season, and there are flights as low as $328/590 (don't make the mistake of buying the high-season one-way ticket for US$1092!). Flights also leave from Baltimore, Boston and Orlando. The flights go via Reykjavík, where you could stop over and visit Iceland (not many people can say they've done that). There's no extra charge, but you must either buy one of Icelandair's special package deals or make your own arrangements for accommodation. Icelandair also flies between JFK and Luxembourg for US$556 return or US$278 one way regardless of the season. The train and/or bus to Amsterdam is not included.

Canada

Travel CUTS is a chain of budget travel agents with offices throughout Canada. The main office is in Toronto (☎ 416-977 3703) but you can also ring on ☎ 800-667 2887 or consult the Web site at www.travelcuts.com. Flights to Amsterdam start at C$599/750 return in the low/high season for students (or rather, those aged under 27), but there are some insane discounts during the low season – keep an eye on the Web site or stop by occasionally. Once again, KLM offers the most frequent flights.

For courier flights, contact FB On Board Courier Services in Montreal (☎ 514-631 7925).

Australia & New Zealand

There's a big difference between low and high-season fares, and unlike trans-Atlantic flights, where prices rise and fall gradually on either side of the high season, the increases and decreases are more sudden. Book well ahead if you intend to fly close to the crossover dates around April/May and September. One-way flights cost about two-thirds of return flights.

Discounted return fares on mainstream airlines through a reputable budget agency like STA Travel or Flight Centres International cost around A$1500/2500 in the low/high season. KLM flies between Amsterdam and Sydney three times a week, with a one-hour stop in Singapore, for A$1870/2480 return in the low/high season (Ansett connecting flight to/from Melbourne included) – the most hassle-free option if you can afford it. It often has cheaper specials. A budget airline such as Garuda could be cheaper still but you might spend 36 hours or more getting to Amsterdam from Sydney, rather than the already gruelling 21 hours with KLM.

Between November and March, no-frills Britannia Airways flies between Sydney/Melbourne/Adelaide/Brisbane/Perth and London/Manchester for A$999–1759 return depending on the date. One-way fares are half the return fare and fares from Perth are about A$100 cheaper. Contact the UK Flight Shop (☎ 02-9247 4833), 7 Macquarie Place, Sydney 2000.

From New Zealand, fares start at NZ$2059/2445 return in the low/high season. A round-the-world ticket could be cheaper still and this is sometimes also the case from Australia.

Airline Offices

Airline offices in Amsterdam, listed under *Luchtvaartmaatschappijen* (Aviation Companies) in the pink pages of the phone book, include:

Aer Lingus (☎ 623 86 20) Heiligeweg 14
Aeroflot (☎ 627 05 61) Weteringschans 26-III
Air France (☎ 446 88 00) Evert van der Beekstraat 7, Schiphol
Air India (☎ 624 81 09) Papenbroeksteeg 2
Air UK (KLM-UK; ☎ 474 77 47) Planetenweg 5, Hoofddorp
Alitalia (☎ 577 74 44) Paulus Potterstraat 18
British Airways (☎ 554 75 55) Neptunusstraat 33, Hoofddorp
British Midland (☎ 662 22 11) Strawinskylaan 721
Cathay Pacific (☎ 653 20 10) Evert van der Beekstraat 18, Schiphol
China Airlines (☎ 646 10 01) De Boelelaan 7
Delta Air Lines (☎ 661 00 51) De Boelelaan 7

El Al (☎ 644 01 01) De Boelelaan 7-VI
Garuda Indonesia (☎ 627 26 26) Singel 540
Icelandair (☎ 627 01 36) Muntplein 2-III
Japan Airlines (☎ 305 00 60) Jozef Israelskade 48E
KLM (☎ 474 77 47) Amsterdamseweg 55, Amstelveen
Lufthansa (☎ 560 81 00) Wibautstraat 129
Malaysia Airlines (☎ 626 24 20) Weteringschans 24A
Northwest Airlines (☎ 648 71 11) Weteringschans 85C
Qantas (☎ 683 80 81) Stadhouderskade 6
Singapore Airlines (☎ 548 88 88) De Boelelaan 1067
South African Airways (☎ 554 22 88) Polarisavenue 49, Hoofddorp
Thai Airways (☎ 622 18 77) Singel 466–468
Transavia (☎ 601 56 66) Westelijke Randweg 3
United Airlines (☎ 504 05 55) Strawinskylaan 831-B8

BUS

Amsterdam is well connected to the rest of Europe, Scandinavia and North Africa by long-distance bus. For information about regional buses in the Netherlands, for instance to places not serviced by the extensive train network, call the transport information service on ☎ 0900-92 92 (f0.75 a minute).

Eurolines

The most extensive European bus network is maintained by Eurolines, a consortium of coach operators with offices all over Europe. Its Web site, www.eurolines.com, has links to each national Eurolines Web site.

Returns from London to Amsterdam start from UK£39 for those aged under 26 or UK£44 for those aged 26 and over, and the journey takes 10 to 12 hours. Fares may rise or fall considerably depending on cutthroat competition among cross-Channel services. You can reach Eurolines UK on ☎ 0990-143 219. Some Eurolines buses cross the Channel via Calais in France; travellers using this service should check whether they require a French visa.

In Amsterdam, tickets can be bought at most travel agencies as well as at the Netherlands Railways (NS) Reisburo (Travel Bureau) in Centraal Station. The most convenient Eurolines Amsterdam

GETTING THERE & AWAY

office (Map 4; ☎ 560 87 87) is at Rokin 10 near Dam Square. Free timetables with fare information are cheerfully supplied, and fares are consistently lower than the train. Buses leave from the bus station (☎ 694 56 31) next to Amstelstation (Map 1), easily accessible by metro.

Cities like Bruges, Paris, Berlin, Copenhagen and Budapest are also easily accessible by Eurolines bus. The buses to Paris and London travel overnight, allowing you to save a night's hotel bill coming and going.

Busabout

Busabout (UK ☎ 020-7950 1661, fax 7950 1662), 258 Vauxhall Bridge Road, London SW1V 1BS, is a UK-based budget alternative to Eurolines. Though aimed at younger travellers, it has no upper age limit. It runs coaches along five interlocking European circuits, including one through Munich. It has a Web site at www.busabout.com.

A Busabout pass costs UK£249 (UK£199 for youth and student-card holders) for 15 days or as many of the five circuits as you like. There are also passes for 21 days at UK£345/275, one month at UK£425/325, two months at UK£595/485 and three months at UK£895/720, as well as Flexipasses entitling you to between 10 and 30 days' travel in a two-month period.

The main drawback is that buses on most loops travel in one direction (ie, from Amsterdam to Berlin, but not vice versa), and that you can't just jump on a bus to the next city without buying one of the above passes.

The Busabout service to/from Amsterdam runs from mid-April to the end of October. Coaches stop at Hotel Hans Brinker in Kerkstraat, smack in the middle of the city.

Gullivers

The Berlin-based Gullivers Reisen (Germany ☎ 030-311 02 11) covers a few international destinations to/from Amsterdam, including Amsterdam (nine hours, DM100, or DM90 for youth and student-card holders) and London-Victoria (16½ hours via Amsterdam, DM185/165). Its Web site is at www.gullivers.de.

TRAIN

Amsterdam's main train station is Centraal Station, commonly known as CS, which has regular and efficient train connections to most corners of the country and to all neighbouring countries. Eurail, Inter-Rail, Europass and Flexipass tickets are valid on Dutch trains, which are run by the Nederlandse Spoorwegen (NS). See Getting Around the Country in the Excursions chapter for more information about trains within the country.

Information

For international train information and reservations, use the NS international reservations office inside the station, open from 6.30 am to 10.30 pm daily, but be prepared for number-taking and long waits. There's another international reservations office at Amstelstation, open from 10 am to 5 pm daily, which is far less crowded though it is a bit out of the way. In peak periods it's wise to reserve international seats in advance. You can buy tickets to Belgium, Luxembourg and Germany at the normal ticket counters.

For international train information, you can also ring the Teleservice NS Internationaal on ☎ 0900-92 96 (f0.50 a minute) but the information can be a bit dodgy.

For national trains, simply turn up at the station: you'll rarely have to wait more than an hour for a train to anywhere.

Main Lines

There are two main lines south from Amsterdam. One passes through The Hague and Rotterdam and on to Antwerp (f52, 2¼ hours, hourly trains) and Brussels (f62, three hours, hourly trains) and then on to either Paris (f154 plus a f7 EuroCity supplement, six hours, 10 per day) or Luxembourg City (f102, six hours).

The other line south goes via Utrecht and Maastricht to Luxembourg City (f90, six hours) and on to France and Switzerland, or branches at Utrecht and heads east via Arnhem to Cologne (f83 plus a f7 EuroCity supplement, 2½ hours, every one to two hours) and farther into Germany. The main line east eventually branches off to the north-east of the country or continues east to Berlin, with a branch north to Hamburg. There's also a line north from Amsterdam to Den Helder in the tip of Holland.

All these fares are one way in 2nd class; people aged under 26 get a 25% discount. Weekend returns are much cheaper than during the week. For instance, a weekend return Amsterdam-Brussels (departure all day Friday, and returning any time on Monday, or for travel any time in between) costs f75 compared to the normal f124.

The high-speed train, the *Thalys*, runs four times a day between Amsterdam and Antwerp (f61, two hours), Brussels (f72, 2½ hours) and Paris (f161, 4¼ hours). Those aged under 26 get a 45% discount and seniors with a Rail Europe Senior (RES) card are entitled to 30% off stretches outside the Netherlands.

A special weekend deal, a so-called Tourist Ticket, gets you a return on the *Thalys* to Paris for f161 or the EuroCity to Cologne for f90, but demand is high so you need to reserve one to two weeks in advance.

The UK

Rail Europe (☎ 0990-848 848) will get you from London to Amsterdam using the highly civilised Eurostar passenger train service from Waterloo Station through the Channel Tunnel to Brussels, with an onward connection from there. This takes about five hours and starts from UK£80 return in 2nd class with special deals. There is a Web site at www.raileurope.com.

Train-boat-train combos are cheaper but take a fair bit longer. Stenaline (☎ 0990-707 070) has return fares from London to Amsterdam starting at UK£60 (for those aged under 26) or UK£80 (for those over), including the 3½ hour ferry crossing. The company's Web site www.stenaline.com has details.

CAR & MOTORCYCLE

Freeways link Amsterdam to The Hague (A4/E19 and A44), Rotterdam (A4/E19) and Utrecht (A2/E35) in the south, and

Amersfoort (A1/E231) and points farther east and north-east. The A10/E22 ring freeway encircles the city, with tunnel sections under the IJ. Amsterdam is about 480km (six hours' drive) from Paris, 840km from Munich, 680km from Berlin and 730km from Copenhagen.

The ferry port at Hook of Holland is about 80km away, the one at IJmuiden is just up the road along the North Sea Canal (see the following Boat section for ferry details). Coming from the UK it's slightly cheaper to take the ferry rather than the shuttle through the Tunnel, though the latter might save a few hours travelling time – contact Eurotunnel (☎ 0990-353 535) for the latest prices. Its Web site is at www.eurotunnel.com.

Vehicles, obviously, have to be roadworthy, registered and insured. The standard European road rules and traffic signs apply. Trams always have the right of way unless you're on a right-of-way road. Speed limits are 50km/h in built-up areas, 80km/h in the country, 100km/h on major through-roads and 120km/h on freeways (sometimes 100km/h, clearly indicated). The blood-alcohol limit when driving is 0.05%. Petrol is very expensive.

For more information about driving (or rather, not driving) in Amsterdam and about rental cars, see Car & Motorcycle in the Getting Around chapter.

Documents

Anyone driving a car or riding a motorcycle in the Netherlands must be able to show a valid licence as well as the vehicle's registration papers on the spot. With rental cars the registration papers usually live in the dashboard compartment; take them with you whenever you park, to avoid theft. Foreign-registered vehicles must have proof of third-party insurance in the form of a Green Card.

The Dutch automobile association ANWB (Map 6; see under Tourist Offices in the Facts for the Visitor chapter) provides a wide range of information and services if you can show a letter of introduction from your own association.

BICYCLE

The Netherlands are extremely bike-friendly; once you're in the country you can pedal most of the way to/from Amsterdam on dedicated bicycle paths. Everything is wonderfully flat, but that also means powerful wind and it always seems to come from ahead. Beware that mopeds use bike paths too and might be travelling well in excess of their 40km/h speed limit (30km/h in built-up areas). Bikes (or mopeds) are not allowed on freeways at all. Only competition cyclists or posers wear bicycle helmets.

If you want to bring your own bike, consider the high risk of theft in Amsterdam – rental might be the wiser option. You can bring it along on the train for a nominal charge and (most) ferries charge nothing. Airlines usually treat it as normal accompanied luggage – inquire in advance, and also ask what to do if bike and luggage exceed your weight allowance or you could be charged a fortune for the excess.

For organisations offering local advice and support, see Bicycle & Moped in the Getting Around chapter.

HITCHING

Hitching is never entirely safe in any country and we don't recommend it. Travellers who decide to hitch should understand that they are taking a small but potentially serious risk.

Many Dutch students have a government-issued pass allowing free public transport (though this is under review). Consequently the number of hitchhikers has dropped dramatically and car drivers are no longer used to the phenomenon. Hitchers have reported long waits.

On Channel crossings from the UK, the car fares on the Harwich–Hook of Holland ferry as well as the shuttle through the Channel Tunnel include passengers, so you can hitch to the Continent for nothing at no cost to the driver (though the driver will still be responsible if you do something illegal).

Looking for a ride out of the country? Try the notice boards at the Science and Economics complex at Roetersstraat 11, the main public library at Prinsengracht 587, the Tropenmuseum or youth hostels. People also advertise to share fuel costs in the classifieds paper *Via Via* published on Tuesday and Thursday.

BOAT

Several companies operate car/passenger ferries between the Netherlands and the UK, and one of them also sails to/from Norway via the UK. For information on train-ferry-train services, see the earlier Train section. Most travel agents have information on the following services but might not always know the finer points – it's easier to catch eels with your bare hands than to pin down who's doing what exactly when it comes to ferries. Once again, expect prices and deals to fluctuate madly depending on cross-Channel competition. Reservations are essential for motorists, especially in the summer high season, though motorcycles can often be squeezed in at the last moment.

Stenaline (☎ 0990-707 070) sails between Harwich and Hook of Holland and has both a day and night service (about 3½ hours). Foot passengers pay upwards of UK£25 return. Fares for a car with up to five people range from UK£90 to UK£130 depending on the season (extra passengers pay the foot-passenger fare). Options such as reclining chairs and cabins cost extra and are compulsory on night crossings. Stenaline also sails to/from Ireland but this is almost getting into cruise-ship territory. Its Web site is at www.stenaline.com.

P&O North Sea Ferries (☎ 01482-377 177) operates an overnight ferry every evening (takes 14 hours) between Hull and Europoort (near Rotterdam). Return fares start at UK£67 for a foot passenger and UK£280 for a car with up to four passengers. There is a Web site at www.ponsf.com.

DFDS Scandinavian Seaways (☎ 0990-333 111) sails between Newcastle and IJmuiden, the closest port to Amsterdam, departing Newcastle on even-numbered dates (14 hours). Fares start at UK£60 for a (foot) passenger plus UK£100 for a car and include reclining seats (cabins cost extra). Expect to pay about 80% more in

the high season. Its Web site is at www
.dfdsseaways.co.uk.

The same company also sails between
IJmuiden and Kristiansand (Norway) via
Newcastle. From IJmuiden, fares cost
f170/205/290 for a car in low/middle/high
season, while passengers pay f155/215/300.
The trip takes 39 hours, including a six-
hour stopover in Newcastle.

TRAVEL AGENTS

Many travel agents specialise in discounted
fares; more of them don't but still manage
to be competitive with interesting packages.
The best advice is to shop around, beginning with the following agents:

Amber Reisbureau (Map 4; ☎ 685 11 55) Da
Costastraat 77 – open from 10 am to 5 pm
weekdays, to 3 pm Saturday; has a great travel
bookshop and good prices on tickets to Asia

Ashraf (Map 2; ☎ 623 24 50, fax 622 90 28)
Haarlemmerstraat 140, 1013 EZ Amsterdam –
runs overland adventure tours to Africa, Asia
and Latin America for young people

Budget Air (Map 4; ☎ 627 12 51) Rokin 34 – free
brochure published every two months with 700
exact fares for cheap flights to cities around the
world; pick up a copy for comparison, do your
homework and don't rely on staff to give you
the best deals

D-Reizen (Map 7; ☎ 200 10 12) Linnaeusstraat
112 – open from 9.30 am to 6 pm weekdays (to
8 pm Thursday), from 10 am to 3 pm Saturday;
really friendly service and some good last-
minute deals from Lufthansa, Sabena, KLM and
others

Flyworld/Grand Travel (☎ 657 00 00, fax 648
04 77) Wallaardt Sacrestraat 262, Schiphol –
cheap long-haul flights, all bookings by phone
or fax

Kilroy Travels (Map 4; ☎ 524 51 00) Singel 413
– special deals for those aged under 33

NBBS, with an office at the main post office, Singel 250 (Map 4; ☎ 423 44 33), and several
branches around town including Haarlemmerstraat 115 (Map 2; ☎ 626 25 57) and the head
office at Van Baerlestraat 82 (☎ 673 21 76) – the
official student travel agency; prices are not the
best, so compare other discount travel agencies
before booking here.

Getting Around

THE AIRPORT

Amsterdam's airport, Schiphol, is 18km south-west of the city centre. It lies 5m below sea level on the bottom of a former lake, the Haarlemmermeer, drained in 1852. The spacious yet surprisingly compact, one-terminal design ensures that everything is within easy reach, and the signposting couldn't be much clearer.

The arrivals hall, built around a V-shaped concourse with shops called Schiphol Plaza, is on the ground floor, with the Holland Tourist Information office (open from 7 am to 10 pm daily) in the far left corner as you emerge from the passenger area. The departures hall is upstairs. Passengers travelling to/from Schengen countries (see Visas in the Facts for the Visitor chapter) are kept separate from other passengers and don't go through passport control, though they should carry their passport as a means of identification and to transfer from Schengen to non-Schengen lounges.

On arrival, yellow signs and transfer information monitors direct you to the transfer gates or desks (if you don't already have a boarding pass for your onward flight), green signs to the various amenities.

Schiphol is world-renowned for its tax-free shopping; the scale and variety of goods are second to none and many prices are beaten only by airports such as Dubai and Abu Dhabi. In addition there's every facility you'd expect (and even some you wouldn't) of one of the world's leading international airports – it consistently rates near or at the top of business travel surveys. There's an interesting aviation museum nearby (see Amsterdam for Children in the Facts for the Visitor chapter) and even a casino in the passenger-only section of the non-Schengen departure lounge, open from 6 am to 8 pm, accessible to passengers aged over 18 with a valid boarding pass.

For airport and flight information, ring ☎ 0900-01 41 (f1 per minute) or check www.schiphol.nl on the Web.

Left Luggage

Luggage up to 30kg can be left at the staffed counter (☎ 601 24 43) in the basement, under the plaza, for a minimum of a day and a maximum of a month. This costs f6 to f8 per day depending on the length of time. The counter is open from 6.15 am to 10.45 pm but staff may be called through the intercom at other times. Lockers in the same area (f6 per day for small items, f15 for large) are available for a maximum of seven days.

TO/FROM THE AIRPORT

A taxi into the city takes 20 to 45 minutes (maybe longer in peak-hour traffic) and costs about f65. Trains to Centraal Station leave every 15 minutes, take 15 to 20 minutes and cost f6.50 (f10.75 return). Train-ticket counters are in the central court of Schiphol Plaza – buy your ticket before taking the escalator down to the subterranean platforms (you might want to buy a *strippenkaart* for public transport while you're at it – see the following Public Transport section). If your hotel is some way out of the city centre, it could be worth taking a train to one of the other stations around the city (see Train in the following section) and transferring to a taxi from there. Trains also connect Schiphol to 75% of train stations in the country either direct or with one change, and to major cities in Belgium, France and Germany.

Free shuttle buses travel to the Bastion, Hilton, Ibis, Golden Tulip, Holiday Inn, Dorint and Mercure airport hotels. A KLM shuttle bus runs between the airport and about 15 major hotels in the city every 30 minutes from the early morning to mid-evening at a cost of f17.50 one way, f30 return. For information, contact the Transport Desk (open from 7.30 am to 11.30 pm), the Holland Tourist Promotion desk, or ring Connexxion on ☎ 649 56 51. Bus No 172 maintains a regular service between the airport and Centraal Station but there are many other bus services that could better suit your needs – ring ☎ 0900-92 92 (f0.75 a minute).

There are also buses to other parts of the country.

Car-rental offices at the airport are in the right corner near the central exits of Schiphol Plaza. One of the country's main road arteries, the A4 freeway linking Amsterdam, The Hague and Rotterdam, tunnels under one of the airport runways. Just north of the airport is the A9 to/from Haarlem in the west, which runs south of the city and connects with the A2 to Utrecht and the south-east of the country. A bit farther north of the A9 is the intersection with the A10 ring road around Amsterdam.

Parking

The P1 and P2 short-term parking garages (under cover) charge f3.50 per half-hour for the first three hours, then f4 per hour. The maximum charge is f47.50 a day for the first two days, f25 a day thereafter. Pay at the machines before going to your car. Credit card holders can also use the P7 garage directly under the terminal at a cost of f15 for the first hour, then f10 per hour to a maximum of f65 a day. The P3 long-term parking area (open-air) is a fair distance from the terminal (follow the signs 'P – Lang Parkeren') but is connected by 24-hour shuttle bus. The parking charge is f85 for up to three days (minimum charge) and f7.50 for each day thereafter – a worthwhile alternative to parking in the city.

PUBLIC TRANSPORT

Amsterdam is compact and you can get to a lot of places on foot, but public transport (tram, *sneltram*, bus and metro), run by the GVB (Gemeentevervoerbedrijf – Municipal Transport Company), is comprehensive and efficient; see the Transport System map at the back of the book. The only problem is within the canal belt: trams and buses stick to the 'spoke' roads, so if you want to cover distance along a canal you'll have to take a tram or bus into the centre and another back out again.

The hub of the transport system is Centraal Station (CS), where most tram and bus lines and the metro converge. The GVB information office (Map 2) in front of the station is open from 7 am to 9 pm weekdays (to 7 pm from late October to March), from 8 am on weekends, and sells all types of tickets and passes. Pick up the free *Tourist Guide to public transport Amsterdam* booklet and several free transport maps; the complete transport map covering all of Amsterdam costs a token f1.50.

For transport information, call ☎ 0900-92 92 from 6 am to midnight weekdays, from 7 am weekends. This costs f0.75 a minute, which can add up quickly if your query is complicated. Expect to be put on hold for a couple of minutes as other calls are answered ahead of you.

Tickets & Passes

Ticketing is based on zones. Most of Amsterdam proper (the canal belt and surrounding districts) is one zone; travel to the older suburbs is two, and to the newer, outer suburbs is three.

The strip ticket *(strippenkaart)* is valid on all buses, trams and metros in the country, as well as trains within municipal areas (though in Amsterdam's case Schiphol is *not* included). Fold the ticket to the relevant strip and stick it into the yellow machine to cancel two strips for the first zone and an additional strip for each additional zone – always one strip more than the number of zones. Any number of people can travel on the one ticket, so long as you cancel the appropriate number of strips for each person. When you get to the bottom of the ticket, cancel the last strip and proceed with the next ticket. The validity for one, two or three zones is one hour, during which time you can transfer as often as you like.

Strip tickets (f11.75 for 15 strips, f34.50 for 45) are available at tobacco shops, post offices, train-station counters and ticketing machines, many bookshops and newsagencies, and special outlets such as the GVB offices in front of Centraal Station and the GVB head office in the Scheepvaarthuis (Map 5), Prins Hendrikkade 108–114 (the latter is open from 9 am to 4.30 pm weekdays). Drivers and conductors only sell two/three/eight-strip tickets for f3/4.50/12, or a day pass for f12 (actually an eight-strip

GETTING AROUND

ticket stamped vertically). Children and pensioners pay f7 for a 15-strip ticket that has to be bought in advance. Travelling without a valid ticket (frequent spot checks) incurs a fine of f60 plus the ticket price, and playing the ignorant foreigner won't work.

The GVB offices also sell day passes valid for all zones at f10 for one day, f15 for two and then in f4 increments up to f43 for nine days; those eligible for a discount pay f6 for one day, f10 for two days and then in f2.50 increments up to f27.50 for nine days. Passes valid for one zone cost f17.75 a week or f58.75 a month (f10.50 or f37 with discount). The GVB offices can advise of several other options.

Night buses take over when regular transport stops running shortly after midnight. Drivers sell single tickets for f4, or you can stamp three strips off your strip card and pay a f2 supplement (which works out to be more expensive). Day passes are valid during the night(s) following the day(s) indicated on the pass but attract the same f2 supplement. Five-journey cards for night buses bought in advance cost f17.50. The privately run Connexxion night buses cost more.

Tram

Most trams can be entered or exited through any of the doors, where there are yellow machines to stamp strip tickets. If you need to buy a ticket, enter at the front by the driver. Some trams have a separate conductor in the back and can only be entered through the rear doors (there are one-way bars at the others); in that case, show your ticket to the conductor. When getting in or out, the bottom step locks the door in the open position and prevents the tram from leaving.

There are also a few *sneltram* ('fast tram', or light rail) lines in the southern and south-eastern suburbs. Tickets are cancelled the same way as in ordinary trams except where the sneltram shares the metro line, in which case you use the yellow machines at the stairways to the platforms.

Always assume that pickpockets are active on busy trams.

Circle Tram Tram No 20 is the very useful Circle Tram that does a wide loop through the city along all the major tourist sights in either direction from Centraal Station about every 10 minutes from 9 am to 6 pm. It accepts normal strip tickets (one zone, ie, two strips) and passes.

Bus

Trams don't venture to Amsterdam North and only a few go to the outer suburbs, so you're likely to need a bus there. Board a bus through the front door and present your ticket to the driver.

Metro

The metro is useful mostly for getting to the international bus station at Amstelstation (one zone) or to the Bijlmer (three zones). In the city there's only one line (at least, until the north-south line comes into operation in 2006) but after Amstelstation it branches into three lines – one to the southern suburbs of Buitenveldert and Amstelveen and two to the south-eastern suburb of Bijlmer. Cancel your strip ticket at the machines near the stairways to the platforms.

Anyone interested in seeing another side of Amsterdam should hang around Weesperplein metro station during the morning or afternoon rush hours when people from the Bijlmer change from the metro to trams at this station. The scene is just like a little New York!

Train

You're most likely to use the train in Amsterdam when travelling to/from Schiphol airport. The options are Centraal Station, at the hub of the public transport system; Lelylaan, De Vlugtlaan and Sloterdijk in the western suburbs; Zuid WTC and RAI (near the exhibition centre) in the southern suburbs; or Duivendrecht and Diemen-Zuid in the south-eastern suburbs. A sneltram connects RAI station to Amstelstation for trains to/from Utrecht and the east of the country, though such trains also call at Centraal Station.

You can use strip tickets to travel on trains in the Amsterdam region – cancel your ticket at the machines near the stairways to the platforms. Muiderpoort and Amstelstation are two strips to/from Centraal Station; Diemen, Diemen-Zuid, Duivendrecht, RAI, Zuid WTC, Lelylaan, De Vlugtlaan and Sloterdijk are three strips; and Bijlmer is four strips. Strip tickets are *not* valid to/from Schiphol, which requires a normal train ticket.

For more about train travel, see Train in the Getting There & Away chapter, and Getting Around the Country in the Excursions chapter.

CAR & MOTORCYCLE

See Car & Motorcycle in the Getting There & Away chapter for general information about road rules, documents etc.

Central Amsterdam's narrow canalside streets were not built for heavy vehicular traffic, and driving into the city is actively discouraged by the authorities with their *autoluw* ('car-sheltered') policy. Of course, the most effective way to reduce the number of cars is by limiting parking space. There's absolutely no free parking in Amsterdam (the only exceptions are way outside the A10 ring road), and even if it looks like the parking is free because no warning signs are posted, there's a hungry automatic ticketing machine in the vicinity. This disgorges a receipt that you should place on the dashboard inside the car (check that it stays there when you slam the door shut). In the city centre and some of the 19th-century neighbourhoods, parking charges are payable Monday to Saturday between 9 am and 11 pm, Sunday between noon and 11 pm. It costs f5/3 per hour inside/outside the centre Monday to Saturday from 9 am to 7 pm, and f3 per hour at other times regardless of location (check the notice on the machine: fees and conditions change frequently).

The ticketing machine may not be visible immediately but do find it, otherwise a bright yellow *wielklem* (wheel clamp) will be attached to your car and it will cost f130 to have it removed. Don't expect to talk your way out of this: they've heard it all before. The infringement notice on your windscreen will give the location of the nearest City Surveillance *(Stadstoezicht)* office, where you must go in person if you want to pay cash. Foreigners with a credit card can pay at their car by ringing the number indicated on the notice.

There are two City Surveillance offices that can remove wheel clamps (and a third to be announced): Weesperstraat 105A (head office), between Weesperplein and Waterlooplein on the corner of Nieuwe Prinsengracht; and Beukenplein 50, out east near the Oosterpark. The Weesperstraat office is open from 8 am to 8 pm seven days; the Beukenplein office is open the same hours but closed Sunday. The notice will indicate what to do outside those hours.

If you don't report to one of these offices within 24 hours your car will be towed away and a f300 towing charge plus f94 per 12 hours garage fee will be collected in addition to the parking fine, which can make things very expensive indeed. Towed cars are taken to the Daniel Goedkoopstraat 7–9 in the south-eastern suburbs (metro: Spaklerweg or Overamstel), so before jumping to the conclusion that your vehicle has been stolen, call ☎ 555 30 333 (general information number, 24 hours).

You can easily avoid these potential problems by parking your car in the outer suburbs and entering the city by tram or metro, as many people do. For undercover parking, the Transferium parking garage (☎ 400 17 21) under the Arena stadium in the Bijlmer charges f2.50 per hour or f12.50 per day, including transfers to the metro and two return tickets to Centraal Station – an excellent deal, even (or especially) long-term. There's a similar parking garage (same deal) in front of the VVV office at Stadionplein in the south-western outskirts of the city.

It's also possible to buy a city parking permit at any of the above offices for f33/185.50 a day/week (two-thirds price for areas outside the canal belt or museum quarter). Monthly permits are also available. The ticketing machines issue day permits but you have to go to one of the above-mentioned offices for other permits.

euro currency converter f1 = €0.45

Tip: any ticket bought from a machine after 11 pm is valid the next day, so you don't have to rush out at 8.55 am to 'top up' your ticket. Some hotels issue three-day tourist passes for f90/60 inside/outside the canal belt, and a few luxury hotels have their own arrangements that aren't cheap.

Parking garages in the city centre (eg, on Damrak, near Leidseplein and under the Stopera) are often full and cost more than a parking permit, though they do provide shelter and some security against theft and vandalism. Alternatively, you could book into your hotel and then leave the car in the Transferium, in the Stadionplein garage or the long-term parking area at Schiphol airport for the duration of your stay, which is probably the wisest option (see the earlier The Airport section and compare prices with the above-mentioned Transferium, bearing in mind that the Transferium and Stadionplein are undercover).

Drivers with a disability and the appropriate windscreen marker may park free of charge in designated parking spots – but beware of spots with a registration number reserved for local residents because your car will be towed away.

Motorcyclists don't face parking problems: they can park on the pavement (sidewalk) free of charge provided they don't obstruct anybody. Security is a big problem with any parked vehicle, however, irrespective of the time of day, so you shouldn't leave luggage on the bike nor rely on the steering lock.

Car Rental

There's no point renting a car to tour the city but it's a good way to make excursions into the countryside. The car-rental market is fluid, and prices and deals change by the week. The following list represents a snapshot of what was available at the time of research, but it pays to ring around to find the deal that suits you best. Make sure you bring a credit card.

Local companies are usually cheaper than the multinationals (Avis, Budget, Hertz, Europcar) but don't offer as much backup or flexibility (eg, one-way rentals

within or outside the Netherlands). Rentals at Schiphol airport incur an extra f70.50 'airport company tax' which none of the companies are happy about.

Avis (☎ 683 60 61) Nassaukade 380, not far from Leidseplein; (☎ 644 36 84) President Kennedylaan 783; (☎ 430 95 11) Klokkenbergweg 15; international reservations ☎ 430 96 09 weekdays only – f205 a day for the cheapest car with unlimited kilometres, insurance and tax included; otherwise it's f127 a day plus f0.40 per kilometre (the first 200km are free), tax and insurance included

Budget (☎ 612 60 66) Overtoom 121; (☎ 604 13 49) Schiphol Plaza; central number ☎ 0800-05 37 (free call); international reservations ☎ 070-384 43 85 – f210 a day for the cheapest car, unlimited kilometres, insurance and tax included; this is expensive but Budget also offers one of the cheapest deals in the country through the post office – see below. A Renault Cariole specially adapted for a wheelchair in the back costs f90 a day but should preferably be booked a week in advance

Europcar (☎ 683 21 23) Overtoom 197; (☎ 316 41 90) Schiphol Plaza; international reservations ☎ 070-381 18 91 (weekdays only) – a Renault Twingo for f67 a day plus f0.35 a kilometre (the first 200km are free)

Hertz (☎ 612 24 41) Overtoom 333; (☎ 623 61 23) Engelsesteeg 4; international reservations ☎ 504 05 54 (seven days from 8 am to 8 pm) – f74 a day for a Seat Ibiza with 200km free (f0.30 per extra kilometre); the branch at Schiphol Plaza has cars from f201 a day with unlimited kilometres

Kuperus BV (☎ 693 87 90, fax 665 98 78) Middenweg 175 on the south-eastern side of town (tram No 9) – cheapest car is f53 a day including insurance, tax and 100km (f0.29 per extra kilometre); cars with unlimited kilometres begin at f264 for three days, all-inclusive

Safety Rent-a-Car (☎ 636 63 63) Papaverweg 3B near the Galaxy Hotel, Amsterdam North – cheapest car is f73 a day plus f0.22 per kilometre (after the first 100km), tax and insurance included; unlimited kilometre rentals also available, depending on where you want to go

The cheapest arrangement of all involves a post office, where you buy a voucher that gets you the smallest Budget car for only f55 a day or f85 a weekend including insurance, tax and 200km (f0.20 per extra kilometre). The vouchers are valid for six months and you must book your car directly at a Budget office no less than 24 hours in advance. For more information, call ☎ 0900-15 76 from 8 am to 8 pm weekdays, and to 5 pm Saturday.

Camper Van Purchase

Braitman & Woudenberg (☎ 622 11 68), Droogbak 4A at Singel diagonally opposite Hotel Ibis, sells camper vans to travellers with a guaranteed repurchase agreement. A good VW Westfalia costs f10,000, and if you return it in good condition within three months you'll get 75% back, within six months 65%, and within a year 60%; longer periods are negotiable. Occasionally there are cheaper vans at around f5000.

Buying and selling a vehicle privately is possible if you have sufficient time and expertise. You can transfer registrations at the post office but don't forget about motor vehicle tax for Dutch-registered vehicles, which is due quarterly. For information about registration documents, call the Department of Road Transport on ☎ 0598-62 42 40 from 8 am to 5 pm weekdays. The Central Office for Motor Vehicle Tax is on ☎ 0800-07 49 (free call), also from 8 am to 5 pm weekdays.

Motorcycle Rental

Renting a car is cheaper than renting a motorcycle but sometimes a car just won't do, will it? For instance, you might want to visit the Dutch TT at Assen on the last weekend in June. Ring around:

KAV Autoverhuur (☎ 614 14 35) Johan Huizingalaan 91 in the south-west of the city – 47 different types of motorcycles ranging in price from f70 a day plus f0.25 per kilometre (first 100km free) to f218 a day and f0.40 per kilometre (after the first 100km), tax included; insurance waiver f29.50 a day; credit card and international driving permit required

Kuperus BV (☎ 668 33 11) Van der Madeweg 1–5 – Yamaha Virago at f99 a day including insurance, tax and 100km (extra kilometres f0.25 each); three-day, unlimited-kilometre hire is f425 all-inclusive; a Honda VT750, CB750 or Suzuki Marauder costs f164 a day including 100km; credit card and international driving permit required

Motorsport Selling (☎ 465 66 67) Spaklerweg 91 – a range of big touring bikes at f105 a day plus f0.25 per kilometre (the first 125km are free), tax and insurance included; on a weekly basis it's f840 with 875km free; f1000 deposit required; cash is fine

TAXI

Amsterdam taxis are among the most expensive in Europe and the drivers are rude, but you'd be rude too if you had to put up with such frequent traffic delays and road closures. To call a taxi anywhere in the city, dial ☎ 677 77 77 (soon to become ☎ 0900-677 77 77); apart from the cost of the call, this is no more expensive than walking to a taxi stand. You're not supposed to hail taxis on the street but nobody seems to care much; the taxi is available if the roof sign is illuminated. Taxis cost the same day or night, and a tip of 5% to 10% is expected.

The excellent train-taxi service (see Getting Around the Country in the Excursions chapter) only operates to/from Amsterdam Zuid WTC station and is limited to Amstelveen, Buitenveldert and a few other outlying areas – call ☎ 645 18 52.

BICYCLE & MOPED

See Bicycle in the previous chapter for general information about road rules etc.

Amsterdam has 550,000 bicycles, an ideal way to get around because nothing within the canal belt (and sometimes a fair way beyond) is more than 10 minutes by bike. Most bikes carry a couple of locks that are worth more than the thing itself, indicative of the fact that 200,000 bicycles are stolen each year.

An alternative to renting a bike (see the following section) is to buy one, which is worth considering if you're spending more than a month or so in town. Bicycle shops sell second-hand bikes for f140–200; add f60–100 for one or two good locks to attach the frame and front wheel (not just the front wheel) to a bridge railing or something solid. Drug addicts might offer bikes for considerably less – as little as f25 if they're desperate – but Amsterdam residents boycott such activity and detest

GETTING AROUND

tourists who 'acquire' their vehicle this way. It's also highly illegal and can land you in big trouble if the owner recognises their bike (which happens more often than you'd think).

If you arrive with your own bicycle, the Dutch automobile association ANWB (Map 6; see under Tourist Offices in the Facts for the Visitor chapter) provides information and services if you can show a letter of introduction from your automobile association (or your cycling association, but that seems to depend on the person behind the counter). The letters ANWB stand for General Netherlands Cyclists' Federation – that's how it started and cyclists haven't been forgotten completely.

Some of the bicycle rental agencies mentioned below organise tours and can help with cycling maps. See also Organised Tours later in this chapter. Map shops such as Pied à Terre, Jacob van Wijngaarden and à la Carte (see Books – Travel in the Shopping chapter) have an extensive range of cycling maps. Serious cyclists who are into cycling policy and legislation can contact the local cyclists' association, the ENFB (☎ 685 47 94), Wilhelmina Gasthuisplein 84, 1054 BC Amsterdam (advice on activities, rental, purchase, tours, train transport etc, after 10 am weekdays).

Bicycle Rental

Many visitors rent a bike towards the end of their stay and wish they had done so sooner, but the chaotic traffic can be challenging. Amsterdam cyclists have been weaving through this mess all their lives, and believe with justification that the embarrassingly obvious rental bikes spell trouble. Take care, and watch those tram tracks: if they catch a wheel you'll go down and it will hurt.

All the companies listed below require ID plus a credit card imprint or a cash deposit. The NS (railways) Rijwielshop and Amstel Stalling are the cheapest but their bicycles can be a bit run-down towards the end of the tourist season (rent one in April). They're cheaper still if you buy a *huurfiets-dagkaart* (rental-bicycle day card) with your train ticket, or show your ticket at the counter of your destination station and buy it there. This costs a mere f7.50; a *huurfiets-weekkaart* for one week costs f30. In both cases you'll also need to pay a deposit that varies with the station (between f50 and f200). This excellent system applies to 100 train stations around the country – worth remembering for excursions.

Prices are for standard, 'coaster-brake' bikes (no gears, brake in the rear hub operated by pedalling backwards); gears and hand brakes cost more:

Amstel Stalling (Map 1; ☎ 692 35 84) Amstel-station – f9.50/38 a day/week, f100 deposit
Bike City (Map 4; ☎/fax 626 37 21) Bloemgracht 68–70 in the Jordaan opposite the Anne Frankhuis – f12.50/50 a day/week, f50 deposit and no embarrassing advertising on the bikes, so you can pretend you're a local
Damstraat Rent-a-Bike (Map 4; ☎ 625 50 29) Pieter Jacobsdwarsstraat 7–11 near Dam Square – f15/67.50 a day/week, f50 deposit
Holland Rent-a-Bike (Map 4; ☎ 622 32 07) Damrak 247 in the Beurs van Berlage – f12.50/50 a day/week, f50 deposit with a passport or f200 without
MacBike (Map 4; ☎ 620 09 85) Mr Visserplein 2 next to Waterlooplein market – f12.50/60 a day/week, f50 deposit or a credit card imprint, passport required. Another MacBike outlet is at Marnixstraat 220 (Map 4; ☎ 626 69 64) next to the Europarking complex
Rijwielshop (Map 2; ☎ 624 83 91) Stationsplein 12 – access from the outer side of Centraal Station at the far east end of the building near the city bus stops; f9.50 a day, f38 a week, f200 deposit

Moped Rental

Moped Rental Service (Map 4; ☎ 422 02 66), Marnixstraat 208, rents neat little mopeds from f12.50 an hour or f35/60 a half/full day including insurance and a full tank of petrol – a fun way to get out of Amsterdam for a spin. You don't have to wear a helmet on the simplest type of moped but you do need a licence (car licence will do). The place is open 9 am to 7 pm daily in summer, to 6 pm in winter.

WALKING

The cliche 'Venice of the north' is apt: like Venice, Amsterdam is a joy to discover on

Two-Wheeled Obstruction

Scene: Vijzelstraat during afternoon peak hour.

Plot: Loud swearing in the most guttural Dutch. A gentleman on a bicycle has stopped for a red light; other cyclists swerve to avoid colliding into the back of him. 'Idiot! Scrotum! Can't you just keep going? You're a road hazard!'

The gentleman in question? The mayor of Amsterdam, Schelto Patijn.

foot, and most of the sights are within easy walking distance in the compact city centre. You can also get lost as in Venice, but never as comprehensively. There's a lot of irregular brick or cobblestone paving, so avoid high heels – and watch out for dog-shit.

Accident statistics show that the Netherlands is the safest country in Europe for pedestrians, who are more than twice as likely to be run over by a car in Britain. Beware of bicycles though: they have traffic rights separate to those of a pedestrian. A lot of them zigzag through Amsterdam, ignoring road rules in the same way that pedestrians ignore pedestrian lights. Paving that is coloured reddish is reserved for cyclists, who can get quite angry (there are very few polite cyclists) when pedestrians get in the way, which foreigners often do inadvertently.

BOAT
Ferries

The free ferry to Amsterdam North for pedestrians, bicycles and mopeds, marked *Buiksloterwegveer* (*veer* means ferry), goes straight across the IJ from the landing between Piers 8 and 9 at the rear of Centraal Station. A round trip would be an interesting way to kill 45 minutes or so while waiting for a train. It operates every five minutes from 6.30 am to 9 pm, then every 10 minutes from 9 pm to 6.30 am daily, and only takes a few minutes to get across. The *Adelaarswegveer* from Pier 8 goes diagonally across the IJ and takes a bit longer. It operates every seven or 15 minutes from

6.27 am to 8.57 pm weekdays, every 15 minutes Saturday, but not Sunday.

Canal Boat, Bus & Bike

For information about regular canal tours, see Canal Tours in the following Organised Tours section.

The Lovers Museum Boat (Map 2; ☎ 622 21 81) leaves every 30 or 45 minutes (the schedules vary) from in front of Centraal Station at Prins Hendrikkade, opposite No 26, and stops at all the major museums. A day ticket for unlimited travel costs f25 (f15 if you buy it after 1 pm). If you only join for a single stop it costs f7.50, two stops cost f10, and three or four stops f12.50. The day ticket gives 10% to 50% admission discounts to most museums en route. If you're the sort of person who can handle several museums in a day it's not a bad deal because expert commentary is part of the package and you save on a canal tour.

The Canal Bus (☎ 623 98 86) does a circuit of the tourist centres between Centraal Station and the Rijksmuseum between 10.15 am and 6.45 pm. A day pass costs f22 (f32.50 including entry to the Rijksmuseum). Canal 'bikes' (☎ 626 55 74) can be hired from kiosks at Leidseplein, Keizersgracht/Leidsestraat, the Anne Frankhuis and the Rijksmuseum, with two/four-seaters costing f25/40 an hour.

Water Taxi

Amsterdam's canals are sadly under-utilised for transport – there's no equivalent of the Venetian *vaporetto*, *traghetto* or *gondola*. The closest you'll get is the overpriced water taxi that operates from 8 am to midnight from its home base at the Lovers terminal in front of Centraal Station (Prins Hendrikkade opposite No 26). Prices vary depending on the number of people and the duration. Simple food can be supplied on board, or you can go for an aquatic running dinner (three courses at three restaurants). Advance bookings are essential on ☎ 622 21 81.

ORGANISED TOURS

The following organisations offer tours that provide a quick overview of the sights.

euro currency converter f1 = €0.45

GETTING AROUND

Prices may vary depending on special exhibitions at the Rijksmuseum:

Holland International (☎ 625 30 35) Damrak 90 – 3½-hour bus tour includes the Rijksmuseum and a diamond factory; at 2.30 pm daily (f48)

Keytours (☎ 623 50 51) Dam 19 next to Thomas Cook and the Krasnapolsky Hotel – 3½-hour city sightseeing tours in summer: the morning tour at 9.30 am is by bus and boat (f40) while the afternoon tour at 2.30 pm is by bus to the Rijksmuseum and a diamond factory (f48); only afternoon tours in winter

Lindbergh Tours (☎ 622 27 66) Damrak 26 – 2½-hour city sightseeing tours by bus at 10 am and 2.30 pm daily in summer (f27.50, or f35 bus plus one-hour canal boat tour, though these prices are likely to increase); only afternoon tours in winter

On public holidays and Sundays from mid-June to mid-September, the GVB operates a historic 1920s Tourist Tram that leaves from opposite the Victoria Hotel in front of Centraal Station and trundles past the sights in the city centre. There's also a candlelight dinner tram, and several bus tours around the city and beyond. Inquire at the GVB office in front of Centraal Station, or ring ☎ 460 53 53.

Canal Tours

It might come as a surprise that many if not most Amsterdammers have never taken a canal tour. Little do they realise they're missing a totally different and very worthwhile perspective of the city. A horde of operators leave from in front of Centraal Station, along Damrak and Rokin and near the Rijksmuseum, and charge around f15 for a one-hour cruise. They're all fairly similar so choose whichever is convenient. Advance bookings are unnecessary unless you're planning something special.

The operators run slightly different routes, so if there's a canal you desperately want to see from the water, ask. There are evening cruises by candlelight, with wine and cheese (or even five-course dinners) to enhance the experience.

You can save money on a regular day cruise by going to one of the two official youth hostels (the Stadsdoelen or Vondelpark

– see Hostels in the Places to Stay chapter) and buying your ticket from the receptionist. This will get you a 40% discount on the normal price and you don't need to be staying at the hostel or to show a HI or IYHF card to obtain such a ticket. The Lovers boat opposite Centraal Station charges f10 for students.

Other Water Tours

On Sundays and public holidays from mid-April to mid-October, the GVB runs a harbour ferry that leaves from behind Centraal Station and takes you on a two-hour trip of the harbour at noon, 2 and 4 pm – tickets (f12.50, or f9 for children) are available at the GVB information office in front of Centraal Station, or ring ☎ 460 53 53. There are trips by hydrofoil and catamaran to other destinations, including Lelystad and Almere.

More ambitious cruises are offered by Rederij Naco (☎ 626 24 66) from Pier 7 behind Centraal Station. From May to mid-September its six-hour cruise to the historic fort of Pampus and the castle at Muiden leaves at 10 am every Thursday and Sunday (f39, children f22.50). Take along some sandwiches to avoid being dependent on the shipboard restaurant (drinks are reasonably priced). In May, June and September there's a Tuesday cruise from 10 am to 4 pm along the picturesque Vecht River with its historic country mansions south-east of the city. Cruises vary each year; ring to find out what's on offer.

Bicycle Tours

Several operators offer bike tours from April to October. Yellow Bike Tours (☎ 620 69 40), Nieuwezijds Kolk 29 off Nieuwezijds Voorburgwal, is the largest of its kind and offers three-hour bicycle tours around town for f32.50, or longer 6½-hour tours to Broek in Waterland north of Amsterdam which cost f42.50.

Let's Go (☎ 600 18 09) offers 6½-hour bike tours to Edam and Volendam, or a Castle & Windmills tour east of the city, for f45 (train tickets not included). Tours start at the VVV office in front of Centraal

Station and you take the train to the bikes. Several readers have recommended these tours highly. Its Web site (www.come.to /letsgo) has details.

Cycletours Holland (☎ 627 40 98, fax 627 90 32), Keizersgracht 181, 1016 DR Amsterdam, offers a variety of overnight tours around the Netherlands by bicycle and barge-boat sleeping 15 to 30 people. It caters mostly to people who have booked in advance from abroad, so it's best to write ahead for a brochure – it may have moved by the time you read this, so check www.cy cletours.com on the Web. A one-week tour from Saturday to Saturday costs f1195 (two-berth cabin with shower and toilet); there are also four or five-day tours from f605 (same facilities).

Things to See & Do

Amsterdam is one of those places where you never get bored going for a walk. It's full of hidden gems and unexpected delights. The attractions described in this chapter are the more 'important' ones, but visitors as well as residents keep finding interesting things that don't make it into guidebooks or tourist publications. No doubt you'll find some of your own, and begin to understand what keeps drawing people back to the city.

HIGHLIGHTS

According to the VVV, the most popular attractions in Amsterdam are (in order):

1. Canal tour
2. Artis zoo
3. Rijksmuseum
4. Diamond factory visit
5. Van Gogh Museum
6. Holland Casino Amsterdam
7. Concertgebouw
8. Anne Frankhuis
9. Stedelijk Museum
10. Seksmuseum Amsterdam ('De Venustempel')

This ranking includes Dutch as well as foreign visitors. A subjective listing on behalf of foreigners might read as follows:

1. Canal tour
2. Rijksmuseum
3. A few 'brown cafés'
4. Nederlands Scheepvaartmuseum (maritime history)
5. Stedelijk Museum
6. Aimless wandering within the canal belt
7. Albert Cuyp market
8. Begijnhof
9. People-watching at Leidseplein
10. Free summer concert in the Vondelpark

THINGS TO AVOID

Some of the popular sights are overrated, such as Madame Tussaud Scenerama on Dam Square (the one in London is better); Holland Experience next to the Rembrandthuis (an overpriced multimedia hype-fest that could have been so much more convincing); the casino off Leidseplein (why come to Amsterdam for a casino?); and even the Anne Frankhuis (a pilgrimage to this place in summer is ruined by the queues – visit the Joods Historisch Museum instead). Other things to avoid include:

- A canal cruise with a bunch of school kids screaming through the commentary
- The Kalverstraat and Nieuwendijk shopping streets on Saturday and Sunday – far too busy then, and a domain of pickpockets
- Taxis – rude drivers and very expensive
- Driving a car within the canal belt – you'll get stuck behind a truck unloading beer barrels and

Amsterdam for Free

It's easy to spend a fortune in Amsterdam but some of the most enjoyable things cost nothing. The following free activities and sights are described in this chapter in the following order:

- Catch a ferry across the IJ
- Hear a carillon recital while walking along a canal (the VVV has up-to-date schedules)
- Wander through the red-light district and try to admire the architecture
- Stroll through the Civic Guard Gallery
- Enjoy peace and quiet in the Begijnhof
- Admire the view at the intersection of Keizersgracht and Reguliersgracht
- Take a tour of a diamond factory
- Visit the Zuiderkerk
- See the NAP display in the Stopera
- Wander through the Rijksmuseum garden
- Catch a free lunch-time concert in the Concertgebouw or the Stopera
- Go to an open-air concert in the Vondelpark in summer
- Join over 2000 in-line skaters on a skate through the city each Friday night (weather permitting); meet outside the Nederlands Filmmuseum in the Vondelpark at 8 pm
- Watch horses being trained indoors at the Hollandse Manege

you won't be able to park without blowing the budget; if you do park, the car will get broken into
- Brightly coloured hire bikes with embarrassing rent-a-bike signs – Amsterdammers consider them a traffic hazard (not that Amsterdammers stick to road rules themselves but at least they know what they're doing); ask for something less obvious if you have a choice
- Paying by credit card – many proprietors refuse cards, or charge a hefty 'administration fee'
- Taking photos of prostitutes or loiterers in the red-light district
- Buying drugs on the street

Central Amsterdam

The city within the canal belt is referred to as Amsterdam Centrum. One of the charms of this part of town is that its history is still so evident in its layout. The Damrak, Dam Square and Rokin, which run down the middle of the old medieval core, used to form the final stretch of the Amstel River. The city arose around the dam built across the Amstel at what is now Dam Square. The east bank was called Old Side (Oude Zijde), the west bank was the New Side (Nieuwe Zijde).

The marshy environment required drainage canals to create reasonably solid land. Eventually the Old Side was bordered by the Kloveniersburgwal and Gelderse-kade, and the New Side by the Singel (Moat), which marked the extents of the medieval city. In the late 1400s and early 1500s this modest area received a city wall, with fortified gates at strategic points.

A century later the feudal wall that cost so much to build was torn down again as the city spilled into the surrounding marshes; some of the old fortified gates remain today. Towards the end of the 16th century, habitable islands were built to the east. These form the current Nieuwmarkt neighbourhood, which lies east of the square of the same name.

Finally, in the 17th century, an enormous urban construction project resulted in the semicircular canal belt, enclosed by the Lijnbaansgracht and the zigzag Buitensingel (outer moat) now known as the Singelgracht.

A Medley of Museums

Everyone should find something to enjoy in Amsterdam's wide range of museums. Weekends tend to be the busiest times, along with Wednesday afternoons when many primary schools have the afternoon off and children are herded into museums. Many museums are closed on Monday.

Display captions may be in Dutch only – ask for an English-language brochure (often free) when you buy your ticket. Even so, captions are often short and you may wish to buy one of the guidebooks in the museum shop that explain things in more detail. Many museums have pleasant cafés (sometimes even restaurants) with gardens or courtyards – good places to relax and read up on the items on display.

A handful of museums are free but most charge admission and you might have to pay extra for special exhibitions. Discounts are frequently available for those aged over 65 or under 18, for students (rare), CJP Pass holders (see Student & Youth Cards in the Facts for the Visitor chapter) and holders of several other passes.

The Museumjaarkaart (Museum Year Card) gives you free entry to 400 museums around the country for a year at f55 (f25 for those aged 24 and under, f45 for those aged 55 and over). It's valid for most museums in Amsterdam including the major ones (Rijksmuseum, Van Gogh Museum, Stedelijk Museum, Scheepvaartmuseum etc) but not the Anne Frankhuis. At the others you'll usually get a discount, though special exhibitions might be an exception. After five or six museums the card will have paid for itself. Inquire at participating museums or the VVV (one photo required).

The Museum Boat is also worth considering for the discounts offered with its day card (see Boat in the Getting Around chapter), but if you want the discounts to work it's probably better to visit the Rijksmuseum separately because this can take a large chunk out of your day.

THINGS TO SEE & DO

DAMRAK, DAM SQUARE & ROKIN (MAP 4)

Most visitors arrive at **Centraal Station** (1889), a Dutch-Renaissance edifice with Gothic additions built to a design by Pierre Cuypers, who was also responsible for the Rijks-museum, and AL van Gendt, who designed the Concertgebouw. Its structure – a central section flanked by square towers with wings on either side – is indeed similar to Cuypers' Rijksmuseum. It influenced the designers of Tokyo's central station. Note the intricate gilded facade.

The site for the station was hotly debated at the time. Most council members favoured a station at Leidseplein or in the rapidly expanding southern suburbs, but the national government held the purse strings and went for the current site, on three artificial islands in the IJ. This cut the city off from its historical harbour, though the focus of the harbour had already shifted eastwards and would later move well to the west.

You can leave Centraal Station at the rear, harbour side, hop on one of the free passenger ferries to Amsterdam North and experience the expanse of the IJ. It's quiet now, but in the 17th and 18th centuries this was the busiest harbour in the world.

Leaving the station at the front, city side, the cupola and twin towers of the neo-baroque **St Nicolaaskerk** (1887) are to your left. Designed by AC Bleijs, it is the city's main Catholic church but is under threat of closure. The interior (wooden vaulting with square pillars of black marble) contains many paintings and a high altar with the crown of Holy Roman Emperor Maximilian I, but don't bother if you're pressed for time.

Damrak

The Damrak ('Dam Reach') stretches out in front of you towards Dam Square. This used to be the original harbour but soon became unsuitable for larger ships that tied up to

AMSTERDAMS HISTORISCH MUSEUM

Procession of the Lepers, Dam Square, painted by Adriaen van Nieulandt in 1633. Left to right: the old city hall, the Nieuwe Kerk, the Weigh House and the Damrak with small freighters drying their sails. The procession, to gather donations, was last held in 1603.

How to Murder Music: Street Organs & Carillons

Street organs and carillons are to the Dutch what bagpipes are to the Scots, and they elicit the same mixed feelings.

The elaborate street organs (*draaiorgels*, literally barrel organs) developed out of the hand-held barrel organs that were once popular throughout Europe but have now all but disappeared. Their atrocious tuning and repetitive repertoire contributed to their demise: people tended to pay organ grinders to stop rather than continue.

One of the factors that ensured their survival in the Netherlands was a leasing system established in Amsterdam in 1875: grinders leased their organs from

ROB VAN DRIESUM

Richly decorated street organ

owners who looked after maintenance and tuning, which ensured reasonable standards upheld by strict licensing laws. Even today, grinders are assigned limited hours in particular areas of the city so they are evenly distributed, and they can spend five minutes on the same spot before having to move on.

The repertoire includes anything from *Tulips from Amsterdam* and *The Blue Danube* to wacky renditions of the latest Top 40 hits. Fluctuations in temperature and humidity still play havoc with tuning, especially in the critical bourdon register where each tone is represented by two pipes tuned a few hertz apart for the desired vibrato, sometimes resulting in a cat's-wail effect. Is it music? Who knows, but most will agree that a street organ at full tilt is a pretty impressive bit of machinery. They used to be operated by hand but now little generator motors do the hard work.

The Dutch infatuation with mechanical instruments extends to the out-of-tune carillons that adorn many public buildings, especially church towers. They're usually operated by machines, though a select group of carillonneurs pound the keys during occasional concerts. These live interpretations of the works of classical and modern composers are often played with a surprising amount of feeling if you consider the natural limitations of the instrument.

Carillons are wonderfully quaint and attractive in passing, but if your accommodation is in the shadow of a church that has one, the repetitive time chimes every 15 minutes can drive you up the wall. Thank God they fall silent at night.

---

palisades along what is now Centraal Station and unloaded onto lighters. Today the Damrak is an agonising stretch of gaudy souvenir shops, exchange bureaus and claustrophobic hotels. At No 18 is **Seksmuseum Amsterdam** (also known as 'De Venustempel'), open daily from 10 am to 11.30 pm and well worth the f4.50 admission fee for its bizarre collection of pornographic material. Welcome to Amsterdam!

In the late 19th century the southern half of the Damrak was filled in for the new exchange building, the 1903 **Beurs van Berlage** (☎ 530 41 41), named after the architect HP Berlage who was still designing it after work began. The functional lines and stark, square clock tower contrast with the more exuberant designs of the age, but it is considered one of the most important landmarks of Dutch city architecture. You'll understand why when you look more closely at the clever details inside and out. The large central hall, with its steel and glass roof, was the commodities exchange where coffee, tobacco, sugar, wine and colonial merchandise were traded. (The traders eventually deserted the building in favour of the neoclassical **Effectenbeurs** (Stock Exchange), built in 1913 by Centraal Station's Pierre Cuypers on the east side of Beursplein.)

In the 1970s the foundations of Berlage's bourse were sinking and it was slated for

euro currency converter f1 = €0.45

demolition, but it was saved by popular outcry. It is now a cultural centre (home to the Netherlands Philharmonic Orchestra) with concert performances and changing exhibitions such as Picasso's paintings, Frank Lloyd Wright's designs and Karel Appel's works that are too large for regular museums. The public entrance is on the Damrak side, next to the bicycle shop. It's open Tuesday to Sunday from 10 am to 4 pm and entry costs f6 (f4 with discounts). Climb the clock tower for the view. In summer there's a pleasant café on the Beursplein side.

Dam Square

The Damrak ends in Dam Square (usually referred to simply as the Dam) where the original dam was built across the Amstel, giving the city its name. It was the central market square where everything happened. It used to be much smaller than today, reaching its current size only after buildings on all sides were gradually demolished. It seems empty now, inhabited by thousands of cheeky pigeons and the occasional fun fair.

The original dam was at the eastern end of the current square, with a sluice alongside so ships could pass through. From 1611 they had to lower their masts to pass under the new stock exchange built over the sluice, which was filled in for good in 1672.

The stock exchange itself was demolished in 1838 and the eastern end of the square is now dominated by a phallic obelisk, the **Nationaal Monument**. This was built in 1956 in memory of those who died during WWII and who are still honoured every year on 4 May. In the late 1960s the monument was a camping spot for hippies until angry marines chased them away. By the early 1990s it had become seriously weakened by rain and frost and was in danger of falling apart, but it has recently been restored by…a German firm. The statues symbolise war (the four male figures), peace (woman with child) and resistance (men with dogs); the 12 urns at the rear contain earth from the 11 provinces and the Dutch East Indies.

The imposing hulk at the western end of the Dam is the **Royal Palace**, or Koninklijk Paleis (completed 1665, in use since 1655),

which started life as the grand new city hall of republican Amsterdam. It replaced the old city hall on the same spot which conveniently burned down. No costs were spared by the architect, Jacob van Campen, for this display of Amsterdam's wealth that rivalled the grandest European buildings of the day. A century-and-a-half later it became the palace of Napoleon's brother king, who contributed one of the world's richest collections of Empire furniture but had the historic Weigh House in front of the building demolished because it spoiled his view.

The building then passed to the House of Orange who stayed here occasionally. In 1935 the national government bought and restored it for state functions (officially Queen Beatrix lives here and pays f1 a year rent, though she really lives in The Hague). The stunning interior, particularly the richly decorated Civic Hall, is much more lavish than the stark exterior suggests and is well worth visiting. The limited opening times vary throughout the year and depend on official functions. You might be lucky between 12.30 and 5 pm, but ring ☎ 624 86 98

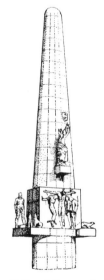

TAMSIN WILSON

Nationaal Monument

to check. Admission costs f7 (or f5 with discounts).

Next to the Royal Palace is the **Nieuwe Kerk** (New Church; early 15th century), the coronation church of Dutch royalty. This late-Gothic basilica is only 'new' in relation to the Oude Kerk (Old Church), with which it competed to be the grandest church in the city. It was gutted by fire several times, and the planned, exceptionally high tower was never completed because funds were diverted to the city hall next door.

Of interest are the magnificently carved oak chancel, the bronze choir screen, massive organ, stained-glass windows, and mausoleum of the city's greatest naval hero, Admiral Michiel de Ruijter, who died in 1676 fighting the French at Messina. Several other famous Amsterdammers are buried here, including the poets Joost van den Vondel and Pieter Cornelisz Hooft. The building is used for exhibitions and for organ concerts, no longer as a church. Opening hours and admission fees vary depending on what's on – ring the information line on ☎ 638 69 09 to find out.

Rokin

Beyond the Dam, the Damrak becomes the Rokin (a corruption of *rak-in*, 'inner reach'), most of which was filled in the 19th century. It is considerably more upmarket than the Damrak, with office buildings (the modern Options Exchange at No 61), prestigious shops (the wood-panelled tobacconist Hajenius at No 92) and art dealers (Sotheby Mak van Waay at No 102 – probably moved by the time you read this). A **column** on the pavement at Wijde Kapelsteeg commemorates the Miracle of Amsterdam that made the city a place of pilgrimage in medieval times (see Early Trade in the History section of the Facts about Amsterdam chapter). The chapel built on the spot where the miracle of the incombustible Host took place has been demolished, but it occupied this small block between Wijde and Enge Kapelsteeg.

At Grimburgwal, where the water begins again, the bank opposite the Rokin is called Oude Turfmarkt. Near the Grimburgwal

corner, at Oude Turfmarkt 127, is the University of Amsterdam's **Allard Pierson Museum** (☎ 525 25 56), with the world's richest university collection of archaeological material. It's not in the same league as the country's largest collection of antiquities in Leiden, let alone the British Museum or the Louvre, but the exhibits (Egyptian, Mesopotamian, Roman and Greek, among others) are far less overwhelming and provide a good insight into daily life in ancient times. The museum is open Tuesday to Friday from 10 am to 5 pm, weekends from 1 pm; entry costs f9.50 (f7 for students and seniors). The museum's Web site is www.uba.uva.nl/apm.

The Rokin terminates at Muntplein, a busy intersection dominated by the **Munttoren** (Mint Tower). This was part of the 15th-century Regulierspoort, a city gate that burned down in 1619. On what was left of the gate, the architect and tower-specialist Hendrick de Keyser built the tower that received its current name in 1672–73, when the French occupied much of the republic and the national mint was transferred here from Dordrecht for safekeeping.

OLD SIDE (OUDE ZIJDE) (MAP 4)

East of the Damrak-Rokin axis is the Old Side of the medieval city. The name is misleading because the New Side to the west is actually older – see the following New Side section.

In the 1380s the Old Side began to expand eastwards towards the Oudezijds Voorburgwal ('front fortified embankment') and soon farther towards to the Oudezijds Achterburgwal ('rear fortified embankment').

Originally the city didn't extend farther south than Grimburgwal, where the filled-in part of the Rokin ends today. In the 1420s, however, the newly dug Geldersekade and Kloveniersburgwal added more space for the growing population.

Warmoesstraat

One of the original dykes along the Amstel – and thus one of the oldest streets in town – is Warmoesstraat, which runs parallel to Damrak behind the former warehouses that line the east bank of the river (the southern extension beyond the Dam is called Nes). The city's wealthiest merchants, and anyone else who could afford to, lived here. Today it's a run-down strip of restaurants, cheap hotels and sex shops, with the busiest police station in town (No 44–50). **Geels & Co** (☎ 624 06 83) at No 67 is a tea and coffee shop with an interesting little museum upstairs (free admission). The shop is open normal hours but you can only visit the museum on Tuesday, Friday and Saturday between 2 and 4 pm.

Oude Kerk

A few paces east of here, through Enge Kerksteeg, is the mighty Oude Kerk, the Gothic Old Church built early in the 14th century in honour of the city's patron saint, St Nicholas – the 'water saint', protector of sailors, merchants, pawnbrokers and children. It's the oldest surviving building in town, sadly demeaned by the red-light district that now surrounds it. The original basilica was replaced in 1340 by an intricately vaulted triple-hall church of massive proportions that was miraculously undamaged by the great fire of 1452.

Further extensions ground to a halt as funds were diverted to the Nieuwe Kerk, and a century later Calvinist iconoclasts smashed and looted many of the priceless paintings, statues and altars. The newly Calvinist authorities kicked out the hawkers and vagabonds who had made the church their home, and changed the official name from St Nicolaaskerk to Oude Kerk (as it was commonly known anyway). In the mid-17th century the Nieuwe Kerk took over as the city's main church.

Note the stunning Müller organ (1724), the gilded oak vaults (with remains of paintings above the southern aisle) and the stained-glass windows (1555). Check the lively 15th-century carvings on the choir stalls – some of them are downright rude.

As in the Nieuwe Kerk, many famous and not so famous Amsterdammers lie buried here under worn tombstones, including Rembrandt's first wife, Saskia van Uylenburgh (died 1642). The church is open daily from 11 am to 5 pm, Sunday from 1 pm, and admission costs f5 (f3.50 with discounts). A Dutch Reformed service is held Sundays at 11 am (door closes at 11 am sharp).

The church's **tower** (1565) is arguably the most beautiful in Amsterdam and is well worth climbing for the magnificent view. The 47-bell carillon, installed by the carillon master François Hemony in 1658, is considered one of the finest in the country. The bell in the top of the tower dates from 1450 and is the city's oldest.

The only problem is that the tower can only be visited by guided tours organised in advance at a cost of f65 per hour (maximum 25 people). If you can get a group together to share expenses, ring ☎ 612 68 56.

Red-Light District

The city's (in)famous red-light district is bordered by Warmoesstraat in the west, Zeedijk/Nieuwmarkt/Kloveniersburgwal in the east and Damstraat/Oude Doelenstraat/Oude Hoogstraat in the south. The area, known colloquially as the *wallen* or *walletjes* for the canals that run down the middle, has been sending sailors broke since the 14th century with houses of ill repute and countless distilleries. The distilleries have gone but prostitutes now display themselves in windows under red neon lights, touts at sex theatres lure passers-by with 'live show fucky-fucky podium', and sex-shop displays leave nothing to the imagination. Several years ago three men installed themselves behind windows in a sociological experiment; there was intense media interest and not a single woman dared enter. One of the prostitutes declared the experiment 'filthy'.

The ambience is laid-back and far less threatening than in red-light districts elsewhere. Crowds of sightseers both foreign and local mingle with would-be pimps, drunks, weirdos, drug dealers and Salvation Army soldiers; police patrolling on foot chat with prostitutes. Streetwalking is illegal, so female sightseers are not automatically assumed to be soliciting and tend to be left alone if they exercise big-city street sense. Advice to all: don't take photos of prostitutes or loiterers, and don't enter into conversation with a drug dealer.

The mainly self-employed prostitutes are taxed on their earnings, undergo mandatory health checks and have a vocal union. Beneath the well-regulated veneer, however, is a world of exploitation, drug addiction and misery – for every happy hooker there's an unhappy one, perhaps a young Eastern European without the right papers, sucked into a vicious circle of high hopes and extortion.

The *wallen* area is actually a very pretty part of town and well worth a stroll for the architecture, if you need that sort of excuse. For a scenic view, face north on the bridge across Oudezijds Voorburgwal linking Lange Niezel and Korte Niezel.

Immediately to your left from here, at Oudezijds Voorburgwal 40, is the **Museum Amstelkring** (☎ 624 66 04), home to **Ons' Lieve Heer op Solder** (Our Dear Lord in the Attic), one of several 'clandestine' Catholic churches established after the Calvinist coup in 1578. Church property was confiscated and Catholics were only allowed to worship in privately owned real estate so long as it wasn't recognisable as a church and the entrance was hidden. The wealthy hosier Jan Hartman had the house built in 1663, complete with a small church in the attic dedicated to St Nicholas. It remained in use until 1887, when the large St Nicolaaskerk on Prins Hendrikkade diagonally opposite Centraal Station opened its doors.

It then became a museum with the city's richest collection of Catholic church art, although occasional services, weddings and organ concerts are still held here. The museum is worth visiting for the 17th-century living quarters, including the Dutch Classical *Sael* or reception hall (note the matching rectangular patterns on the floor, walls and ceiling), and of course for the church in the attic – one of the few 'clandestine' churches that has remained intact. The museum is open daily from 10 am to 5 pm, Sunday

from 1 pm, and admission is fl0 (f7.50 with discounts).

Other places worth considering in the red-light district include the **Hash & Marihuana Museum** (☎ 623 59 61), Oudezijds Achterburgwal 148; and the renowned **Tattoo Museum** (☎ 625 15 65), Oudezijds Achterburgwal 130. The **Erotic Museum** (☎ 624 73 03), Oudezijds Achterburgwal 54, is less entertaining than Seksmuseum Amsterdam on Damrak (see the earlier Damrak, Dam Square & Rokin section).

Zeedijk

North of the red-light district is the Zeedijk, the original sea dyke that curved from the mouth of the Amstel to Nieuwmarkt Square and continued from there along what are now St Anthoniesbreestraat, Jodenbreestraat and Muiderstraat. The house at **Zeedijk 1** dates from the mid-1500s and is one of two timber-fronted houses still left in the city (another, older one is in the Begijnhof).

The Zeedijk used to be (and to some extent still is) a street of wine, women and song, the first port of call for sailors after their long voyages. In the 1950s, wine and song predominated and many of the world's great jazz musicians played in pubs such as the Casablanca at No 26. In the 1970s the street's dubious reputation hit rock-bottom when it became the centre of Amsterdam's heroin trade. A massive police campaign in the mid-1980s restored some of the old merriment and legitimate business is beginning to pick up again, but so too is the heroin trade at the Nieuwmarkt end of the street.

East of the Zeedijk is the Geldersekade, and at the tip of this canal is a small brick tower, dating from around 1480, that used to form part of the city fortifications. It's the oldest such tower still standing and is called the **Schreierstoren** from an old Dutch word for 'sharp', a reference to this sharp corner that jutted out into the IJ. Tourist literature calls it the 'wailing tower' (from *schreien*, to weep or wail) and claims that sailors' wives stood here and cried their lungs out when ships set off for distant lands, which makes a far more interesting story. The women even have a plaque dedicated to them.

THINGS TO SEE & DO

The Winner by a Narrow Margin

Canal-boat commentators and other tourist guides like to point out the narrowest house in Amsterdam. They account for the phenomenon by explaining that property was taxed on frontage – the narrower the house the lower the tax, regardless of the height. There is some truth in this, but it seems as if each guide has a different 'narrowest' house. So which house holds the record?

The house at Oude Hoogstraat 22 east of Dam Square is 2.02m wide and 6m deep. Occupying a mere 12 sq metres it could well be the least space-consuming self-contained house in Europe (though it's a few storeys high). The house at Singel 7 is narrower still, consisting of just a door and a slim, 1st-floor window, but canal-boat commentators fail to point out that it's actually the rear entrance of a house of normal proportions. Farther along and on the other side of Singel at No 144 is a house that measures only 1.8m across the front; it widens to 5m at the rear and experts with nothing better to do will argue whether this counts.

The Kleine Trippenhuis (Small Trippenhouse) at Kloveniersburgwal 26 is 2.44m wide. It's opposite the 22m-wide house of the Trip brothers at No 29, one of the widest private residences in the city. The story goes that their coachman exclaimed, 'If only I could have a house as wide as my masters' door!' and that his wish was granted.

ROB VAN DRIESUM

Oude Hoogstraat 22

The tower attracts plaques: another one explains that the English captain Henry Hudson set sail from here in 1609 in his ship the *Halve Maen* (Half Moon). The United East India Company had enlisted him to find a northern passage to the East Indies, but instead he bought Manhattan and explored the river that bears his name. On the return voyage his ship was seized in England and he was ordered never again to sail for a foreign nation. His reports, however, made it back to base, and in 1614 the Dutch established a fort on Manhattan that developed into a settlement called New Amsterdam. In 1664 the West India Company's local governor, the fanatically Calvinist Pieter Stuyvesant, surrendered the town to the British who promptly renamed it New York. Stuyvesant retired to the market garden called Bouwerij (Agriculture), now known as the Bowery section of New York City.

Nieuwmarkt Square

In the 17th century, ships used to sail from the IJ down Geldersekade to the Nieuw-markt (New Market) to take on board new anchors or load and unload produce. (Nobody adds the world *plein* or 'square' to the name, which is confusing because the whole neighbourhood to the east and south-east is also known as Nieuwmarkt.)

The Nieuwmarkt's imposing **Waag** (Weigh House) dates from 1488, when it was known as St Anthoniespoort (St Anthony's Gate) and formed part of the city fortifications. A century later the city had expanded farther east and the gate lost its original function. A section of Kloveniersburgwal was filled in to create the St Anthonies-markt (now the Nieuwmarkt). The central courtyard of the gate was covered and it became the city weigh house – the one on the Dam had become too small. Guilds occupied the upper floor, including the surgeons' guild who commissioned Rembrandt to paint *The Anatomy Lesson of Dr Tulp* (displayed in the Mauritshuis in The Hague) and added the octagonal central tower in 1691 to house their new Anatomical Theatre.

Public executions took place at the Waag from the early 19th century, after Louis

Napoleon decreed that his palace on Dam Square was no longer a suitable spot for such gory displays. In later years it served other purposes – fire station, vault for the city archives, home to the Amsterdam Historical Museum and the Jewish Historical Museum. Today it houses an overpriced bar-restaurant illuminated by huge candlewheels for medieval effect, and combines the medieval with the future as the Society for Old & New Media (see Internet Cafés in the Facts for the Visitor chapter).

The area east and south-east of Nieuwmarkt Square was the centre of Jewish Amsterdam, which was virtually wiped out during the German occupation. Jews were assembled in front of the Waag for deportation.

South of Nieuwmarkt Square

Just south of the Nieuwmarkt, on the east side of Kloveniersburgwal at No 29, is the **Trippenhuis**. It was built in 1660–64 to house the wealthy Trip brothers, Lodewijk and Hendrik, who made their fortune in metals, artillery and ammunition. The greystone mansion with Corinthian pilasters consists of two separate houses with false middle windows, and the chimneys are shaped like mortars to indicate their owners' trade. Note the narrow house across the canal at No 26 (see the boxed text 'The Winner by a Narrow Margin').

On the west side of Kloveniersburgwal beyond the intersection with Oude Hoogstraat (an extension of Damstraat) is the **Oostindisch Huis**, the former head office of the mighty VOC, the United East India Company. You'd walk straight past if you didn't know it was here – there's no sign or plaque to identify it. The complex of buildings, attributed to Hendrick de Keyser, was

built between 1551 and 1643. It was rented to the VOC in 1603 and now belongs to the University of Amsterdam. Enter the courtyard through the small gate at Oude Hoogstraat 24. Even here nothing indicates the historical significance of the place except for the small VOC emblem above the door ahead of you across the courtyard. Along the Kloveniersburgwal frontage, note the gables that defy convention by tilting backwards, which makes them seem higher.

Old Side, Southern Section

The Old Side south of Damstraat/Oude Doelenstraat/Oude Hoogstraat is distinctly residential and the red-light district seems miles away. The southern end of Oudezijds Voorburgwal used to be known as the 'velvet canal' for the wealthy people who lived here. Both the Oudezijds canals end at Grimburgwal and the junction is one of the strongholds of the University of Amsterdam, as evidenced by the chaotic jumble of parked bicycles.

The former municipal university (not to be confused with the orthodox-Calvinist Free University in the southern suburbs) has no central campus as such; its buildings are spread throughout the city but there's a large concentration of them here.

At the south end of Oudezijds Voorburgwal, at No 231, is the **Universiteitsmuseum De Agnietenkapel** (☎ 525 33 39), with changing exhibitions on the history of the university, open weekdays from 9 am to 5 pm (ring the door bell; admission f3.50). The complex started life as a convent of St Agnes in 1397 and the beautiful Gothic chapel was added in 1470. When the Calvinists took over it was used as an admiralty warehouse.

In 1632 it also became home to the city library (moved from the Nieuwe Kerk) and the Athenaeum Illustre, the Illustrious Athenaeum, an offshoot of the University of Leiden. Classes (history and philosophy, later also law, medicine and theology, and finally physics and chemistry) were conducted in Latin to prepare students for higher education elsewhere. In 1864 the Athenaeum moved to Singel 421 (part of

TAMSIN WILSON

Facade detail of the Oostindisch Huis

the present university library) and in 1877 it became the fully fledged Municipal University of Amsterdam – a long gestation for the university of such an eminent city.

Just south of the Agnietenkapel, where the three 'fortified embankments' *(burgwallen)* meet, is the **Huis aan de Drie Grachten** (House on the Three Canals), a beautiful building dating from 1609 that was owned by a succession of prominent Amsterdam families. It's now a bookshop catering for linguistics and literature students.

Across Oudezijds Achterburgwal, just before the corner with Grimburgwal, is a small, arched gateway called the **Oudemanhuispoort** (Old Man's House Gate) leading to a passage of the same name that extends to Kloveniersburgwal. Note the spectacles above the gateway: an almshouse for elderly men and women was built here in 1601 from the proceeds of a public lottery. It was rebuilt in the mid-18th century and in 1879 it became the seat of the university. The administration has since moved to other premises but the buildings here, referred to simply as 'de Poort', can lay claim to being the heart of the university.

A market has operated in the passage since the mid-1700s, specialising in gold, silver, books and knick-knacks but now devoted entirely to second-hand books – it's well worth a browse. Halfway along, an entrance leads to a lovely 18th-century courtyard dominated by a bust of Minerva (originally there was a bust of Rembrandt but the Roman goddess of wisdom was considered more apt). The university lecture rooms surrounding the courtyard are closed to the public – nobody will pull you up for going inside but they hold little of general interest.

A few steps south of the Oudemanhuispoort, at the end of Grimburgwal, another gateway leads to the former inner-city hospital, the **Binnengasthuis**, dating from 1582. In 1981 the university took over and the area is now a mini campus, with university buildings, living quarters, a large refectory *(mensa)* and an information centre (see Universities in the Facts for the Visitor chapter).

NEW SIDE (NIEUWE ZIJDE) (MAPS 2 & 4)

West of the Damrak-Rokin axis is the New Side of the medieval city. It was actually settled slightly earlier than the Old Side – the names date from the construction of the Nieuwe Kerk  and the division of the city into two parishes.

In the early 14th century the western boundary was formed by a watercourse running along Nieuwezijds Voorburgwal (filled in 1884), but this was soon extended westwards to the Nieuwezijds Achterburgwal (now also filled and known as Spuistraat). Around 1450 the Singel (Moat) was cut. This linked up with the Geldersekade and Kloveniersburgwal in the east to complete the moat around the medieval city, which received proper walls with fortified gates some 50 years later.

Nieuwendijk

The very first houses in Amsterdam probably stood on a strip of raised land, no more than 25m wide, on the western bank of the Amstel between the Dam and Oudebrugsteeg. This, the oldest dyke in the city, parallel to the current Damrak, later acquired the name of its northern extension, Nieuwendijk. It used to link up with the road to Haarlem, and its shops and other businesses became adept at fleecing travellers on their way to Amsterdam's market on Dam Square. Today this pedestrianised shopping street still suffers from a distinctly downmarket image, though some of the narrow streets leading to the west can be as picturesquely medieval as it gets.

Singel, Northern Section

The top section of Nieuwendijk, between Martelaarsgracht and Singel, is sometimes referred to as Korte Nieuwendijk (Short Nieuwendijk). Head south from here along the east (odd-numbered) side of Singel, where the former city wall used to run, and you'll pass a house at No 7 (next to the

Liberty Hotel) that's no wider than its door – except that this is actually the rear entrance of a house of normal proportions.

The domed church next door is the **Ronde Lutherse Kerk** (Round Lutheran Church), built in 1668–71 to replace the old Lutheran church on Spui Square. It's the only round Protestant church in the country and is pure 17th-century baroque, though the white interior is suitably sober. The church was rebuilt after a disastrous fire in 1822 but falling attendances forced its closure in 1936 (ironically the old church on Spui Square is still in use by Lutherans). It now serves as a conference centre for the nearby Renaissance Hotel, and opens to the public during free chamber-music performances on Sunday morning.

Across the canal, tied up at No 40, is the **Poezenboot** (Cat Boat) owned by an eccentric woman who looks after several hundred stray moggies. They seem endearingly content with life on the water, and visitors are welcome to stroke them daily between 1 and 3 pm in return for a donation towards cat food.

Farther along Singel is **Torensluis**, one of the widest bridges in the city. Here used to stand a tower that formed part of the city fortifications; the bridge was later built around it. The tower was demolished in 1829, leaving a 42m-wide esplanade. The view northwards is camera material.

The ghastly statue that dominates the bridge represents Multatuli (Latin for 'I have suffered greatly'), the pen name of the brilliant 19th-century author Eduard Douwes Dekker, who would indeed suffer greatly if he stood here now. A local captain's son who served in the East Indies colonial administration, Multatuli exposed colonial narrow-mindedness in a novel about a coffee merchant. After being sacked he wrote letters and essays. The nearby **Multatuli Museum** (☎ 638 19 38), Korsjespoortsteeg 20, is free but only open Tuesday from 10 am to 5 pm and weekends from noon. It's a must for fans of Dutch literature.

Magna Plaza

Back towards Dam Square at Nieuwezijds Voorburgwal 182, facing the Royal Palace,

is the imposing orange-and-white facade of Magna Plaza. This was the former GPO, built in 1895–99 by the government architect CH Peters, a pupil of Pierre Cuypers. It used to be one of the grandest post offices in Europe but has now been converted into a luxurious shopping centre dominated by clothing boutiques. Pop inside to admire the grand hall and look at some of the interesting shops. There's an extensive Virgin Megastore in the basement. Several decades ago the Nieuwezijds Voorburgwal itself was the country's 'Fleet Street' where many newspapers had their head offices (they're now out in the suburbs).

Kalverstraat

South of Dam Square is Kalverstraat, the extension of Nieuwendijk. This was one of the original dykes along the Amstel – together with Nieuwendijk, Warmoesstraat and Nes – which makes it one of the oldest streets in the city. The name (Calves Street) presumably refers to the cattle that were led to market on Dam Square. (In the 15th century there was a cattle market in the southern section of Kalverstraat beyond Spui Square but the name is older.)

Like Nieuwendijk, pedestrianised Kalverstraat has traditionally been a shopping street, albeit a more upmarket one that's well worth visiting on weekdays (it's too busy on Saturdays and not much better on Sundays). The southern tip between Kalverstraat and Singel near Muntplein has been transformed into a shopping complex called the **Kalvertoren** (Kalver Tower); it's worth visiting the snack bar at the top of the tower for the 360° rooftop view enjoyed by pigeons, though not for the food (better to use the Vroom & Dreesmann food court downstairs).

South along Kalverstraat from Dam Square, about two-thirds of the way to Spui Square, is a gateway to the right at No 92 that leads to the **Amsterdams Historisch Museum** (on the opposite side of Kalverstraat used to be the chapel commemorating the Miracle of Amsterdam). This is a surprisingly interesting museum with attractive displays about the history of the city, housed in the former civic orphanage that existed here till 1960. The restaurant (free entry) serves delicious pancakes. The museum (☎ 523 18 22) is open weekdays from 10 am to 5 pm, weekends from 11 am, and admission is f11 (various discounts). Ask for the English-language booklet. The Web site www.ahm.nl has details.

If you want to give this a miss, it's still worth walking into the courtyard (note the cupboards in which the orphans stored their possessions) and from there to the Begijnhof through the **Civic Guard Gallery** (free, open same hours as the museum). The huge group portraits of civic guards displayed here will help you appreciate Rembrandt's ground-breaking interpretation of the genre in *The Nightwatch*, which is displayed in the Rijksmuseum. The gallery used to be a ditch separating the boys' and girls' sections of the orphanage.

Begijnhof

Hidden behind the intersection of Spui and Nieuwezijds Voorburgwal is the enclosed Begijnhof (also spelled Bagijnhof), a former convent dating from the early 14th century – the Nieuwezijds Voorburgwal curved westwards to include it in the city boundary. It's a surreal oasis of peace, with tiny houses grouped around a well-kept courtyard. Amsterdam has many such enclosed *hofjes* (literally 'little courtyards'), or almshouses (old people's homes run by charities), but this is the only one where the public is still welcome. It's open during the day but not for tour groups or camera crews.

Linger a while to recover from the hustle and bustle of the city. Note the house at **No 34**: it dates from around 1465, making it the oldest maintained wooden house in the country. There's a collection of biblical wall tablets on the blind wall to the left.

The Beguines were a Catholic order of unmarried or widowed women from wealthy families who cared for the elderly and lived a religious life without taking monastic vows; the last true Beguines died in the 1970s. They owned their houses, so these could not be confiscated after the Calvinist coup. Their **Gothic church** at the southern end of the courtyard, however, was

Wall Tablets

Before street numbers were introduced in 1795, many of Amsterdam's residences were identified by their wall tablets. These painted or carved stone plaques (dating from the mid-17th century) were practical decorations used to identify not only the inhabitants' house but also their origin, religion or profession.

Beautiful examples of these stones are still found on many of the buildings along the main canals. Occupations are the most frequently occurring theme: tobacconists, milliners, merchants, skippers, undertakers and even grass-mowers are represented.

As well as being colourful reminders of the city's former citizens, these tablets also provide historical hints about the city's past. A stone depicting a mail wagon at Singel 74 commemorates the commencement of the postal service between Amsterdam and The Hague in 1660. Farther down the street a tablet portraying the scene of Eve tempting Adam with an apple attests to the time when that part of the street operated as a fruit market (known as the 'apple market').

Many wall tablets dotted throughout the city celebrate the life of famous citizens like the maritime hero Michiel Adriaenszoon de Ruyter and biologist Jan Swammerdam, but the most appealing are memorials to domestic life and common vocations of the age.

taken away from them and they were forced to worship in the **'clandestine' church** opposite (note the dogleg entrance), where paintings and stained-glass windows commemorate the Miracle of Amsterdam. The Gothic church was eventually rented out to the local community of English and Scottish Presbyterian refugees – the Pilgrim Fathers worshipped here – and still serves as the city's Presbyterian church. Some of the pulpit panels were designed by a young Piet Mondriaan.

Spui Square

Until 1882, the elongated Spui Square (usually referred to simply as the Spui) used to be water. In the 14th century it marked the southern end of the city, together with Grimburgwal, its north-eastern extension across Rokin. The name means 'sluice' (or rather, the area inside a sluice) and it connected the Amstel with the watercourse running along Nieuwezijds Voorburgwal, the western side of the city, and later with the Singel.

A book market is held Fridays on the section of the square in front of the Begijnhof entrance, where the Beguines used to have an outer garden, but the heart of the square is its western part where Nieuwezijds Voorburgwal and Spuistraat meet. The statuette in the middle is an endearing rendition of an Amsterdam street-brat called the *Lieverdje* (Little Darling). It was donated by a cigarette company and became the focal point for Provo 'happenings' in the mid-1960s. The area is now a meeting point for the city's intelligentsia, who congregate in the pubs at the western end of the square and in the surrounding bookshops, including the landmark Athenaeum bookshop and newsagency.

The classicist building between Voetboogstraat and Handboogstraat is the **Maagdenhuis**, the Virgins' House built in 1787 as a Catholic orphanage for girls and now the administrative seat of the university. In 1969 it was occupied by students, a watershed in the development of students' rights in the country. Police cordoned off the building but the occupiers held out for five days, with supplies ferried across a bridge that supportive workers built over the alley. The handsome **Lutheran Church** next door, on the corner of Singel, was built in 1633. It is still used as a church but also by the university for ceremonies such as doctoral promotions, which benefit from its good acoustics.

Singel, Southern Section

Around the corner, in the row of buildings at Singel 421–425, is the current **University Library**. Citizen's militias used to meet here: the 'hand-bow' militia in No 421 and the 'foot-bow' militia in No 425 (the latter also served as headquarters for the West India Company and is now obliterated by the modern facade). Their firing ranges at the rear reached to Kalverstraat – the current Handboogstraat and Voetboogstraat are named after the militias. The building at No 423 was constructed by Hendrick de Keyser in 1606 as the city arsenal and was later used as royal stables.

On the opposite side of the canal are the soaring turrets of the neo-Gothic **Krijtberg** ('chalk mountain') church, officially known as the St Franciscus Xaveriuskerk, completed in 1883 to a design by Alfred Tepe. It replaced a 'clandestine' Jesuit chapel on the same site. The lavish paintings and statuary make this one of the most beautiful churches in the city, and it has all just been restored to its full glory. You can visit daily during Mass between noon and 1 pm or 5 and 6 pm, or attend Latin Mass on Sunday at 9.30 and 11 am. One of the houses that stood here belonged to a chalk merchant, hence the common name.

You could turn left here to go back to Kalverstraat along the **Heiligeweg**, the Holy Way travelled by pilgrims on their annual procession to the chapel of the Miracle of Amsterdam. The route used to extend all the way from the village of Sloten, southwest of the city, along what is now the Overtoom (once a canal for towboats carrying produce) and through the current Leidsestraat, but only this final section has retained the original name. A procession still takes place every year on the Sunday closest to 15 March and attracts Catholics from Holland and abroad.

Halfway to Kalverstraat is a gateway on your right, dating from the early 17th century and attributed to Hendrick de Keyser. This once gave access to the Rasphuis, a model penitentiary where beggars and delinquents were put to work to ease their return to society. One of their back-breaking jobs was to rasp brazil wood for the dyeing industry – hence the name, Rasp House. Later it became a normal prison and in 1896 a public swimming pool; now it's a gateway to the Kalvertoren shopping complex.

Back along Singel, the opposite side of the canal towards Muntplein is occupied by the floating **Bloemenmarkt** (Flower Market), open Monday to Saturday from

euro currency converter f1 = €0.45

Mad about Tulips

A search on the Internet for the term 'Tulipmania' will turn up lots of articles about the speculative nature of Internet and e-commerce stocks. Indeed, when it comes to investment frenzy, the Dutch tulip craze of 1636–37 stands alongside the South Sea Bubble of 1720 and the boom preceding the Great Crash of 1929 as the greatest folly of all time.

Tulips originated as wild flowers in Central Asia and were first cultivated by the Turks, who filled their courts with these beautiful spring blossoms ('tulip' is Turkish for turban). In the mid-1500s, the Habsburg ambassador to Istanbul brought some bulbs back to Vienna where the imperial botanist, Carolus Clusius, learned how to propagate them. In 1590, Clusius became director of the Hortus Botanicus in Leiden – Europe's oldest botanical garden – and had great success growing and cross-breeding tulips in Holland's cool, damp climate and fertile delta soil.

The exotic flowers with their frilly petals and 'flamed' streaks of colour attracted the attention of wealthy merchants, who put them in their living rooms and hallways to impress visitors. As wealth and savings spread downwards through society so too did the taste for exotic products, and tulips were no exception. Growers rose to service the demand.

Ironically, the frilly petals and colour streaks were symptoms of an infection by the mosaic virus transmitted by a louse that thrived on peaches and potatoes – healthy tulips are solid, smooth and monotone. Turks already knew that the most beautiful tulips grew under fruit trees but the virus itself wasn't discovered until the 20th century.

The most beautiful tulips in 17th-century Holland were also the weakest due to heavy cross-breeding and grafting, which made them even more susceptible to the virus no-one knew about. They were notoriously difficult to cultivate and their blossoms unpredictable. A speculative frenzy ensued, and people paid top florin for the finest bulbs that would change hands many times before they sprouted. Vast profits were made and everyone joined in. Speculators fell over themselves to out-bid each other. The fact that such bidding often took place in taverns and was fuelled by alcohol no doubt added to the enthusiasm.

At the height of the Tulipmania in November 1636, a single bulb of the legendary *Semper augustus* fetched the equivalent of 10 years' wages for the average worker; a couple of *Viceroy* bulbs cost the equivalent of an Amsterdam canal house. One unfortunate foreign sailor made himself rather unpopular with his employer by slicing up what he thought was an onion in order to garnish his herring. An English amateur botanist was intrigued by an unknown bulb lying in his host's conservatory, proceeded to bisect it, and was put in jail until he could raise 4000 florins.

This bonanza couldn't last, and when several bulb traders in Haarlem failed to fetch their expected prices in February 1637, the bottom fell out of the market. Within weeks many of the country's wealthiest merchants went bankrupt and many more people of humbler origin lost everything they thought they had acquired. Speculators who were stuck with unsold bulbs, or with bulbs that had been reserved but not yet paid for (the concept of options was invented during the Tulipmania), appealed for government action but the authorities refused to become involved in what they considered to be gambling.

The speculation and stockjobbery disappeared, but love of the surprising tulip endured and it remained an expensive flower. Cool-headed growers perfected their craft. To this day, the Dutch continue to be the world leaders in tulip cultivation and supply most of the bulbs planted in Europe and North America. They also excel in other bulbs such as daffodils, hyacinths and crocuses.

So what happened to the flamed, frilly tulips of the past? They're still produced but have gone out of fashion, and are now known as Rembrandt tulips because of their depiction in so many 17th-century paintings.

MARTIN MOOS

Detail of the Rijksmuseum's facade

RICHARD NEBESKY

Neo-Gothic Krijtberg church on Singel

JON DAVISON

Nighttime illumination enhances the beauty of Amsterdam's canals.

EDWARD AM SNIJDERS

Panoramic view from Westerkerk's bell tower

LEANNE LOGAN

Contrast of old and new along the Rokin

RICHARD NEBESKY

Amsterdam residential architecture: each house is distinctly different

9 am to 5 pm. Amsterdam has had many flower markets since the Tulipmania in the 17th century (see the boxed text 'Mad about Tulips' for the story of this speculative madness). The market here dates from the 1860s and specialises in flowers, bulbs, pots, vases and some plants. It's a very pretty sight and the place is packed with tourists and pickpockets. Prices are steep by Amsterdam standards but the quality is good.

WESTERN CANAL BELT (MAPS 2 & 4)

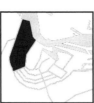

Towards the end of the 16th century, the city burst out of its medieval walls with a flood of Jewish refugees from Portugal and Spain and Protestant refugees from Antwerp. In the 1580s, after the Calvinists took power and reassessed the city's needs, new land was reclaimed from the IJ and Amstel in the east (see the Nieuwmarkt Neighbourhood section later in this chapter), while in the west the Singel became a residential canal with the addition of a new moat that was to become Herengracht.

In 1613 the authorities embarked on an ambitious expansion project that more than tripled the city's area. Based on a plan drawn up by the city carpenter, Hendrick Jacobsz Staets, Amsterdam received a belt of parallel canals from the IJ to the IJ, one after the other like layers of an onion around the medieval city core. These canals with their many bridges and connecting roads (intended as shopping streets) were all built in one huge effort. Parcels of land were sold along the way to finance the project and buildings arose gradually. The whole city was enclosed by a new outer moat, the zigzag Buitensingel (outer moat), now known as the Singelgracht. The moat's outer quays became the current Nassaukade, Stadhouderskade and Mauritskade.

Work began at the north-western end adjoining the new harbour works and headed south from the radial Brouwersgracht. By 1625 the western canal belt was completed down to the radial Leidsegracht when money ran out. The project was picked up again later but at a much slower pace, and by the end of the 17th century it petered out just short of its original goal (see the Southern Canal Belt section later in this chapter).

These new canals clearly segregated society into haves and have-nots. Until then, merchants lived more or less in their warehouses, mingling with their labourers and suppliers in the thick of the city's activities.

Bending the Golden Rules

Amsterdam has always had a shortage of land suitable for building purposes. When the authorities embarked on their expensive canal-belt project, they drew up detailed regulations to ensure that this scarce commodity would return maximum revenue. Parcels of land had to be large enough to attract top guilder, but small enough to maximise the number of sales flowing to the municipal coffers rather than to speculators.

On the outer bank of Herengracht, for instance, plots were limited to a width of 30 feet and a depth of 190 feet (these were pre-metric days). There were no limits to the height of buildings over the first 110 feet, but anything erected on the remaining 80 feet had to be less than 10 feet high to ensure the unprecedented luxury of large gardens (even today, the gardens behind many Herengracht houses are magnificent). Buyers also had to pay for the brick quayside in front of their plots but the city paid for the street. Subdivisions were prohibited in order to keep these properties desirable and maintain their value.

So much for the theory. In practice, the very wealthiest Amsterdammers got dispensation, as can be seen in the immense palaces along the 'Golden Bend' of Herengracht between Leidsestraat and Vijzelstraat. Elsewhere, regulations were interpreted creatively – for instance, by buying two adjacent plots and building one house with two fronts; or by building one house with two entrances, subdividing the edifice into upstairs and downstairs and selling the two separately.

Now the wealthiest among them escaped the sweat and the stench by building residential mansions along the delectable Herengracht (named after the Heeren XVII, the '17 Gentlemen' of the United East India Company). The Keizersgracht (the 'emperor's canal' in honour of Maximilian) was similarly upmarket, though the houses along its later extension beyond Leidsegracht were a bit more pedestrian. Businesses that could be annoying or offensive were banned, and bridges were fixed to exclude large vessels – though this didn't prevent barges from unloading and loading goods at the warehouses that were built even along these canals.

The Prinsengracht (so named to keep the House of Orange happy) was a 'cheaper' canal with smaller residences, warehouses and workshops. It acted as a barrier against the downmarket Jordaan that lay beyond – a housing estate for the city's many labourers, including those employed in this massive extension project.

Western Islands (Map 2)

The wharves and warehouses of the Western Islands (Westelijke Eilanden), built into the IJ north of the western canal belt, were a focus of the harbour in the first half of the 17th century. The wealthy Bicker brothers, mayors of Amsterdam, even built their very own **Bickerseiland** to cater for their ships.

The area has a character all its own and is well worth a wander. Many warehouses have been converted to residences, and the ones that haven't had much done to them are in demand as studios for sculptors and painters. The **Prinseneiland** and **Realeneiland** (named after the 17th-century merchant Reynier Reael) are the prettiest of the islands – the narrow bridge linking the two, the Drieharingenbrug (Three Herrings Bridge), is a modern replacement for the pontoon that used to be pulled aside to let ships through.

By all means visit the photogenic **Zandhoek**, the 17th-century sand market on the eastern waterfront of Realeneiland. The Zandhoek escaped demolition this century thanks to Jan Mens' 1940 novel *De Gouden Reael*, named after the bar-restaurant at No

14. Galgenstraat (Gallows Street), which runs across Prinseneiland to Bickerseiland, used to provide a view over the IJ to the gallows at Volewyck, the uninhabited tip of what was to become Amsterdam North, where bodies of criminals executed on Dam Square were propped up and left to the mercy of crows and dogs.

Haarlem Quarter (Map 2)

The Haarlem Quarter (Haarlemmerbuurt) between the Western Islands and Brouwersgracht gets few visitors, which is just as well because it offers a glimpse of life in central Amsterdam without tourists. **Haarlemmerstraat** and its western extension, **Haarlemmerdijk**, were part of the original sea dyke along the IJ, from the Zeedijk in the east all the way to the western extremities of the IJ north of Haarlem. They have become a lot quieter now that the road artery to/from Haarlem runs north of here. Pedestrians have flocked back, mainly local residents lured by a good range of shops, pubs and restaurants.

Halfway along Haarlemmerstraat is the **Herenmarkt**, which leads to Brouwersgracht at the head of Herengracht. This was planned as a market in the 1613 canal-belt project but it never took off. Now it's a quiet oasis and a prestigious Amsterdam address. The building at the north end of the square used to be a meat hall before it became the **Westindisch Huis** in 1623, head office of the West India Company. In 1628 Admiral Piet Heyn captured the Spanish silver fleet off Cuba and the booty was stored here in the cellars. Every Dutch person knows the nursery rhyme celebrating Heyn's small name and big deeds, sung by soccer supporters at international matches as a warning not to underestimate this small country.

Walk through the east entrance into the courtyard with its statue of Pieter Stuyvesant, the unpopular governor of New Netherlands, which included the Hudson Valley, Delaware (captured from the Swedes) and several Caribbean islands. Today the building houses the John Adams Institute, a Dutch-US friendship society (see Cultural Centres in the Facts for the

Visitor chapter). In 1654 the WIC moved premises to its quayside warehouse on the corner of Oude Schans and Prins Hendrikkade (west of the current IJ-Tunnel entrance), and from there to Singel 425 (the current University Library).

The busy road to Haarlem led through the **Haarlemmerpoort** (Haarlem Gate) on Haarlemmerplein, where travellers heading into town had to leave their horses and carts. The current structure dates from 1840 and was built as a tax office and a gateway for King William II to pass through on his coronation. It's officially known as the Willemspoort but Amsterdammers never liked the building and still refuse to call it that, even now that it has been converted to housing. It replaced the most monumental of all the city gates, built by Hendrick de Keyser in 1615 but demolished some 200 years later.

In the 17th century a canal was dug from here to Haarlem to transport passengers on horse-drawn barges. In the 19th century the railways took over, but the original canalside road, Haarlemmerweg, is still a major road (which, for obvious reasons, no longer passes through the gate itself). Earlier gateways to Haarlem stood at the Herenmarkt and at the intersection of Nieuwezijds Voorburgwal and Nieuwendijk.

Beyond Haarlem Quarter It's worth going west across the traffic bridge next to the gateway and turning right, past the statue of Ferdinand Domela Nieuwenhuis (1846–1919) – a Frisian minister who converted to socialism and then to anarchism and played a leading role in the militant 19th-century workers' movement – and under the railway bridge. Turn immediately left and follow Zaanstraat for a few minutes until you come to the intersection with Oostzaanstraat, where you'll find a housing estate known as **het Schip** (the Ship), which is one of the highlights of Amsterdam School architecture.

This triangular block, loosely resembling a ship, was completed in 1920 to a design by Michel de Klerk for a housing corporation of railway employees. The post office located at the 'bow' of the 'ship', with its parabolic window, still has the original interior. The pointed tower at the short side of the block has no purpose whatsoever, apart from aesthetically linking the two wings of the complex – and serving as the symbol of the Amsterdam School. There are several other Amsterdam School-designed housing blocks in this area.

Brouwersgracht (Map 2)

The Brewers' Canal, named after the breweries that used to operate here, was an industrious canal full of warehouses, workshops and factories banned from the residential canal belt. These included smelly breweries, distilleries, tanneries, potash works, whale-oil and sugar refineries, and warehouses for spices, coffee and grain.

The buildings were solidly constructed and many were converted to apartments in the 1970s and 1980s. Note the almost uninterrupted row of former warehouses from No 172 to 212. House boats add to the lazy, residential character of this picturesque canal.

Herengracht (Maps 2 & 4)

The first section of Herengracht, south from Brouwersgracht, shows a mixture of expensive 17th and 18th-century residences interspersed with warehouses – note the 18th-century warehouses at Nos 37 and 39, and the early-17th-century warehouses at Nos 43 and 45. On the opposite side of the canal, beyond the pretty Leliegracht and just before the first bend, is the White House at No 168 and the adjacent Bartolotti House at No 170–172.

The **White House**, named for its sandstone facade, was built in 1620 and modified in 1638 to a design by Philips Vingboons. It now houses the **Theatermuseum** (☎ 623 51 04), open Tuesday to Friday from 11 am to 5 pm, weekends from 1 pm (admission f7.50, or f4 with discounts). Even if you're not interested in the history of Dutch theatre, it's well worth visiting for the stunning interior which was completely restyled in the 1730s, with intricate plasterwork and extensive wall and ceiling paintings by Jacob de Wit and Isaac de Moucheron; a magnificent spiral staircase was added then too. All of this has been completely renovated recently, so you'll see it at its best. In summer, the lovely garden out the back is the perfect spot to reflect on life.

The museum spills over into the **Bartolotti House**, which has one of the most stunning facades in the city – a red-brick, Dutch-Renaissance job that follows the bend of the canal. It was built in 1615 by Hendrick de Keyser and his son Pieter by order of the wealthy brewer Willem van den Heuvel, who later assumed the name of his Bolognese father-in-law so he could inherit his bank and develop it into a trading empire. The house was later split down the middle (the Theatermuseum occupies No 170) and both residences were inhabited by prominent Amsterdam families.

Just beyond these houses, Herengracht is crossed by **Raadhuisstraat**, a 'spoke road' built in 1894–96 to link the Jordaan with the Dam. Note the shopping arcade on the far side, which follows the S-bend of Raadhuisstraat towards Keizersgracht. It was designed by AL van Gendt (the Concertgebouw architect) for an insurance company, with sculptures of vicious animals to stress the dangers of life without insurance. Smoke bombs greeted Princess Beatrix's wedding coach as it passed this arcade in 1966.

Continuing along Herengracht, the even-numbered side between Huidenstraat and Leidsegracht shows an interesting mix of architectural styles. The quartet of sandstone neck gables at No 364–370 is known as the Cromhouthuizen, designed in 1662 by Philips Vingboons for Jacob Cromhout. They now house the **Bijbels Museum** (☎ 624 24 36), which even atheists might consider visiting for the beautiful 18th-century ceiling paintings by Jacob de Wit. The museum focuses on biblical archaeology from the Middle East and Egypt, models of temples, and a collection of Dutch bibles including the *Delft Bible* printed in 1477. It's open Monday to Saturday from 10 am to 5 pm, Sunday from 1 pm (admission f5, discounts f3.50).

The house at **No 380–382** is unique in that it's designed like a French chateau in early French Renaissance style (a fairly faithful copy of the chateau at Blois) instead of following Dutch Renaissance lines. It was built in the 1880s for Jacob Nienhuys, who made his fortune as a tobacco planter and wanted to live in the most luxurious canal house that money could buy. It was the first house in Amsterdam with electric lighting and had its own generator room. His neighbours took a dim view of such bright displays and spread the rumour that the authorities had prohibited him placing a solid gold gate in front of the house.

Keizersgracht (Maps 2 & 4)

The three **Greenland warehouses** with their step gables at Keizersgracht 40–44 belonged to the Greenland (or Nordic) Company, which dominated Arctic whaling from the early 17th century when Amsterdam's whalers edged out the Basques. Whalers from Zaandam proved more competitive after the company's monopoly was lifted in 1642, though Amsterdam continued whaling till the early 1800s.

The company established a settlement on an island off Spitsbergen (Svalbard, north of Norway) where harpooned whales were dragged ashore for processing. Whale oil was much sought after for a variety of uses (soap, oil lamps, paint), as was whalebone or baleen (corsets, cutlery). Oil-storage wells in these Keizersgracht warehouses (there were five in a row – the ones at Nos 36 and 38 have been demolished) held 100,000L of the precious stuff, and more barrels sat alongside the whalebone on the top floors. The authorities moved the storage facilities to the Western Islands in 1685 to maintain the upmarket character of the canal belt. Many houses at this end of Keizersgracht used to belong to whaling executives and still bear decorations related to their trade.

Farther south on the opposite side of the canal, halfway between Herenstraat and Leliegracht, is the **House with the Heads** at No 123, one of the finest examples of Dutch-Renaissance architecture. The beautiful step gable, with its six heads at door level representing the classical muses, is reminiscent of Hendrick de Keyser's Bartolotti House on Herengracht. This is not surprising: the original owner, Nicolaas Sohier, was related to the Bartolottis and commissioned De Keyser to design the house, though the architect died in 1621 and the job was presumably completed by his son Pieter a year later. Folklore has it that the heads represent six burglars, decapitated in quick succession by an axe-wielding maid of Sohier's as they tried to break into the cellar. Appropriately, the building now houses the city's conservation office which aims to preserve the city's monuments.

The tall **Greenpeace Building** at No 174–176, which houses the organisation's international headquarters as well as the Dutch branch, is a rare example of Art Nouveau architecture in Amsterdam (The Hague has a much richer collection). It was built in 1905 for a life insurance company – the facade's huge tile tableau shows a guardian angel who seems to be peddling an insurance policy.

On the same side of the canal, note the pink granite triangles of the **Homomonument** at Westermarkt just before you get to Raadhuisstraat. It commemorates those who were persecuted for their homosexuality by the Nazis – homosexuals had to wear a pink triangle, while Jews wore the Star of David. See Gay & Lesbian Travellers in the Facts for the Visitor chapter for more about this monument.

Beyond Raadhuisstraat and still on the same side of the canal, the row of houses from No 242 to 252 became famous as a squatters' fortress known as the **Groote Keyser**. Squatters occupied the empty buildings in November 1978 and couldn't be served with eviction notices until the authorities found out their full names. Notices were served a year later, but the squatters stayed put and could count on a well-organised support network to meet force with force. They fortified the buildings and set up a pirate radio station, the Vrije Keyser (Free Keyser), which scanned the police frequencies and broadcast instructions to their supporters – the station played a key role in the massive riots that accompanied Queen Beatrix's coronation on 30 April 1980. Eventually the owners and authorities

gave up: in October 1980 the council bought the buildings, legalised the squatters and renovated the houses on their behalf.

A bit farther along Keizersgracht, just beyond Berenstraat, is the **Felix Meritis building** at No 324. It was built in 1787 by Jacob Otten Husly for an organisation called Felix Meritis (Latin for 'Happy through Merit'), a society of wealthy residents who promoted the ideals of the Enlightenment through the study of science, arts and commerce. It became the city's main cultural centre in the 19th century. The colonnaded facade served as a model for that of the Concertgebouw, and its oval concert hall (where Brahms, Grieg and Saint Saëns performed) was copied as the Concertgebouw's Kleine Zaal (Small Hall) for chamber music.

The building later passed to a printing company and was gutted by fire in 1932. After WWII it became the headquarters of the Dutch Communist Party (and the offices of the party newspaper), and from 1968 to 1989 the Shaffy Theatre Company staged its avant-garde productions here. Today, the reconstituted Felix Meritis Foundation promotes European performing arts in the building.

Opposite Felix Meritis, at No 317, is the residence where Tsar **Peter the Great** of Russia surprised his host, Christoffel Brants, by sailing right up to the house in the passenger barge from Utrecht to pay his respects. The Brants family used to live in Russia where they shared Peter's interest in ships. In 1697 the young tsar had already paid an incognito visit to the world centre of shipbuilding to serve as an apprentice shipwright; this time, in 1716–17, his visit was official.

The city dignitaries greeted him with compliments in cultured French; he answered in earthy Dutch expletives, drank beer straight from the jug at the evening banquet and spent the night on the floor beside his bed. The next day he moved to the Russian ambassador's house at Herengracht 527 and trashed the place with bouts of drunken revelry over the following months. A similar lot befell Brants' country mansion (called 'Petersburg') along the Vecht River, though Brants received handsome financial recompense and a title.

Prinsengracht (Maps 2 & 4)

Prinsengracht, named for William the Silent, Prince of Orange and forefather of the royal family, is the least upmarket of the main canals and also the liveliest. Instead of stately offices and banks, there are shops and cafés where you can sit outside in summer. The houses are smaller and narrower than along the other canals, and apartments are still relatively affordable by canal standards; houseboats line the quays. Together with the adjoining Jordaan neighbourhood (see the following section), this is an area where anyone can feel comfortable.

The **Noorderkerk** at Noordermarkt, near the northern end of the canal, was completed in 1623 to a design by Hendrick de Keyser as a Calvinist church for the 'common' people in the Jordaan (the upper classes attended his Westerkerk farther south). It was built in the shape of a broad Greek cross (four arms of equal length) around a central pulpit, giving the whole congregation unimpeded access to the word of God in suitably sober surroundings. This design, unusual at the time, would become common for Protestant churches throughout the country. A sculpture near the entrance commemorates the bloody Jordaan riots of July 1934, when five people died protesting the government's austerity measures, including a 12% reduction of already pitiful unemployment benefits.

The **Noordermarkt** has been a market square since the early 1600s. It now hosts a lively flea market on Monday morning where you can find some wonderful bargains. Early on Saturday morning there's a bird market (caged birds, rabbits etc – a holdover from the former livestock market), followed till early afternoon by a 'farmer's market' *(boerenmarkt)* with organic produce, herbs etc.

On the opposite side of Prinsengracht, between Prinsenstraat and Leliegracht, is a row of former **warehouses** stretching from No 187 to 217.

At No 263 is the **Anne Frankhuis**, probably the most famous canal house in Amsterdam with half a million visitors a year. Interest focuses on the *achterhuis*, the 'rear house' or annexe where the Jewish Anne Frank and her family went into hiding from 1942 to 1944 to escape deportation by the Germans. The museum (☎ 556 71 00) is open daily from 9 am to 5 pm (to 7 pm from June to August). Admission costs f10, or f5 with discounts (free for children aged under 10). The queues in summer can be exasperating but they should be OK if you arrive before opening time.

Anne probably couldn't see but could certainly hear the carillon in the tower of the **Westerkerk**, at 85m the highest church tower in the city. It's topped by the imperial crown that Habsburg emperor Maximilian I bestowed to the city's coat of arms in 1489. The tower, the tourist logo of Amsterdam today, affords a tremendous view over the city, including the differing layouts of the

TAMSIN WILSON

The square tower of the Westerkerk

Anne Frank

Anne Frank's father, Otto Frank, was a manufacturer of pectin (a gelling agent used in jam) who had the foresight to emigrate with his family from Frankfurt to Amsterdam in 1933. In December 1940 he bought this house and moved his business from the Singel to here. By then the German occupiers had already tightened the noose around the city's Jewish inhabitants, and even though he signed the business over to his non-Jewish partner, Otto was forced in July 1942 to go into hiding with his family – his wife and daughters Anne (aged 13) and Margot (16).

They moved into the specially prepared rear of the building, along with another couple, the Van Daans, and their son Peter, and were joined later by a Mr van Dussel. The entrance hid behind a revolving bookcase, and the windows of the annexe were blacked out to prevent suspicion among people who might see it from surrounding houses (blackouts were common practice to disorient Allied bombers at night).

Here they survived until they were betrayed to the Gestapo in August 1944. The Franks were among the last Jews to be deported and Anne died in the Bergen-Belsen concentration camp in March 1945, only weeks before it was liberated. Otto was the only member of the family to survive, and after the war he published Anne's diary which was found among the litter in the annexe (the furniture had been carted away by the Nazis). Addressed to the fictitious Kitty, the diary – written in Dutch but translated into 55 languages since – traces the young teenager's development through puberty and displays all the signs of a gifted writer in the making. It has recently been reissued, complete with passages deleted by her father about her awakening sexuality and relationship problems with her mother.

In 1957 the then owner donated the house to the Anne Frank Foundation, who turned it into a museum on the persecution of Jews in WWII and the dangers of present-day racism and antisemitism.

canal belt and the streets in the Jordaan. The climb is strenuous, though.

The church is the main gathering place for Amsterdam's Dutch Reformed community. It was built as a showcase Protestant church for the rich to a 1620 design by Hendrick de Keyser, who copied his design of the Zuiderkerk but increased the scale. De Keyser died in 1621 and the church was completed by Jacob van Campen in 1630. The square tower dates from 1638 – De Keyser would have made it hexagonal or octagonal. The nave, 29m wide and 28m high, is the largest of any Dutch Protestant church and is covered by a wooden barrel vault (the marshy ground precluded the use of heavy stone).

The huge main organ dates from 1686, with panels decorated with biblical scenes and instruments by Gerard de Lairesse. The secondary organ is used for Bach cantatas.

Rembrandt, who died bankrupt at nearby Rozengracht, was buried in the church on 8 October 1669 but no-one knows exactly where – possibly near his son Titus' grave.

The church (☎ 624 77 66) is open from Easter to mid-September, Monday to Friday from 11 am to 3 pm (also Saturday in July and August). The tower is open from 1 April to 30 September, Monday to Saturday from 10 am to 5 pm, and costs f3.

The church stands on **Westermarkt**. Until 1857 the eastern part of the square was dominated by the monumental Westerhal, with a meat hall at ground level and the headquarters of the city watch upstairs. In 1634 the French philosopher **René Descartes** resided in the house at No 6 on the quiet northern side of the square. He was one of many foreign intellectuals who found the freedom to develop and express their ideas in Amsterdam (others included Locke, Comenius, Voltaire and Marx), or who had their works published here. According to Voltaire, the residents were so preoccupied with profit that they would never notice him even if he spent his entire life here.

Farther south along Prinsengracht is the **Pulitzer Hotel**, which started business in

1971 and now occupies the 17 adjoining canal houses between Nos 299 and 331, all connected with internal staircases and passages. The gables have been meticulously restored, along with some of the interior features. A free classical concert is held from barges in the canal in August.

If you continue south along the same (eastern) side of the canal you might notice a number of very narrow **alleyways** between Berenstraat and Leidsegracht, closed off with gates. They were officially intended as side entrances for servants' quarters at the rear but such quarters were rented out as accommodation and workshops to the city's poor. These hidden slums, in damp cellars and clustered around dark courtyards, violated the municipal codes of the canal belt but nobody took much notice, probably because they were opposite the southern reaches of the Jordaan – had they been on Herengracht or Keizersgracht it might have been a different story.

Jordaan (Maps 2 & 4)

The Jordaan neighbourhood was planned and built as a working-class district during the canal-belt project in the early 17th century. Here the canal-diggers and bridge-builders, carpenters and stonemasons settled with their families. Here too came the tanneries, breweries, sugar refineries, smithies, cooperages and other smelly or noisy industries banned from the upmarket canal belt, along with the residences of the artisans and labourers who worked in them.

The name Jordaan wasn't used until a century later and its origin is unclear. The most popular theory is that it's a corruption of the French *jardin* (garden). After all, many French Huguenots settled here in what used to be the market gardens beyond the city walls – the street pattern follows the original grid of ditches and footpaths, and many streets carry names of flowers. Some historians contend that the name had biblical connotations and referred to the Jordan River.

For centuries, the Jordaan remained a thoroughly working-class area and the authorities saw it as the unruly heart of the city. It was the first precinct where tarred roads

replaced brick paving because the latter could be turned into barricades and police-smashing projectiles during riots. Early this century one in seven Amsterdammers lived in the Jordaan, 1000 people packed to the hectare (100x100m) in squalid conditions.

New housing estates in Amsterdam's northern, western and southern suburbs brought some relief after WWI, and in the 1960s and 1970s many Jordanese moved to the outlying 'garden suburbs' and the polders of Flevoland. Their places were taken by students, artists and tertiary-sector professionals who began to transform the Jordaan into a trendy area, though there are still enough working-class and elderly people for it to retain some of its original flavour.

Popular conceptions of the Jordaan linger: it is the 'heart and soul' of the 'real' Amsterdam epitomised in schmaltzy oompah ballads, where life happens on the streets or in the corner pub (rather than in the overcrowded houses) and where common folk still share their experiences; where houses are tiny but tidy, with lace curtains and flowers in window boxes, behind which auntie Greet eyes the street and her front door with the help of a *spionnetje* ('little spy' mirror) attached to the windowsill; and where living, working, shopping, schooling and entertainment are integrated in the one neighbourhood.

Such popular conceptions still hold true, as you will discover when you wander through the Jordaan and soak up the real-life atmosphere of people going about their daily business. Take your time and don't worry if you get lost (which you will): there are plenty of inviting pubs and restaurants, offbeat shops and weird little art galleries to grab your attention.

The Jordaan is over-endowed with lively **markets**, such as:

Noordermarkt – see the earlier Prinsengracht section

Lindengracht – general market on Saturday, very much a local affair

Westermarkt on Westerstraat – clothes and textiles on Monday

De Looier at Elandsgracht 109 – bargain antiques and bric-a-brac at indoor stalls most days from 11 am to 5 pm, Thursday to 9 pm, closed Friday

In the late 19th and early 20th centuries many of the Jordaan's ditches and narrow canals were filled in, mainly for sanitary reasons, though their names remain: Palmgracht, Lindengracht, Rozengracht (now a busy thoroughfare), Elandsgracht. **Bloemgracht** was the most upmarket of the canals (the 'Herengracht of the Jordaan') and, for that reason, was never filled in: here wealthy artisans built smaller versions of patrician canal houses. Note the row of three step gables at No 87–91, now owned by the Hendrick de Keyser Foundation and known as the Three Hendricks, though they were built in 1645, long after the famous sculptor/architect had died.

The southern tip of the Jordaan beyond Rozengracht is quieter than the area to the north and perhaps less interesting for an aimless wander. It was (and to some extent still is) an area of workshops and artists' studios.

The Jordaan also has a high concentration of **hofjes**, almshouses consisting of a courtyard surrounded by houses built by wealthy benefactors to house elderly people and widows – a noble act in the days before social security. Some hofjes are real gems, with beautifully restored houses and lovingly maintained gardens. The entrances are usually unobtrusive and hidden behind doors. Hofjes became such a popular tourist attraction in recent years that residents complained and in theory they are now closed to the public (the one exception being the famous Begijnhof, discussed in the earlier New Side section). If the entrance is unlocked, however, and if there are only one or two of you and you exercise the necessary discretion, most residents probably won't mind if you take a quick peek. Try the following:

Lindenhofje, Lindengracht 94–112 – dating from 1614, the oldest surviving hofje

Suyckerhofje, Lindengracht 149–163 – a charming hofje founded in 1670

Karthuizerhofje, Karthuizersstraat 89–171 – a hofje for widows, dating from 1650 and on the site of a former Carthusian monastery

Claes Claeszhofje, Eerste Egelantiersdwarsstraat 3 – also known as Anslo's Hofje; three courtyards dating from around 1630; inhabited by music students

St Andrieshofje, Egelantiersgracht 107–141 – the second-oldest surviving hofje (finished in 1617), founded by the cattle farmer Jeff Gerritzoon

Venetiae, Elandsstraat 106–136 – founded in the mid-1600s by a trader with Venice; features a very pretty garden

SOUTHERN CANAL BELT (MAPS 4 & 6)

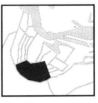

The canal project stopped at the radial Leidsegracht in 1625 through lack of funds but was picked up again later. Even then, work on the southern section progressed much more slowly: it had taken a mere 12 years to construct the canals down from Brouwersgracht, along with their interconnecting roads and the adjoining Jordaan area, but it took another 40 years to complete the southern canal belt towards the Amstel and beyond the opposite bank. Interest then fizzled out and the only canal that ever made it to the eastern IJ was the (Nieuwe) Herengracht.

The corner of Herengracht and Leidsegracht is a tranquil spot, surrounded by 17th and 18th-century houses. You may notice that the buildings along Leidsegracht, as well as those along the southern canal belt, are almost entirely residential: there are very few of the warehouses or combined warehouses and residences found in the western section. The facades are also more restrained and stately, and less boisterously decorated.

Herengracht (Map 4)

Along the southern section of Herengracht more than anywhere else, the buildings are larger than in the western section. By now (mid-17th century) some of Amsterdam's merchants and shipping magnates had amassed stupendous fortunes and they saw to it that the authorities (often these same merchants and magnates) relaxed their restrictions on the size of canalside plots.

The Herengracht between Leidsestraat and Vijzelstraat, known as the **Golden Bend**, was the site of some of the largest private mansions in the city. Most of them now belong to financial and other institutions. Dutch architectural themes are still evident but the dominant styles are Louis XIV, XV and XVI – French culture was all the rage among the city's wealthy class.

You can look at the interior of one of these houses by visiting the **Goethe Institut** at No 470 (see Cultural Centres in the Facts for the Visitor chapter). When this house was built in 1669 it was much larger and included No 468 next door.

Another Golden Bend house open to the public is the **Kattenkabinet** (Cats' Cabinet; ☎ 626 53 78) across the canal at No 497. This museum, devoted to the feline presence in art, was founded by a wealthy financier in memory of his red tomcat, John Piermont Morgan III. Cat fanciers will go gaga over the displays but it's also worth visiting for the magnificent interior and views of the garden. It's open Tuesday to Saturday from 11 am to 7 pm, Sunday from noon, and costs f10.

Back on the even-numbered side of Herengracht, the corner with Vijzelstraat is dominated by the colossal (some would say monstrous) **ABN-AMRO bank building** that continues all the way to Keizersgracht. It was completed in 1923 as head office for the Netherlands Trading Society, a Dutch overseas bank (successor to the United East India Company and West India Company) that became the ABN Bank in the mid-1960s and merged with the AMRO Bank in 1991. The ABN-AMRO is the largest bank in the country and the largest foreign bank in the USA. It ranks only 16th in the world but has one of the biggest international networks (the combination of finance and trade has always been a Dutch speciality).

Beyond Vijzelstraat, past the mayor's residence at No 502, is the **Geelvinck Hinlopen Huis** (☎ 639 07 47) at No 518, a 17th-century house with stylish rooms, a formal garden and art in the coach house. Though not as impressive as Museum Willet-Holthuysen a bit farther along the canal (see later) or the Museum Van Loon (see the following section on Keizersgracht), it's far more serene, and worth a look if you can be bothered organising a private tour for f150 (maximum 15 people).

A few steps past this house is the start of the radial **Reguliersgracht**, the beautiful 'canal of the seven bridges' cut in 1664. You can just about count them all when you stand on the Herengracht bridge. Canal tour boats halt here for photos because it's easier from the water, especially at night when the bridges are lit up and their graceful curves are reflected in the water. This canal was almost filled at the turn of the century to accommodate a tram line.

The Great Art Fraud

Herengracht 470, which currently houses the Goethe Institut, used to include No 468 next door. The house was later split, and during WWII a German art dealer 'acquired' No 468. The Amsterdam painter Han van Meegeren sold him a painting by the 17th century Delft master Jan Vermeer that the German passed on to Nazi ringleader Hermann Göring in return for f2 million-worth of paintings plundered elsewhere.

Van Meegeren was accused of collaboration after the war, but he declared that he had painted the Vermeer himself and in fact had painted the other Vermeers that had appeared out of nowhere in recent years. To prove his case he painted another 'Vermeer' under supervision.

His work completely fooled the art historians of the day, including the prestigious Boijmans-van Beuningen Museum in Rotterdam that bought one of the paintings before the war and gave it top billing. It was the greatest art fraud in Dutch history, all the more remarkable for the fact that Vermeer only produced 35 known paintings in his lifetime. Out of respect for Van Meegeren's talent, and as a warning for gullible art snobs, the judge sentenced him to a lenient one year in prison.

Walk down Reguliersgracht to take in its serenity and lively mix of architectural styles. Sights include:

- the house at No 34 with its massive eagle gable commemorating the original owner, Arent van den Bergh (*arend* is one of the Dutch words for eagle), and its unusual twin entrance against the side walls for the upstairs and downstairs dwellings
- the superb scene back towards Herengracht from the east-west bridge at Keizersgracht, and the photogenic lean of the two houses on the corner (not to mention the 15 bridges visible from here)
- the Dutch/German woodwork fantasy at No 57–59 reminiscent of the city's medieval wooden houses, built in 1879 for a carpentry firm (the same architect, Isaac Gosschalk, designed No 63)
- the Amstelveld with the white, wooden Amstelkerk at Prinsengracht (see the following Prinsengracht section)
- the statuette of a stork set into the corner house at No 92 (storks were a protected species; canalboat operators fantasise that a midwife lived here)

The extension of Reguliersgracht across Herengracht towards the centre of town used to be water but is now **Thorbeckeplein**, with a statue of Jan Rudolf Thorbecke, the Liberal politician who created the Dutch parliamentary system in 1848. He faces outwards and wouldn't like the look of his square, though the second-rate nightclubs have all but disappeared and the banning of cars has made it more pleasant than it used to be. An art market (mostly modern pictorial) is held here Sundays from 10.30 am to 6 pm between mid-March and mid-October.

Beyond Thorbeckeplein is **Rembrandtplein**, originally called Reguliersplein and then Botermarkt because the butter market was held here. The proud statue of the painter, gazing pensively towards the Jewish quarter where he lived until circumstances forced him to the Jordaan, was unveiled in 1852 and the square was renamed in 1876. It's lined with pubs, grand cafés and restaurants, and attracts outer suburbanites looking for a noisy good time.

The street running west from Rembrandtplein to the Munt is Reguliersbreestraat.

(Before the construction of the canal belt, the nuns of the Regulier, or 'Regular', order had a monastery outside the city walls roughly where Utrechtsestraat now crosses Keizersgracht, which explains the frequent use of the name in this area.) About a third of the way along on the left is the **Tuschinskitheater** (☎ 626 26 33) at No 26–28, established in 1921 and still the most glorious cinema in the country. The blend of Art Deco and Amsterdam School architecture with almost camp interior decorations is a visual feast, even before you've seen a film on one of its screens. Guided tours in July and August (Sunday and Monday at 10.30 am) cost f7.50, but you might as well go for the whole experience by watching a film in the main auditorium, Tuschinski 1.

Back at the Herengracht bridge over Reguliersgracht, continue eastwards across **Utrechtsestraat**, a lively street with interesting shops, restaurants and cafés that's worth a wander (turn right for this).

At Herengracht 605 is **Museum Willet-Holthuysen** (☎ 523 18 22), named after Abraham Willet's widow who bequeathed this beautiful house with its sumptuous interior to the city 100 years ago. Dating from 1687, it has been remodelled several times and underwent extensive renovations recently. Some furnishings and artefacts come from other bequests which explains the uncoordinated mix of 18th and 19th-century styles. It's open weekdays from 10 am to 5 pm, weekends from 11 am, and costs f7.50 (f5.50 with discounts). It's all very impressive but a bit unnatural – the Museum Van Loon (see the following Keizersgracht section) gives a better idea of the real thing. You can see the formal French garden with its sundial for free through the iron fence at the Amstelstraat end.

Keizersgracht (Maps 4 & 6)

The intersection of Keizersgracht and Leidsestraat has a couple of remarkable buildings. The **Metz department store** at Keizersgracht 455 was built in 1891 to house the New York Life Insurance Company (hence the exterior and interior eagles) but soon passed to the purveyor of luxury furnishings. The functionalist designer and architect Gerrit Rietveld added the gallery on the top floor where you can have lunch with a view.

Across the canal at No 508 is the former **PC Hooft store**, built for a cigar manufacturer in 1881 by AC Bleijs (the architect of the St Nicolaaskerk near Centraal Station). The name refers to poet, playwright, historian and national icon Pieter Cornelisz Hooft, whose 300th birthday was commemorated in this Dutch-Renaissance throwback with Germanic tower. Note the playful reliefs depicting the various stages of tobacco preparation.

Farther along on this side of the canal, beyond Leidsestraat, is the solid yet elegant **Keizersgrachtkerk** at No 566. It dates from 1888 and was built to house the orthodox-Calvinist Gereformeerd community who left the Dutch Reformed Church two years before (see Religion in the Facts about Amsterdam chapter).

The next side street is **Nieuwe Spiegelstraat**, lined with shops selling luxury antiques and other collectables. Even if you don't have the inclination (or the money!) to buy anything, at least have a look at the goods on offer. The extension of this street, the pretty Spiegelgracht with more antique shops and especially art galleries, leads to the Rijksmuseum.

Farther along Keizersgracht, across windswept Vijzelstraat, is the **Museum Van Loon** (☎ 624 52 55) at No 672, built in 1672 (along with the house next door, No 674) for a wealthy arms dealer. The portraitist Ferdinand Bol, a faithful student of Rembrandt, rented the place for a while. In the late 1800s it was acquired by the Van Loons, one of the most prominent patrician families, who lived in a style befitting their status; their stables across the canal at No 607 now house an art gallery. The house, with its period rooms and family portraits, provides a good impression of canalside living when money was no object, and the rococo rose garden is typical of the greenery Amsterdammers aspired to in the 18th century. The museum is only open Friday to Monday from 11 am to 5 pm and costs f7.50 (f5 with discounts).

Note the austere, two-storey **Amstelhof** on the opposite side of the river where Keizersgracht meets the Amstel. It was built in 1683 as an almshouse and is still in use today for Dutch Reformed elderly women (and men, in the basement). It illustrates how the canal project ran out of steam by the time it reached the Amstel. Much of the land beyond was given over to charities or turned into recreational area: the wealthy had already bought their plots and built their mansions, and the Dutch Republic went into consolidation mode against the British and French, which meant there was little new wealth (only increased wealth for those who already had money).

Prinsengracht (Maps 4 & 6)

The odd and even house numbers along Prinsengracht are more out of step than along the other canals (where they follow one another fairly closely) due to the many Jordaan streets that lead off it. This is exacerbated by additional streets beyond Leidsegracht, and the result is that house No 1133 sits opposite No 868 when Prinsengracht reaches the Amstel.

Near the corner with Leidsegracht is the **Paleis van Justitie** (Court of Appeal) at No 436, a huge, neoclassical edifice modified in 1829 by the city architect Jan de Greef. It started life in 1666 as the city orphanage and was designed for 800 orphans, but by the early 19th century more than half the city's 4300 orphans were crammed in here. A royal decree in 1822 relocated orphans over the age of six to other towns, much to the chagrin of the local authorities who were powerless to act against the 'theft of children'.

A hundred metres or so down Leidsestraat is **Leidseplein**, one of the liveliest squares in the city and the undisputed centre of nightlife. It has always been busy: in the 17th century it was the gateway to Leiden and other points south-west, and travellers had to leave their carts and horses here when heading into town.

The **Stadsschouwburg** (City Theatre) with its balcony arcade at Leidseplein 25 dates from 1894. People criticised the building – as they criticised every city theatre before or since – and the funds for the exterior decorations never materialised. The architect, Jan Springer, couldn't handle this and retired. The theatre is used for large-scale plays and operettas. South across Marnixstraat, the **American Hotel** is an Art Nouveau landmark from 1902 foreshadowing the Amsterdam School's use of brick. No visit to Amsterdam is complete without a coffee in its stylish Café Americain.

The pavement cafés at the north end of the square are perfect for watching interesting street artists and eccentric passers-by. There are countless pubs and clubs in the area that continue till daylight, and a smorgasbord of restaurants in the surrounding streets. There are cinemas and other entertainment venues, and even a casino built in the shape of a roulette table. Everybody finds something to enjoy at Leidseplein.

Back at Prinsengracht, eastwards on the far side of the canal, the ebullient neo-Renaissance facade is all that remains of the former **milk factory** at No 739–741, built in 1876 to a design by Eduard Cuypers. Until then, milk was brought into town from the surrounding countryside in wooden barrels and sold on the streets from open buckets – not very hygienic.

Farther east, beyond the intersection of Prinsengracht and Reguliersgracht, is the Amstelveld with the wooden **Amstelkerk**. The city planners had envisaged four new Protestant churches in the southern canal belt, linked to one another by Kerkstraat, but the only one they actually built was the Oosterkerk, way out on Wittenburgergracht near the IJ (Map 5; see the later Eastern Islands section). The Amstelkerk was a temporary structure, erected in 1670 so the congregation had somewhere to meet while the permanent church arose next to it, but the funds remained elusive and the 'temporary' church still conducts services today. Gothic alterations were made to the interior in the 1840s.

The authorities never completely dropped their plans for a permanent church and kept the **Amstelveld** free of buildings. In 1876 the Monday market moved here from Rembrandtplein. This lively 'free market' had vendors from out of town peddling a wide range of goods (it still operates in the summer

months, focusing on plants and flowers). A small statue by the Amstelkerk commemorates Professor Kokadorus, a.k.a. Meijer Linnewiel (1867–1934), the most colourful market vendor Amsterdam has known. People would buy anything from spoons to suspenders ('to hang up your mother-in-law') just to watch his performances interlaced with satirical comments about the politics of the day. The annihilation of the Jewish community in WWII put an end to the city's rich tradition of creative vending.

In summer the Amstelveld is a pleasant space where children play soccer, dogs run around, and patrons laze in the sun at Café Kort against the south side of the Amstelkerk. The Catholic church across the canal at Prinsengracht 756, **de Duif** (the Dove), was first built in 1796, shortly after the French-installed government proclaimed freedom of religion. It was the first Catholic church with a public entrance for over two centuries, and was rebuilt to its current design in the mid-1800s. In the 1970s the Church authorities wanted to sell the building but the priest and other staff continued to hold services in defiance and saved the church.

Continue to the Amstel, and a couple of interesting sights. To your right are the **Amstelsluizen**, which cross the river to Theater Carré (built as a circus in 1868, rebuilt in brick in 1887 and now used mainly as a theatre). These impressive sluices date from 1674 and allowed the canals to be flushed with fresh water from the Amstel rather than salt water from the IJ, which made the city far more livable (see Ecology & Environment in the Facts about Amsterdam chapter). They were still operated by hand until recently.

To your left is the **Magere Brug** (Skinny Bridge), the most photographed drawbridge in the city. It links Kerkstraat with Nieuwe Kerkstraat and dates from the 1670s, when it was a very narrow pedestrian drawbridge. Rebuilt and widened several times, it was finally torn down in 1929 to make way for a modern bridge, only to be rebuilt again in timber. It's still operated by hand and makes a very pretty sight during the day as well as at night when it's lit up. Stand in the middle and feel it seesaw under the passing traffic.

euro currency converter f1 = €0.45

NIEUWMARKT NEIGHBOURHOOD (MAPS 4 & 5)

For information on Nieuwmarkt Square, see the earlier Old Side section. East of this square is the Nieuwmarkt neighbourhood, enclosed by the Geldersekade and Kloveniersburg-

wal in the west, the Amstel in the south, the Valkenburgerstraat (the feeder road of the current IJ-Tunnel) in the east and the IJ in the north. It was the birthplace in 1975 of the organised squatter movement in response to the metro line. The planned line snaked through much of the neighbourhood and required the demolition of many houses that were derelict or still quite habitable – often depending on one's point of view (see History in the Facts about Amsterdam chapter).

New, subsidised housing estates arose after completion of the line and today the west and south of the neighbourhood are dominated by modern inner-city architecture, some of it interesting and some less than successful.

Until WWII the area was the focal point of Amsterdam's Jews, a thriving community who enjoyed more freedom here than elsewhere in Europe and made the city a centre for diamonds, tobacco, printing and clothing. They also gave Amsterdam an exceptional variety of lively markets, some of which still exist as sad reminders (eg, the flea market on Waterlooplein).

Lastage

The Nieuwmarkt neighbourhood grew haphazardly. Immediately east of Nieuwmarkt Square was an area known as the Lastage, a jumble of wharves, docks, rope yards and warehouses that lay beyond the medieval city wall and the protective sea dyke that ran along the current Zeedijk, St Anthoniesbreestraat, Jodenbreestraat and Muiderstraat. In the 1510s, after an attack by troops from Gelderland, the Lastage was fortified by means of the wide **Oude Schans** canal and guarded by a gun turret,

the **Montelbaanstoren** – its octagonal tower was added in 1606, presumably to a design by Hendrick de Keyser. Today the spot offers panoramic views over expanses of water.

North-west of here, across Waalseilandsgracht on the corner of Binnenkant and Prins Hendrikkade, is the **Scheepvaarthuis**, the Shipping House completed in 1916 to a design by Johan van der Mey. Note the many facade sculptures. This remarkable building, which utilises the street layout to resemble a ship's bow, was the first building in Amsterdam School style and is still one of the finest examples of this architectural movement. It used to house a consortium of shipping companies but is now home to the municipal transport company that runs the trams and buses.

Nieuwmarkt Islands (Map 5)

In the 1580s, the sudden influx of Sephardic Jews from Spain and Portugal prompted the newly Calvinist authorities to reclaim land from the IJ in the form of several rectangular islands east of Oude Schans, one of which, **Uilenburg**, is still recognisable as an island today. Shipyards that operated here soon moved out to the new Eastern Islands (see the Eastern Islands section later in this chapter), making way for another wave of Jewish refugees, this time Ashkenazim from Central and Eastern Europe.

On Uilenburg, the vast Gassan diamond factory (☎ 622 53 33), abutting a synagogue at Nieuwe Uilenburgerstraat 173–175, was the first to use steam power in the 1880s. The factory was recommissioned in 1989 after thorough renovations. See Diamonds in the Shopping chapter for more information about diamonds and free guided tours of diamond factories.

Southern Nieuwmarkt Neighbourhood (Maps 4 & 5)

South of here, inside the sea dyke, the 16th-century authorities reclaimed land from the Amstel: the island of Vlooienburg (the current Waterlooplein), with canals and transverse streets that would become the heart of the Jewish quarter. This was not

Jewish Amsterdam

The Nazis brought about the almost complete annihilation of Amsterdam's Jewish community. Before WWII there were about 140,000 Jews in the Netherlands of whom about 90,000 lived in Amsterdam, where they formed 13% of the population. (Before the 1930s this proportion was about 10% but it increased with Jews fleeing the Nazi regime in Germany.) Only some 5500 of these Amsterdammers survived the war, barely one in 16.

They played an important role in the city over the centuries. In medieval times few Jews lived here but their expulsion from Spain and Portugal in the 1580s brought a flood of Sephardic refugees. More arrived when the Spaniards retook Antwerp in 1585. They settled on the newly reclaimed islands in the current Nieuwmarkt neighbourhood where land was cheap.

The monopolistic guilds kept most trades firmly closed to these newcomers but some of the Sephardim were diamond-cutters, for which there was no guild. Other Sephardic Jews introduced printing and tobacco processing, or worked in similarly unrestricted trades such as retail on the streets, banking and medicine. The majority, however, eked out a meagre living as labourers and small-time traders on the margins of society, and lived in houses they could afford in the Nieuwmarkt area, which developed into the Jewish quarter. Still, they weren't confined to a ghetto and, with some restrictions, could buy property and exercise their religion – freedoms unheard of elsewhere in Europe.

The 17th century saw another influx of Jewish refugees, this time Ashkenazim fleeing pogroms in Central and Eastern Europe. Thus the two wings of the diaspora were reunited in Amsterdam but they didn't always get on well. Sephardim resented the increased competition posed by Ashkenazic newcomers, who soon outnumbered them and were generally much poorer, and the two groups established separate synagogues. Perhaps because of this antagonism, Amsterdam became a major Jewish centre in Europe.

The guilds and all remaining restrictions on Jews were abolished during the French occupation, and the Jewish community thrived in the 19th century. There was still considerable poverty and the Jewish quarter included some of the worst slums in the city; but the economic, social and political emancipation of the Jews helped their burgeoning middle class, who moved out into the Plantage area and later into the suburbs south of the city.

The Holocaust left the Jewish quarter empty, a sinister reminder of its once bustling life. Many of the houses, looted by Germans and local collaborators and deprived of their wooden fixtures for fuel in the final, desperate months of the war, stood derelict until they were demolished in the 1970s.

Some estimates put the current Jewish population of Amsterdam at 30,000, but many are so integrated into Dutch society that they don't consider themselves distinctly Jewish. Amsterdam slang incorporates many terms of Hebrew or Yiddish origin, such as the alternative name for Amsterdam, Mokum (from *makom aleph*, the best city of all); the cheery goodbye, *de mazzel* (good luck); *joetje* (f10, from the 10th letter of the Hebrew alphabet); *gabber* (friend, 'mate') from the Yiddisch *chawwer*, companion; and the ultimate put-down, *kapsones maken* (to make unnecessary fuss, from *kapsjones*, self-importance).

enough, however, to satisfy the needs of the rapidly growing city and two decades later the authorities gave the go-ahead for the ambitious canal-belt project.

The street that runs from Nieuwmarkt Square in the direction of Waterlooplein is St Anthoniesbreestraat, once a busy street that lost its old buildings during the construction of the metro line – the new houses incorporate rubber blocks in the foundations to absorb vibrations caused by the metro. One exception is the **Pintohuis** at No 69 which used to belong to a wealthy Sephardi, Isaac de Pinto, who had it remodelled with Italianate pilasters in the 1680s. In the 1970s a freeway to Centraal Station required the demolition of this building but the controversy stopped the freeway instead. It's now a library annexe – pop inside to admire the beautiful ceilings.

A passageway in the modern housing estate across St Anthoniesbreestraat leads to the **Zuiderkerk**, the Southern Church built by Hendrick de Keyser in 1603–11. His tower, 1m out of plumb, dates from 1614. This was the first custom-built Protestant church in Amsterdam – still a Catholic design but without the choir – and served as a blueprint for De Keyser's Westerkerk. The final church service was held here in 1929 and at the end of WWII it served as a morgue.

It now houses the Municipal Centre for Physical Planning and Public Housing (☎ 622 29 62) with a very interesting exhibit on all aspects of urban planning, open Monday to Friday from noon to 5 pm, Thursday to 8 pm (free admission). A large, computerised laser map answers questions about the city in English. From 1 June to 30 September, you can climb the tower for a great view over the city (Wednesday to Saturday at 2, 3 and 4 pm; cost f3).

The former cemetery east of the church adjoins Theo Bosch's community housing project, the **Pentagon**, completed in 1983, with an arty waterfall along the courtyard wall. You'll either love it or hate it but you can't ignore it. Visiting architects often have a look.

South of here, across the beautiful **Raamgracht** that city planners wanted to fill in the 1950s, is the narrow **Verversstraat** with a

mix of old and new architecture typical of this area. The name, Painters' Street, refers to the polluting paint factories that were limited to this street (originally a canal) beyond the city walls.

The covered walkway over the street used to link sections of the Leeuwenburg sewing-machine factory, slated for demolition but saved by squatters who now live here legally and quite happily (it's an impressive building viewed from the Zwanenburgwal end). At the end of Verversstraat, turn right to the steel drawbridge over the pretty **Groenburgwal**, which affords a good photo opportunity back towards the Zuiderkerk. Note the slight tilt in its tower.

Jodenbreestraat St Anthoniesbreestraat opens on to the wide Jodenbreestraat, a remnant of the freeway-to-be. Note the picturesque, leaning lock-keeper's house on the left, where you can have a quiet beer out in the sun.

Across the road, at Jodenbreestraat 4–6, is **Museum Het Rembrandthuis** (☎ 520 04 00), a beautiful house dating from 1606 where Rembrandt lived (downstairs) and worked (upstairs). He bought the house in 1639 for a fortune thanks to his wealthy wife, Saskia van Uylenburgh, but chronic debt got the better of him and he had to bail out and move to the Jordaan in 1658. The years spent in this house were the high point of his career, when he was regarded as a star and ran the largest painting studio in Holland, but he ruined it all by making enemies and squandering his earnings.

The museum is well worth visiting for the almost complete collection of Rembrandt's etchings (250 of the 280 he is known to have made). There are also several drawings and paintings by his pupils as well as his teacher, Pieter Lastman, and an etching by Albrecht Dürer. Recently refurbished and expanded with a modern section including the entry hall to the left, it is open daily from 10 am to 5 pm. Admission costs f12.50 (various discounts). Check the Web site www.rembrandthuis.nl for more information.

Next to the Rembrandthuis is **Holland Experience** (☎ 422 22 33), Waterlooplein 17.

Pentagon community housing project

Bicycles are everywhere – even on the trains!

CHARLOTTE HINDLE

Opulent 17th century canalside mansion

EDWARD AM SNIJDERS

Royal Palace, on Dam Square, the historic heart of the city

ZAW MIN YU

ZAW MIN YU

Royal Palace facade & bell tower

RICK GERHARTER

Music while you munch, in the Vondelpark

This multimedia hype-fest tries to cram all of this little land's big attractions into an overpriced mish-mash of sights, sounds and smells. A plotless half-hour film lurches from tulips to windmills to threatened dykes, without narration or explanation, but with artless extras parading as cutting-edge entertainment. Cheap perfume is puffed into the auditorium while the tulips are on screen. When an on-screen dyke crumbles, room temperature plummets, the audience is sprinkled with water, and a Sony-augmented thunderstorm rages. A plaster ballerina wobbles on rails in front of a filmed rehearsal of *Swan Lake*. Holland Experience is a superlative example of what can happen with many machines and few ideas, and as entertainment it is very lame. It's open daily from 10 am to 6 pm and costs f17.50 (gulp) with minimal discounts, or f25 in combination with the Rembrandthuis.

Waterlooplein South of this is Waterlooplein, once known as Vlooienburg and the heart of the Jewish quarter. It's now dominated by the gleaming gold front tooth in the canal belt, the **Stopera**, an oversized city hall and music theatre that opened in 1986 after endless controversy. It was designed by the Austrian architect Wilhelm Holzbauer and his Dutch colleague Cees Dam, who won a competition back in 1968 with a submission that, in the words of one critic, 'has all the charm of an Ikea chair'. You might wish to attend a music performance in the theatre, or at least a free lunch-time concert on Tuesday, but in any case have a look at the little display in the arcade between city hall and theatre that shows the country's water levels (for more about this subject, see Sea Level & NAP under Geography in the Facts about Amsterdam chapter).

The original Waterlooplein covered the eastern portion of Vlooienburg and was created in 1882 by filling a couple of canals. This was the site of the major Jewish **flea market** where anything was available. The market itself survived the war and is now held north of the Stopera from Monday to Saturday, with a wide range of goods. It's a popular market, not least among tourists.

Prices are a bit higher than at other markets but it's definitely worth a wander. Beware of pickpockets.

The neoclassical **Mozes en Aäronkerk**, a Catholic church built in 1841 on the northeastern corner of Waterlooplein, shows that this wasn't an exclusively Jewish area. It is still used as a church and also as a centre for social and cultural organisations. It replaced the 'clandestine' Catholic church that occupied two houses named Mozes and Aäron at what is now the rear of the church along Jodenbreestraat.

One of the buildings demolished to make way for the new church was home to the Jewish philosopher **Baruch de Spinoza** (1632–77), who was born in Amsterdam but spent much of his life making lenses in The Hague after the rabbis proclaimed him a heretic. He is best known for his work *Ethics*, which proposes that the concept of God possesses an infinite number of attributes. 'Polytheism!' cried rabbis and Calvinist ministers alike – their approach to religion was, after all, similar in many respects.

Jewish Centres The busy roundabout east of the church is Mr Visserplein ('Mr' stands

Baruch de Spinoza

for *meester*, or 'master', the Dutch lawyer's title). LE Visser was a Jewish president of the supreme court who was dismissed by the Nazis. He refused to wear the Star of David and berated the Jewish Council for helping the occupiers carry out their anti-Jewish policies. He died before the Germans could wreak revenge on him.

On the east side of the square is the majestic **Portuguese-Israelite Synagogue** (☎ 624 53 51), at No 3, built between 1671 and 1675 by the Sephardic community. It was the largest synagogue in Europe at the time and is still impressive. The architect, Elias Bouman, was inspired by the Temple of Solomon but the building's classicist lines are typical of Amsterdam. It was restored after the war and is still in use today. The large library of the Ets Haim seminary is one of the most important Jewish libraries in Europe and contains many priceless works. The synagogue is open Sunday to Friday from 10 am to 4 pm, and admission costs f7.50 (f5 with discounts).

South of the synagogue is the triangular Jonas Daniël Meijerplein, named after the country's first Jewish lawyer (actual name Joune Rintel), who did much to ensure the full emancipation of the Jews in the Napoleonic period.

On the square, Mari Andriessen's statue of the *Dockworker* (1952) commemorates the general strike that began among dockworkers on 25 February 1941 to protest the treatment of Jews. The first deportation round-up had occurred here a few days earlier. The anniversary of the strike is still an occasion for wreath-laying but has become a low-key affair with the demise of the Communist Party.

On the south side of the square at JD Meijerplein 2–4, across busy Weesperstraat, is the **Joods Historisch Museum** (Jewish Historical Museum; ☎ 626 99 45), a beautifully restored complex of four Ashkenazic synagogues linked by glass-covered walkways. These are the Grote Sjoel (Great Synagogue, 1671), the first public synagogue in Western Europe; the Obbene Sjoel (Upstairs Synagogue, 1686); the Dritt Sjoel (Third Synagogue, 1700 with a 19th-century facade); and the Neie Sjoel (New Synagogue, 1752), the largest in the complex, but still dwarfed by the Portuguese Synagogue across the square.

The Great Synagogue contains religious objects as well as displays showing the rise of Jewish enterprise and its role in the Dutch economy. The New Synagogue focuses on different aspects of Jewish identity and the history of Jews in the Netherlands. There's also a kosher coffee shop serving Jewish specialities. The complex is open daily (except Yom Kippur) from 11 am to 5 pm and costs f8 (f4 with discounts); entry fees might be a bit higher during special exhibitions. It's a very interesting and impressive museum. The Web site www.jhm.nl has more information.

The area south-east of here, the 'new' canals (Nieuwe Herengracht, Nieuwe Keizersgracht and Nieuwe Prinsengracht) intersected by the busy Weesperstraat traffic artery, was where the canal-belt project petered out around 1700. The canals on this far side of the Amstel were less in demand among the city's wealthy residents and went to charities or were settled by well-off Jews from the nearby Jewish quarter.

PLANTAGE (MAPS 5 & 7)

In the 19th century, the discovery of diamonds in South Africa led to a revival of Amsterdam's diamond industry and the Jewish elite began to move into the Plantage (Planta-  tion), where they built imposing town villas. Until then the Plantage had been a district of parks and gardens east of the Jewish quarter and north of the 'new' canals.

In the 18th century, wealthy residents rented parcels of land here to use as gardens, and the area developed into a weekend getaway with tea houses, variety theatres and other establishments where the upper class relaxed and enjoyed themselves in green surroundings.

The University of Amsterdam's **Hortus Botanicus** (Botanical Garden; ☎ 625 84 11),

Plantage Middenlaan 2A, was established in 1638 as a herb garden for the city's doctors and moved to this south-west corner of the Plantage in 1682. It became a repository for tropical seeds and plants (ornamental or otherwise) brought to Amsterdam by the West and East India Companies' ships. Commercially exploitable plants such as coffee, pineapple, cinnamon and oil palm were distributed from here throughout the world. The herb garden itself, the so-called Hortus Medicus, won world renown for its research into cures for tropical diseases.

The garden is a must-see for anyone with an interest in botany. The wonderful mixture of colonial and modern structures includes the restored, octagonal seed house; a hyper-modern, three-climate glasshouse (1993) with subtropical, tropical and desert plants; a monumental palm house with a 400-year-old cycad, the world's oldest plant in a pot (it blossomed in 1999, a rare event); an orangery with a very pleasant terrace; and of course the Hortus Medicus, the medicinal herb garden that attracts students from around the globe. The garden is open weekdays from 9 am to 5 pm, weekends from 11 am, in winter to 4 pm. Admission costs f7.50 (children f4.50); guided tours on Sunday at 2 pm cost f1.

The complex of buildings in front of the garden includes the Association for Nature & Environmental Education (☎ 622 81 15), Plantage Middenlaan 2C, which organises guided walks and other educational activities; and the Nature & Environmental Education Centre (☎ 622 54 04), Plantage Middenlaan 2E, an information centre for environmental and nature education.

Several buildings in the area serve as reminders of its Jewish past. The **Nationaal Vakbondsmuseum** (National Trade Union Museum; ☎ 624 11 66) at Henri Polaklaan 9 used to house the powerful General Netherlands Diamond Workers' Union, one of the pioneers of the Dutch labour movement under the chairmanship of Henri Polak. The displays won't be of great interest to foreigners but the building itself is definitely worth a look. The architect HP Berlage designed it as the union's headquarters in 1900

and it soon became known as the 'Burcht van Berlage', Berlage's Fortress – a play on Beurs van Berlage, the bourse along Damrak by the same architect.

Berlage considered it his most successful work and it's easy to see why, from the diamond-shaped pinnacle and the magnificent hall with its brick arches and decorated staircase, to the murals, ceramics and leadlight windows by famous artists of the day. The museum is open Tuesday to Friday from 11 am to 5 pm, Sunday from 1 pm, but is closed Saturday and on public holidays; admission costs f5 (f3 with discounts and for union members).

Around the corner, at Plantage Kerklaan 61A, is the **Verzetsmuseum** (Resistance Museum; ☎ 620 25 35), which provides an excellent insight into the difficulties faced by those who fought the German occupation from within. Labels in Dutch and English help with the exhibits, many of them interactive, that explain such issues as active and passive resistance, how the illegal press operated, how 300,000 people were kept in hiding, and how such activities were funded (a less glamorous but vital detail). The museum shows in no uncertain terms how much courage it takes to actively resist an adversary so ruthless that you can't trust neighbours, friends or even family. It's open Tuesday to Friday from 10 am to 5 pm, weekends from noon, and costs f8 (f4 with discounts). There's also a library.

Across the road, at Plantage Kerklaan 38–40, is the entrance to **Artis zoo** (Map 5; ☎ 523 34 00). The zoo was founded by an association called Natura Artis Magistra (Latin for 'Nature is the Master of Art') back in 1838, which makes it the oldest zoo on the European continent. Famous biologists have studied and worked here among the rich collection of mammals, birds, reptiles, amphibians, insects, fish, trees and plants. Unfortunately some of the cramped enclosures hardly seem to have progressed since the 19th century, but the zoo's layout – with ponds, statues and winding pathways through lush surroundings (remnants of some of the former Plantage gardens) – is very pleasant. Concerts and art exhibitions are also held here to observe the original aim of the association, which was to link nature and art.

A highlight of the zoo is the fascinating aquarium, the oldest in the country (1882) with some 2000 fish; its many exhibits include a cross-section of an Amsterdam canal. There's also a planetarium (Dutch commentary with a summary in English), and zoological and geological museums. The zoo is open daily from 9 am to 5 pm and entry costs f25 (children aged between 4 and 11 pay f17.50, free for toddlers). The fee includes the museums and the hourly shows at the planetarium. Lower prices are charged in September.

The **Hollandsche Schouwburg** (Holland Theatre; ☎ 626 99 45) at Plantage Middenlaan 24 played a tragic role during WWII. Originally it was the house of the director of Artis zoo across the road; it became the Artis Schouwburg in 1892 and was soon one of the centres of Dutch theatrical life. In WWII, however, the Germans turned it into a theatre by and for Jews, and from 1942 they made it a detention centre for Jews awaiting deportation. Some 60,000 of them passed through here on their way to Westerbork transit camp in the east of the country and from there to the death camps.

After the war no-one felt like reviving the theatre. In 1961 it was demolished except for the facade and the area immediately behind it. A 10m-high pylon in the former auditorium commemorates the country's Jews who were killed by the Germans. There's a memorial room and an exhibition room with videos and documents that display the building's tragic history. It's open daily from 11 am to 4 pm and admission is free.

Diagonally across the road, at Plantage Middenlaan 33, is the brightly coloured **Moederhuis** (Mothers' House), a refuge for young, single women awaiting childbirth. It was completed in 1981 to a design by Aldo van Eyck and incorporates the original 19th-century building to the right.

East of the Plantage

At the eastern end of Plantage Middenlaan, past the Artis aquarium and across the canal,

is Alexanderplein with the **Muiderpoort** (Map 7), a grim, Doric city gate dating from 1771. Just north-east of here, along Sarphatistraat, is the 250m facade of the **Oranje-Nassau Kazerne**, barracks built to house the French garrison but only finished in 1814, a year after the French left. They've now been converted to homes, offices and studios. The former drill yard along Singelgracht accommodates a remarkable row of six modern apartment blocks, each designed by an architect from a different country (from the Muiderpoort end: Japan, Greece, France, USA, Denmark, UK).

Just north of here, on Funenkade, stands an 18th-century grain mill known as **De Gooyer**, the sole survivor of five windmills that once stood in this part of the city. Originally it stood south-west of here but was moved to its current spot in 1814 when the Oranje-Nassau barracks stopped the wind. In 1985 the former public baths alongside, at Funenkade 7, were converted into **Bierbrouwerij 't IJ** (☎ 622 83 25), a small brewery producing 10 different beers, some seasonal, that can be tasted in the windmill Wednesday to Sunday from 3 to 7.45 pm. There's a tour of the brewery on Fridays at 4 pm.

North-East of the Plantage

When the Plantage was constructed in the 1680s, the original sea dyke was moved north to what are now the Hoogte Kadijk and Laagte Kadijk (the 'high section' and 'low section' of the 'quay dyke'). The stretch of water between the Plantage and this new sea dyke is the **Entrepotdok**, established in the 1820s as a storage zone for goods in transit. The 500m-long row of warehouses, once the largest storage depot in Europe, has been converted into desirable apartments and studios.

On the outer side of the dyke, at Hoogte Kadijk 147, is **Museumwerf 't Kromhout** (☎ 627 67 77), an 18th-century wharf that still repairs boats in its western hall. The eastern hall is now a museum devoted to shipbuilding and the early marine engines that were designed and built here. Anyone with an interest in marine engineering will love the place; others will probably want to move on. It's open Monday to Friday from 10 am to 4 pm and costs f3.50.

EASTERN ISLANDS (MAP 5)

The rapid expansion of seaborne trade led to the construction of new islands in the east of the harbour in the 1650s: the islands of Kattenburg, Wittenburg and Oostenburg.

The United East India Company set up shop on the eastern island of **Oostenburg**, where it established warehouses, rope yards, workshops and docks for the maintenance of its fleet. Private shipyards and dockworkers' homes dominated the central island of **Wittenburg** – the city architect Daniël Stalpaert's **Oosterkerk** (1671) on Wittenburgergracht was the last, and the least monumental, of the four 'compass churches' (the others were the Noorderkerk, Westerkerk and Zuiderkerk).

Admiralty offices and buildings arose on the western island of **Kattenburg**, and warships were fitted out in the adjoining naval dockyards that are still in use today.

The Republic's naval arsenal was housed in an imposing building at Kattenburgerplein 1, completed in 1656 to a design by Daniël Stalpaert. The admiralty vacated the building in 1973 and since 1981 it houses the **Nederlands Scheepvaartmuseum** (Netherlands Shipping Museum; ☎ 523 22 22), with one of the most extensive collections of maritime memorabilia in the world. If you only visit two or three museums in Amsterdam, make this one of them

It traces the history of Dutch seafaring from the ancient past to the present. Maritime trade, naval combat, fishing and whaling are all explained in interesting displays, including an engaging audiovisual re-enactment of a trip to the East Indies. Less inviting is the jar with bits of skin and flesh belonging to Lieutenant Jan van Speyk, who chose to blow up his ship rather than surrender to Belgian freedom fighters in the port of

Antwerp in 1831. There are some 500 models of boats and ships, and a stunning collection of charts and navigational material.

The full-scale replica of the East Indiaman ship moored alongside the museum was a make-work project for the chronically unemployed and was completed in 1991. It represents the United East India Company's 700-tonne *Amsterdam*, one of the largest ships of the fleet, that set sail on its maiden voyage in the winter of 1748–49 with 336 people on board but got stuck off the English coast near Hastings; there it became a famous shipwreck that has been much researched in recent years. Actors in 18th-century costume do their best to re-create shipboard life.

The museum is open Tuesday to Sunday from 10 am to 5 pm and costs f14.50 (various discounts). Admission to the *Amsterdam* is included in the entry fee. The Web site www.generali.nl/scheepvaartmuseum has more information.

West of this museum, the structure resembling a ship's bow on top of the IJ-Tunnel entrance is the **newMetropolis Science & Technology Center** (☎ 0900-919 11 00, f0.75 per minute), designed by the Italian architect Renzo Piano who also worked on the Centre Pompidou in Paris. It offers many interactive displays that are a delight for both children and grown-ups. Unfortunately it has been beset by financial and organisational problems since it opened in 1997 and its continued existence is by no means certain. It's open Tuesday to Sunday from

DOKKES LULOFS

Tall ships moored in the IJ, in the previous (1995) 'Sail Amsterdam' festival

10 am to 6 pm and costs f20, or f15 for children. Check the Web site www.newmet.nl for further details. The (free) rooftop 'plaza' affords a great view over the city.

Eastern Docklands

The eastern docklands north and east of the Eastern Islands show a lot of building activity – and a lot of to-ing and fro-ing between urban planners, financiers and council politicians over how to reconcile grandiose projects with affordable housing. North of Kattenburg is the **Oostelijke Handelskade** (Eastern Trade Quay), where the new passenger terminal caters for cruise ships. A bridge links this area to the **Java Eiland** farther north, where new housing estates enclose sheltered parks.

The eastern third of this island is known as the **KNSM Eiland**, named after the Royal Netherlands Steamship Company that based its ships here in the late-colonial period. It has now been transformed by an enormous housing project with pleasant, hyper-modern and overpriced apartment blocks that charm visiting architects. Opinions are divided but everybody seems to form one – worth a look. Some interesting cafés have opened up here too.

The **Open Haven Museum** (Open Harbour Museum; ☎ 418 55 22) at KNSM-laan 311 portrays the history of the harbour with creative use of material from the KNSM collection, and is rather boring unless you're interested in harbours, though you do get a great view of the harbour from the Compass Room. It's open Wednesday to Monday from 1 to 5 pm, and admission costs f3.50 (f3 with discounts).

South of here, the former **Sporenburg** and **Borneo** islands now have the highest population density in the country. None of the expensive houses here are freestanding, but they're designed in such a way that privacy is ensured and no-one looks into each other's rooms. The planning motto could be described as 'green is blue', meaning there aren't any trees or parks but lots of water and sky.

A tunnel under the water between Sporenburg and Borneo (the longest tunnel

in the country, which isn't saying much in a country that usually relies on bridges and dykes) links the Eastern Docklands to **IJburg**, a huge new housing project on a string of artificial islands in the IJsselmeer. On completion, IJburg will be home to 40,000 people served by 11 primary schools and its own cemetery. A small majority of Amsterdammers voted against the project in a referendum, but not enough people voted so the plan went ahead. Inhabitants of Durgerdam, a picturesque old village across the water, were livid about losing their view.

19th-Century Districts

The canal belt was a far-sighted project that sufficed for two-and-a-half centuries. There was no real pressure to expand beyond the canals until the 1860s, when the industrial revolution began to attract workers back to the city. In 1830 there were 200,000 inhabitants – 20,000 less than in the 18th century, due to Napoleon's disastrous Continental System. In 1860 this had picked up to 245,000, in 1880 to 320,000, and in 1900 to over 500,000.

This time the city's expansion was uncoordinated. There were several grand plans but none got past the proposal stage; private initiative and speculation reigned supreme. De Pijp, between the Amstel and Hobbemakade, was the first area to be added in the 1860s, full of dreary and shoddily built tenement blocks for the city's labourers. Farther west came the Vondelpark in the 1860s and 1870s, surrounded by upmarket housing. The last two decades of the 19th century were a free-for-all as investors grabbed other land beyond the canal belt and built new residential areas, often with very few restrictions. Old West (Oud West) around Kinkerstraat is a good example, though you'll have to be quick to see the worst buildings here before they're demolished to make way for modern social housing.

OLD SOUTH (OUD ZUID)

This wedge-shaped district is roughly bordered by the Vondelpark in the west and Hobbemakade in the east. Some people call it the Museum Quarter, Concertgebouw area or Vondelpark area, depending on which of these landmarks is closest. Fortunately it escaped the late-19th-century free-for-all. Wealthy investors wanted an upmarket area for themselves and saw to it that tenement blocks or businesses were prohibited here – a suitable spot for a grand national museum (the Rijksmuseum) and an equally grand new concert hall (the Concertgebouw).

In a rerun of the canal-belt scenario, the park and cultural centres were financed by the sale of plots of land to the highest bidders, who proceeded to build private mansions close to these attractive landmarks. It wasn't until the early decades of the 20th century, however, that the wealthy class deserted its mansions along Herengracht and Keizersgracht altogether.

In the 1920s, plots farther south that remained empty were filled with Amsterdam School-designed apartments commissioned by subsidised housing corporations. Good examples can be seen along **JM Coenenstraat** (Map 6; architect JF Staal) and in the adjoining **Harmoniehof** (Map 6), featuring the robust designs of JC van Epen.

Museum Quarter (Map 6)

Rijksmuseum The Museum Quarter's gateway – literally, with its pedestrian and bicycle underpass – is the 1885 Pierre Cuypers-designed Rijksmuseum (☎ 674 70 47). It bears a striking resemblance to Centraal Station, which was designed by the same architect and completed four years later. The museum's style is a mixture of neo-Gothic and Dutch Renaissance. Aspects of the former (towers, stained-glass windows) elicited criticism from Protestants including the king, who dubbed the building 'the archbishop's palace' (Cuypers was Catholic, and proudly so in his approach to architecture).

The Rijksmuseum was conceived as a repository for several national collections, including the royal art collection that was first housed in the palace on Dam Square and then in the Trippenhuis on Kloveniersburgwal. It's the country's premier art museum and one that no self-respecting visitor to Amsterdam can afford to miss – in fact, 1.2 million visitors flock here each year.

Some 5000 paintings are on display in 200 rooms, and many other works of art, so it pays to be selective if you don't want to spend days here. Grab the free floor plan when you buy your ticket and home in on the areas that interest you most – there are five major collections but you'll need the floor plan to find your way around them. The museum shop on the 1st floor sells guidebooks that describe the collections in more detail. Check the Web site at www .rijksmuseum.nl.

The most important collection, Paintings, consists of Dutch and/or Flemish masters from the 15th to 19th centuries, with emphasis on the 17th-century Golden Age. Pride of place is taken by Rembrandt's huge *Nightwatch* (1650) in room 224 on the 1st floor, showing the militia led by Frans Banningh Cocq, a future mayor of the city – the painting only acquired this name in later years because it had become dark with grime (it's nice and clean now). Room 211 shows earlier (and more colourful) works by Rembrandt. Other 17th-century Dutch masters on this floor include Jan Vermeer *(The Kitchen Maid*, also known as *The Milkmaid*, and *Woman in Blue Reading a Letter)*, Frans Hals *(The Merry Drinker)* and Jan Steen *(The Merry Family)*.

The museum's other collections are Sculpture & Applied Art (delftware, beautiful dolls' houses, porcelain, furniture), Dutch History (the Amsterdams Historisch Museum and Nederlands Scheepvaartmuseum do this better), Asiatic Art (including the famous 12th-century *Dancing Shiva*), and finally the Print Room, with changing exhibitions that can be surprisingly interesting depending on which of the 800,000 prints and drawings are on display when you visit.

From 2003 to 2005 most sections of the museum will be closed for a sweeping renovation that will cost several hundred million guilders and bring more 'air' and 'light' into the sometimes rather gloomy rooms. Only the top attractions will be on display and it's not yet clear what will happen with the rest.

The museum is open daily from 10 am to 5 pm and costs f15 (f7.50 with discounts, but no student discount). The main entrance faces the city centre at Stadhouderskade 42.

The **garden** at the back (free entry) has flowerbeds, fountains and an eclectic collection of stone memorabilia comprising statues, pillars and fragments of demolished buildings and monuments from all over the country. It's open Tuesday to Saturday from 10 am to 5 pm, Sunday from 1 pm.

Street musicians perform in the pedestrian and bicycle underpass beneath the museum, their sounds echoing off the cavernous walls. This passage leads to the large **Museumplein**, which hosted the World Exhibition in 1883 and hasn't had a clear purpose since. It has recently been transformed into a huge park, with an underground Albert Heijn supermarket under the 'dog-ear' bulge opposite the Concertgebouw. The name of the square is somewhat misleading because none of the museums actually face it.

Van Gogh Museum The next museum down, with its main entrance at Paulus Potterstraat 7, is the recently refurbished and expanded Van Gogh Museum (☎ 570 52 00) designed by Gerrit Rietveld (the recent expansion onto Museumplein, a separate exhibition wing designed by Kishio Kurosawa, is commonly known as 'the Mussel'). It opened in 1973 to house the collection of Vincent's younger brother Theo, which consists of about 200 paintings and 500 drawings by Vincent and his friends or contemporaries, such as Gauguin, Toulouse-Lautrec, Monet and Bernard.

Vincent van Gogh (pronounced 'khokh', rhyming with Scottish 'loch') was born in 1853 and had a short but very productive life. He didn't begin painting until 1881 and produced most of his works in the four years he spent in France, where he shot himself to escape mental illness in 1890 (he had already cut off his own ear after an argument with Gauguin). Famous works on display include *The Potato Eaters* (1885), a prime example of his sombre Dutch period, and *The Yellow House in Arles* (1888), *The Bedroom at Arles* (1888) and several self-portraits, sunflowers and other blossoms that show his vivid use of colour in the intense Mediterranean light. One of his last paintings, *Wheatfield with Crows* (1890), is an ominous work foreshadowing his suicide.

His paintings are on the 1st floor; the other floors display his drawings and Japanese prints as well as works by friends and contemporaries, some of which are shown in rotation. The museum is open daily from 10 am to 6 pm and costs f15.50 (f5 for children, free under 12 years). The library, with a wealth of reference material for serious study, is open Monday to Friday from 10 am to 12.30 pm and 1.15 to 5 pm.

Stedelijk Museum Next to the Van Gogh Museum is the Stedelijk Museum (☎ 573 29 11) at Paulus Potterstraat 13, the Municipal Museum that focuses on modern art – paintings, sculptures, photography and anything else that qualifies – from 1850 to the present. It's one of the world's leading museums of modern art, though this wasn't always the case: when the Dutch-Renaissance building opened its doors in 1895 it housed the private collection of art patroness Sophia de Bruijn, mainly bric-a-brac that was thrown out in subsequent years. Before WWII it evolved into the national museum of modern art, and under the driving force of its postwar curator, Willem Sandberg, it amassed the eclectic collection you can enjoy today.

This includes works by Monet, Van Gogh, Cézanne, Matisse, Picasso, Kirchner and Chagall as well as other modern 'classics', including a unique collection of some 50 works by the Russian artist Malevich. There are abstract works by Mondriaan, Van Doesburg and Kandinsky, and a large, post-WWII selection of creations by Appel (great mural in the café-restaurant), De Kooning, Newman, Ryman, Judd, Warhol, Dibbets, Baselitz, Dubuffet, Lichtenstein, Polke and Rietveld's furniture. Sculptures include works by Rodin, Renoir, Moore, Laurens and Visser. Some of these are on display in the sculpture garden overlooked by a pleasant café-restaurant that draws the glitterati of the (inter)national arts scene.

The museum displays most of its permanent collection in the summer months. At other times of the year many of the works make way for changing exhibitions that some people will consider pretentious nonsense while others will be ecstatic, though the planned expansion onto Museumplein should provide space for everything. It's open daily from 11 am to 5 pm and costs f9 (f4.50 with discounts); special exhibitions might cost extra. Grab a floor plan from the information desk to your left as you enter. Phone or check the Web site www.stedelijk.nl for lectures and art history courses.

Concertgebouw (Map 6)

The Concert Building at the end of Museumplein, at Concertgebouwplein 2-6, was completed in 1888 to a neo-Renaissance design by AL van Gendt. In spite of his limited musical knowledge, he managed to give the Grote Zaal (Great Hall) near-perfect acoustics that are the envy of concert hall designers worldwide.

The Concertgebouw attracts some 800,000 visitors a year, making it the busiest concert hall in the world. The best conductors and soloists consider it an honour to perform here – a far cry from the 1870s, when Brahms tried to knock the musicians in the Felix Meritis building into shape and had to admit they were lovely people but lousy musicians. Under the 50-year guidance of composer and conductor Willem Mengelberg (1871–1951), the Concertgebouw Orchestra (with the epithet 'Royal' since 1988) developed into one of the world's finest orchestras.

In the 1980s the Concertgebouw threatened to collapse because its 2000 wooden piles were rotting. Thanks to new technology the piles made way for a concrete

foundation, and the building was thoroughly restored to mark its 100th anniversary. The architect Pi de Bruin added a glass foyer along the south side that most people hate though everyone agrees it's effective.

The Grote Zaal seats 2000 people and is used for concerts. Recitals take place in the 19x15m Kleine Zaal (Small Hall), a replica of the hall in the Felix Meritis building.

Tickets are available on ☎ 671 83 45 daily between 10 am and 5 pm, or at the door till 7 pm (after 7 pm you can only get tickets for that evening's performance). The VVV and Amsterdam Uitburo (see Tourist Offices in the Facts for the Visitor chapter) also sell tickets. For free lunch-time concerts, turn up on Wednesday at 12.30 pm.

Vondelpark & Surroundings (Maps 1 & 6)

This English-style park, with ponds, lawns, thickets and winding footpaths, is about 1.5km long and 300m wide. Laid out on marshland beyond the canal belt in the 1860s and 1870s as a park for the bourgeoisie when the existing city park, the Plantage, became residential, it was soon surrounded by upmarket housing. It's named after the poet and playwright Joost van den Vondel (1587–1679), the Shakespeare of the Netherlands.

In the late 1960s and early 1970s the authorities turned the park into an open-air dormitory to alleviate the lack of accommodation for hordes of hippies who descended on Amsterdam. The sleeping bags have long since gone and it's now illegal to sleep in the park, but there's still evidence of Italian, French and Eastern European tourists stuck in the '70s.

The park is now used by joggers, in-line skaters, children chasing ducks or flying kites, couples in love, families with prams, acrobats practising or performing, teenagers playing soccer – in short, by anybody who enjoys very pleasant, green surroundings. It can get crowded on weekends but never annoyingly so. From June to August the park hosts free concerts in its **open-air theatre** (☎ 523 77 90 for information), an experience not to be missed, and there are always people performing music throughout the park. The functionalist **Round Blue Teahouse** (1936) serves coffee and cake. A stand near the Amstelveenseweg entrance at the south-western end of the park rents in-line skates and gloves for about f7 an hour.

At Vondelpark 3, close to Constantijn Huygensstraat, is the former Vondelpark Pavilion (1881), now home to the **Nederlands Filmmuseum** (☎ 589 14 00) which could well be moving to Rotterdam in the next few years. It has a large collection of memorabilia and a priceless archive of films that are screened in two theatres, often with live music and other accompaniments. One theatre contains the Art-Deco interior of Cinema Parisien, an early Amsterdam cinema. It's not a real museum as such with displays etc, but you can wander in from 10 am to 5 pm (closed Monday) and entry is free though there's a charge for film screenings (with discounts for students). The museum's charming Café Vertigo (☎ 612 30 21) is a popular meeting place, and an ideal spot to spend a couple of hours watching the goings-on in the park; on summer evenings there are films on the outdoor terrace.

The impressive **library** and study centre (☎ 589 14 35) adjoining the museum at Vondelstraat 69–71 is open Tuesday to Friday from 10 am to 5 pm, Saturday from 11 am. In 1980, the house at Vondelstraat 72, along with the intersection with Constantijn Huygensstraat, were the scene of one of the most dramatic episodes in the history of the squatter movement – see History in the Facts about Amsterdam chapter.

Also in Vondelstraat, near the Filmmuseum, is the **Vondelkerk** (1880), built to a design by Pierre Cuypers, which now accommodates offices. A few steps down the road at Vondelstraat 140 is the neoclassical **Hollandse Manege** (1882) designed by AL van Gendt, an indoor riding school inspired by the famous Spanish Riding School in Vienna. The building was fully restored in the 1980s, and it's worth walking through the passage to the door at the rear and up the stairs to the café, where you can sip a cheap beer or coffee while enjoying the beautiful interior and watching the instructor put the

horses through their paces. The school should be open daily but times vary – ring ☎ 618 09 42 to avoid disappointment.

Beyond the opposite side of the park is narrow, 19th-century **PC Hooftstraat**, a shopping street for the cream of society and the nouveau riche (note the parked Daimlers and Ferraris).

Beyond the south-western extremities of the park, at Amstelveenseweg 264 just north of the Olympic Stadium, is the former Haarlemmermeer Station which houses the **Tram Museum Amsterdam** (☎ 673 75 38). Historic trams sourced from all over Europe run between here and Amstelveen – a great outing for kids and adults. A return trip (f5, or f2.50 with discounts) takes more than an hour and skirts the large Amsterdamse Bos recreational area. Services operate on Sunday from 11 am to 5 pm between April and October, and Wednesday afternoon between May and September – contact the museum for a schedule.

DE PIJP (MAPS 1 & 6)

This district is enclosed by the Amstel in the east, Stadhouderskade in the north, Hobbemakade in the west and the Amstelkanaal in the south – it's actually a large island connected to the rest of the city by 16 bridges. The district's name, 'the Pipe' (originally the 'YY neighbourhood'), presumably reflects its straight, narrow streets that are said to resemble the stems of old clay pipes, but nobody really knows. There are a surprising number of attractions for an area that has so often been derided as the city's first 19th-century slum.

Its shoddy tenement blocks, some of which collapsed even as they were being built in the 1860s, provided cheap housing not just for newly arrived workers drawn by the city's industrial revolution, but also for students, artists, writers and other poverty-stricken individuals. In the 1960s and 1970s, as many of the working-class inhabitants left for greener pastures, the government began refurbishing the tenement blocks for immigrants from Morocco, Turkey, the Netherlands Antilles and Suriname. Now these immigrants are also moving out and the Pijp is attracting a slightly wealthier breed of locals who are doing up apartments and lending the neighbourhood a more gentrified air.

In the past as now, the Pijp has often been called the 'Quartier Latin' of Amsterdam thanks to its lively mix of people – labourers, intellectuals, new immigrants, prostitutes (in the city's other and very depressing redlight district along Ruysdaelkade opposite Hobbemakade), and now an increasing number of higher-income professionals.

This interesting array is best viewed at the **Albert Cuyp market**, Amsterdam's largest and busiest market, Monday to Saturday along Albert Cuypstraat. The emphasis is on food of every description and nationality but clothes and other general goods are on sale too, often cheaper than anywhere else. If you want to experience the 'real' Amsterdam at its multicultural best, this market is not to be missed. As always at busy markets, beware of pickpockets.

The surrounding streets hide cosy neighbourhood cafés and small (and usually very cheap) restaurants that offer a wide range of cuisines.

Many tourists head for the **Heineken Museum** (☎ 523 94 36) at Stadhouderskade 78, still commonly known as the Heineken Brewery. Tours of the former brewery complex are offered at 9.30 and 11 am weekdays all year, and from 1 June to 15 September extra tours are laid on at 1 and 2.30 pm. A token f2 donation to charity is collected at the door. The visit ends with a beer 'tasting' session at which several glasses per person may be consumed (they aren't stingy), and the green Heineken baseball caps sold at the exit for f7.50 make great souvenirs. Heineken's Web site is www.heineken.nl.

The brewery closed in 1988 due to inner-city congestion and since then the building has been used only for the tours and administration; the company's directorate is in the low-key premises across the canal.

Heineken beer is now brewed at a larger plant in 's-Hertogenbosch (Den Bosch) in the south of the country that opened in 1950, and since 1975 also at the largest brewery in Europe at Zoeterwoude near Leiden. The Heineken tours are a great favourite among beer-swilling backpackers who often come several times during their stay. If you can prove it's your birthday you get a free Delft-blue beer mug.

South of Albert Cuypstraat is the **Sarphatipark**, an English-style park named after the energetic 19th-century Jewish doctor and chemist Samuel Sarphati (1813–66). His diverse projects (a waste-disposal service, a slaughterhouse, a factory for cheap bread, trades and business schools, the Amstel Hotel, a mortgage bank) exasperated the dour city council, though many of these ventures survive to this day.

The street along the south side of the park is Ceintuurbaan, a traffic artery that holds little of interest except the so-called **Kabouterhuis** (Gnome House), near the Amstel at No 251–255. Its whimsical woodwork facade incorporates a couple of gnomes playing ball, a reference to the surname of the original owner, Van Ballegooijen ('of ball-throwing').

South of here, at Amsteldijk 67, is the neo-Renaissance **Gemeentearchief** (Municipal Archives; ☎ 572 02 02), housed in the former town hall of Nieuwer Amstel, a town annexed by Amsterdam during the late-19th-century expansion. Anyone interested in their family history or the history of the city can peruse the archives free of charge, and occasionally there are surprisingly interesting exhibitions. It's open Monday to Saturday from 10 am to 5 pm (closed Saturday in July and August).

South of Ceintuurbaan, the Pijp contains some of the most interesting examples of early-20th-century housing estates built in the Amsterdam School style. The imposing **Cooperatiehof**, surrounded by Burgemeester Tellegenstraat, was designed for the socialist housing corporation De Dageraad (The Dawn) by one of the main Amsterdam School architects, Piet Kramer. Another leading architect, Michel de Klerk, designed the idiosyncratic housing estates at Henriëtte Ronnerplein and Thérèse Schwartzeplein. As with other architecture of this school, the eccentric details are worth noting: vertically laid bricks, letterboxes as works of art, asymmetric windows, oddly shaped doorways, funny chimneys, creative solutions for corners and so forth.

OOSTERPARK DISTRICT (MAP 7)

This south-eastern district, named after the lush, English-style park lying at its centre, was built in the 1880s. At the time, the city's diamond workers suddenly found they had money to spare thanks to the discovery of diamonds in South Africa. About a third of Jewish families worked in the diamond industry in one way or another, and many of these could finally afford to leave the Jewish quarter for this new district beyond the Plantage (the delectable parklands where only the wealthiest could afford to live). Signs of this district's lower-middle-class heritage have long since disappeared and now it's depressingly similar to the other 19th century slums that arose around the canal belt.

The only exception, apart from the park, is the **Tropenmuseum** (☎ 568 82 00) at Linnaeusstraat 2, an impressive complex completed in 1926 to house the Royal Institute of the Tropics, still one of the world's leading research institutes for tropical hygiene and agriculture. Part of the building became a museum for the institute's collection of colonial artefacts, but this was overhauled in the 1970s to create the culturally aware and imaginatively presented displays you see today.

A huge central hall with galleries over three floors offers reconstructions of daily life in several tropical countries (a north African street, Javanese house, Indian village, African market etc). Separate exhibitions focus on music, theatre, religion, crafts, world trade and ecology, and there are special exhibitions throughout the year. Expert guides introduce children to tropical cultures in the separate children's section (☎ 568 82 33) reserved for six to 12-year-olds – book ahead, especially if you want your kids entertained in English (well worth the effort). There's an extensive library (☎ 568 82 54), a shop selling books and gifts and unique CDs, a pleasant café, a restaurant serving Third World cuisine, and the Tropeninstituut Theater (☎ 568 85 00), a theatre that screens films but also hosts music, dance, plays and other performances by visiting artists. Check the Institute's well-designed Web site at www.kit.nl.

The museum itself is open Monday to Friday from 10 am to 5 pm, weekends from noon, and costs f12.50 (f7.50, various discounts). It's a good place to spend a lazy Monday when most of the other museums are closed. There's a useful notice board for travellers, with lift shares, people looking for travel partners etc. The theatre has a separate entrance – phone for information and bookings (Monday to Friday between 10 am and 4 pm). The library is open Monday to Friday from 10 am to 4.30 pm, Sunday from noon.

Greater Amsterdam

The city's population stabilised at around 700,000 by 1920, which is still more or less the figure today. The authorities at the time didn't foresee this of course and cautiously expected 950,000 by the year 2000. Despite a slight pause during the Depression and WWII, the city kept gobbling up one outlying town after another as increased mobility fuelled urban sprawl.

NEW SOUTH (NIEUW ZUID) (MAP 1)

The Housing Act of 1901 set minimum standards for new houses and allowed the compulsory purchase and demolition of old houses that didn't meet these standards. The act also forced municipal authorities to come up with proper blueprints for city

THINGS TO SEE & DO

expansion. One such plan was the Plan Zuid of 1917 for the south of the city, drawn up by the progressive architect Berlage and insti- gated by the labour party alderman FM Wibaut. The result was New South, be- tween the Amstel and what was to become the Olympic Stadium.

Urban planners, architects and municipal authorities had not worked together so closely since the canal-belt project, suc- cessfully integrating solid housing and wide boulevards that enclosed quiet neighbour- hoods with cosy squares. There was even a canal linking the Amstel in the east with the Schinkel in the west: the Amstelkanaal that split in two about halfway along and re- joined again behind the Olympic Stadium. Subsidised housing corporations provided funding for innovative designs by architects of the Amsterdam School. Many of these architects worked for the city housing department, and the council preferred their designs to the functionalist designs of Berlage himself.

Funding cutbacks in the 1930s meant that these architects couldn't be as creative as they had been in their earlier designs, but even today the area is as elegant as it was then. Streets such as Churchillaan, Apollo- laan and Stadionweg are 'good' addresses. The area's main shopping street, Beethov- enstraat, is lined with expensive shops and other establishments for elderly women in fur coats.

Among the first residents were Jewish refugees from Germany and Austria, many of them writers and artists, who settled around Beethovenstraat. The Frank family lived at Merwedeplein farther to the east, where Churchillaan and Rooseveltlaan merge around the **'Skyscraper'** (1930), a 12-storey building with spacious luxury apartments designed by JF Staal.

South-west of here is the **RAI** exhibition and conference centre (☎ 549 12 12, fax 646 44 69) at Europaplein 8, the largest

such complex in the country. It opened in the early 1960s and new halls are still being added. There's always some sort of exhib- ition or trade fair going on: cars, two- wheelers, boats, camping gear – ring to find out. The name comes from the regular exhibitions hosted earlier this century by the Rijwiel & Automobiel Industrie (Bicycle & Car Industry).

AMSTELVEEN (MAP 1)

This suburb south of Amsterdam has a long history. In the 12th century it was a moor drained by the Amstel (*veen* means peat). Local farmers built canals to drain the land for agricul-

ture, thus turning the Amstel into a clearly defined river. As the soil along the Amstel compacted, the farming community moved farther west, which is why the west bank of the Amstel at this latitude is relatively uninhabited today. There's not much to draw you to Amstelveen, but a couple of attractions are worth considering.

First there's the **Amsterdamse Bos** (Am- sterdam Woods), a large recreational area built as a work-creation project in the 1930s. Amsterdammers flock here on week- ends but it's so huge (940 hectares) that it never gets too crowded. It's open 24 hours a day free of charge, and its only drawback is that it's close to Schiphol and a lot of low-flying aircraft.

The visitors centre (☎ 643 14 14) is at Nieuwe Kalfjeslaan 4 and is open daily from 10 am to 5 pm. There are lakes, wooded areas and meadows, an animal enclosure with bison, a goat farm, paths for walking, cycling and horse-riding, a rowing course (the Bosbaan, with several water craft for hire), an open-air theatre (☎ 638 38 47) with plays in summer, a sport park, a pancake house, a forestry museum (☎ 645 45 75, open daily from 10 am to 5 pm, Sun- day from 1 pm, free admission; displays about the construction, and flora and fauna, of the area) and much more. You can get

THINGS TO SEE & DO

here by historic tram from the Haarlem-mermeer Station (see the earlier Vondelpark & Surroundings section) or with bus No 170, 171 or 172 from Centraal Station. Rent a bike at the main entrance at Van Nijen-rodeweg.

The other main attraction is the **CoBrA Museum** (☎ 547 50 50), Sandbergplein 1–3 just north of the A9 freeway's Amstelveen exit and opposite the Amstelveen bus terminal (bus No 170, 171 or 172 from Centraal Station, or tram No 5 but that's a 10-minute walk). The CoBrA artistic movement was formed in the postwar years by artists from Denmark, Belgium and the Netherlands – the name consists of the first letters of their respective capital cities. Members included Asger Jorn, Corneille, Constant and the great Karel Appel (see Painting in the Facts about Amsterdam chapter). The Stedelijk Museum has a good collection of their work but this museum in Amstelveen is the treasure trove with paintings, ceramics, statuary, creative typography, the lot. It's open Tuesday to Sunday from 11 am to 5 pm and costs f7.50 (f5 or f3.50 with discounts).

AMSTERDAM NORTH (NOORD) (MAPS 1 & 3)

In the dim, dark past, the area across the IJ now known as Amsterdam North was marshland with shifting contours. Roman sentries may have stared at it and glimpsed the barbar-ians beyond their empire. Several hundred years ago its tip was known as Volewyck, a place where executed criminals were left to be devoured by crows and dogs. Few people actually lived here.

As ships became larger and the sandbanks in the IJ posed more of a problem, engineers built an 80km canal, the Noordhollands Kanaal (North Holland Canal), from Volewyck right up to Den Helder in the northern tip of Holland. It opened in 1824 but by 1876 it was replaced by the more

efficient Noordzeekanaal (North Sea Canal) west to IJmuiden. Amsterdam North wasn't properly colonised until the turn of the 20th century, and the opening of the IJ-Tunnel in 1968 finally established a fixed connection.

The area is predominantly working-class, offering glimpses of authentic Dutch life away from the tourists in the old town. Forget about it if you're pressed for time, but otherwise it's worth spending half a day exploring the older parts of the area on foot or by bicycle (preferably by bicycle if the weather is less than perfect).

Take the free pedestrian ferry marked 'Buiksloterwegveer' (between Pier 8 and Pier 9) from behind Centraal Station across the IJ to the Shell Oil installations at Buiksloterweg, where you'll disembark next to the **Noordhollands Kanaal**. Climb up onto the first lock, the Willemsluis near the ferry wharf, for the view. Return to the main street and walk north 10 minutes on Van der Pekstraat. Ahead you'll eventually see the massive Golden Tulip Waterfront Hotel, formerly Amsterdam North's general hospital. Today it's used mostly by European tourists on bus tours.

A passageway to the right of the hotel leads into **Mosveld** where a large public market is held on Wednesday, Friday and Saturday (the best days to do this walk). The market is used almost exclusively by local residents and seldom sees any tourists.

To return to central Amsterdam, catch bus No 34 or 35 from the stop next to the large **Egyptian Coptic Church** (the only one in Holland) on Mosplein. These buses go through the IJ-Tunnel straight back to Centraal Station.

If you have a bit more time, take any street east to the Noordhollands Kanaal, which you follow north through **Florapark**. You'll pass a public swimming pool and reach a small bridge which crosses another lock on the canal. The old road on both sides of this bridge is lined with picturesque little Dutch cottages. Don't cross the canal but continue north along its west bank and you'll come to a large windmill, the **Krijtmolen**, originally used to grind chalk, with a children's animal park alongside (free).

Just north of here is Amsterdam North's massive public hospital where you can catch bus No 34 back to town. This interesting walk could easily fill a morning or afternoon; by bicycle it would take a couple of leisurely hours.

'GARDEN CITIES'

The outer suburbs west of Amsterdam – **Geuzenveld**, **Bos en Lommer**, **Slotermeer**, **Osdorp** and **Slotervaart** – were planned in the 1930s as part of the city's grand General Extension

Plan and were fully established after WWII to meet the continued demand for housing, made ever more acute by the demographic shift away from extended families. These spacious new estates, known as 'garden cities' *(tuinsteden)*, with carefully planned traffic systems, lakes, sporting fields, greenery and abundant natural light, represented the latest thinking in suburban living but seem rather dreary and windswept today.

Similar concepts dominated the massive Bijlmermeer housing project south-east of the city, now simply called the **Bijlmer**. The huge apartment blocks, laid out in a honeycomb pattern around artificial parks, were considered most progressive when the foundations were laid in the mid-1960s. By the time they were finished in the early 1970s, however, most people with a choice in the matter avoided such an environment and the area was doomed to become an instant slum, inhabited by Creole immigrants from the Netherlands Antilles, black immigrants from newly independent Suriname, and anyone else who couldn't afford to live elsewhere.

In October 1992 the Bijlmer made world headlines when an El Al freighter jumbo crashed into one of the apartment complexes after take-off from Schiphol, just as residents were settling in to their evening meals. Officially 45 people died in the inferno but the figure was probably higher, despite the subsequent amnesty on illegal immigrants.

Activities

Soccer, ice skating, cycling, tennis, swimming and sailing are just a few activities that keep the locals fit – and of course jogging, which is popular in the Vondelpark and other parks. The Amsterdamse Bos has several walking and jogging trails for serious exercise. Het Twiske, near Landsmeer north of Amsterdam (bus No 91 or 92 from Centraal Station), is another recreational area with nature trails, cycle routes, rentals of water craft, beaches and a children's swimming pool and playground; for information, ring Het Twiske on ☎ 075-684 43 38.

The whole coast of Holland, from the Hook of Holland right up to Den Helder, is one long beach, backed by often picturesque dunes that are ideal for walks. The closest seaside resort is Zandvoort (see the Excursions chapter) which can get packed in summer (forget about parking then – take the train), but more pleasant resorts can be found farther north, such as Castricum north of IJmuiden, or Egmond and Bergen a bit farther north near Alkmaar.

For information about sport and leisure activities and venues, visit the city hall information centre (☎ 624 11 11) at Amstel 1 in the arcade between the Stopera and the city hall, or ring the Amsterdam Sport Service on ☎ 552 24 90. Local community centres (consult the phone book under *Buurtcentrum*) organise fitness courses.

See Spectator Sports in the Entertainment chapter for details about soccer, field hockey or the Dutch sport of korfball.

FITNESS CENTRES

These are listed in the pink pages of the phone book under *Fitnesscentra*. To pump iron, head for Barry's Fitness Centre (☎ 626 10 36), Lijnbaansgracht 350, though the loud disco music might not be to everyone's taste. A day card is f20 and a monthly pass is f110. For aerobics and feelgood activities, including sauna, massage, physiotherapy and dietary advice, try The Garden Gym (☎ 626 87 72), Jodenbreestraat 158. A one-day pass ranges from

Walking Tours

Amsterdam is tailor-made for walking. You could simply follow your nose or, if a particular area takes your fancy, you could explore it with the previous text.

Alternatively, you could follow one or more of the official VVV walks designed by the ANWB (the Dutch automobile association) that are indicated on the maps in the back of this book and on occasional public maps at points en route. They take you through the most interesting parts of the city, though by necessity they do bypass some of the sights (make your own detours). Obviously they can be walked in either direction and you can combine them or jump from one to the other:

- **Red route** – probably gives the best overview of some of the most attractive areas. Starts at Centraal Station and goes along Nieuwendijk, the Dam, Kalverstraat, Spui Square (Begijnhof), Leidsestraat, Leidseplein, and finally Museumplein, ending at the Concertgebouw. You could return via the Grey route.
- **Blue route** – a bit of a west-east marathon. Starts at the Westerkerk (Anne Frankhuis) and heads into the city along Raadhuisstraat; passes Dam Square and continues east through the red-light district; on to Jodenbreestraat and the Jewish quarter; up towards the old harbour area north-east of the Plantage and on to the Tropenmuseum.
- **Green route** – shorter alternative to the Blue route. Starts at Centraal Station and follows the Zeedijk to Nieuwmarkt Square (detour for the red-light district), through the Jewish quarter and then the Plantage before ending at the Tropenmuseum. It could be tacked on to the Blue route to make a full day trip.
- **Grey route** – combines the old medieval centre with glimpses of authentic daily life just south of the canal belt; starts at Centraal Station and goes down Damrak and Rokin to Rembrandtplein; along beautiful Reguliersgracht; then past the Heineken Museum to the Albert Cuyp market (multicultural Amsterdam at its best); and on to the Concertgebouw (detour southwards to Harmoniehof for Amsterdam School architecture); could return via the Red route.
- **Purple route** – starts at either the ship-passenger terminal or Centraal Station and goes past the IJ-Tunnel entrance (newMetropolis Science & Technology Center) to Waterlooplein; then on to Rembrandtplein and Muntplein, and through Nieuwe Spiegelstraat (antiques) to Leidseplein; return via the Brown route or latch on to the Red route.
- **Brown route** – goes past and through the Jordaan area (make your own detours), starting at Centraal Station and ending at Leidseplein.

f16.50 to f23.50, a monthly pass from f77.50 to f122.50.

New Age

Oininio (Map 2; ☎ 553 93 55) at Prins Hendrikkade 20–21, near Centraal Station opposite Hotel Ibis, is a New Age activities centre offering esoteric reflection in a high-tech mould. Downstairs is a grand café, tea garden, specialist bookstore and ditto supermarket, upstairs are several therapeutic centres (yoga etc), and on the top floor is a sauna. There's also a vegetarian restaurant overlooking the café. The Oininio Passage leads into the same complex from Nieuwendijk 25. It's definitely worth a visit,

even if you don't consider yourself a New Age type, though it's beset by financial difficulties and may have closed by the time you read this (which would be a real shame).

Saunas

Saunas are mixed and there's no prudish swimsuit nonsense, though they do cater for people who have a problem with this – ask.

Deco (Map 4; ☎ 623 82 15), Herengracht 115, is a respectable, elegant sauna with good facilities including a snack bar. The building itself is an early creation of the architect HP Berlage and its Art-Deco furnishings used to grace a Parisian department store. It's open Monday to Saturday from

AMERENS HEDWICH

Rijksmuseum, the grand national museum of the Netherlands, is a must-see for art lovers.

AMERENS HEDWICH

The ubiquitous canal house souvenirs

ELLIOT DANIEL

Reliefs on the former PC Hooft store, showing aspects of tobacco preparation

AMERENS HEDWICH

ZAW MIN YU

ELLIOT DANIEL

ELLIOT DANIEL

Trumpet player and singer
CHET BAKER
died here on May 13th 1988
He will live on in his music
for anyone willing
to listen and feel

From phallic monuments to fake Romans – spot the real human (clue: he's clothed).

11 am to 11 pm, Sunday from 1 to 6 pm. There's a reduced admission of f19.50 weekdays from 11 am to 2 pm, at other times it's f27.50. You can also have massages and beauty therapies.

In the Oininio complex (see preceding section), the top-floor sauna (☎ 553 93 11) costs f23.50 to use before 5 pm, or f29 thereafter. The rickety, antique elevator is an experience in itself. After your sauna, relax in a hammock on the huge roof terrace and enjoy the splendid view.

The Eastern Bath House/Hammam (☎ 681 48 18), Zaanstraat 88 in the northwest beyond the Haarlemmerpoort, is a Turkish bath house for women only (Sunday and Monday men only).

Gay Mandate (Map 4; ☎ 625 41 00), Prinsengracht 715, is a beautiful 18th-century canal house with a very modern, gay-only sport school and sauna; it's open weekdays from 11 am to 10 pm, Saturday from noon to 6 pm and Sunday from 2 to 6 pm. The large Thermos Day Sauna (Map 4; ☎ 623 91 58), Raamstraat 33, is a popular place for sexual contacts, with porn movies and private (or not so private) areas; it's open weekdays from noon to 11 pm, weekends to 10 pm, and admission costs f30. The Thermos Night Sauna (Map 4; ☎ 623 49 36), Kerkstraat 58–60, is similar to the day sauna except there's no restaurant; admission also costs f30 and it's open from 11 pm to 8 am.

SWIMMING POOLS

There are indoor pools and summer outdoor pools. It's always best to ring ahead to ensure the pool is open to the general public (English is almost always spoken) because there are often restricted sessions – nude, Muslim, children, women, seniors, clubs, swimming lengths etc. Of course that might just be what you're after, but schedules for these sorts of sessions change constantly.

Flevoparkbad (Map 1; ☎ 692 50 30), Zeeburgerdijk 630, east of the city centre – outdoor pool only; open May to September from 10 am to 5.30 pm

Brediusbad (Map 1; ☎ 682 91 16), Spaarndammerdijk 306, north-west of the city centre – outdoor pool only; open May to September from 10 am to 5 pm

Marnixbad (Map 2; ☎ 625 48 43), Marnixplein 5–9, at the western end of Westerstraat – indoor pool only, closed in July and August, admission f4.75/4 for adults/children

Jan van Galenbad (Map 1; ☎ 612 80 01), Jan van Galenstraat 315, west of the city centre – outdoor pool only, open mid-May to August

Sloterparkbad (Map 1; ☎ 613 37 00), Slotermeerlaan 2, in the western suburbs next to the terminus of tram No 14 – in an attractive recreational area with yacht harbour etc; both indoor and outdoor pools (on cold, rainy days in summer the indoor pool will also be open); outdoor pools can get overcrowded but there's a less frequented nudist island reached by walking straight back past the pools and across a causeway; admission is f5 for anyone aged over 3

De Mirandabad (Map 1; ☎ 642 80 80), De Mirandalaan 9, south of the city centre – tropical 'aquatic centre' complete with beach and wave machine; indoor and outdoor pools; open all year; f6.25 for anyone aged over 3

Bijlmersportcentrum (Map 1; ☎ 697 25 01), Bijlmerpark 76, Bijlmer – indoor and outdoor pools; open all year except public holidays; f5.25/4.75 for adults/children

Floraparkbad (Map 1; ☎ 632 90 30), Sneeuwbalweg 5, Amsterdam North – indoor and outdoor pools; open all year; f6.35/5.30 for adults/children

SAILING

Keen sailors shouldn't miss Sail 2000 from 24 to 28 August 2000, when more than 1000 sailing ships from around the world will converge on Amsterdam to strut their stuff up and down the IJ and attend the finish of the Cutty Sark Tall Ships' Race. See Public Holidays & Special Events in the Facts for the Visitor chapter.

The Dutch are avid sailors – windsurfing in particular is a national sport. On weekends a fleet of restored flat-bottomed boats, called the 'brown fleet' because of their (reddish) brown sails, crisscross the watery expanse of the IJsselmeer. Some are privately owned but many are rented, and sailing one is an unforgettable experience. The cheapest options are *botters*, former fishing boats with long, narrow leeboards and sleeping space (usually for around eight people) below deck. Larger groups could rent a converted freight barge known as a *tjalk*, originally with jib and spritsail rig though modern designs are made of steel and have diesel motors. Other vessels include anything from ancient pilot boats to massive clippers.

Costs are quite reasonable if you can muster a group of fellow enthusiasts. Some places only rent boats for day trips but it's much more fun to go for the full weekend experience. The usual arrangement is that you arrive at the boat Friday at 8 pm, sleep on board, sail out early the next morning, and visit several places around the IJsselmeer before returning on Sunday between 4 and 6 pm. Food is not included in the packages, nor is cancellation insurance (trips are cancelled if wind is stronger than 7 Beaufort), but you do get a skipper.

Contact the following companies to find the deal that suits you best, and bear in mind that everything is negotiable:

Hollands Glorie (☎ 0294-27 15 61, fax 26 29 43), Ossenmarkt 6, Muiden – weekend trips from 8 pm Friday to 5 pm Sunday; in the high season (May to September) a tjalk costs f1400 (maximum 14 people), and a clipper for a large group of people costs f4700; there are also weekly arrangements, eg, a tjalk from Monday to Sunday from f3000, and many other options; in March, April and October prices are discounted by 10%

Zeilcharter Volendam (☎ 0299-36 97 40, fax 36 34 42), Enkhuizerzand 21, Volendam – a botter costs f800 per day (10 am to 6 pm, maximum 12 people); there are also more expensive boats, eg, a modern yacht for up to eight people at f995 per day (f2400 for a weekend, f4890 for a week)

Holland Zeilcharters (☎ 0299-65 23 51, fax 65 36 18), Monnickendam – botters from f700 per day (12 to 14 people) and many other options

Muiden Jacht Charter (☎ 0294-26 14 13, fax 26 10 04), Naarderstraat 10, Muiden – has four botters costing from f600 per day (10 am to 6 pm, maximum 20 people); a weekend costs from f1250

ICE SKATING

When the canals freeze over in winter (which doesn't happen often enough) everyone goes for a skate. Lakes and waterways in the countryside also fill up with colourfully clad skaters making trips tens of kilometres long. It's a wonderful experience, though painful on the ankles and butt if

DOEKES LULOFS

Awaiting a beer on ice

you're learning. Be aware also that people drown under ice every year. Don't take to a patch of ice unless you see large groups of people, and be very careful at the edges and under bridges (such areas often don't freeze properly).

You can only rent skates at a skating rink. A pair of simple hockey skates costs upwards of about f100 at a department store (sports shops might have a wider selection but tend to be more expensive). Hockey skates are probably the best choice for learners: figure skates (with short, curved blades) are difficult to master, and speed skates (with long, flat blades) put a lot of strain on the ankles – though they're definitely the go if you want to make serious trips. Check for second-hand skates on notice boards at supermarkets or at the Centrale Bibliotheek (Central Library), Prinsengracht 587. Old wood-framed skates that you tie under your shoes can be picked up cheaply at antique and bric-a-brac shops. Don't dismiss them: they're among the fastest skates around if they're freshly sharpened, and make great souvenirs.

The Jaap Edenbaan (Map 1; ☎ 694 98 94), Radioweg 64 in the eastern suburb of Watergraafsmeer (tram No 9), has an indoor and outdoor rink.

TENNIS & SQUASH

The huge Borchland Sportcentrum (☎ 563 33 33), Borchlandweg 8–12, next to the Arena stadium in the Bijlmer (metro:

Duivendrecht or Strandvliet, or the Ouder-kerk aan de Amstel exit of the A2/E35 free-way towards Utrecht), has tennis, squash and badminton courts, bowling alleys and other facilities including a restaurant.

Tenniscentrum Amstelpark (☎ 301 07 00), Karel Lotsylaan 8, has 42 open and covered courts and runs the country's biggest tennis school. It's conveniently close to the World Trade Center and RAI exhibition buildings.

Squash City (Map 2; ☎ 626 78 83), Ketelmakerstraat 6 at the railway line at Bickerseiland (west of Centraal Station), charges f28 (f37 in the evenings) for two people to use a squash court; a combination ticket for court plus gym and sauna is f23.50 per person (f28.50 in the evenings).

More courts are listed under *Tennisbanen* and *Squashbanen* in the pink pages of the phone book.

CHESS
The Max Euwe Centrum (Map 6; ☎ 625 70 17), Max Euweplein 30A1 off Leidseplein, has a permanent exhibition devoted to the history of chess and to the country's one and only world chess champion, for whom the centre is named. You can play against live or digital opponents. Admission is free and it's open from 10.30 am to 4 pm Tues-day to Friday plus the first Saturday of the month. At other times, chess enthusiasts can be found in Schaakcafé 't Hok (☎ 624 31 33), Lange Leidsedwarsstraat 134.

GOLF
The main problem with golf in this country is lack of space and the consequent lack of affordable golf courses. The sport was long derided as something for the elite but has become increasingly popular in recent years.

Golfcenter Amstelborgh (☎ 563 33 33), Borchlandweg 6 adjoining the Borchland Sportcentrum (see the earlier Tennis & Squash section), has nine holes and charges f20; club rental is f15 for half a set. It's open daily all year (closed 1 January and 25 December). Openbare Golfbaan Sloten (☎ 614 24 02), Sloterweg 1045 on the south-west side of town (bus No 142), also

has nine holes and charges f21.50 weekdays or f27.50 weekends (play as many rounds as you like); club rental is f12.50 for half a set. It's open weekdays all year and in sum-mer on weekends too.

Look under *Golfbanen* in the pink pages of the phone book for several other options.

BUNGY JUMPING
Bungy Jump Holland (Map 3; ☎ 419 60 05), Oostelijke Handelskade 1 at the waterfront half a kilometre east of Centraal Station, offers jumps from a crane suspended 75m above the water, from noon to 9 pm seven days a week in July and August (Thursday to Monday in May and June, Thursday to Sunday in October). It's expensive (f100 for the first jump, f75 for the second or f400 for 10) but if you can keep your nerves under control you'll never forget the view.

Courses

The Foreign Student Service is a support agency for foreign students that supplies information about study programs and in-tensive language courses. For more details about this organisation, or about study at academic level, see Universities in the Facts for the Visitor chapter.

LANGUAGE COURSES
Dutch is a close relative of English but that doesn't make it easy to learn. Regular courses take months and intensive courses last several weeks. Plan ahead and make inquiries well in advance.

The Volksuniversiteit Amsterdam (☎ 626 16 26), Rapenburgerstraat 73, 1011 VK Amsterdam, offers a range of day and evening courses that are well regarded and don't cost a fortune. The Tropeninstituut (Royal Institute for the Tropics) has in-tensive training courses with a large component of 'cultural training', aimed specifically at foreigners moving to the Netherlands; they're fairly expensive but very effective. Contact the Language Train-ing department (☎ 568 85 59) at Postbus 95001, 1090 HA Amsterdam (or visit the

THINGS TO SEE & DO

Web site www.kit.nl). The British Language Training Centre (☎ 622 36 34), Nieuwezijds Voorburgwal 328E, 1012 RW Amsterdam, is also expensive and has a good reputation.

OTHER COURSES

The above-mentioned Volksuniversiteit offers a range of courses, some in English. The Amsterdam Summer University (☎ 620 02 25), Keizersgracht 324, 1016 EZ Amsterdam, conducts all its courses and workshops in English. Subjects focus on arts and sciences, as befits the traditions of the Felix Meritis building that houses it.

Also inquire at museums: the Stedelijk Museum, for instance, conducts courses in art history.

For courses in yoga, relaxation massage, acupuncture, herbalism and so forth, contact the Oininio centre (Map 2; ☎ 553 93 55), Prins Hendrikkade 20–21 diagonally opposite Centraal Station.

The city hall information centre (☎ 624 11 11), Amstel 1 in the arcade between the Stopera and the city hall, has lots of information about informal courses and workshops (cooking, pottery, needlework, car repairs, stamp-collecting – you name it). Most or all of these are in Dutch but that shouldn't be an insurmountable problem. To find out about similar activities in your neighbourhood, contact the nearest community centre listed under *Buurtcentrum* in the phone book.

Places to Stay

Amsterdam attracts many tourists throughout the year – book ahead if you want a 'good' place to stay. Even camping grounds can be filled to capacity in summer. It's worth paying a bit extra for something reasonably central so you can enjoy the nightlife without having to rely on night buses or the most expensive taxis in Europe. This doesn't mean having to stay within the canal belt: accommodation in the Museum Quarter or around the Vondelpark, for instance, is well within walking distance of the lively Leidseplein area.

Theft is not uncommon at camping grounds or in dormitories (bring your own padlock for the locker) but is rare in 'normal' hotel rooms. It's always wise to deposit valuables for safe keeping at the reception desk. Some hotels have coin-operated safety deposit boxes in the rooms (f1 per usage).

Ask about parking if travelling by car. In almost all cases parking is a major problem and the most you'll get is a (payable) parking permit out on the street – with all the attendant headaches and security risks – or a referral to the nearest parking garage (at up to f60 a day) that may be a fair distance away. The top-end hotels have their own expensive parking arrangements but like to be warned in advance.

CAMPING GROUNDS

There are several camping grounds in and around Amsterdam, but the four listed here seem to be the most popular and accessible. The Vliegenbos and Zeeburg sites attract crowds of young people, the other two sites are more suited to older campers and families. At the time of research none of these camping grounds had finalised their rates for the coming season, so expect prices to be slightly higher than quoted here. The Vliegenbos, Zeeburg and Amsterdamse Bos sites also rent out cabins with different bed configurations that can work out as cheaply as f15 to f25 per person – ideal for families.

Camping Vliegenbos (Map 3; ☎ 636 88 55, fax 632 27 23, Meeuwenlaan 138), in Amsterdam North, is open from April to September and is probably the most convenient camping ground for people without a car. Tent campers pay f14.25 per person, tent site included (car is f5.50 extra). From Centraal Station, take bus No 32 or night bus No 72. Alternatively, hop aboard the free *Adelaarswegveer*, the ferry from Pier 8 behind Centraal Station (bicycles and mopeds are also carried free). From the other side, it's a 20-minute walk or five-minute ride by bicycle. When this ferry doesn't operate (see Boat – Ferries in the Getting Around chapter), take the larger, 24-hour *Buiksloterwegveer* (between Piers 8 and 9) straight across the IJ and walk across the locks of the Noordhollands Kanaal, which adds five minutes to the trip on foot.

Camping Zeeburg (Map 1; ☎ 694 44 30, fax 694 62 38, Zuider IJdijk 20) is in an industrial area on an artificial island east of the city, near a huge bridge over the IJ (bus No 22 from Centraal Station or No 37 from Amstelstation, or tram No 14 from Dam Square). It's not as bad as it sounds: the nearby Flevopark has walking trails, a swimming pool and sporting facilities. Camping costs f7.50 per person, f5 per tent, and parking is f7.50. It's open from March to December.

Camping Het Amsterdamse Bos (☎ 641 68 68, fax 640 23 78, Kleine Noorddijk 1, Aalsmeer) is open from April to October. It's a long way south-west of town in the southern extremities of the Amsterdamse Bos, but bus No 171 from Centraal Station provides a painless connection. The noise from nearby Schiphol airport can be annoying but the recreational facilities in the Amsterdamse Bos are great. It costs f8.75 per person, f5.50 per tent and f4.75 per car.

Gaaspercamping (☎ 696 73 26, fax 696 93 69, Loosdrechtdreef 7, Gaasperdam) is in a large park-cum-recreational area in the south-eastern suburbs (metro to Gaasper-plas, then a 500m walk). It costs f6.75 per person, f7.25 per tent and f6.25 per car, and is open from mid-March to December. This place is also pleasant for backpackers.

HOSTELS
Official Youth Hostels

The head office of the Netherlands Youth Hostel Association (NJHC; Map 7; ☎ 551 31 33, fax 639 01 99) is at Professor Tulpplein 4, 1018 GX Amsterdam (ironically, in front of the Amstel Inter-Continental Hotel, the most luxurious hotel in the country). The association uses the Hostelling International logo for the benefit of foreigners but has kept the 'youth hostel' name. For information about youth hostels, call ☎ 551 31 55.

A youth hostel card (or rather, an International Guest Card) costs f30 at this office or at the hostels; alternatively, nonmembers pay an extra f5 a night for a bed and after six nights they're a member. HI or NJHC members can get discounts on international travel (eg, 10% discount on Eurolines tickets) and pay less commission on money exchange at the GWK (official exchange) offices. Members and nonmembers have the same rights at the hostels and there are no age limits.

Bookings are strongly advised in summer – a phone call to the hostel is enough. Apart from the usual dormitories there are rooms for two, four, six and eight people that are often used by families (single rooms are normally reserved for bus drivers). These should be booked well ahead in busy periods (spring, summer and autumn holidays) and rates vary considerably – inquire at the hostel.

The **Stadsdoelen Youth Hostel** *(Map 4; ☎ 624 68 32, Kloveniersburgwal 97)*, near the red-light district in the old town, is very central and charges f28 for members. There's a 2 am curfew, though the door is opened at a quarter past the hour to let people in and out.

The **City Hostel Vondelpark** *(Map 6; ☎ 589 89 96, Zandpad 5)*, which is more or less in the Vondelpark, is probably the most pleasant of the two HI hostels and is certainly the busiest, with 300,000 guests a year. There have been quite a few reports of theft, so mind your valuables. Members pay f33.75/38 for a dorm bed in the low/high season including breakfast, and double rooms go for f90/125. There's no curfew.

The **Haarlem Youth Hostel** *(☎ 023-537 37 93, Jan Gijzenpad 3)*, in Haarlem, charges f28, with surcharges for double and quad rooms. Rules include 10 pm silence but there's no curfew (the room key is also the front door key). It's a 10-minute walk from Santpoort Zuid train station (trains to/from Amsterdam pass every half-hour and take 24 minutes) or you can take bus No 2 to/from Haarlem Centraal (more frequent trains).

Other Hostels

'Unofficial' hostels are reluctant to take bookings over the phone and seem to prefer walk-in trade. Try getting there by 10 am and you should stand a reasonable chance.

Christian backpackers will feel right at home in **Christian Youth Hostel Eben Haëzer** *(Map 4; ☎ 624 47 17, fax 627 61 37, Bloemstraat 179)* in the Jordaan. A bed costs f23 including breakfast, there's a 2 am curfew, and the age limit is 35. A similar setup is **Christian Youth Hostel 'The Shelter'** *(Map 4; ☎ 625 32 30, Barndesteeg 21)* in the red-light area. A bed is f23/25 in the low/high season (including breakfast), the age limit is 35, and curfew is at midnight (1 am on weekends).

Bob's Youth Hostel *(Map 4; ☎ 623 00 63, fax 675 64 46, Nieuwezijds Voorburgwal 92)*, only four blocks from Centraal Station, is devoid of Christian leanings and has a very relaxed policy on dope. A bed is f26 including breakfast, and there's no age limit though they prefer people in their 20s. It's a basic and convenient place to crash if you roll into Amsterdam exhausted and don't wish to search further, but with a little effort you'll do better.

The **Flying Pig Downtown Hostel** *(Map 4; ☎ 420 68 22, fax 421 08 02, Nieuwendijk 100)* is run by backpackers and is a popular choice. Dorm beds cost f26.50 to f41.50 depending on the number of beds in the room, and doubles go for f120 with shower and toilet, breakfast included.

The **Flying Pig Palace Hostel** *(Map 6;* ☎ *400 41 87, fax 421 08 02, Vossiusstraat 46)*, at the Vondelpark, has similar rates. It's not as central as the one downtown but is the more pleasant of the two.

Apart from these dedicated hostels, also check the budget and 'lower middle' hotels on the following pages: many have dorm beds at similar prices, in a less 'institutional' environment where you'll meet much the same people.

HOTELS
Ratings & Facilities
The star-rating system for hotels goes up to five stars; accommodation rating less than one star can call itself a pension or guesthouse but not a hotel. The ratings are not very helpful because they have more to do with the amenities – lifts (elevators), phones in the rooms, mini bar etc – and the number of rooms than with the quality of the rooms themselves.

Many hotels (like many of the houses) have steep and narrow stairs but no lifts, which make them inaccessible for people with mobility problems. Check when you make inquiries. Of course the top-end hotels do have lifts, and some mid-range ones too.

Rooms usually come with TV, though in the cheaper places you might have to feed coins into a timer to help pay for the cable subscription. Then again, there might be no room TV even in some expensive hotels, so if this means a lot to you, check when making inquiries.

Hotels tend to be small – any hotel with more than 20 rooms is 'large' – so if you book a room with shower or toilet down the corridor you probably won't have to share it with too many other guests. If you book a room with private shower, this will usually include a toilet but not always. Rooms in hotels in the top price bracket have their own bathrooms with real baths; cheaper hotels tend to have showers but might have a few rooms with baths for the same price – ask.

Bookings
The VVV offices in front of and inside CS, or the GWK (money exchange office) inside,

have hotel-booking services that can save you a lot of hunting around during busy periods. The VVV offices charge a f6 commission plus a f10 deposit on the price of the room; the GWK office charges f5 commission and you pay 10% of the room charge in advance. The Netherlands Reservation Centre (☎ 070-419 55 19, fax 419 55 44), Postbus 404, 2260 AK Leidschendam, accepts hotel bookings from abroad. Check the Web site at www.hotelres.nl.

Hotels tend to charge a bit more if you come to them through these services – you can save money by booking directly with the hotel. Many of them won't accept credit card details over the phone (if they accept cards at all) and may insist on a down payment by cheque or money order before they'll confirm the booking.

When booking for two people, make it clear whether you want a twin (two single beds) or double (a bed for two). It should make no difference to the price, but the wrong bed configuration could be impossible to fix on the spot when rooms are fully booked in summer.

Many hotels now have their own Web sites: try keying in www.(hotelname).nl.

Prices
Generally you get what you pay for and you don't get much. Hotels in the lowest price bracket (below f125 for a double) can be run-down and invariably seem to suffer from mouldy smells due to the damp climate, coupled with the Dutch aversion to decent ventilation. Still, they can be good value, especially if they've just been renovated. Hotels above this price bracket are more pleasant, and may even have doubles for less than f125 depending on the season and whether or not you want breakfast or a shower in the room. Breakfast in the hotel is a good idea because few food establishments open early (see the Places to Eat chapter).

Single rooms cost about two-thirds of the rates quoted here for doubles; add a third to a half for triples. Hotels that accept children (many of them don't) often have special rates for families. Prices at many hotels drop a bit in the low season (which is roughly

PLACES TO STAY

October to April excluding Christmas/New Year and Easter) but it's always worth asking for 'special' rates, especially if you're staying a few nights. Top-end hotels, on the other hand, often rely on business travellers and tend to be cheaper in the summer months and on weekends.

Most of the quoted rates include a 5% city hotel tax; at the most expensive hotels, however, this is added separately to the bill.

Hotels – Budget (Doubles under f125)

These places are popular with backpackers, and some have lounges filled with happy smokers who would be in jail if this weren't Amsterdam. Some hotels, however, are very strict about this sort of thing and lighting a joint could lead to instant expulsion.

Budget hotels often won't take bookings over the phone. Start door-knocking at 10 am, or book into whichever place will have you and find something better at your leisure.

Inside the Canal Belt Off Damrak, *Frisco Inn (Map 4; ☎ 620 16 10, Beursstraat 5)* is a youth hotel with doubles for f90 with or without shower (luck of the draw); triples/quads with bunk beds cost f40 to f45 a head. Breakfast is not included. There's a bar downstairs. Next door, *Hotel Beursstraat (Map 4; ☎ 626 37 01, fax 690 90 12, Beursstraat 7)* has doubles without/ with shower for f100/125, breakfast not included. The place is slightly more respectable than others in this area.

Centrumhotel (Map 4; ☎ 624 35 35, fax 624 86 66, Warmoesstraat 15), near Centraal Station, charges f90 for a double with shared shower, f115 with private shower, f135 with shower and toilet. All rooms have TV and there's a bar downstairs.

Hotel Kabul (Map 4; ☎ 623 71 58, fax 620 08 69, Warmoesstraat 42), next to the red-light district's police station, is popular and really packs the customers in. A dorm bed starts at f35 and a double room at f125, both including breakfast. *Hotel Winston (Map 4; ☎ 623 13 80, fax 639 23 08, Warmoesstraat 123)*, a block from the Dam, is also a multimedia centre with a trendy bar.

Brightly coloured doubles with facilities in the corridor cost f95 and go up from there; breakfast is f10 per person extra.

Hotel Crown (Map 4; ☎ 626 96 64, fax 420 64 73, Oudezijds Voorburgwal 21), in the red-light area, has tidy doubles with shared shower for f100 to f120 depending on the season, or f110 to f130 with private shower – good value for the location, even though breakfast costs extra. The dorm beds for f30 to f50 are a worthwhile alternative to those offered in the more 'institutional' hostels. The bar downstairs is only closed from 5 to 8 am but noise levels seem OK.

Hotel Brian (Map 4; ☎ 624 46 61, Singel 69), near Centraal Station, is somewhat shabby but friendly enough, and it's hard to argue with a canalside location charging f40 per person in doubles, triples or quads, breakfast included. The *Liberty Hotel (Map 2; ☎ 620 73 07, Singel 5)*, owned by the same people, has the same prices and setup. Avoid these places if you can't handle funny or even normal smoke.

Hotel Groenendael (Map 2; ☎/fax 624 48 22, Nieuwendijk 15), near Centraal Station, has doubles without/with shower for f95/110, breakfast included. So long as you don't expect too much, it's one of the better kept hotels in this bargain-basement price category.

Around the corner, back towards the station, *Hotel BA (Budget Amsterdam; Map 2; ☎ 638 71 19, fax 638 88 03, Martelaarsgracht 18)* has doubles with shared shower for f75 to f120 depending on the season, including breakfast, and dorm beds start at f25 to f35. The doubles are in a separate section at No 12, and the dorms are at No 18 with the breakfast room downstairs.

Near the Westerkerk, the curving, red-brick arcade along the S-bend of Raadhuisstraat has a few hotels worth checking, all of them up steep flights of stairs. It's a busy street with noisy trams, so a room at the back is preferable. *Hotel De Westertoren (Map 4; ☎ 624 46 39, fax 618 74 17, Raadhuisstraat 35)* has doubles without/with shower from f95/110, breakfast included. *Hotel Pax (Map 4; ☎ 624 97 35, Raadhuisstraat 37)* has doubles without shower or toilet from f85, breakfast included. *Hotel Clemens* (Map 4; ☎ 624 60 89, fax 626 96 58, Raadhuisstraat 39) has doubles without shower from f90, including breakfast; it's full all summer though it's no better than the other hotels in this row.

The *International Budget Hotel* (Map 4; ☎ 624 27 84, fax 626 18 39, Leidsegracht 76) is a popular backpacker hang-out in an attractive old canal house. A double without shower will set you back f120, and a bed in a four-bed dorm starts at f35 depending on the season; breakfast is not included.

The *Euphemia Budget Hotel* (Map 6; ☎/fax 622 90 45, ✆ euphemiahotel@budge thotel.A2000.nl, Fokke Simonszstraat 1) is on a quiet street just off busy Vijzelgracht. It's a former monastery – the institutional layout still attests to that. Double rooms without shower cost f70 to f150 depending on the season, with shower f90 to f150; buffet breakfast is f8.50 per person extra. Using email to book your stay will earn you a 10% discount.

In the north-eastern corner of the canal belt, *Hotel Pension Hortus* (Map 5; ☎ 625 99 96, fax 416 47 85, Plantage Parklaan 8) faces the Botanical Garden. Small doubles with or without shower (luck of the draw) are f90 including breakfast. A bed in a quad dorm costs f45 including breakfast. It's a relaxed place on a quiet side street, and the clientele includes young and happy smokers in the lounge. *Hotel Pension Kitty* (Map 5; ☎ 622 68 19, Plantage Middenlaan 40) has double/triple rooms with shared shower for f120/160. This includes breakfast (but not on weekends because 'the guests wake up too late').

Outside the Canal Belt South of Leidseplein, *Hotel PC Hooft* (Map 6; ☎ 662 71 07, fax 675 89 61, PC Hooftstraat 63) is an OK place but you get what you pay for (which isn't much). A double costs f110 without shower or f120 with (toilets in the corridor), breakfast included. It's above a pavement café near the museums.

Hotel Bema (Map 6; ☎ 679 13 96, fax 662 36 88, Concertgebouwplein 19B) has spacious doubles for f110/125 without/with

shower; breakfast in bed is included. It's a friendly place but faces a noisy tram line (ask for a room at the back). On a quiet street nearby is *Hotel Peters* (Map 6; ☎ 673 34 54, fax 623 68 62, Nicolaas Maesstraat 72). It's a private home where they've done little to create a hotel 'feel', which could be a plus or a minus depending on your preferences. A double with or without shower is f100 (rooms with shower are smaller), or f130 with shower and toilet, breakfast included; all rooms have a TV and fridge.

Hotels – Lower Middle (f125 to f200)

Hotels in this price range are pleasant enough for most people, though not all rooms will be worth the money compared with some of the better rooms in the previous category.

Inside the Canal Belt The *Amstel Botel* (Map 5; ☎ 626 42 47, fax 639 19 52, Oosterdokskade 2–4) is a floating hotel alongside the district post office, a few minutes walk east of Centraal Station. Double rooms cost f147 on the land side, f157 on the water side. All rooms have shower, toilet, TV and phone; breakfast is f12 per person. This is a safe choice.

Hotel Continental (Map 4; ☎ 622 33 63, fax 626 51 57, Damrak 40–41), near Centraal Station, has small rooms but is clean and bright. Doubles with shower and breakfast range from f150 in the off season to f175 on a weekend night at the height of summer; a single with shower in the corridor costs f60.

Keizersgracht Hotel (Map 2; ☎ 625 13 64, fax 620 73 47, Keizersgracht 15) has doubles with shower (but shared toilet) for f135, and breakfast is f12.50 per person. Formerly the International Student Center, now it's a regular tourist hotel with two stars. Rooms on the canal side are quite OK for this price.

Hotel Belga (Map 4; ☎ 624 90 80, fax 623 68 62, Hartenstraat 8) charges f140 to f190 for a double with shower, toilet and TV, or f125 to f160 without, breakfast included. The rooms are a bit stuffy but they're decent enough and you pay for the location.

euro currency converter f1 = €0.45

Hotel van Onna (Map 4; ☎ 626 58 01, *Bloemgracht 102–108)* consists of 41 rooms in three houses along a beautiful, quiet canal in the Jordaan. Clean, well-kept, modern doubles cost f140 with shower and toilet, breakfast included. There are no phones or TVs in the rooms and they don't accept credit cards. Ask for a room on the canal side (no mark-up in price) only if you're a heavy sleeper: the nearby Westerkerk's bells peal every half-hour until 1.30 am and start again at 6.30 am. Owner Loek van Onna is very helpful and the place is friendly and relaxed. Book ahead because it's often full.

Across from the Westerkerk is *Hotel Nadia* (Map 4; ☎ 620 15 50, fax 428 15 07, *Raadhuisstraat 51–53)*. The rooms are a bit smaller than those in the cheaper, neighbouring hotels in this red-brick arcade but they're well furnished and all come with shower, toilet, TV and phone. Doubles cost f200 and triples f260, with breakfast. The front rooms have a balcony. Part of the hotel faces Keizersgracht – ask for a room overlooking the canal.

Hotel Hoksbergen (Map 4; ☎ 626 60 43, fax 638 34 79, *Singel 301)* is a cheaper alternative to the beautiful Hotel Estheréa next door. It looks attractive from the outside and you can't beat the location, but the doubles for f185 are small and cramped.

Hotel Agora (Map 4; ☎ 627 22 00, fax 627 22 02, *Singel 462)*, off Koningsplein near the Flower Market, has doubles without shower for f120 to f150, or f175 to f215 with, breakfast included. It's a comfortable hotel in an old building with a large, stylish lobby and breakfast area.

Hotel Hans Brinker (Map 6; ☎ 622 06 87, fax 638 20 60, *Kerkstraat 136)* is a large, slick place with an institutional feel – excited groups of preteens mingle with middle-aged Irishmen worried about where to park the car. The hotel has built an advertising campaign around its spartan rooms and lack of facilities or service ('No car park, no room service, no minibars, no hole in your pocket'), but it's not that bad and is often filled to capacity. Small, clean doubles with shower and toilet cost f145 (with a f2.50 surcharge per person if you only stay

one night), including breakfast; dorm beds are considerably cheaper at f41.50 (same surcharge for one night).

There is a string of hotels in this price category along Leidsekade, close to the many entertainment options around Leidseplein. They're all similar, slightly run-down and musty, but offer reasonable value. *Hotel Impala* (Map 4; ☎ 623 47 06, fax 638 92 74, *Leidsekade 77)* has doubles without shower for f120 to f130, with shower for f150, and with toilet and shower for f160. *Hotel Kooyk* (Map 4; ☎ 623 02 95, fax 638 83 37, *Leidsekade 82)* has doubles without shower for f130, breakfast included, and four-bed family rooms for f225 (f275 for five). *Hotel King* (Map 4; ☎ 624 96 03, fax 620 72 77, *Leidsekade 86)* has doubles without shower for f115 to f135, depending on the season, breakfast included. *Hotel Titus* (Map 4; ☎ 626 57 58, fax 638 58 70, Leidsekade 74) charges f160 for a double with shower and TV including breakfast, and seems to offer a bit more style than the others.

Hotel Nes (Map 4; ☎ 624 47 73, fax 620 98 42, Kloveniersburgwal 137–139) has doubles with bath or shower from f175 all the way up to f350. It looks fancy from the outside but some of the rooms are below average for that sort of money – check before you commit yourself.

Hotel Eureka (Map 4; ☎ 624 66 07, fax 624 13 46, 's-Gravelandseveer 3–4), around the corner from Hotel Nes, has doubles with shower from f175 up to f295, breakfast included. The rooms aren't magnificent but the view over the Amstel is. Small, dark doubles at the back of the building (no view) cost f125 to f225 depending on the season, and for that sort of money you can do better.

The Veteran (Map 4; ☎ 620 26 73, fax 625 35 06, Herengracht 561), at Thorbeckeplein, has doubles without/with shower for f120/140, breakfast included, but it's not a particularly pleasant hotel. You're better off spending marginally more at *Hotel De Admiraal* (Map 4; ☎ 626 21 50, fax 623 46 25, Herengracht 563) on the opposite corner. Doubles without shower go for f125 to f135, with shower for f145 to f150, and with toilet and shower for f155 to f185; breakfast is an extra f10 per person.

A good choice in this area is the *City Hotel (Map 4; ☎ 627 23 23, fax 638 47 93, Utrechtsestraat 2)*, off Rembrandtplein above the Old Bell pub. A double without shower costs f125 to f140 depending on the season, or f165 to f180 with shower (some rooms with bath) and toilet, breakfast included. Other options include six-bed rooms for f300 to f320. It's clean and good value, certainly considering the location.

Better still is *Hotel Prinsenhof (Map 6; ☎ 623 17 72, fax 638 33 68, Prinsengracht 810)*, near Utrechtsestraat, a beautiful old canal house with an electric hoist through the central staircase for luggage. As is often the case in canal houses, every room is different – the two attic rooms with their diagonal beams are the most popular (mind your head!). Doubles without shower cost f125, with shower f175; breakfast is included and is served in the pleasant breakfast room.

Hotel de Munck (Map 6; ☎ 623 62 83, fax 620 66 47, Achtergracht 3), off Frederiksplein, is not bad either. Well-kept, clean doubles without shower or toilet start at f145, or f155 with both; triples and quads start at f225 and f310, respectively. Prices include breakfast.

Nearby, *Hotel Asterisk (Map 6; ☎ 624 17 68, fax 638 27 90, Den Texstraat 14–16)* is in a quiet street across the canal from the Heineken Museum. Doubles with shower and toilet cost f175, and if you pay cash this includes breakfast (otherwise it's another f12.50 per person). It's a tidy hotel and even has a lift. Across the road, *Hotel Kap (Map 6; ☎ 624 59 08, fax 627 12 89, Den Texstraat 5B)* has doubles with shower for f140, or more spacious doubles with shower and toilet for f160, including breakfast. The slight price differential with Hotel Asterisk is reflected in the rooms and the lack of a lift, but it's still a perfectly comfortable, safe choice.

Around the corner from here, *Hotel Nicolaas Witsen (Map 6; ☎ 626 65 46, fax 620 51 13, Nicolaas Witsenstraat 4–8)* has double rooms with shower and toilet for f175 (f195 with bath), including breakfast,

and there's a lift as well. This place is up a notch from the previous two in price and ambience.

Hotel Adolesce (Map 4; ☎ 626 39 59, fax 627 42 49, Nieuwe Keizersgracht 26) is in a quiet location just off the Amstel. It charges f130 for a double without shower or f160 with shower and toilet; breakfast in the sunny patio is included. You could ask for a room at the front overlooking the canal but one of the two rooms behind the patio would be just as pleasant. It's closed from November to mid-March. *Hotel Fantasia (Map 4; ☎ 623 82 59, fax 622 39 13, Nieuwe Keizersgracht 16)* has doubles with shower, toilet and breakfast for f135 to f165. It's closed in January.

In the Plantage area near the Botanical Garden and Artis zoo, try *Hotel Rembrandt (Map 5; ☎ 627 27 14, fax 638 02 93, Plantage Middenlaan 17)*. Smallish doubles without shower cost f110, larger doubles with bath or shower are f160. This includes breakfast in the stunning, wood-panelled breakfast room with 17th-century paintings on the linen wall coverings, which alone makes this hotel worth staying at. It faces a noisy tram line; ask for a room at the back.

Outside the Canal Belt At *Hotel Smit (Map 6; ☎ 676 63 43, fax 662 91 61, PC Hooftstraat 24)* there are doubles with bath and toilet for f180 to f220 depending on the season, including breakfast. It's clean, reasonably new and well kept, and there's a lift. It's not a bad choice, close to Leidseplein and the museums.

Hotel Museumzicht (Map 6; ☎ 671 29 54, fax 671 35 97, Jan Luijkenstraat 22), by the Rijksmuseum, has doubles without/with shower for f125/165, breakfast included. It faces a noisy tram line but is well kept. A bit farther along, *Hotel Acro (Map 6; ☎ 662 05 26, fax 675 08 11, Jan Luijkenstraat 44)* has clean doubles with shower and toilet for f175, breakfast included, and is a slightly better proposition than Hotel Museumzicht if you can afford the little bit extra.

Hotel Acca International (Map 6; ☎ 662 52 62, fax 679 93 61, Van der Veldestraat 3A), near the Van Gogh and Stedelijk

PLACES TO STAY

museums, has doubles with shower (or bath) and toilet for f195; breakfast costs f10 extra. All rooms are similar so you won't have any nasty surprises – a safe choice, though the same sort of room could be had elsewhere for f20 less.

Hotel Parkzicht *(Map 6; ☎ 618 19 54, fax 618 08 97, Roemer Visscherstraat 33)*, adjoining the Vondelpark, is OK, with double rooms for f140 to f160 including shower, toilet and breakfast. The **Hotel Sipermann** *(Map 6; ☎ 616 18 66, fax 618 53 72, Roemer Visscherstraat 35)* next door is similar.

Hotel De Filosoof *(Map 1; ☎ 683 30 13, fax 685 37 50, Anna van den Vondelstraat 6)* is a stately hotel in a quiet street next to the Vondelpark. Rooms are decorated in different philosophical themes – a Nietzsche room, a Wittgenstein room, a Humanism room etc. A double with bath or shower and TV costs f195, including breakfast.

Hotel Arena *(Map 7; ☎ 694 74 44, fax 663 26 49, 's-Gravesandestraat 51)*, near the Tropenmuseum, is a huge complex (400 beds in 121 rooms) in the lush Oosterpark. It was originally a monastery, then a hospital, and not so long ago it was known as the Sleep-In. The dorms have gone and now the place is more upmarket with double rooms, all with own shower and toilet, for f150 to f210 in summer and f110 to f160 in winter. Rooms for four cost f175/250 in winter/summer. There's wheelchair access throughout. Parking costs f5 whenever you leave the parking area, which is great value if you take the tram or rent a bike. Attractions include a café and restaurant, live music in the bar, and dance nights on Thursday, Friday and Saturday.

Hotel Van Bonga *(Map 1; ☎ 662 52 18, fax 679 08 43, Holbeinstraat 1)*, off Stadionweg south-west of the city centre, has double rooms with bath for f145 including breakfast – worth considering for an exhibitor needing a place near the RAI exhibition centre.

Hotels – Upper Middle (f200 to f275)

Hotels in this category are comfortable without being formal, and, with the exception of Hotel Ibis, are small enough to offer

personal attention. All of the following are within the canal belt.

Hotel Ibis Amsterdam Centre *(Map 2; ☎ 638 99 99, fax 620 01 56, Stationsplein 49)* is an 11-storey high-rise attached to Centraal Station, convenient for business travellers. A double with shower costs f274, breakfast included.

RHO Hotel *(Map 4; ☎ 620 73 71, fax 620 78 26, Nes 11–23)*, just off the Dam, has doubles with bath for f195/230 in the low/high season, including breakfast. You could do better if you had the time to hunt around, but the rooms are OK and you can't beat the location.

The **Singel Hotel** *(Map 2; ☎ 626 31 08, fax 620 37 77, Singel 15)*, next to the Round Lutheran Church, charges f275 for doubles, breakfast included. If you get a room at the front overlooking the beautiful canal you'll get your money's worth, otherwise you could find a similar room for less elsewhere.

The **Canal House Hotel** *(Map 4; ☎ 622 51 82, fax 624 13 17, Keizersgracht 148)* is an old-world sort of place spread over three grand canal houses. It's the pick of the bunch in this price category, though many rooms already fall in the next category. All rooms are different and have been kept as original as possible with antique furniture and no TVs (though there are computer sockets for email etc). A double with bath costs f265 to f345, breakfast included.

Hotel Toren *(Map 4; ☎ 622 60 33, fax 626 97 05, Keizersgracht 164)*, near the Westerkerk, has doubles with shower and toilet from f235 and luxury rooms up to f425, without breakfast. Some rooms are fairly small – ask to see a few before committing yourself.

The **Waterfront Hotel** *(Map 4; ☎/fax 421 66 21, Singel 458)*, near Koningsplein, has doubles with shower for f195 to f220, depending on whether there's a view of the canal. The place is a bit too ragged to charge that sort of money, but the rooms are decent enough and it's a good spot.

Near Rembrandtplein, the **Seven Bridges** *(Map 6; ☎ 623 13 29, Reguliersgracht 31)* has nine double rooms with shower and toilet for f200 to f350; breakfast on fine china, delivered to your room, is included. The well-kept, beautiful rooms are tastefully decorated with expensive furniture. It's a lovely hotel on one of the loveliest canals, but many people know this and you're unlikely to get in if you don't book well ahead.

Hotels – Top End (Doubles from f275)

Hotels in this category constantly change their rates to meet the competition, and calling around to ask if they have any 'specials' going could save a few hundred guilders on a stay of several nights; if they think you're in town on business and the company is paying you may be charged more. All rooms have bathrooms with proper bath, shower and toilet.

Inside the Canal Belt The *Swissôtel Amsterdam (Map 4; ☎ 626 00 66, fax 627 09 82, Damrak 96)* has smallish doubles for f310 to f550 that lack character but are comfortable enough. The hotel itself is spotless and it's a top location.

The family-owned *Hotel Estheréa (Map 4; ☎ 624 51 46, fax 623 90 01, Singel 305–307)* occupies three canal houses. It has doubles for f260 to f365 depending on the season; breakfast is an extra f27.50. The rooms have recently been renovated and come with all the mod cons.

The *Ambassade Hotel (Map 4; ☎ 626 23 33, fax 624 53 21, Herengracht 341)* is a stylish, almost grand hotel spread over 10 canal houses. All rooms are different and tastefully appointed with beautiful furniture. Check the antique clock (1750) in the lounge, with its rocking ships and mermaids. Doubles cost f350 and breakfast another f27.50. There's also a suite with two bedrooms for f550, and an apartment with kitchen for f525.

Outside the Canal Belt The *Bilderberg Garden Hotel (Map 1; ☎ 664 21 21, fax 679 93 56, Dijsselhofplantsoen 7)*, across from the Hilton Hotel, south-west of the centre, has doubles with jacuzzi for f250 to f590; breakfast is an extra f37.50. It's a relatively small hotel in a low-rise building (the smallest five-star hotel in Amsterdam), and prides itself on its informality and home-away-from-home ambience.

The *Golden Tulip Waterfront Hotel (Map 1; ☎ 634 43 66, fax 636 03 45, Distelkade 21)*, in Amsterdam North, has doubles for f310 including breakfast. It's a former hospital and rooms lack character, but it's popular with Europeans on bus tours and there's plenty of parking space.

Hotels – Over the Top

Hotels in this category have all the facilities that the international jet-setter would expect – fitness centres, conference rooms, business centres (or at least 'desks') – and they'll probably be able to park your car, which is saying something in Amsterdam. Breakfast, too mundane to be included in the price, will cost another f25 to f45. They often have weekend deals – something to keep in mind for that special occasion.

Hotels with the most 'character' are the Krasnapolsky, Pulitzer, Grand, De l'Europe, American, Schiller and the undisputed king, the Amstel Hotel.

Inside the Canal Belt The *Victoria Hotel (Map 4; ☎ 627 11 66, fax 627 42 59, Damrak 1–5)*, in the imposing building opposite Centraal Station (entrance along Prins Hendrikkade), has modern doubles with bath from f510 to f560 (extra bed f80, breakfast f32.50), and all the mod cons including swimming pool and business centre.

The *Golden Tulip Barbizon Palace (Map 4; ☎ 556 45 64, fax 624 33 53, Prins Hendrikkade 59–72)*, to your left opposite Centraal Station, is a sterile, six-storey building with a Fit Palace Fitness Club on the premises. Doubles cost f520 to f650, or f420 on the weekend with breakfast. Call ahead to inquire about 'specials', and check elsewhere at the same time.

The *Grand Hotel Krasnapolsky (Map 4; ☎ 554 91 11, fax 622 86 07, Dam 9)*, behind the national monument, is an elegant, historic hotel on Amsterdam's main square. It's a bit of a monument itself and charges accordingly: doubles are f545 to f660. The focal point of the hotel is the renowned

euro currency converter f1 = €0.45

'winter garden' with its steel and glass roof (constructed in 1879).

The *Pulitzer Hotel (Map 4; ☎ 523 52 35, fax 627 67 53, Prinsengracht 315–331)* occupies a row of 17th-century canal houses with beautifully restored facades and some original (restored) interiors. Doubles (only deluxe) are f695.

The *Grand Westin Demeure (Map 4; ☎ 555 31 11, fax 555 32 22, Oudezijds Voorburgwal 197)* is housed in the former admiralty building that served as city hall until the late 1980s. Queen Beatrix's civil wedding took place here in 1966. The listed monument has been restored to its former grandeur and charges f730 for doubles. Weekend deals go for f590, or f650 including an excellent dinner in one of the eight banquet chambers. There are all the usual five-star accoutrements including indoor swimming pool.

Hotel De l'Europe (Map 4; ☎ 531 17 77, fax 531 17 78, Nieuwe Doelenstraat 2–8) has doubles for f630 to f730. It's an impressive red-brick building near Muntplein that oozes Victorian elegance. The attached Excelsior Restaurant is very good.

The Art-Deco *American Hotel (Map 6; ☎ 556 30 00, fax 556 30 01, Leidsekade 97)*, just off Leidseplein, is a listed monument built in 1902. Doubles cost f565 to f650, and breakfast in the stylish Café Americain is another f35. Cheaper deals are available when booked in conjunction with a KLM flight to Amsterdam.

Another Art-Deco monument, the *Golden Tulip Schiller (Map 4; ☎ 554 07 00, fax 624 00 98, Rembrandtplein 26–36)*, has recently been restored to its original 1912 splendour. Works by the artist-hotelier Frits Schiller adorn the walls. Tastefully furnished doubles go for f420 to f495.

The *Amstel Inter-Continental Hotel (Map 7; ☎ 622 60 60, fax 622 58 08, Professor Tulpplein 1)* has an imposing location overlooking the Amstel. It was extensively renovated in 1992 and is probably the finest hotel in the country, with prices to match. A double with bath on the river side costs f650 on weekend days (f600 on the less interesting land side) but on weekdays you're looking at f995 (f895 on the land side). Breakfast is another f48.50 per person. Rooms go right up to f5250 for the royal suite. The hotel has all the facilities you could imagine, including limousine service, health club and swimming pool. It also boasts La Rive, Amsterdam's first (and so far only) restaurant with two Michelin stars.

Outside the Canal Belt The *Golden Tulip Amsterdam Centre (Map 6; ☎ 685 13 51, fax 685 16 11, Stadhouderskade 7)*, at Leidseplein, has doubles for f395 to f540. It's a fine hotel with nothing in particular to recommend it apart from the location. The same applies to the slightly more luxurious *Marriott Hotel (Map 6; ☎ 607 55 55, fax 607 55 11, Stadhouderskade 21)*, off Leidseplein, which has doubles for f415 to f595.

The *Hilton Amsterdam (Map 1; ☎ 710 60 00, fax 710 60 80, Apollolaan 138–140)*, south-west of the city centre, has doubles for f445 to f576. It's your standard Hilton in a 10-storey building, but it's in a stately area and boasts a marina with 'authentic traditional' boats for hire. In the late 1960s it became famous when John Lennon and Yoko Ono stayed in bed here for world peace, waving at screaming fans out on the street.

The *Okura Hotel (Map 1; ☎ 678 71 11, fax 671 23 44, Ferdinand Bolstraat 333)* has doubles for f425 to f595. It's a 22-storey hotel next to the Amstelkanaal, not far from the RAI exhibition centre – a good choice for an exhibitor who wants to be near the RAI and isn't overly concerned about room prices.

Gay & Lesbian Hotels

Hotels are pretty relaxed about same-sex couples (and would be breaking the law if they refused them) but some cater specifically for them.

The *Aerohotel (Map 4; ☎ 622 77 28, fax 638 85 31, Kerkstraat 49)*, in the middle of the gay action, is a popular gay hotel that charges f110 to f175 for a double. Another favourite is *Hotel Orfeo (Map 6; ☎ 623 13 47, reception ☎ 622 81 80, Leidsekruisstraat 14)*, which charges f100 for a double.

The **Stablemaster Hotel** *(Map 4; ☎ 625 01 48, fax 624 87 47, Warmoesstraat 23)* caters for the leather crowd and has doubles for f160.

The sole women-only establishment in town is **Liliane's Home** *(Map 7; ☎ 627 40 06, Sarphatistraat 119)*, which has three rooms from f185 for a double. It's not really a hotel but a private home and isn't geared up for walk-in trade – best to write in advance.

Hotel Quentin *(Map 6; ☎ 626 21 87, fax 622 01 21, Leidsekade 89)* is popular with lesbians, though heteros and gays also stay here; a double costs f125 to f130 with private shower, f97.50 without.

LONG-TERM RENTALS

Rental accommodation costing less than f1107 a month unfurnished is subject to a housing permit. This is only issued to legal residents who are bound to the region through work or study, and the price and size of the dwelling must match their income and needs. This means that as a foreigner you'll usually pay more – say, f1500 a month for a smallish, two-bedroom flat in the Vondelpark area – and you might not like what you get.

Apartments tend to be small so sharing is rare. Housing permits are not required in Amsterdam Zuidoost (south-east) but that's because it's a rather unattractive area.

Residents usually procure accommodation through housing corporations. Others have more luck through property ads in the daily newspapers *De Telegraaf* (especially Wednesdays) and *De Volkskrant* or *Het Parool* (especially Saturdays – look under *Te Huur*, For Rent), or through the classifieds paper *Via Via* (published Tuesdays and Thursdays). The national organisation of real-estate agents lists properties at www.nvm.nl but only in Dutch.

Speaking English can work against you in a variety of ways when apartment-hunting, so get a Dutch friend to help, and act swiftly because it's very much a seller's market. The owner will probably want a deposit of a month's rent, and the previous tenant may demand key money disguised as take-over costs for furnishings or recent handiwork.

Official information on renting is supplied by the Information Centre for Physical Planning and Housing in the Zuiderkerk (☎ 622 29 62), Zuiderkerkhof 72, Monday to Friday from noon to 5 pm (Thursday to 8 pm). The central information telephone line for those seeking housing (☎ 665 91 71) operates Monday to Thursday from 8.30 am to 3 pm, to noon on Friday. They might not be too helpful if you're not a resident. Try the following agents:

IDA Housing Services (☎ 624 83 01, fax 623 38 44, ✆ ida@ida-housing.demon.nl) Den Texstraat 30 – furnished apartments from f1800 a month, minimum six months (sometimes shorter in summer).

Goudsmit Estate Agents (☎ 644 19 71, fax 644 23 76) AJ Ernststraat 735 – furnished apartments from f2000 a month, minimum rental one year.

Riverside Apartments (☎ 627 97 97, fax 627 98 58, ✆ geuje@worldonline.nl) Weteringschans 187E – specialises in 'exclusive executive accommodation in central Amsterdam'; rates start at f1000 a week or f1500 a month.

All-Inn Apartment Service (☎ 428 23 00, fax 428 23 04) Singel 315 – furnished apartments throughout the city from f2500 a month or f4000 for 'luxurious canalside apartments', minimum rental six months.

Intercity Room Service (☎/fax 675 00 64) Van Ostadestraat 348 – only if you're desperate: single rooms from f350 a month, also for shorter periods, occasionally apartments too; commission two weeks' rent (one month for apartments longer than six months). Agencies operating in this price bracket need a municipal permit, which this one has.

PLACES TO STAY

Places to Eat

FOOD

Dutch food in the traditional sense is not exactly world famous but international influences have made modern Dutch cuisine quite palatable. In fact, in recent years Amsterdam has undergone a bit of a culinary revolution and you can eat very well indeed. If you prefer traditional Chinese, Italian, Thai or Mexican, for example, you'll find it here too. Prices are very reasonable by European standards and servings are generous.

Smoking is still an entrenched habit in restaurants. A few places have nonsmoking sections but even vegetarian establishments have trouble banning smokers altogether.

Where & When

Don't overlook the many *eetcafés*, pubs that also serve meals – see Cafés (Pubs) in the Entertainment chapter: most of them could just as well be listed here as places to eat and many are good to excellent, though they don't always take reservations. They're affordable and lively, and if you enjoy the ambience you can hang around for drinks afterwards. The grand cafés in particular are good places for lunch.

The main meal of the day is dinner, from around 6 to 9.30 pm. Amsterdammers like to eat out, and the more popular places fill up by 7 pm (the Dutch eat early). Book ahead or arrive early, or be prepared to wait at the bar. You could try arriving late: films, concerts and other performances usually start at 8.30 or 9.30 pm and tables may become available then for a 'second sitting', but keep in mind that some kitchens close at 10 pm (though the restaurants stay open longer). Vegetarian restaurants tend to close earlier.

Lunch is more modest, with sandwich and salad menus, though you'll find places that serve full meals if you really want one.

The streets around Leidseplein (Lange Leidsedwarsstraat and Korte Leidsedwarsstraat) are packed with restaurants, a culinary United Nations. They cater for tourists and most of them are OK, though few stand out. Walk along and pick whatever takes your fancy.

There's a high staff turnover in cafés and restaurants, and some of the places mentioned here may have declined in quality. Don't despair: there's plenty to choose from, and for every place that has gone bad there will be a new one doing its best to attract customers.

Cuisines

Cuisines such as Italian, Spanish, Mexican, Thai, Chinese, Indian and Turkish will be similar to what you're used to, though they might be adapted a bit to suit the Dutch palate and ingredients available locally. Vegetarians are well catered for and most restaurants have one or more vegetarian dishes on the menu, though we also list several dedicated vegetarian places.

Dutch The standard Dutch meal consists of potatoes, meat and vegetables in large portions (though meat is expensive, so don't expect plate-filling steaks). Few restaurants serve exclusively Dutch cuisine but many places have several Dutch staples on the menu, especially in winter, that are filling and good value for money:

stamppot ('mashed pot') – potatoes mashed with vegetables (usually kale or endive) and served with smoked sausage or strips of pork

hutspot ('hotchpotch') – similar to stamppot, but with carrots, onions and braised meat

erwtensoep – thick pea soup (a spoon stuck upright in the pot should fall over slowly) with smoked sausage and bacon

asperges – asparagus (always white, very popular in spring), served with ham and butter

kroketten – croquettes: dough-ragout with meat (sometimes fish or shrimp) that's crumbed and deep-fried; often in the form of small balls called *bitterballen* served with mustard – a popular pub snack

mosselen – mussels, popular (and best eaten) from September to April; cooked with white wine, chopped leeks and onions, and served in a bowl

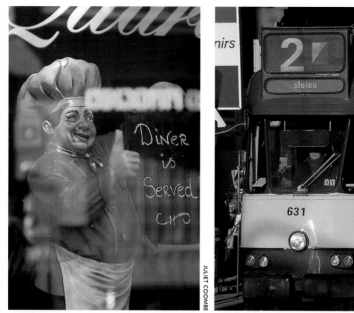

Grub's up!

Trams are a handy way to get around town.

Centraal Station, the hub of Amsterdam's public transport network

CHARLOTTE HINDLE

AMERENS HEDWICH

JULIET COOMBE

AMERENS HEDWICH

RICHARD NEBESKY

ANTHONY PIDGEON

Countless colourful clogs – cliched but cute

Traditional Dutch Dishes

Winter may be the best season to cook up one of these hearty, homy Dutch dishes.

Dutch Pea Soup

This thick soup tastes even better the next day. Serve with hot, crusty bread.

Ingredients
3 cups split green peas
1 pig's trotter
1 pig's ear
1 cup diced bacon
1kg potatoes
2 leeks
2 onions
1 celeriac
4 frankfurters
salt and pepper to taste

Cooking Instructions
* Wash peas, place in bowl, cover with water and soak overnight.
* Boil softened peas in 3L of water for one hour.
* Add pig's trotter, ear and bacon and continue to cook for two hours.
* Add sliced potatoes, diced leeks, diced onions and diced celeriac and simmer for a further one hour.
* Add sliced frankfurters to soup for the last five minutes.
* Season with salt and pepper.

Mashed Potatoes with Crispy Bacon

Ingredients
1 cup diced bacon
1kg floury potatoes
2 tbsp butter
milk to mix
cracked pepper and salt to taste

Cooking Instructions
* Fry the bacon until crispy, set aside, reserve the fat.
* Peel and quarter potatoes; place in a large saucepan with water and bring to the boil.

* Once boiling, reduce to a medium heat and continue cooking for 20 minutes.
* Drain and mash potatoes with butter and milk to soften.
* Return to heat and fold through bacon and remaining fat. Season as required.

Dutch *Appeltaart*

Ingredients
1 packet shortcrust pastry
1½ tsp gelatine
1kg apples
1 tbsp lemon juice
2 tbsp sugar
2 tsp cinnamon
150g dried fruit soaked in 3 tbsp rum
¼ cup butter
1 tsp caster sugar
½ cup whipped cream

Cooking Instructions
* Use a 24cm greased round cake tin.
* Preheat oven to 175°C/350°F.
* Use three-quarters of the shortcrust pastry dough to line base and sides of tin; sprinkle with the gelatine.
* Peel and core apples, slice thinly, sprinkle with lemon juice and mix in sugar and 1 tsp of cinnamon.
* Place alternate layers of apple slices and dried fruit in tin, sprinkling each layer with some cinnamon and sugar. Use apples for the top layer and dot with butter.
* Roll the remaining dough into a rectangle, cut into 1cm-wide strips and lay in a lattice over fruit, sealing at ends; brush with some milk, and sprinkle caster sugar mixed with remaining cinnamon on top.
* Bake for 45 minutes or till golden.
* Cool and serve with a generous amount of whipped cream.

PLACES TO EAT

or cooking pot with a side dish of French fries *(frites* or *patat)*; use an empty shell as a pincer to pluck out the bodies; don't eat mussels that haven't opened properly as they can be poisonous

Seafood doesn't feature as prominently as one might expect in a seafaring nation, though there's plenty of it. Popular fish include *schol* (plaice), *tong* (sole), *kabeljauw* (cod) and freshwater *forel* (trout). *Garnalen* (shrimps, prawns) are also found on many menus, often large species known by their Italian name of *scampi. Haring* (herring) is a national institution, eaten lightly salted or occasionally pickled but never fried or cooked; *paling* (eel) is usually smoked. Don't dismiss herring or eel until you've tried them – see Fast Food later in this chapter.

Typical Dutch desserts are fruit pie (apple, cherry or other fruit), *vla* (custard) or pancakes. Many snack bars and pubs serve *appeltaart* (apple pie) and coffee throughout the day.

Fusion A new food trend sweeping Amsterdam, this is the sort of food that Australians, Californians and, more recently, Londoners have been enjoying for years. The idea is to combine Asian/Pacific-Rim ingredients and cooking techniques with local produce on the one plate. Sometimes it works wonderfully, other times it's a miserable melange of too many flavours and textures. Listed on the following pages are a few restaurants where the experiment is working successfully.

Indonesian This is a tasty legacy of Dutch colonial history. Some dishes, such as the famous *rijsttafel* ('rice table' – white rice with heaps of side dishes; take your time), are colonial concoctions rather than traditional Indonesian, but that doesn't make them less appealing.

One slight problem, however, is that most places serving Indonesian food are Chinese-Indonesian, run by Chinese (some with Indonesian backgrounds) who have perfected bland dishes to suit Dutch palates. The food is OK and can be great value, but if you want the real thing, avoid places that call themselves *Chinees-Indonesisch* (or order Chinese dishes there instead).

Even at 'genuine' Indonesian restaurants, rijsttafel can be a bit of a rip-off and the ingredients don't always taste authentic – once you've had a really good one you'll know the difference. A few good rijsttafel places are mentioned in this chapter, but it's an expensive dish and if you eat elsewhere you're better off ordering *nasi rames* (literally, boiled rice), a plate of rice covered in several accompaniments that would be served in separate bowls in a rijsttafel. The

same dish with thick noodles (more a Chinese-Indonesian variant and quite filling) is called *bami rames*.

Gado-gado (lightly steamed vegetables and hard-boiled egg, served with peanut sauce and rice) feels good in all respects. *Saté* or *sateh* (satay) is marinated, barbecued beef, chicken or pork on small skewers; unfortunately it's often cooked electrically and smothered in peanut sauce. Other stand-bys are *nasi goreng* (fried rice with onions, pork, shrimp and spices, often topped with a fried egg or shredded omelette) and *bami goreng* (the same thing but with noodles).

Indonesian food is usually served mild for sensitive Western palates. If you want it hot (*pedis*, pronounced 'p-DIS'), say so but be prepared for the ride of a lifetime. It's better to play it safe by asking for *sambal* (chilli paste), if it isn't already on the table, and helping yourself. Usually it's *sambal oelek*, which is red and hot; the dark-brown *sambal badjak* is based on onions and is mild and sweet. If you overdo it, a spoonful of plain rice will quench the flames; drinking distributes the oily sambal and only makes things worse.

Indonesian food should be eaten with a spoon and fork (chopsticks are Chinese) and the drink of choice is beer or water.

International Many restaurants fall into this category, which mixes cuisines from different parts of the world depending on the skill or preference of the cook. Dishes might represent a genuine mixture, eg, Italian fettuccine topped with Provencale ratatouille and meat stir-fried in soy sauce, or Dutch braised beef served with North African couscous, but more often the menu will simply list an international range of dishes. These are variations on the potatoes-meat-vegetables theme but might include dishes such as an indeterminate curry, a spaghetti bolognese, a beef stroganoff, a plate of Mexican corn chips (nachos) or a bowl of mussels. Main dishes usually come with salads that can be quite imaginative.

Surinamese Food from this former South American colony is similar to Caribbean food – a unique African/Indian hybrid – with Indonesian influences contributed by indentured labourers from Java. Chicken features strongly, along with curries (chicken, lamb or beef), potatoes and rice, and delicious *roti* (unleavened bread pancakes). Steer clear of this type of food if you can't handle hot and spicy, but it's always wholesome and good value.

Costs

The prices quoted in this chapter are probably the minimum you'll end up spending; add the cost of something to drink and one or two other dishes and you could spend twice as much. Drinks other than draught beer *(pils)* will pad out the bill, and wine can be a blatant rip-off, with bottles that cost f10 in the shops going for anything up to f45. 'House wines' are no different: a half-litre carafe of acidic house red will cost at least f15, though some restaurants do serve drinkable stuff.

Many places list a *dagschotel* (dish of the day) or *dagmenu* that will be good value, but don't expect a culinary adventure. On the other hand, the trend in many places is to limit the menu to two or three options that change daily, in which case the food can be quite exciting.

Service is included in the bill and tipping is at your discretion, though most people leave small change (5% or so) if the service hasn't been bad enough to warrant customer revenge. The protocol is to say how much you're paying in total as you settle the bill.

Beware that many restaurants do *not* accept credit cards; ask in advance to avoid disappointment.

DRINKS
Nonalcoholic

Amsterdam tap water is fine but it does have a slight chemical taste, so mineral and soda waters are popular. Dairy drinks include chocolate milk, Fristi (a yoghurt drink), *karnemelk* (buttermilk) and of course milk itself, which is good and relatively cheap. A wide selection of fruit juices and all the international soft drinks are available too.

Tea & Coffee For a city with such a rich tradition in the tea and coffee trade, tea is a bit of a disappointment. It's usually served as a cup of hot water with a tea bag, though many places do offer a wide choice of bags. If you want milk, ask *'met melk, graag'* (with milk, please); many locals prefer to add a slice of lemon instead.

Coffee: From Yemen to You

The coffee plant is said to have come from Ethiopia, but it was the Yemenis who first commercialised the product. In 1616 a Dutch visitor to Al-Makha, a Red Sea port in Yemen, noted a caravan of 1000 camels carrying goods including fruit, spices, pottery and coffee – the latest craze in Europe – grown in the Yemeni mountains. Two years later the Dutch built Al-Makha's first coffee factories.

By the 1630s coffee houses were operating in Amsterdam and elsewhere, and the demand for coffee rose to such heights that Yemen was unable to meet demand. Prices soared, bringing prosperity to the coffee merchants of Al-Makha, who built gorgeous villas in the city. During those years Yemen had a virtual world monopoly on the beans, and the term 'mocha' (*mokka* in Dutch) has survived to the present day to indicate the strongly flavoured, dark-brown coffee from Arabia, or an equally dark and tasty mixture of coffee and cocoa.

Eventually, however, the plant was smuggled out by the Dutch and, after being studied and propagated in Amsterdam's Hortus Botanicus, it was cultivated in Ceylon (Sri Lanka) and Java by the early 1700s. With its monopoly broken, Al-Makha began a slow decline.

Coffee is still grown in the mountains of Yemen, although farmers derive greater profits from *qat*, the mild stimulant used daily by almost every adult Yemeni in the mountainous northern districts. The restoration of the coffee trade is a much-debated issue. Foreigners working in development-aid projects want to see coffee plants once again covering Yemeni mountain slopes instead of qat. The ideal growing regions of the two plants overlap only slightly and both could prosper in the country.

PLACES TO EAT

The hot drink of choice is coffee, which should be strong and can be excellent if it's freshly made or horrendous if it has been simmering in the jug for a couple of hours. If you simply order *koffie* you'll get a sizeable cup of the black stuff with a separate jug (or small airline container) of *koffiemelk*, a slightly sour-tasting cream similar to unsweetened condensed milk that enhances the flavour. *Koffie verkeerd* (coffee 'wrong') comes in a bigger cup or mug with plenty of real milk. If you order *espresso* or *cappuccino* you'll be lucky to get a decent Italian version; most cappuccinos are just covered in watery froth, though the blandness may be disguised by a sprinkle of cinnamon.

Alcoholic

Lager beer is the staple, served cool and topped by a two-finger-thick head of froth – supposedly to trap the flavour. Requests of 'no head please' will meet with a steely response. *Een bier* or *een pils* will get you a normal glass; *een kleintje pils* is a small glass and *een fluitje* is a small, thin, Cologne-style glass. Many places also serve half-litre mugs *(een grote pils)* to please tourists, but somehow draught lager doesn't taste the same in a mug and soon goes flat if you don't hurry up!

Popular brands include Heineken, Amstel, Grolsch, Oranjeboom, Dommelsch, Bavaria and the cheap Brouwersbier put out by the Albert Heijn supermarket chain. They contain 5% alcohol by volume in the bottle and close to 5% on tap, so a few of those seemingly small glasses can pack quite a wallop. Tasty and stronger Belgian beers, such as Duvel and Westmalle Triple, are also very popular and are reasonably priced. *Witbier* is a somewhat murky, crisp beer drunk in summer with a slice of lemon; the dark, sweet *bokbier* is available in autumn.

Dutch gin *(genever)* is made from juniper berries and is drunk chilled from a tiny glass filled to the brim. Most people prefer *jonge* (young) genever, which is smooth and relatively easy to drink; *oude* (old) genever has a strong juniper flavour and can be an acquired taste. A common combination, known as a *kopstoot* (head butt), is a glass

of genever with a beer chaser – few people can handle more than two or three of those. Brandy is known as *vieux* or *brandewijn*. There are plenty of indigenous liqueurs, including *advocaat* (a kind of eggnog) and the herb-based *Beerenburg*, a Frisian schnapps.

Wines in all varieties are very popular thanks to European unity, which has given French vintners and their overpriced products a run for their money. The average Amsterdam supermarket stocks wines from every corner of Europe (with excellent value from Spain and Bulgaria) and many countries farther afield, such as Chile, South Africa and Australia. The most expensive bottle in a supermarket rarely costs more than f12.50 and will be quite good. Australians may discover that a so-so wine at home commands top guilder here for its snob appeal.

BREAKFAST & LUNCH

Amsterdam wakes up late and you'll have trouble finding places other than hotels that serve anything before 9 or even 10 am. Dutch hotel breakfasts typically consist of a selection of breads and toast with butter, cheese and meats (ham, roast beef, salami), jam, and coffee or tea. A soft-boiled egg is sometimes part of the package, and Anglo-American eggs and bacon might be available on request. The Dutch version of fried eggs and meat, the *uitsmijter* served in snack bars and some pubs (see Fast Food), is not commonly eaten for breakfast but will keep you going for hours.

Despite the lack of early-morning eateries, you can still have breakfast if you know where to look (and don't get up too early). Amsterdam has a plethora of small, inexpensive restaurants serving hearty breakfasts and good quality sandwiches, soups and cakes for lunch. The more interesting ones are in the smaller side streets inside the canal belt and in the Jordaan and Nieuwmarkt neighbourhoods. Some are only open for breakfast and lunch, while others open at 8 am and serve food through to 10 pm. Most don't serve alcohol, but some have fully stocked bars.

Nielsen (Map 4; ☎ 330 60 06, Berenstraat 19) is worth a visit for breakfast. Its bright interior is often filled with vases of fresh flowers. The set breakfast – eggs, toast, fruit, juice and coffee for f13.75 – is hard to beat. During lunch a large variety of tasty salads and sandwiches are served. The extra big turkey club sandwich (f12.50) is fantastic. Nielsen is open Tuesday to Saturday from 8 am to 5 pm and from 9 am on Sunday.

Hein *(Map 4; ☎ 623 10 48, Berenstraat 20)* just across the street also does wonderful breakfasts. It's open Wednesday to Monday from 9 am to 6 pm. The owner, Hein, will cook just about anything that takes your fancy, in her open, industrial-style kitchen. A strong coffee and a *croque monsieur* are a good way to start the day.

In the Jordaan, **Foodism** *(Map 4; ☎ 427 51 03, Oude Leliestraat 8)* is a hip little joint run by a fun crew of chefs and waiters who are just as happy to work as sit at your table and have a chat. Open daily from 11 am to 10 pm, it serves filled sandwiches and all-day breakfasts, and pasta at night. Try the appropriately named Miss Piggy – egg and bacon fettucine for f15.50.

Close by, to the west of Dam Square, is **Villa Zeezicht** *(Map 4; ☎ 626 74 33, Torensteeg 7)*, on the corner with Singel. It's packed during the week with students from the arts faculty around the corner and on weekends with people enjoying the terrace tables. The fact that it serves some of the best apple pie in the city ensures return patronage: for f5 you get a mountain of cooked apples dusted in cinnamon powder and surrounded by warm flaky pastry – perfect for afternoon tea.

Dimitri's *(Map 2; ☎ 627 93 93, Prinsenstraat 3)* looks like a mini Parisian brasserie, but it has an international menu with lots of salads, pastas and burgers. Mornings see fashionable media types nibbling on croissants or, if they're feeling particularly perky, ordering the champagne breakfast (coffee, juice, toast, pancakes, smoked salmon and a glass of bubbly) for f22.50. Just opposite is **Vennington** *(Map 2; ☎ 625 93 98, Prinsenstraat 2)*, where an artier crowd munch on toasted bagels and slurp fresh fruit shakes while listening to the hip music. It's open

from 8 am to 4 pm Wednesday to Monday, and from 9.30 am Sunday.

Barney's *(Map 2; ☎ 625 97 61, Haarlemmerstraat 102)* is the place to head if you need a joint with your morning juice. Originally a coffeeshop, it now also does a roaring trade in all-day breakfasts, served daily from 7 am to 8 pm. Although the interior, a decorative mix of sci-fi fantasy and New Age mysticism, is best appreciated after a spliff, it's still worth a visit for the huge set breakfasts (Dutch, American, Irish, vegan or vegetarian from f13.50 to f25). **New Deli** *(Map 2; ☎ 626 27 55, Haarlemmerstraat 73)* is close by but attracts a thoroughly different crowd. Slick, hip couples congregate at this modern and minimal café to read the design magazines and share Asian-inspired dishes like chicken in red curry (f15). It's open daily from 10 am to 10 pm.

Goodies *(Map 4; ☎ 625 61 22, Huidenstraat 9)*, just west of Spui, is open Monday to Saturday from 9.30 am to 10.30 pm and Sunday from 11 am. It looks a little like a 1970s country kitchen and serves big sandwiches during the day and pasta at night. It's very popular with students and office workers who munch away on filled bagels named after cartoon characters. **Café Reibach** *(Map 2; ☎ 626 77 08, Brouwersgracht 139)* is a charming gay and straight-friendly establishment that serves a massive breakfast for f22.50. Expect a platter laden with Dutch cheese, paté, smoked salmon, eggs, coffee and fresh juice. The pear tart (f5) is so popular that it sells out within minutes of coming out of the oven.

Metz & Co Café *(Map 4; ☎ 520 70 36, Keizersgracht 455)*, on the top floor of the swanky department store, has panoramic views of the city centre. You'd assume that such a wonderful location would bump up the price of the food, but you'll be pleasantly surprised. Substantial set breakfasts, brunches and afternoon teas cost between f19.50 and f22.50. Alternatively, order a Dutch cheese platter (f12.50) and a glass of beer (f4) and drink in that amazing view.

Around the corner, **Café Morlang** *(Map 4; ☎ 625 26 81, Keizersgracht 451)* offers a quiet retreat from the shopping mayhem of

PLACES TO EAT

, Grab a fashion magazine, order ... ~aesar salad (f16) and take in the gigantic portraits of staff members painted on the back wall. Just next door is *Café Walem (Map 4; ☎ 625 35 44, Keizersgracht 449)*. It's a popular, modern, industrial-style café open daily from 10 am to 1 am. Toasted sandwiches (f7.50 to f13.50) are the speciality and it has a variety of set menus for breakfast (f16.50 to f18.50). If the weather is nice, ask to sit in the garden courtyard.

Over near the Stopera, *Puccini (Map 4; ☎ 620 84 58, Staalstraat 21)* is a small, corner sandwich bar that stays open for dinner until 8 pm when there is an opera on at the Stopera. Otherwise it's open daily from 10 am to 6 pm. Various Italian-inspired sandwiches and salads (filled with lots of sun-dried ingredients) are prepared in an open, industrial-style kitchen.

DINNER RESTAURANTS

For ease of use, the following restaurants are listed by location and then by cuisine, but Amsterdam is quite small and you don't need much initiative to visit a worthwhile restaurant wherever it is.

Medieval Centre

Argentinian There are quite a few Argentinian steak houses and you'll find at least one or two dotted along the tourist eat streets. They all feature big grilled steaks, spareribs and salad bars. Some have live South American bands on the weekend. *Gauchos (Map 4; ☎ 626 59 77, Geelvincksteeg 6)*, in a side street by the floating Flower Market, plates up three sizes of rib-eye steaks (f26.50 to f47) and as many spareribs as you like for f26.50. It's part of a chain of six Gauchos around town.

Chinese For 'real' Chinese, with the freshest ingredients at affordable prices, visit the strip of Chinese restaurants along the Zeedijk near Nieuwmarkt Square. Don't worry about reservations – if a place is full, the one next door will have space. *Hoi Tin (Map 4; ☎ 625 64 51, Zeedijk 122)* is open daily from noon to midnight. It's far from glamorous but it is always packed with people tucking into honestly priced Cantonese cuisine. The menu features over 200 dishes with most mains priced around f17.

Oriental City (Map 4; ☎ 626 83 52, Oudezijds Voorburgwal 177–179), on the corner of Oude Doelenstraat (the extension of Damstraat), is a large, efficient Chinese restaurant serving tasty main dishes from f17.50 to f45. Many Chinese eat here.

Si-Chuan Kitchen (Map 4; ☎ 420 78 33, Warmoesstraat 17–19), next to Centrumhotel, is a cut above the average, with spicy Sechuanese main dishes at around f20.50.

Dutch Once a place where Dutch tourists stopped for a meal on their way home via Centraal Station, *De Roode Leeuw (Map 4; ☎ 555 06 66, Damrak 93)* attracts a wider clientele these days but the food is still well prepared, with main dishes under f35.

d'Vijff Vlieghen Restaurant (Map 4; ☎ 624 83 69, Spuistraat 294–302) is a large restaurant spread over several canal houses, catering for splurging foreigners keen to sample Dutch food in authentic surroundings (the food and surroundings are good indeed). Mains start at f48 and there are four-course menus for f82.50. Book ahead. *Dorrius (Map 4; ☎ 420 22 24, Nieuwezijds Voorburgwal 5)* serves a wide range of Dutch dishes in old-world surroundings that were transferred intact when the business moved premises a few years ago. It's one of the city's premier venues for Dutch cuisine, and the prices (many main dishes under f40) are worth it.

Haesje Claes (Map 4; ☎ 624 99 98, Nieuwezijds Voorburgwal 320) is slightly cheaper but no worse, with dark wooden panelling to enhance the experience. It's open daily from noon to 10 pm and reservations are recommended.

If you're running out of money, you'll survive at the *Keuken van 1870 (Map 4; ☎ 624 89 65, Spuistraat 4)*, not far from Centraal Station, a former soup kitchen still serving dirt-cheap meals from an old-fashioned open kitchen in a spacious locale. Nothing is over f21, and the set menu on weekdays is f12. It's open weekdays from 12.30 to 8 pm, weekends from 4 to 9 pm.

For Dutch pancakes, try **Pannenkoeken-huis Upstairs** *(Map 4; ☎ 626 56 03, Grim-burgwal 2)*, above the 3-D Hologrammen shop, which serves filling pancakes for f8 to f14. It's one of the smallest restaurants you're ever likely to see, up a 45-degree flight of stairs. Opening hours are limited – weekdays from 10 am to 7 pm, weekends to 5 or 6 pm – but it's great for lunch.

Fusion For a real treat, try **Tom Yam** *(Map 4; ☎ 622 95 33 Staalstraat 22)*. Former Michelin-star chef Jos Boomgaardt has turned his sights east and now dishes up fragrant, Thai-inspired soups, curries and noodle dishes. The set menu for f55 is a good option. It's open daily 6 to 10 pm.

Greek You wouldn't think of Amsterdam as a great place to try Greek food, but an exception is **Grekas** *(Map 4; ☎ 620 35 90, Singel 311)*. It's actually a catering shop selling delectable take-home dishes and meals, but you can also sit down for gener-ous portions of the best Greek home cooking with the freshest ingredients. Low over-heads (snack-bar ambience) ensure very reasonable prices.

Indonesian At **Kantjil en de Tijger** *(Map 4; ☎ 620 09 94, Spuistraat 291)* food is served in an Art-Deco environment. Some locals consider it one of the best Indonesian restaurants in the city, especially for its rijsttafel (f45 for 22 dishes), but others think you could eat better elsewhere for the money – check for yourself.

At **Sukasari** *(Map 4; ☎ 624 00 92, Damstraat 26)*, near the Dam, most dishes are under f23 (the nasi rames 'Sukasari' makes a good mini-rijsttafel for f20.75). It has seen better days before it discovered tourists but is still not a bad choice.

International Behind Centraal Station, **Pier 10** *(Map 2; ☎ 624 82 76, De Ruijter-kade Steiger 10)*, at the end of a pier on the IJ, offers a great view of the harbour as you dine by candlelight – freight barges pass right by your window. The French/Dutch/Italian dishes served here are on the pricey

side (mains around f40) but worth the money. The delicious plunger coffee fills three cups and comes with a huge plate of sweets. Book a table in the rotunda at the tip of the pier and watch the sun set over the North Sea Canal.

The **Supper Club** *(Map 4; ☎ 638 05 13, Jonge Roelensteeg 21)* is an extraordinary place where they transform the interior according to the cuisine they are serving on the night. You may find yourself in downtown Naples with the laundry hang-ing from the ceiling, or a sophisticated Paris salon. Menu prices vary according to the day of the week: f85 on Wednesday, Thursday and Sunday and f95 on Friday and Saturday (when there's live music and a DJ).

Eetcafé de Staalmeesters (Map 4; ☎ 623 42 18, Kloveniersburgwal 127) should actually be listed under Cafés (Pubs) in the next chapter but most people come here for the food. It's a small place with only a handful of tables, and the food is inventive and very reasonably priced for the quality, with mains under f30 and a three-course menu for f39.50. You'll leave here feeling satisfied.

Italian At **Caprese** *(Map 4; ☎ 620 00 59, Spuistraat 261)* you'll get good and afford-able Italian food, and not just pizzas and pasta either. Many Italians eat here.

North American For a modern take on burgers and bagels, head to **Caffe Esprit** *(Map 4; ☎ 622 19 67, Spui 10)*. Gorgeous waiters (they're all models) scurry around the terrace area serving mega-size club sandwiches to too-thin glamour girls. The salads (from f11.75 to f19.75) are meals in themselves.

Seafood The fast-food chain **De Visscher** *(Map 4; ☎ 623 73 37, Kalverstraat 122)* serves inexpensive, good seafood, open from 10 am to 7.30 pm, Thursday till 9.30 pm.

Vegetarian The smokefree vegetarian restaurant in the **Oininio** complex *(Map 2; ☎ 553 93 26, Prins Hendrikkade 20–21)*

PLACES TO EAT

serves excellent food, though snacks and meals in the café downstairs are cheaper.

Western Canal Belt

Dutch Located near the Haarlemmerpoort, *Moeder's Pot Eethuisje (Map 2; ☎ 623 76 43, Vinkenstraat 119)* has seen better days but still serves up solid, inexpensive meals. It's a small, kitsch place with only a few small tables, open Monday to Saturday from 5 to 9.30 pm. The proprietor might seem gruff but he's been doing the food and the caustic comments for some 30 years.

The Dutch know how to make delicious, filling pancakes (savoury or sweet) and one of the best places to try them is *The Pancake Bakery (Map 2; ☎ 625 13 33, Prinsengracht 191)*, in the basement of a restored old warehouse. It has dozens of kinds of pancakes for f8 to f19, as well as omelettes, soups and desserts. The kitchen is open daily from noon to 9.30 pm.

French The somewhat pretentious *Tout Court (Map 4; ☎ 625 86 37, Runstraat 13)* has tasty mains around f45 and menus from f57.50 to f120.

Jean Jean (Map 2; ☎ 627 71 53, Eerste Anjeliersdwarsstraat 12), in the Jordaan, has meat and fish dishes for under f33, as well as crepes, soups and salads. It's nothing special but honest and affordable.

Bordewijk (Map 2; ☎ 624 38 99, Noordermarkt 7), also in the Jordaan, has an interior so minimal that you have little to do but appreciate the spectacular French/Italian cooking. Prices are substantially less than you pay at most French restaurants that are this good, with a range of three-course set menus costing between f60 and f80. It's open for dinner only, Tuesday to Sunday from 6.45 to 11 pm.

Amsterdam has a long list of really upmarket French restaurants, and one of the most famous is *Christophe (Map 4; ☎ 625 08 07, Leliegracht 46)*. A Michelin star ensures that Jean Christophe's subtly swanky restaurant is constantly filled with diners supping on dishes like warm oysters with saffron and caviar (f45) and roasted lobster with sweet garlic and potatoes (f60).

Fusion *!Zest (Map 2; ☎ 428 24 55, Prinsenstraat 10)* is popular with local media types and business diners. It's open daily from 6 to 11.30 pm. Dishes like prawns atop a coriander and coconut coulis (f36.50) are served in a beautifully understated deluxe room. Reservations are essential.

Summum (Map 2; ☎ 770 0407, Binnen Dommersstraat 13) is a small restaurant with crisp white-linen tablecloths and napkins. The quiet formality of the room contrasts with the punchy Italian and Thai dishes coming out of the kitchen. Mains are priced from f22 to f37.

Lof (Map 2; ☎ 620 29 97, Haarlemmerstraat 62) is a successful restaurant whose popularity has surely helped promote the growth of fusion cooking. It does wonders with seafood, combining South-East Asian and Mediterranean flavours marvellously. It's open Tuesday to Sunday from 6.30 to 11 pm. Be sure to book.

Indian In the Jordaan, *Koh-I-Noor (Map 4; ☎ 623 31 33, Westermarkt 29)* has a pretty gaudy interior but serves good curries, tandoori and biryani dishes. Mains are around f25 and it's open daily from 5 to 11 pm.

Indonesian Good Indonesian food is served at *Restaurant Speciaal (Map 4; ☎ 624 97 06, Nieuwe Leliestraat 142)*, though this can vary. *Cilubang (Map 4; ☎ 626 97 55, Runstraat 10)* has a reasonable, filling rijsttafel for f38.

International It's worth visiting *De Belhamel (Map 2; ☎ 622 10 95, Brouwersgracht 60)* for its Art-Nouveau interior alone but the French-inspired food is good too and affordable, with most mains under f37 (the entrance is around the corner in Binnen Wieringerstraat).

Nearby in the Jordaan, *Stoop (Map 2; ☎ 639 24 80, Eerste Anjeliersdwarsstraat 4)* has a reputation for serving some of the best bistro-style food in Amsterdam at modest prices. Tasty mains like lamb shanks on mashed potatoes (f32.50) and moreish desserts (f11.50) ensure that bookings are essential. It's open daily from 6.30 to 11 pm.

Italian The always-busy *Toscanini Caffè* *(Map 2; ☎ 623 28 13, Lindengracht 75)*, in the Jordaan, is a convivial place in a former courtyard, with mains under f33 and three-course menus for f57.50. Book ahead. Also in the Jordaan, *Burger's Patio (Map 4; ☎ 623 68 54, Tweede Tuindwarsstraat 12)* serves Italian food in the evenings only. The three-course set menu (Tuscan tomato soup, grilled lamb cutlets and tiramisu) for f40 is good value. Despite the name, hamburgers are not the speciality and there is no patio, but a small garden courtyard.

Mexican Located in the Jordaan, *Rozen & Tortillas (Map 4; ☎ 620 65 25, Prinsengracht 126)* fills up quickly each night with students and locals sharing dishes like chicken quesadillas (f18.50) and beef fajitas (f28.50 for two). Be sure to order a *caipirinha*, an icy blend of sugar-cane rum and freshly squeezed limes (f7.50). After two of these you'll salsa out into the night.

Seafood A good fish restaurant, also in the Jordaan, is *Albatros (Map 2; ☎ 627 99 32, Westerstraat 264)*. It has somewhat camp decor and a smokefree section. Main courses cost f32.50, three-course menus start at f53, and the kitchen is open from 6 to 11 pm (closed Wednesday).

Spanish It might not look like much, but *Casa Juan (Map 2; ☎ 623 78 38, Lindengracht 59)* does fantastic Spanish food – some say the best in Amsterdam and they could well be right – at very reasonable prices. It's hard to get a table early in the evening but the 'second sitting' should be quieter.

Duende (Map 2; ☎ 420 66 92, Lindengracht 62) is the place to head for a convivial night. Flamenco music, big shared tables and reasonably priced tapas (between f3.50 and f9.50) guarantee its popularity, though the food isn't quite as good as at Casa Juan. It's open daily from noon to 1 am and to 3 am on the weekend. *Paso Doble (Map 2; ☎ 421 26 70, Westerstraat 86)*, also in the Jordaan, almost matches Casa Juan in the quality of its food.

Thai Good, busy and cheap, *Pathum Thai (Map 2; ☎ 624 49 36, Willemsstraat 16)*, in the northern Jordaan, has mains for around f24. *Rakang Thai (Map 4; ☎ 627 50 12, Elandsgracht 29)*, in the southern Jordaan, is a hip restaurant with over-the-top decorations and delicious cooking. Mains are around f30.

Turkish The Turkish eetcafé *Avare (Map 2; ☎ 639 31 67, Lindengracht 248)*, in the Jordaan, is decked out with wonderfully kitsch interior trimmings found in old-fashioned Jordaan cafés. The food isn't bad either.

Turqoise (Map 4; ☎ 624 20 26, Wolvenstraat 22) is another Turkish eetcafé, less over-the-top than Avare but the food is good, the service is great and it's cheap.

Vegetarian The popular, homy little *De Vliegende Schotel (Map 4; ☎ 625 20 41, Nieuwe Leliestraat 162)*, in the Jordaan, has a blackboard menu with inexpensive meals (under f15), which are served daily from 5.30 to 10.15 pm.

De Bolhoed (Map 2; ☎ 626 18 03, Prinsengracht 60–62) is one of the most popular vegetarian restaurants in town. It serves organic food and amazing cakes in arty surroundings. It's open daily from noon to 10 pm (dinner menu after 5 pm) and has a three-course dagmenu for f35. Lunch is soup and salad, dinner a choice of casserole or Mexican dishes.

Southern Canal Belt

Chinese For an upmarket experience, try *Sichuan Food (Map 4; ☎ 626 93 27, Reguliersdwarsstraat 35)*. The formal setting and Michelin star attract people who want a 'proper' night out, and that's exactly what they get. The food is adapted to Western palates and isn't as spicy as you'd expect from this part of China, but it does taste great and you can pile on a selection of chilli pastes. Mains cost between f30 and f40 and banquets are twice that. There's a large selection of great fish dishes.

Dutch *De Blauwe Hollander (Map 6; ☎ 623 30 14, Leidsekruisstraat 28)* is a cosy

PLACES TO EAT

euro currency converter f1 = €0.45

little place that serves the types of dishes you might get in a Dutch home. It's open daily from 5 to 10 pm. All plates are under f30 – good value in this part of town, which helps to explain why it's always full.

At **Hollands Glorie** *(Map 6; ☎ 624 47 64, Kerkstraat 220–222)*, off Vijzelstraat, the 'authentic' 17th-century interior puts you in the right mood to enjoy the well-prepared dishes (most main plates under f36) – a good choice.

French For a worthwhile splurge in quiet surroundings, try **Zuidlande** *(Map 6; ☎ 620 73 93, Utrechtsedwarsstraat 141)*. The chef, who served his apprenticeship with Paul Bocuse, prepares creative French and Mediterranean food with an excellent balance of flavours. Main dishes (generous servings) are under f40.

Indian There are a few Indian restaurants in town, and one of the best is **Memories of India** *(Map 4; ☎ 623 57 10, Reguliersdwarsstraat 88)*. This clone from London has great vegetarian menus for f35, nonvegetarian for f39.50, and main dishes around f29. It's a bit more expensive than the average Indian restaurant but worth it.

Indonesian One of the few places that does a really good rijsttafel, including properly marinated and barbecued satay that isn't smothered in peanut sauce, is **Indonesia** *(Map 4; ☎ 623 20 35, Korte Leidsedwarsstraat 18)*. Prices start at f39.50 for the small *rijsttafel nasi kuning* (yellow rice) that is big enough to fill most stomachs. Book ahead, and be prepared for over-eager service.

Nearby, **Bojo** *(Map 6; ☎ 622 74 34, Lange Leidsedwarsstraat 51)* is open daily from 5pm to 2 am (4 am on weekends) and is an institution among late eaters. The quality is uneven but it's surprisingly cheap for the Leidseplein area.

Tempo Doeloe *(Map 6; ☎ 625 67 18, Utrechtsestraat 75)* is regarded as one of the best Indonesian restaurants in the city and charges accordingly (though the food can be quite variable, depending on who's on duty). Unless you specifically ask for mild

food it will be served quite spicy but in such a way as to enhance the subtle flavours, not kill them – a skill only mastered by the best Indonesian cooks. The wine list is quite extraordinary, with well-chosen New World wines and a stunning collection of rare bottles. Reservations are essential.

Tujuh Maret *(Map 6; ☎ 427 98 65, Utrechtsestraat 73)*, right next door, is less upmarket but, dare we say it, just as good and more consistently so. You sit on wobbly wicker chairs and the toilet is straight through the kitchen (they have nothing to hide). Mains cost around f25 and the food can be spicy – don't ask for more than 'medium' unless you know what you're doing.

Down the street, **Coffee & Jazz** *(Map 6; ☎ 624 58 51, Utrechtsestraat 113)* is a hip little joint open from 9 am to 8 pm Tuesday to Friday and 10 am to 4 pm on Saturday. Get cosy on a couch, order the spicy chicken curry (f19), an extra large mango juice (f10) and chill out to the great jazz music.

International The restaurant **Dwars** *(Map 6; ☎ 620 66 90, Derde Weteringdwarsstraat 17)* proves that the Dutch can cook very well indeed. Eight tables are served from a small, one-chef open kitchen. A limited-selection, three-course menu best described as Dutch/international costs f47.50, or f50 for the 'chef's surprise' *Carte Blanche*. Everything is fresh (the menu claims that the only items kept in the freezer are vodka and ice cream) and quite delightful so long as the owner himself is cooking (try Saturday). It's closed Sunday.

Szmulewicz *(pronounced 'smoolerwitch'; Map 4; ☎ 620 28 22, Bakkersstraat 12)*, off Rembrandtplein, has a filling dish of the day for f19.50; other dishes are around f25. The food – a smattering of Mexican, American and European dishes – is really well priced and the ambience is lively, with live bands playing on the terrace during summer.

Not far from here is **Sluizer** *(Map 4; ☎ 622 63 76, Utrechtsestraat 43–45)*, which consists of two restaurants: a fish restaurant at No 45 and a 'meat' restaurant at No 43, though both menus are offered in either, including the upstairs 'spillover' area. One of its specialities is spareribs at f29.75; other mains cost around f35. It's an Amsterdam institution along a street of interesting little restaurants. The place is lively and always busy so book ahead; ask to be seated in the romantic, enclosed garden terrace at the back of the restaurant.

Pygma-lion (Map 4; ☎ *420 70 22, Nieuwe Spiegelstraat 5A)* is a South African bistro plating up all those animals you normally go to a game park to see. Expect antelope curry (f38.50), crocodile in sage sauce (f39.50) and sandwiches filled with oven-roasted zebra (f10.75). Alternatively, order coffee and cake and take in the bistro's screaming pink interior.

Italian One of the busiest Italian places in the touristy Leidseplein area is *Piccolino (Map 6;* ☎ *623 14 95, Lange Leidsedwarsstraat 63).* It's open daily from noon to midnight and is most affordable – and always packed. Bookings are essential. Try the pizza calzone (f16). *Panini (Map 6;* ☎ *626 49 39, Vijzelgracht 3–5)* serves delicious focaccias for lunch and equally tasty meals like homemade fettucine with ricotta cheese and tomato sauce in the evenings. Most mains are under f25.

Pastini (Map 4; ☎ *622 17 01, Leidsegracht 29),* on the corner of Keizersgracht, is a small, romantic restaurant overlooking two canals. The antipasto starters (f19.50 for five dishes) are substantial as are the perfectly cooked pasta dishes (f17.50 to f22.50). *Pasta e Basta (Map 4;* ☎ *422 22 26, Nieuwe Spiegelstraat 8)* offers a real night of entertainment. Opera singers serenade you whilst serving a variety of antipasto and pasta. The camp rococo interior adds to the fun as do the reasonable prices (f60 for a three-course set menu). It's open daily from 6 pm to midnight, but you need to book weeks ahead.

Zet Isie (Map 4; ☎ *623 42 59, Reguliersdwarsstraat 23)* looks like a set designer's vision of a rustic trattoria – all whitewashed walls and wooden tables set with bowls of fresh vegetables (decoration only) and crusty focaccia with three varieties of olive oil. The menu offers modern interpretations of Mediterranean dishes like carpaccio, pasta and tiramisu. It's open Tuesday to Sunday from 6 to 11 pm.

Japanese Sushi bars are a recent phenomenon in Amsterdam and they're popping up all over the place. *Bento (Map 6;* ☎ *622 42 48, Kerkstraat 148),* at Nieuwe Spiegelstraat, serves organic Japanese cuisine in a subdued room decorated with rice-paper skylights and bamboo trees. For a treat, order the royal bento box (f65) filled with sushi, sashimi, grilled fish, vegetables, miso soup and rice. It's open Tuesday to Sunday from 6 to 10.30 pm.

Yoichi (Map 6; ☎ *622 68 29, Weteringschans 128)* has a selection of set menus ranging from f65 to f90. Enjoy fastidiously prepared sushi and sashimi in the upstairs tatami room. It's open 6 to 10.30 pm (closed Wednesday).

Mexican One of the first Mexican restaurants in town, *Rose's Cantina (Map 4;* ☎ *625 97 97, Reguliersdwarsstraat 38)* is still as busy as ever. Big main portions à la Dutch go for around f28, and litre pitchers of margarita for f56.50. You can't reserve but it's worth waiting for a table. Food is served from 5.30 to 11 pm daily (the bar stays open until 1 or 2 am).

North American Amsterdam's very own *Planet Hollywood (Map 4;* ☎ *427 78 27, Reguliersbreestraat 35)* is housed in a former cinema and has its own real cinema screen – few (if any) of the other branches around the world can claim such appropriate surroundings. It serves expensive hamburgers, Mexican dishes and bad pasta.

Gary's Muffins (Map 4; ☎ *420 24 06, Reguliersdwarsstraat 53)* is open daily from noon to 3 am and on weekends to 4 am. It serves great fresh bagels, warm chocolate brownies and sweet and savoury muffins to all those clubbers who need healthy late-night snacks. There are several Gary's Muffins around town, including at Marnixstraat 121, Prinsengracht 454, Jodenbreestraat 15 and in the basement of the American Book Center at Kalverstraat 185.

PLACES TO EAT

Seafood The seafood dishes at *Sluizer* *(Map 4; ☎ 622 63 76, Utrechtsestraat 43–45)* are acclaimed. See the preceding International section.

Le Pêcheur (Map 4; ☎ 624 31 21, Reguliersdwarsstraat 32) is renowned for its beautiful garden courtyard and wonderfully prepared fish. The mixed seafood platter is well priced at f39.50 and if you're not too full try the tarte tatin with caramel ice cream for dessert. It's open Monday to Friday from noon to midnight, Saturday from 5 pm, and bookings are advisable.

Spanish Both an eyeful and a mouthful of fun is *Pata Negra (Map 6; ☎ 422 62 50, Utrechtsestraat 142)*. The building's alluringly tiled exterior is matched by equally beautiful painted tiles inside. It's quite a scene on the weekends with groups having a fun (and loud) time sharing jugs of sangria and tapas plates. It's open daily from 6 pm to midnight.

Thai The modern, all-white *Take Thai (Map 6; ☎ 622 05 77, Utrechtsestraat 87)* plates up some of the best Thai food in the city. Choose from a variety of curries spiced according to your palate ('soft, spicy or killing,' as the menu puts it). The roast duck in chilli sauce (f34.50) is a winner as is the fish steamed in lemongrass (f32.50).

Dynasty (Map 4; ☎ 626 84 00, Reguliersdwarsstraat 30) is a lavish restaurant, decorated with colourful, over-the-top murals and rice-paper fans hanging from the ceiling. It serves South-East Asian cuisine, specialising in Thai and seafood. The soups are particularly good – try the coconut chicken for f16.

Vegetarian Near the Rijksmuseum is *Deshima Proeflokaal (Map 6; ☎ 625 75 13, Weteringschans 65)*, part of the macrobiotic Kushi Institute. It provides lunch on weekdays from noon to 2 pm. The shop downstairs is open weekdays from 10 am to 6 pm, Saturday to 5 pm.

A bit farther east, *De Vrolijke Abrikoos (Map 6; ☎ 624 46 72, Weteringschans 76)* isn't fully vegetarian (it also serves meat and fish) but all ingredients are organic. Dishes are under f33, and it's open daily from 5.30 to 9.30 pm.

Golden Temple (Map 6; ☎ 626 85 60, Utrechtsestraat 126) has an international menu with a choice of Indian thali, Middle Eastern or Mexican platters for f22.50 as well as pretty wicked banana cream pie. It's open daily 5 to 9.30 pm.

Nieuwmarkt Neighbourhood

Fusion The sunny, ultra-modern *Zosa (Map 4; ☎ 330 62 41, Kloveniersburgwal 20)* serves a mix of French/Italian dishes with a definite Asian influence. Starters like Vietnamese rice-paper rolls (f12.50) and desserts like flambeed figs stuffed with almonds and apples (f12.50) are particularly good.

International If cheese fondue is your thing, try *Café Bern (Map 4; ☎ 622 00 34, Nieuwmarkt 9)*; book ahead. Also in this area is *Hemelse Modder (Map 4; ☎ 624 32 03, Oude Waal 9)*, a popular, beautifully decorated, modern restaurant serving international dishes at less than upmarket prices. The chocolate mousse ('heavenly mud', hence the name of the place) is a calorific delight. Most mains are under f30 and the three-course set menu costs f47.50.

Eastern Islands

Dutch For simple, cheap fare, try the *Koffiehuis van den Volksbond (Map 5; ☎ 622 12 09, Kadijksplein 4)*, south of the Scheepvaartmuseum. It started life as a charitable coffee house for dockers and still offers good value, with mains around f21 served to a youngish clientele.

International At the lively *Gare de l'Est (Map 1; ☎ 463 06 20, Cruquiusweg 9)* you get a five-course menu of the day for f48 and nothing else, and it's a different menu every day of the year. Four chefs who normally work elsewhere take it in turns to prepare what they want, depending on what's seasonally available. The food can vary from Mediterranean to Asian to North African to Dutch-international and sometimes it's a mixture – you take your chances but won't be disappointed. Check what's on offer when you ring to book. The interesting building, with an eclectic mix of interior decorations, is an old coffee house that served the surrounding industrial area, such as the defunct meat works across the road and the rail yards nearby (hence the name).

Old South

French At the hip and glamorous *Le Garage* *(Map 6; ☎ 679 71 76, Ruysdaelstraat 54)*, all those mirrored walls make it easy to spy local and international celebrities enjoying the French regional cuisine. It's open for lunch weekdays from noon to 2 pm and nightly for dinner from 6 to 11 pm. Be sure to book, because the food is excellent (if slightly expensive) and people come from afar to eat here.

De Pijp

This somewhat bohemian part of town sees relatively few tourists in its often busy eateries. You'll mingle with the locals.

Assyrian Just off the Sarphatipark is *Eufraat (Map 6; ☎ 672 05 79, Eerste van der Helststraat 72)*, which serves Middle Eastern food, but the speciality, as the name almost suggests, is Assyrian. The service is friendly and the food excellent and good value, with mains around f23 and three courses for under f35.

French/International At *District V (Map 6; ☎ 770 08 840, Van der Helstplein 17)* there's a three-course menu for f47.50 and choice is limited – you eat whatever is going. The place has a southern French feel, roughly in keeping with the food, and the ambience is lively. It's often packed, so book ahead. Everything you see – plates, tables, lamps – is made by local artists and is for sale. 'District five' is the old police reference to the Pijp neighbourhood.

International The food is delectable at *De Ondeugd (Map 6; ☎ 672 06 51, Ferdinand Bolstraat 13–15)*, just south of the Heineken Museum, though slightly more expensive than the average Pijp eatery – mains are

around f38. The place is always busy, so book ahead.

Surinamese Surinamese restaurants are small and specialise in takeaway food, though there might be a few tables and chairs. They close early and some are only open during the day (eg, for lunch). Stroll around the backstreets near the Albert Cuyp market, or try *Albert Cuyp 67 (Map 6; ☎ 671 13 96, Albert Cuypstraat 67)* or *Albina (Map 6; ☎ 675 51 35, Albert Cuypstraat 69)* next door.

Vegetarian The fully vegetarian *Harvest (Map 6; ☎ 676 99 95, Govert Flinckstraat 251)* purchases its ingredients at the nearby Albert Cuyp market. Dagschotels are under f22, and there's a terrace out the back and a nonsmoking section. It's open Monday to Saturday from 5.30 to 11.30 pm (kitchen closes at 9.30 pm).

For a macro-gourmet dinner party cooked for you in a convivial setting, call Sandra Herceg *(☎ 673 65 69, Rustenburgerstraat 399)*. She creates organic dinners in her home (everything from Japanese to Mediterranean) Wednesday to Saturday. Bookings are essential – call before midday to organise dinner that night.

Other Areas

French Those searching for the perfect venue for an out-to-impress business lunch or dinner should look no further than *La Rive (Map 7; ☎ 622 60 60, Professor Tulpplein 1)* in the Amstel Inter-Continental Hotel. Two Michelin stars and a formal dining room are sure to impress. The six-course set menu costs f150.

Surinamese For some of the best Surinamese Indian and ditto Indonesian cuisine in town, seek out *Riaz (Map 1; ☎ 683 64 53, Bilderdijkstraat 193)*, a totally unpretentious local eatery with sterile decor. It's a bit out of the way but the food is surprisingly good and three courses will come to less than f25. Apart from meat dishes you can also have Surinamese and Indian vegetarian (the Surinamese dishes are larger).

euro currency converter f1 = €0.45

The place is halal, so there's no pork or alcohol. Arrive early: it closes at 9 pm and is closed all day Saturday.

Third World *Soeterijn Café-Restaurant (Map 7; ☎ 568 83 92, Linnaeusstraat 2)* is part of the Tropenmuseum. People often have dinner here before attending a performance in the adjacent theatre and the specials of the week coincide with the performers' country of origin. It's open Monday to Saturday from 5 to 8.30 pm (also open for lunch Tuesday to Friday) and you're advised to reserve.

GAY & LESBIAN RESTAURANTS
The following places are popular among the gay and lesbian community.

Getto (Map 4; ☎ 421 51 51, Warmoesstraat 51) offers a campy interior, funky music (DJ) and very attentive service. Solid, American/English meals are good value for around f18.50 but people don't really come here for the food. Tuesday from 7 pm is 'Getto Girls' women's night.

La Strada (Map 4; ☎ 625 02 76, Nieuwezijds Voorburgwal 93–95) has a mixed lesbian, gay and hetero clientele. There's a pleasant ambience with a reasonable kitchen and very friendly service. Three-course menus start at f28.50, and mains à la carte are under f33. Another gay-friendly place is *Spanjer en van Twist (Map 4; ☎ 639 01 09, Leliegracht 60)*, with romantic canal-side tables that make it a popular destination on summer evenings. It serves sandwiches for lunch, and a main meal at night will set you back about f22.

SELF-SERVICE CAFETERIAS
The *Hema department store (Map 4; ☎ 623 41 76, Nieuwendijk 174)*, a couple of blocks south of Centraal Station, has a good, inexpensive cafeteria upstairs. It's open Monday to Friday from 11 am to 5.15 pm, Thursday to 8.15 pm, Saturday to 4.45 pm, Sunday from noon to 4.15 pm. It's also good for coffee and ice cream.

Other department stores, like *Vroom & Dreesmann* and *Bijenkorf*, also have worthwhile cafeterias. See also the following Self-Catering section for supermarkets that do good takeaway food.

The *Atrium (Map 4; ☎ 525 39 99)* is a student refectory (mensa) in the Binnengasthuis university complex, off the southern end of Oudezijds Achterburgwal. A student magazine rated the food 4½ out of 10 but where else can you eat for well under f10? It's open weekdays from noon to 2 pm and 5 to 7 pm.

FAST FOOD
There are any number of sandwich shops *(broodjeszaken)* or snack bars to still your immediate hunger. The latter serve greasy junk food (French fries etc) but the former do a reasonable job with buns rather than sandwiches. If you're in a particularly healthy mood, ask for a *bruin broodje gezond* (brown bun healthy), with salad filling.

Vlaamse frites (Flemish fries) are French fries made from whole potatoes rather than the potato pulp you'll get if the sign only says 'frites'. They're supposed to be smothered in mayonnaise (though you can ask for ketchup or *pindasaus*, peanut sauce) and will fill your stomach for around f3. One of the best places to try them is at the *Vlaams Friteshuis (Map 4; Voetboogstraat 31)* off Spui Square, Monday to Saturday from 11 am to 6 pm, Sunday noon to 5.30 pm.

An *uitsmijter* (literally 'bouncer') is fried eggs – sunny, often gluggy, side up – with cheese or meat (usually ham, sometimes beef) and garnish. Many cafés and snack bars serve this and it makes a filling breakfast or inexpensive lunch for under f10.

Also try seafood at one of the seafood stalls around town. Raw, slightly salted herring (about f4, cut into bite-sized bits and served with optional onion and gherkin) might not sound appealing, but you may think differently once you've tried it. The same applies to smoked eel, which, like herring, is quite filling, especially if taken in a bun. If you still can't bear the thought, go for shrimps or *gerookte makreel* (smoked mackerel).

Israeli or Lebanese snack bars specialise in *shoarma*, a pitta bread filled with sliced lamb from a vertical spit, salad and a choice of sauces, which makes a filling snack. In some parts of the world it's known as a *gyros* or *doner kebab*. Such places also do a mean *felafel* (spiced chickpea patties, deep-fried).

Poffertjes are miniature pancakes, heaped on a plate and topped with butter and sprinkled with caster sugar – absolutely delicious. They're not a dessert but a snack served at special stalls or parlours using supposedly secret recipes. Try them at the *Carrousel* at Weteringcircuit *(Map 6)*.

SELF-CATERING

Albert Heijn (AH), the country's dominant supermarket chain, seems pretty much to have sewn up the centre of Amsterdam, with branches at Nieuwezijds Voorburgwal 226 behind the Royal Palace (with great stand-up or takeaway meals), Koningsplein 6 near Leidsestraat, Vijzelstraat 117, Haarlemmerdijk 1, Museumplein (underground under the 'dog-ear' in front of the Concertgebouw), Nieuwmarkt 18, Jodenbreestraat 21, Westerstraat 79–87 and Van Woustraat 148–150, among others. They've driven many neighbourhood shops and other supermarkets out of business, and the lack of competition shows in their occasional shabbiness and uninterested service. Still, they're well stocked and open long hours, including weekends.

Other food shops include *Hema (Map 4; ☎ 623 41 76, Nieuwendijk 174)*, a department store with a good food section at the back, and *Dirk van den Broek (Map 6; ☎ 673 93 93, Eerste van der Helststraat 25)*, behind the Heineken Museum with another entrance at Marie Heinekenplein 25 – this is one of the country's least expensive supermarket chains, and beats AH on price. *Aldi Supermarket (Map 6; Nieuwe Weteringstraat 28)*, near Vijzelgracht, is cheaper than any of the above but quite depressing.

As you're paying at a supermarket the clerk may ask, *Wilt u zegels?* (Do you want stamps?). Say *nee* (no) because the stamps cost money and are only a nuisance. Beer bottles, crates and plastic soft-drink containers are returnable for a deposit (added to the purchase price when you buy them) – you'll usually find a bottle-return machine near the supermarket turnstiles.

Bring your own shopping bag: for environmental reasons, supermarkets charge f0.25 to f0.50 for a plastic bag.

PLACES TO EAT

Entertainment

Amsterdam is many things to many people but no-one in their right mind would call it boring. It's one of the entertainment capitals of Europe, with wonderful pubs; music, theatre and film programs to suit all tastes; and frantic nightlife that arouses even the most jaded party animals.

CAFÉS (PUBS)

When locals say *café* they mean a pub, also known as a *kroeg*, and there are over 1000 of them in the city. Proprietors prefer the term *café* (yes, they serve coffee as well, but very much as a sideline). See Drinks in the Places to Eat chapter for a summary of popular drinks.

Many cafés have outside seating on a *terras* (terrace) that may be covered and heated in winter. These are great places to relax and watch passers-by, soak up the sun, read a paper or write postcards for a few hours. Once you've ordered a drink you'll be left alone but you might be expected to order the occasional top-up. If all tables are occupied, don't be shy about asking if a seat is taken and sharing a table.

A good tradition in many cafés, especially the so-called grand cafés, is the indoor reading table with the day's papers and news magazines, including one or two in English.

The price for a standard beer varies from around f2.75 in the outer suburbs to f4.50 in the popular Leidseplein and Rembrandtplein areas. If you occupy a table or sit at the bar, it's common to put drinks on a tab and to pay when you leave. If things are busy or you sit outside you'll probably have to pay per service.

Types of Cafés

Once upon a time cafés only served a few perfunctory snacks but many these days have proper menus. Those that take their food seriously (or would like their customers to think they do) call themselves *eetcafé* and their food can be very good indeed. Many cafés in the following categories serve food.

The most famous type is the **brown café** *(bruin café)*. The true specimen has been in business for a while, is stained by smoke (recent aspirants simply slap on the brown paint), has sand on the wooden floor, and provides an atmosphere conducive to deep and meaningful conversation. There might be Persian rugs on the tables to soak up spilled beer.

Grand cafés are spacious with comfortable furniture. They're all the rage, and any pub that installs a few solid tables and comfortable chairs will call itself a grand café. Some are grand indeed, and when they open at 10 am they're perfect for a lazy brunch with relaxing chamber music tinkling away in the background.

Theatre cafés attract performing artists and other types who do a lot of drinking. There are also a few **tasting houses** *(proeflokalen)* that used to be attached to distilleries (a holdover from the 17th century when many small distilleries operated around town), where you can try dozens of *genevers* and liqueurs.

Some cafés straddle these categories and others don't really fit in, such as the relatively new phenomenon of Irish pubs.

Opening hours depend on whether the café has opted to be a 'day business' (7 am to 1 am, weekends to 3 am), an 'evening business' (8 pm to 3 am, weekends to 4 am) or a 'night business' (10 pm to 4 am, weekends to 5 am). Cafés are free to adjust their hours within these limits but very few open before 9 am.

Brown Cafés

Medieval Centre There are more brown cafés here than elsewhere but many are newcomers that pander to tourists. One of the oldest and prettiest in the Nieuwmarkt area is *Lokaal 't Loosje (Map 4; ☎ 627 26 35, Nieuwmarkt 32–34)*. It has beautiful etched-glass windows and tile tableaus on the walls. It's a student pub in the evening with mixed Nieuwmarkt clientele during the day.

ENTERTAINMENT

Near Spui Square are quite a few brown cafés worth seeking out. The **Pilsener Club** *(Map 4; ☎ 623 17 77, Begijnesteeg 4)*, popularly known as the Engelse Reet, is small, narrow and ramshackle. You can't do anything here but drink and talk, which is what a 'real' brown café is all about. It only started in 1893 but has hardly changed since then. Beer comes straight from the vat behind the draughting alcove and connoisseurs say they can taste the difference (most places have vats in a cellar or side room with long hoses to the bar). **De Schutter** *(Map 4; ☎ 622 46 08, Voetboogstraat 13–15)* is a student eetcafé open daily from 11 am but the kitchen operates from 5.45 to 10 pm; inexpensive *dagschotels* (dishes of the day) start at f15 and mains go up to f17.50. There are several lively bars along this street.

On Spui Square itself, visit **Hoppe** *(Map 4; ☎ 420 44 20, Spui 18)*, one of the best-known cafés in the city. It has been enticing drinkers behind its thick curtain for more than 300 years – the entrance is to the right of the pub-with-terrace of the same name. The crowd spills over onto the pavement in summer and helps Hoppe achieve one of the highest beer turnovers in the city; they wear smart business suits and coexist peacefully with left-wing journalists and writers at **Café De Zwart** *(☎ 624 65 11)* across the alley.

Within the Canal Belt The Jordaan area and adjoining Prinsengracht are packed with wonderful cafés. **Het Papeneiland** *(Map 2; ☎ 624 19 89, Prinsengracht 2)*, on the corner of Brouwersgracht, is a 17th-century gem with its Delft-blue tiles and central stove. The name, Papists' Island, goes back to the Reformation when there was a clandestine Catholic church across the canal, allegedly linked to the other side by a secret tunnel. You won't be the only tourist visiting this café, and with good reason. Nearby is **De II Prinsen** *(Map 2; ☎ 624 97 22, Prinsenstraat 27)*, on the corner of Prinsengracht. Its large windows, mosaic floor and big terrace on Prinsengracht create a pleasant setting.

De 2 Zwaantjes *(Map 4; ☎ 625 27 29, Prinsengracht 114)* is an authentic Jordaan café where locals meet to play cards. On Friday, Saturday and Sunday nights it's sing-along Dutch ballads. It's hilarious to join over a hundred people squished into the small, smoky room merrily belting out torch and pop standards. Note the imposing and unique leadlight awning over the bar (backlit for effect).

Almost next door, **De Prins** *(Map 4; ☎ 624 93 82, Prinsengracht 124)* is a pleasant, popular and unassuming brown café that does good lunchtime sandwiches and a terrific blue cheese fondue (f22.50). The charming **Café 't Smalle** *(Map 4; ☎ 623 96 17, Egelantiersgracht 12)* just around the corner has such a pretty and convivial terrace that it's packed from early morning to late at night during summer. It opened in 1786 as a genever distillery and tasting house. The interior was restored during the 1970s with antique porcelain beer pumps and leadlight windows.

In the Jordaan itself, **Café Nol** *(Map 2; ☎ 624 53 80, Westerstraat 109)* is the epitome of the Jordaan café, a place where the original Jordanese (ie, before students, artists and professionals moved in) still sing oompah ballads with drunken abandon. The kitsch interior is so over-the-top that it's a must-see. Diagonally opposite, the slightly scruffy **Café 't Monumentje** *(Map 2; ☎ 624 35 41, Westerstraat 120)* is always full of barflies, backgammon players and locals. It's a good spot for a beer and a snack after shopping at the Westermarkt.

De Tuin *(Map 4; ☎ 624 45 59, Tweede Tuindwarsstraat 13)* is a good place to start the evening. Its youngish clientele enjoys the wide selection of Belgian beers and the funky soul music. **De Reiger** *(Map 4; ☎ 624 74 26, Nieuwe Leliestraat 34)* was one of the first brown cafés to serve food. It's narrow at the front but the noisy dining section at the back is more spacious.

A bit farther south on Prinsengracht is **Van Puffelen** *(Map 4; ☎ 624 62 70, Prinsengracht 377)*, a café-restaurant popular among students and other intellectual types. The restaurant area, with food prices marked

ENTERTAINMENT

on blackboards, is quieter than the pub (in most places it's the other way round). It's open weekdays from 3 pm, weekends from noon, and the kitchen opens at 6 pm.

Café Het Molenpad (Map 4; ☎ 625 96 80, Prinsengracht 653) is close to the main public library and attracts artists, students and tourists. The walls are lined with art work (changes monthly) and the food is above average, especially the teriyaki beef and vegetable salad (f16.50).

De Doffer (Map 4; ☎ 622 66 86, Runstraat 12–14) is another popular student café with affordable food. The dining room with its old Heineken posters, large wooden tables and fresh flowers is particularly ambient at night. There's also an adjoining bar which opens between 1 and 4 am on Friday and Saturday.

De Pieper (Map 4; ☎ 626 47 75, Prinsengracht 424) is small and unassuming but unmistakably old (from 1664), and is considered by some to be the king of the brown cafés.

On Leidseplein, venerable *Reynders (Map 4; ☎ 623 44 19, Leidseplein 6)* has recently introduced an Irish menu and Guinness on tap, but still retains its old-world charm and has a pleasant terrace (heated in winter) that makes it a good place for people-watching.

Eylders (Map 4; ☎ 624 27 04, Korte Leidsedwarsstraat 47), a few buildings up from Reynders, is an artists' café with exhibits and attractive leadlights. During WWII it was a meeting place for artists who refused to toe the cultural line imposed by the Nazis, and the spirit lingers.

In the southern corner of the canal belt is *De Fles (Map 6; ☎ 624 96 44, Vijzelstraat 137)*; its entrance is down the stairs on Prinsengracht. It's a somewhat forgotten but proud café, with an open kitchen that served meals long before it became fashionable for pubs to do so. You'll eat well for less than f30, but they really should fix that kitchen ventilation.

Not far from here, *Oosterling (Map 6; ☎ 623 41 40, Utrechtsestraat 140)* is as authentic as it gets and is steeped in history (it started in the early 1700s as a tea and coffee outlet for the United East India Company).

Things get busy at the end of the working day, when employees from the Nederlandsche Bank come across the road to swap bills for drinks. It's one of the very few cafés with a bottle-shop (liquor-store) permit.

Outside the Canal Belt A typical Pijp eetcafé, *Koffiehuis Dusart (Map 1; ☎ 671 28 18, Dusartstraat 53)* has a kitsch interior, frequented by taxi drivers and other locals. There's a large menu with mains for around f21. Try the spareribs: it doesn't proclaim them the speciality for nothing.

Grand Cafés

The *Oininio* centre *(Map 2; ☎ 553 93 26, Prins Hendrikkade 20–21)* is diagonally opposite Centraal Station. Its future has been under a cloud in recent years, which is a pity because it's a peaceful retreat in an otherwise commercial and touristy neighbourhood. The complex includes a Japanese tea garden and a spacious, tropical-style grand café serving delicious vegetarian food.

To the west is *Café de Vergulde Gaper (Map 2; ☎ 624 89 75, Prinsenstraat 30)*, a former pharmacy decorated with old chemists' bottles and vintage posters. The pleasant terrace is busy late afternoons with media types meeting for after-work drinks. Farther west is *Dulac (Map 2; ☎ 624 42 65, Haarlemmerstraat 118)*. This former bank building has been outrageously decorated in a mixture of styles (Turkish, Art Nouveau, Amsterdam School) and is definitely worth a visit. It's open from 4 pm to 1 am (to 3 am weekends).

Café de Jaren (Map 4; ☎ 625 57 71, Nieuwe Doelenstraat 20) is a huge, bright grand café overlooking the Amstel from its balcony and water terraces. It attracts a slightly yuppyish crowd in their 20s and 30s. Service can be slow but it's a pleasant place to have brunch on a Sunday (be sure to try the banana cream pie, f5.75). The café's great reading table has some foreign publications.

The glitzy *Café-Restaurant Dantzig (Map 4; ☎ 620 90 39, Zwanenburgwal 15)*, nearby, in the Stopera on the Amstel, has a great riverside terrace that's always busy in summer and affords good views over the water and lots of sunlight. It's just the place to unwind after shopping at Waterlooplein market.

The pearl of the grand cafés is *Mediacafé De Kroon* (Map 4; ☎ 625 20 11, Rembrandtplein 17-1) which attracts people of all ages. Walk through the recessed entrance and up the stairs to the 1st floor or take the lift. It has an appealing, neocolonial design with a biological bent (ancient microscope on the counter, cabinets with pinned butterflies and skeletons), and a beautiful covered balcony terrace with a good view over Rembrandtplein. The food in the restaurant section (mains around f38) is worth trying. The rest of the building houses radio and TV studios.

On Spui Square, stop at *Luxembourg* (Map 4; ☎ 620 62 64, Spui 22–24), a brown café on a grand scale with an interesting mix of people. Watch the goings-on in the square from the terrace. The menu includes tasty breakfasts, great sandwiches and other lunchtime surprises like the 'Royale' snack platter (f29.50) which comprises cured meats, Dutch cheese and deep-fried croquettes. Check the reading table or buy a paper at Athenaeum newsagency and read it in the morning sun.

A few doors up the street is *Café Dante* (Map 4; ☎ 638 88 39, Spuistraat 320), a big, Art-Deco-style space with an art gallery on the 1st floor. It's quite peaceful during the day, but between 5 and 9 pm weeknights it transforms into a boisterous bar where stockbrokers and suits come to unwind.

Farther north is *Café ter Kuile* (Map 4; ☎ 639 10 55, Torensteeg 4). Its large terrace is always busy with students, businesspeople and ladies-who-lunch enjoying a coffee and cake or more extravagant dishes like lobster with bechamel sauce (f17.50).

The oldest and by far the most stylish grand café is *Café Americain* (Map 6; ☎ 556 32 32, Leidsekade 97), under the American Hotel just off Leidseplein (entrance on the Leidseplein side). This Art-Deco monument opened in 1902 and was extensively renovated in 1993. It's the sort of place that attracts rafts of celebrities, as a visit to the Nightwatch bar will attest (the walls are lined with photos of stars like Paul Weller, Lenny Kravitz and Eric Clapton). Prices are stiff but it's worth visiting at least once for a coffee, beer or snack; meals are fine but expect to pay between f75 and f100 for a three-course dinner. The reading table is a serious affair, and there's a nonsmoking section.

Irish & English Pubs

Irish bars are currently so popular in Amsterdam that many pubs are undergoing extensive renovations and reopening with Guinness on tap and some Gaelic decorations. There's also a preponderance of rather formulaic Irish chain pubs around Damstraat and Leidseplein catering mainly to office workers.

Mulligans (Map 4; ☎ 622 13 30, Amstel 100), near Rembrandtplein, is probably the most 'authentic', at least music-wise. There's live Irish music and dancing most nights at 9 pm (no cover charge), Guinness on tap (of course) and a congenial atmosphere. *O'Donnell's* (Map 6; ☎ 676 77 86, Ferdinand Bolstraat 5), at Marie Heinekenplein, just south of the Heineken Museum, is a large Irish pub with a few snugs (great if you can grab one). In the red-light district, try *Durty Nelly's* (Map 4; ☎ 638 01 25, Warmoesstraat 117), which attracts many foreign visitors from the cheap hotels in the area. Irish breakfasts are served from 9 am, Friday to Monday, and it has dorm beds too.

Other reputable Irish pubs include *The Blarney Stone* (Map 2; ☎ 623 38 30, Nieuwendijk 29), beloved for its country-style interior; *The Dubliner* (Map 6; ☎ 679 97 43, Dusartstraat 51), one of the oldest Irish bars in town; and *Molly Malone's* (Map 4; ☎ 624 11 50, Oudezijds Kolk 9), which is regularly packed with Irish expats.

Nearby is the *Last Waterhole* (Map 4; ☎ 624 48 14, Oudezijds Armsteeg 12), a popular place for young, mainly English-speaking travellers. It has three pool tables, a giant video screen, jam sessions weeknights at 9 pm, and rock or blues groups Friday and Saturday at 10 pm. There's also a happy hour from 8 to 10 pm and hostel beds for f25 to f35.

ENTERTAINMENT

Homesick English visitors might wish to sample a pint at the ***Old Bell*** *(Map 4; ☎ 624 76 82, Rembrandtplein 46)* on the corner of Utrechtsestraat, a comfortable English pub that has barely changed since it opened in the 1960s. It's popular among businesspeople and staff from the nearby banks, and of course tourists, but is rather less appealing on weekends when brazen Dutch youth take over.

Tasting Houses

Just off Dam Square, ***Proeflokaal Wijnand Fockinck*** *(Map 4; ☎ 639 26 95, Pijlsteeg 31),* through an arcade behind Grand Hotel Krasnapolsky, is a small tasting house without seats or stools, where you can try scores of different genevers and liqueurs – some are quite expensive and all are potent! Behind the tasting house is a pretty garden courtyard where well-prepared lunch and snacks are served daily from 10 am to 6 pm.

Nearby is ***De Drie Fleschjes*** *(Map 4; ☎ 624 84 43, Gravenstraat 18),* behind the Nieuwe Kerk. The place dates from 1650, and is dominated by old vats that are rented out to groups whose members can help themselves. Be sure to have a look in the glass-fronted cupboard which houses a collection of *kalkoentjes,* small bottles with hand-painted portraits of the city's former mayors. It's open Monday to Saturday from noon to 8.30 pm, Sunday from 3 to 7 pm.

Theatre Cafés

De Smoeshaan in Theater Bellevue *(Map 4; ☎ 625 03 68, Leidsekade 90)* gets pretty lively with theatre visitors and artists. There's a good restaurant upstairs. The ***Felix Meritis Café*** *(Map 4; ☎ 626 23 21, Keizersgracht 324)* is housed in a beautiful and refined room dominated by a dramatic cast-iron chandelier. Performing artists from around Europe and the city's cultural cognoscenti gather to imbibe and converse. It's open Monday to Friday 9 am to 7 pm.

Another theatre café worth checking is ***Blincker*** *(Map 4; ☎ 627 19 38, Sint Barberenstraat 7–9),* in the Frascati theatre complex, in an alley off Nes. It has an attractive modern design in steel and marble with plants and an open mezzanine floor. There's a large collection of wines and decent food.

De Brakke Grond *(Map 4; ☎ 626 00 44, Nes 43)* is part of the Flemish Cultural Centre and does an honest trade in Flemish beer and food.

Women's Cafés

Saarein II *(Map 4; ☎ 623 49 01, Elandsstraat 119),* in the south of the Jordaan, was a focal point of the feminist movement during the late 1970s. The venue itself dates from the early 1600s and the stunningly beautiful interior has been kept intact except for the paintwork. It's no longer run by a women's collective and is now a 'mixed gay' café where anyone is welcome, though it's still a premier meeting place for lesbians. There's a small menu with tapas and a dish of the week.

In the north of the Jordaan is ***Vandenberg*** *(Map 2; ☎ 622 27 16, Lindengracht 95),* a cosy eetcafé popular among older lesbians but men come here too. A meal will set you back about f25, or you can just have a drink.

Vivelavie *(Map 4; ☎ 624 01 14, Amstelstraat 7),* off Rembrandtplein, is one of the more popular 'lipstick lesbian' cafés in town. It's a lively place, with loud music and large windows so everyone can see out or in. In summer the outdoor terrace is very sceney (especially on the weekend). It's open from 3 pm to 1 am Thursday and Sunday, and to 3 am on Friday and Saturday.

Sarah's Grannies *(Map 6; ☎ 624 01 45, Kerkstraat 176)* is a cosy, women-friendly place serving snacks, salads and warm meals with classical music in the background. Works by artists enliven the walls. The food is good and relatively inexpensive.

Other Cafés

In de Wildeman *(Map 4; ☎ 638 23 48, Kolksteeg 3),* between Nieuwendijk and Nieuwezijds Voorburgwal, is a former distillery tasting house transformed into a beautiful 'beer café' with over 200 bottled beers and a separate smokefree area.

Himalaya *(Map 4; ☎ 626 08 99, Warmoesstraat 56)* is a New-Age tearoom with a vegetarian and vegan menu, open Monday from 1 to 6 pm, and Tuesday to Saturday from 10 am to 6 pm (Thursday to 8.30 pm) – just the place to put some yin back into your yang.

North of Spui Square is **Gollem** *(Map 4;* ☎ *626 66 45, Raamsteeg 4)*, the pioneer of Amsterdam's 'beer cafés'. Choose from 200 beers on tap or in the bottle. Its small interior is covered in beer paraphernalia (old coasters, bottles and posters) and the ambience is never dull.

Close by, on Nieuwezijds Voorburgwal, are three of the city's hippest 'see and be seen' bars. **Bar Bep** *(Map 4;* ☎ *626 56 49, Nieuwezijds Voorburgwal 260)* looks like a 1950s Eastern European cabaret lounge, with olive-green vinyl couches and ruby-red walls. It serves food during the day but really starts heating up after 6 pm, with groovy film makers, photographers and artists. Next door is **Diep** *(Map 4;* ☎ *420 20 20, Nieuwezijds Voorburgwal 256)*, a similar style of bar with an ever-changing array of art work and decoration. This may include chandeliers made of bubble-wrap, a 6-foot fibreglass hammerhead shark and illuminated electronic signs above the bar. The crowd is as quirky as the interior. Farther down the street is **Seymour Likely** *(Map 4;* ☎ *627 14 27, Nieuwezijds Voorburgwal 250)*, a late-night club/lounge which attracts a 'hipper-than-thou' crowd and plays a laid-back mix of reggae and hip-hop.

Maximiliaan *(Map 4;* ☎ *626 62 80, Kloveniersburgwal 6–8)*, off Nieuwmarkt Square, is a rambling brewery pub with copper kettles. It opened in 1992 on the site of a former monastery brewery and is one of only two breweries that still operate in the city (the other is Bierbrouwerij 't IJ – see East of the Plantage in the Things to See & Do chapter). It has a restaurant, tasting area, tours and beer seminars, and several home-brewed beers on tap (some seasonal).

The most impressive café in the Nieuwmarkt area has to be **de Waag** *(Map 4;* ☎ *422 77 72, Nieuwmarkt 4)*, in the middle of the square. The former 15th-century weigh house is now a café which combines old-world charm (over 300 candles hang from wrought-iron candelabras) with new-world technology (free Internet access with your drink). It's open from 10 am to 1 am daily and serves pretty good sandwiches and salads.

Café-Restaurant Kapitein Zeppo's *(Map 4;* ☎ *624 20 57, Gebed Zonder End 5)*, just off Grimburgwal, has a mixed clientele including young students, and is one of the livelier pick-up joints in town. There's regular live music, and first Sunday in the month is 'café chantant' where anyone can get up and sing with real big-band backing. The food is OK but it's the atmosphere that attracts the crowds.

At Rembrandtplein, **Café Schiller** *(Map 4;* ☎ *624 98 46, Rembrandtplein 26)* – not to be confused with the terrace under the hotel of the same name – is worth a visit for its stylish, Art-Deco interior with portraits of Dutch actors and cabaret artists from the 1920s and '30s. It's a smallish place with a clientele of journalists, artists and students, and does good food, with dagschotels from f20. It's open from 4 pm to 1 am Sunday to Thursday, to 2 am on Friday and Saturday.

South of here, **Kort** *(Map 6;* ☎ *626 11 99, Amstelveld 12)*, along the southern wall of the Amstelkerk, has a wonderful, quiet terrace looking out over Prinsengracht where you can spend peaceful hours in summer. An international menu is served in two upmarket rooms resplendent with fresh flowers and interesting art work.

South-east of the canal belt is **Café De IJsbreker** *(Map 7;* ☎ *665 30 14, Weesperzijde 23)*, on the Amstel beyond the Amstel Inter-Continental Hotel and through the pedestrian underpass under Mauritskade. This pleasant café belongs to the IJsbreker centre for contemporary music and has a great riverside terrace in summer where you can mix it with the country's leading experimental musicians – at least until 2002 when the centre moves to the Eastern Docklands. Service can be incredibly slow.

Café Thijssen *(Map 2;* ☎ *623 89 94, Brouwersgracht 107)*, in the Jordaan, has a lovely Art-Deco-inspired interior with stained-glass windows. It's busy on the weekends with groups of friends meeting up for a late brunch and staying on till dinner.

euro currency converter f1 = €0.45

Out towards the west, in the Westergas-fabriek complex beyond the Haarlem Quarter, is *Café West Pacific (Map 2; ☎ 488 77 78, Haarlemmerweg 8–10)*. It's a large café with a restaurant and lots of character, and is popular with trendy young things. It's open from 11.30 to 1 am (to 3 am on weekends) and after 11 pm it functions as a club (speed garage, big beat and hip-hop music).

Farther west is *Café-Restaurant Amsterdam (Map 1; ☎ 682 26 66, Watertorenplein 6)*, housed in a former water-processing plant. It's one of the city's hippest eateries. Expect classic French brasserie food (steak bearnaise f30, crepes f7) served in a vast, industrial-style space; the food is OK but the surroundings are better. Note the 100-foot wooden ceilings, hooks and chains and the 22 huge floodlights rescued from the former Ajax and Olympic stadiums. It's open daily from 11 am to 1 am.

COFFEESHOPS

Many establishments that call themselves *koffieshop* (as opposed to *koffiehuis*, espresso bar or sandwich shop) are in the cannabis business, though they do serve coffee. There are also a few *hashcafés* serving alcohol that are barely distinguishable from pubs.

You'll have no trouble finding a coffeeshop: they're all over town, seemingly on every corner. The ubiquitous hemp leaves have been taken down to appease concerned politicians (see Drugs in the Facts for the Visitor chapter), but it's a safe bet that an establishment showing palm leaves and perhaps Rastafarian colours (red, gold and green) will have something to do with cannabis – take a look at the clientele and ask at the bar for the list of goods on offer, usually packaged in small bags for f25.

Another concession to politics is that 'space' cakes and cookies are sold in a rather low-key fashion, mainly because tourists had problems. If you're unused to their effects, or the time they can take to kick in and run their course, you could indeed be in for a rather involved experience. Ask the staff how much you should take and heed their advice, even if nothing happens after an hour. Many coffeeshops sell magic mushrooms, which is quite legal because it's an untreated, natural product (though this may change, with the argument that drying the mushrooms is a treatment, which makes them illegal).

Cannabis products used to be imported but these days the country has top-notch home produce, so-called *nederwiet* (NAY-der-weet) developed by horticulturists and grown in greenhouses with up to five harvests a year. Even the police admit it's a superior product, especially the potent 'superskunk' with up to 13% of the active substance THC (Nigerian grass has 5% and Colombian 7%). According to a government-sponsored poll of coffeeshop owners, nederwiet has captured over half the market and hash is in decline even among tourists.

Listed here are some of the more popular coffeeshops and a few quirky ones too. Price and quality are OK – you won't get ripped off in a coffeeshop like you would on the street. Most shops are open from 10 am to 1 am Sunday to Thursday, to 3 am Friday and Saturday.

Barney's (Map 2; ☎ 625 97 61, Haarlemmerstraat 102) – this coffeeshop serves huge breakfasts all day from 7 am to 8 pm; the interior is a mixture of trippy New-Age art and *Lord of the Rings*-inspired furniture

The Bulldog (Map 4; ☎ 627 19 08, Leidseplein 13–17) – the most famous coffeeshop chain has five branches around town; this is the largest, with Internet facilities, two bars, pool tables and a café serving food

Global Chillage (Map 4; ☎ 639 11 54, Kerkstraat 51) – a small shop near Leidsestraat, with chilled-out music (African and jazzy beats), trippy murals and happy smokers relaxing on comfortable couches

Greenhouse (Map 4; ☎ 627 17 39, Oudezijds Voorburgwal 191) – the recipient of many awards at the annual High Times festival, this Indonesian-inspired coffeeshop is one of the most popular in town; smokers love decorative details like the undersea-themed bathrooms and, of course, the high-quality weed and hash

Grey Area (Map 4; ☎ 420 43 01, Oude Leliestraat 2) – owned by a couple of laid-back American guys, this tiny shop next door to Foodism introduced the extra-sticky, flavourful 'Double Bubble Gum' weed to the city's smokers

Homegrown Fantasy *(Map 4; ☎ 627 56 83, Nieuwezijds Voorburgwal 87A)* – quality Dutch-grown product, pleasant staff and good tunes make this venue a popular choice; be sure to visit the toilets for a visual treat

Kadinsky *(Map 4; ☎ 624 70 23, Rosmarijnsteeg 9)* – hidden away near Spui Square, this attractive, well-decorated coffeeshop has a good selection of hash and grass; the music selection is always groovy

Pi Kunst & Koffie *(Map 4; ☎ 622 59 60, Tweede Laurierdwarsstraat 64)* – canalside coffeeshop with art works on the wall, Internet facilities, backgammon and chess sets and computers for gamers in the basement

Rokerij *(Map 2; no phone, Singel 8)* – African and South American vibes predominate at this beautiful coffeeshop close to Centraal Station; the painted mural/collage on the wall is sure to trip you out after a smoke of the strong 'White Widow' grass (f17.50 a gram)

La Tertulia *(Map 4; no phone, Prinsengracht 312)* – this mother-and-daughter-run coffeeshop in the Jordaan is a backpackers' favourite; relax by the fish pond, play some board games and enjoy the Van Gogh-inspired murals; the organic food is pretty fine as well

MUSIC

For a description of the local music scene, see Music in the Facts about Amsterdam chapter. At many of the venues listed below, just turn up at the door and pay to get in. You might want to book ahead, however, for famous acts or highbrow performances – check the *Uitkrant* (see Useful Publications in the Facts for the Visitor chapter) to see what's happening where, or consult the weekly agenda in the *Parool* newspaper's Saturday *PS* magazine. Apart from the *Uitkrant*, the Amsterdam Uitburo also publishes a bimonthly pop and jazz listing available free from record shops, cafés and music venues. For further information and bookings, contact the venues direct, or the Uitburo (Map 6; Leidseplein 26) which is open daily from 10 am to 6 pm (Thursday to 9 pm), or ring the Uitlijn on ☎ 0900-01 91 (f0.75 per minute) which operates daily from 9 am to 9 pm.

Classical & Contemporary

A pleasant feature of the Amsterdam music scene is the free lunchtime concert, usually chamber music, from 12.30 to 1.30 pm (not in June, July or August when everyone goes on holidays). The Muziektheater offers free concerts of 20th-century music on Tuesday in the Boekmanzaal; on Wednesday the Concertgebouw has chamber music or classical concerts (often public rehearsals), sometimes also jazz, but you won't be the only visitor taking advantage of this; and Friday the Bethaniënklooster puts on anything from medieval to contemporary, while the IJsbreker specialises in contemporary music.

Bethaniënklooster *(Map 4; ☎ 625 00 78, Barndesteeg 6B)* – small former monastery near Nieuwmarkt Square; ticket office open half an hour before performances

Beurs van Berlage *(Map 4; ☎ 627 04 66, Damrak 243)* – two small concert halls housed in the former commodities exchange; ticket office open Tuesday to Friday from 2 to 5 pm and 75 minutes before performances

Churches – check the Amsterdam Uitburo for performances (not just organ recitals) in the Oude Kerk, Nieuwe Kerk, Engelse Kerk (the English/Scottish Presbyterian church in the Begijnhof), Round Lutheran Church, Waalse Kerk (the Walloon Church at Oudezijds Achterburgwal 157), Amstelkerk etc

Concertgebouw *(Map 6; ☎ 671 83 45, Concertgebouwplein 4–6)* – world-famous concert hall with near-perfect acoustics; ticket office open daily from 10 am to 7 pm (telephone only to 5 pm); after 7 pm you can only get tickets for that evening's performance

Koninklijk Theater Carré *(Map 7; ☎ 622 52 25, Amstel 115–125)* – opera, operetta, ballet, musicals, cabaret; ticket office open daily from 10 am to 7 pm (Sunday from 1 pm)

Muziekcentrum De IJsbreker *(Map 7; ☎ 693 90 93, Weesperzijde 23)* – centre for contemporary music; ticket office open daily from 9.30 am to 5.30 pm, and from 7.45 pm on performance nights; will move to a new complex in the Eastern Docklands (near the ship-passenger terminal) in 2002, together with the Bimhuis jazz centre

Muziektheater *(Map 4; ☎ 625 54 55, Waterlooplein 22)* – large-scale ballet and opera in the Stopera; ticket office open Monday to Saturday from 10 am to 6 pm, Sunday and public holidays from 11.30 am

Stadsschouwburg *(Map 4; ☎ 624 23 11, Leidseplein 26)* – opera and operetta; ticket office open Monday to Saturday from 10 am to start of performances

euro currency converter f1 = €0.45

ENTERTAINMENT

Rock

Information and tickets are available at the Amsterdam Uitburo or at the venues direct, but for large pop concerts you can also ring the Ticketlijn on ☎ 0900-300 12 50.

Arena Stadium in the Bijlmer (☎ 311 13 33 for information) – the ultimate stadium venue (seats 52,000) with shows that are big on lights, screens and production, and performers who are tiny little dots; for the top crowd-pullers (Michael Jackson, Tina Turner, Pavarotti, Celine Dion etc)

Jaap Eden Hal (Map 1; ☎ 694 98 94, Radioweg 64) – ice skating rink used two or three times a year for rock concerts; take tram No 9 from Centraal Station

De Koe (Map 4; ☎ 625 44 82, Marnixstraat 381) – the place to check what's happening in the Amsterdam pop scene, with regular band performances on Sunday from 4 pm (free admission)

Korsakoff (Map 4; ☎ 625 78 54, Lijnbaansgracht 161) – still grungy after all these years, hard rock and alternative music venue attracting a young clientele; could be difficult to get in; open daily from 10 pm to 4 am

Melkweg (Milky Way; Map 4; ☎ 624 17 77, Lijnbaansgracht 234) – membership f5 a month, extra admission depending on what's on; cinema, art gallery, café, multimedia entertainment; live music almost every night (often world music, from Aboriginal to Eskimo); the place remains as stoned as ever and the police station across the road doesn't mind

Paradiso (Map 6; ☎ 626 45 21, Weteringschans 6) – membership f5 a month, extra admission for live music, housed in a former church; big-name groups have been appearing here since the 1960s, everyone from the Rolling Stones to Prince and Public Enemy; opens between 8 and 10 pm when there's a concert, 11.30 pm when it's a club

Westergasfabriek (Map 2; Haarlemmerweg 8–10) – a former gas factory that hosts two or three rock concerts a year in the old, round gasholder, as well as the Drum Rhythm Festival, other arts events, raves etc; contact the Amsterdam Uitburo, or Café West Pacific (see the earlier Cafés section)

Jazz, Blues & Latin American

Jazz is popular in Amsterdam and there's a lot happening in cafés around town; blues thrives less. The world's largest jazz festival is the North Sea Jazz Festival in The Hague in July (see Public Holidays & Special Events in the Facts for the Visitor chapter), and throughout that month many international greats take the opportunity to strut their stuff in Amsterdam too.

Bamboo Bar (Map 4; ☎ 624 39 93, Lange Leidsedwarsstraat 64) – live jazz, blues, pop and sometimes salsa, nightly; open Sunday to Thursday from 9 pm to 3 am, Friday and Saturday to 4 am, music from 10 pm

Bimhuis (Map 4; ☎ 623 33 73, Oude Schans 73–77) – Amsterdam's main jazz venue for over 25 years (Dutch and international jazz greats play here), excellent auditorium and pretty spiffy bar; open 8 pm Thursday to Saturday, concerts start at 9 pm, closed Sunday and all of July and August; planning to move to a new location in the Eastern Docklands (near the ship passenger terminal) in 2002, together with the IJsbreker centre for contemporary music

Bourbon Street Jazz & Blues Club (Map 6; ☎ 623 34 40, Leidsekruisstraat 6–8) – blues, funk, rock and roll; open weekdays from 10 pm to 4 am, weekends to 5 am

Canecão (Map 4; ☎ 626 15 00, Lange Leidsedwarsstraat 70) – samba and salsa to live Brazilian music; open from 10 pm to 4 am Sunday to Thursday, to 5 am Friday and Saturday

Casablanca (Map 4; ☎ 625 56 85, Zeedijk 26) – jazz café with an illustrious history since it opened in 1946; its glory days are over, and apart from jam sessions on Sunday and the jazz and big-band performances on Monday and Wednesday nights, it's mainly a karaoke bar, albeit a fun one with little of the sadness normally attached to such establishments; open from 4 pm daily

Heeren van Aemstel (Map 4; ☎ 620 21 73, Thorbeckeplein 5) – office workers and somewhat elitist students; convincing grand café interior (it used to be the Moulin Rouge nightclub); also an eetcafé; open daily from 3 pm, live music beginning around 10 pm (pop and jazz)

Jazz Café Alto (Map 6; ☎ 626 32 49, Korte Leidsedwarsstraat 115) – chill out to live jazz and blues at this small brown café; music from 10 pm to 3 am Sunday to Thursday, and to 4 am Friday and Saturday; catch tenor saxophonist Hans Dulfer on Wednesday night

Maloe Melo (Map 4; ☎ 420 45 92, Lijnbaansgracht 163) – this small, smoky venue is home to the city's blues scene; local and international acts play live roots and blues nightly; pub opens at 9 pm, the hall at 10.30 pm, and live music begins at 11 pm

Meander (Map 4; ☎ 625 84 30, Voetboogstraat 5) – ever-popular salsa nights on Sunday at this multilevel club; other nights DJs play funk, garage, soul and jazzy beats; open Monday to Thursday 8.30 pm to 3 am, to 4 am Friday and Saturday

World Music

Amsterdam is a major European centre for music from exotic parts of the world. See Music in the Facts about Amsterdam chapter for information sources, or contact the Amsterdam Uitburo about gigs in the venues listed below, as well as at Melkweg, Paradiso and Latin bars.

Akhnaton *(Map 4; ☎ 624 33 96, Nieuwezijds Kolk 25–27)* – bills itself as a 'centre for world culture'; music styles range from hip-hop to jazz, salsa, Middle Eastern and African; ring for details; f10 admission, f15 if there's a band (no fee after 3 am); open Friday and Saturday from 11 pm to 5 am, with live music every Friday

Melkweg *(Milky Way; Map 4; ☎ 624 17 77, Lijnbaansgracht 234)* – the premier venue for world music; membership f5 a month, extra admission depending on what's on

Tropeninstituut Theater *(Map 7; ☎ 568 85 00, Linnaeusstraat 2)* – in the Tropenmuseum; mostly South American, Indian and African music with admissions varying from f12 to f30; phone operates Monday to Saturday from noon to 4 pm; the adjoining restaurant serves food to suit the performances

CLUBS

Not much happens before 10 pm and some places don't start bopping till well after midnight. Many clubs are *alleen voor leden* (only for members) but you can 'join' at the door if the bouncer likes the look of you and the place isn't packed. Dress standards are casual and with one or two exceptions you'll be out of place if you dress up, though some people do put effort into looking casual.

The venues listed below close at 4 or 5 am. Pill-poppers head for recovery parties in different parts of town from 5 or 6 am till noon – keep an eye out for fliers (printed or human) at clubs or ask around at closing time.

Only in Amsterdam: staff from the Adviesburo Drugs frequent the club circuit and check ecstasy pills for purity for a fee of f2.50. Or you can contact the Adviesburo Drugs, ☎ 623 79 43, Entrepotdok 32A,

Tuesday to Friday from 2 to 5 pm, in which case the test costs f5.

The following clubs could be worth trying:

Arena *(Map 7; ☎ 694 74 44, 's-Gravesandestraat 51)* – club parties with large crowds at Hotel Arena; two floors of tunes (everything from rock and house to techno); Thursday to Saturday 10 pm to 5 am (entry f12.50 to f15)

Dansen bij Jansen *(Map 4; ☎ 620 17 79, Handboogstraat 11)* – popular student club that's been going for 25 years; the DJs' popular (some say safe) music selection means that it's often too busy to dance; happy hour from 11 pm to midnight; ***d'Oude Herbergh*** bar next door *(Map 4)* gets lively with fraternity students

Escape *(Map 4; ☎ 622 11 11, Rembrandtplein 11)* – this commercial club is the largest in Amsterdam with a capacity of 2000; Saturday's house/techno night 'Chemistry' is wildly popular (especially when international DJs like Derrick May play); expect a dressed-up crowd, laser shows and heavy security at the door; open from 10 pm to 4 am Thursday to Saturday; admission f25 to f45

iT *(Map 4; ☎ 625 01 11, Amstelstraat 24)* – originally a gay club, this huge venue, housed in a former cinema, now attracts a flamboyant crowd of glam club kids, professional dancers and drag queens; closed down for a while by the police for alleged pill dealing at the door and not quite back to its former glory since it reopened; open Thursday to Sunday from 11 pm (Saturday gays only); admission f12.50 to f17.50

Mazzo *(Map 4; ☎ 626 75 00, Rozengracht 114)* – relatively small club featuring nights devoted to progressive house, trance and drum'n'bass; popular with a less sceney crowd who just want to dance; open Wednesday to Sunday from 11 pm to 4 am; admission f12.50 to f20

Melkweg *(Milky Way; Map 4; ☎ 624 17 77, Lijnbaansgracht 234)* – regular club nights (Thursday and Saturday) and one-off parties at this multimedia centre; admission f10 plus membership fee

Odeon *(Map 4; ☎ 624 97 11, Singel 460)* – 'three floors of dancing' with house, hip-hop and a jazz cellar; a mix of students, tourists and youngish office workers enjoy the relaxed scene here; open nightly at 11 pm

Paradiso *(Map 6; ☎ 626 45 21, Weteringschans 6)* – this popular live music venue off Leidseplein also operates as a club from Friday to Sunday; expect future funk, big-beat, hip-hop and classic house; the young, friendly crowd is decked out in everything from streetwear to designer labels; open 11.30 pm to late

Seymour Likely *(Map 4;* ☎ *627 14 27, Nieuwe-zijds Voorburgwal 250)* – club-style lounge for hipsters; the music (down-tempo house, reggae and hip-hop) makes it a pretty good place to chill post-club; don't even think of arriving before midnight

Sinners in Heaven *(Map 4;* ☎ *620 13 75, Wagenstraat 3–7)* – if you're itching to mix it with Dutch celebrities or at least a few well-dressed thirty-somethings, this is the place; decorated to resemble a castle/dungeon; expect to pay big prices for drinks; open Thursday from 11 pm to 4 am, Friday and Saturday to 5 am; admission f15 to f25

Soul Kitchen *(Map 4;* ☎ *620 23 33, Amstelstraat 32)* – next to iT; retro soul and funk music popular among 'elderly youngsters' (minimum age for admission 25) who love the club's friendly vibe and wicked, African-inspired interior; Thursday to Sunday from 11 pm; admission f5 Thursday, f12.50 Friday and Saturday

Trance Buddha *(Map 4;* ☎ *422 82 33, Oudezijds Voorburgwal 216)* – if you've just got to get back to Goa but can't afford the airfare, head to Amsterdam's biggest trance club; increases in admission prices have somewhat ruined the 'everyone welcome' vibe; open nightly from 11 pm to 4 am, to 5 am Friday and Saturday

Café West Pacific *(Map 2;* ☎ *488 77 78, Haarlemmerweg 8–10)* – this hip and happening restaurant/café transforms into a club each night after dinner; music varies from hip-hop to house and funk classics

Hotel Winston *(Map 4;* ☎ *623 13 80, Warmoesstraat 123)* – this café transforms into a popular club on the weekends; changing theme nights and a fine line-up of local DJs make it a good alternative to the commercial venues close by

CINEMAS

There are only 14 cinemas in Amsterdam but many have several theatres and there's always a good choice of films, including a high proportion of 'art' movies for the discerning viewer. The 'film ladder' – the listing of what's on at cinemas around town – is pinned up at cinemas and in many pubs, or you can check it in the paper on Thursdays when weekly programs change. *AL* means *alle leeftijden*, all ages, and 12 or 16 indicates the minimum age for admission.

Films are almost always screened in their original language with Dutch subtitles; the exceptions are children's matinees where the latest Disney creation may come with Dutch voices.

Roxy Burns

The lyrics *'Burn baby burn, disco inferno'* must have come to mind as over 4000 people watched in horror as Amsterdam's most famous nightclub, the Roxy – originally a cinema, near the Muntplein end of Kalverstraat – burnt down one sunny July afternoon in 1999.

Fireworks were let off in the club during a party held after the funeral of the Roxy's designer and co-founder, Peter Giele, whose body had been sailed down the Amstel to its resting place accompanied by flame-cannons. The flamboyant Giele had been quite entranced by the theme of fire, being one of the first promoters to introduce fireworks shows *inside* a club (quite legal, apparently). Sparks entered the ventilation system and within minutes the club was ablaze. All that remained were the walls and the facade.

Nightclubbers and industry insiders always knew that Peter Giele and the Roxy were inextricably linked, but no-one could have predicted that the demise of one would be so connected with the destruction of the other.

The mainstream Hollywood cinemas around Leidseplein have half-price matinee tickets for their first screening on weekdays, but check beforehand. The following cinemas may be worth seeking out:

Bellevue/Calypso *(Map 4;* ☎ *623 48 76, Marnixstraat 400–402)* – two comfortable mainstream cinemas screening Hollywood fare

Cinecenter *(Map 4;* ☎ *623 66 15, Lijnbaansgracht 236)* – interesting films, no blockbusters

Desmet *(Map 5;* ☎ *627 34 34, Plantage Middenlaan 4A)* – art cinema showing gay and avant-garde European films

Kriterion *(Map 7;* ☎ *623 17 09, Roetersstraat 170)* – Amsterdam School/Art-Deco building showing cult movies, with occasional 'sneak previews' of not-yet-released films; lively café worth visiting in its own right; popular among students from the university faculties across the road

The Movies *(Map 2;* ☎ *638 60 16, Haarlemmerdijk 161)* – 'interesting', often highbrow films without intermission (visit the toilet beforehand); beautiful Art-Deco interior, a real classic; there's also a restaurant

Nederlands Filmmuseum *(Map 6;* ☎ *589 14 00, Vondelpark 3)* – films shown daily; admission f10 to f17.50; live jazz in the café Sunday afternoons in summer; has a large terrace overlooking the park (a good place to arrange to meet someone)

Tuschinskitheater (Map 4; ☎ 626 26 33, Reguliersbreestraat 26) – a monument worth visiting for its sumptuous Art-Deco interior; the facade offers only a hint of what's inside

De Uitkijk (Map 4; ☎ 623 74 60, Prinsengracht 452) – the city's oldest surviving cinema, a cosy affair in an old canal house

THEATRE

There are about 50 theatres – the ones listed below are merely a selection. Performances are often in Dutch, sometimes in English (especially in summer) and sometimes it doesn't matter. Check the *Uitkrant*, the Saturday *PS* magazine in the *Parool* newspaper, contact the Amsterdam Uitburo (Map 6; Leidseplein 26), open daily from 10 am to 6 pm (Thursday to 9 pm), or ring the Uitlijn on ☎ 0900-01 91 (f0.75 per minute) which operates daily from 9 am to 9 pm.

Amsterdamse Bos Theatre (Map 1; ☎ 626 36 47) – large, open-air amphitheatre in the park with plays (Chekhov, Shakespeare) in summer

De Balie (Map 6; ☎ 623 29 04, Kleine Gartmanplantsoen 10) – international productions focusing on multicultural and political issues for intellectuals; political debates, short film festivals, new media facilities and a stylish bar (see Cultural Centres in the Facts for the Visitor chapter)

Theater Bellevue (Map 4; ☎ 624 72 48, Leidsekade 90) – experimental theatre, cabaret and dance, mainly in Dutch

Boom Chicago (Map 4; ☎ 423 01 01, Leidseplein 12) – English-language stand-up and improv comedy throughout the year in the former Leidseplein Cinema; the foyer café, Nonsense, serves fresh, reasonably priced food from 11 am to 9 pm daily

Brakke Grond (Flemish Cultural Centre; Map 4; ☎ 626 68 66, Nes 45) – Flemish theatre with pleasant café for pre or post-show drinks

Felix Meritis (Map 4; ☎ 623 13 11, Keizersgracht 324) – the former cultural centre of the city, now with experimental theatre, music and dance; lots of co-productions between Eastern and Western European artists

Frascati (Map 4; ☎ 626 68 66 day, or ☎ 623 57 23 evening, Nes 63) – experimental theatre where young Dutch directors, choreographers and producers get to strut their stuff; lots of

multicultural dance and music performances, as well as a monthly hip-hop, rap and breakdancing night

De Kleine Komedie (Map 4; ☎ 624 05 34, Amstel 56) – 500-seat theatre concentrating on concerts, dance and cabaret, sometimes in English

Koninklijk Theater Carré (Map 7; ☎ 622 52 25, Amstel 115–125) – the largest theatre in town (1700 seats), with mainstream international shows, musicals, cabaret, circuses etc; backstage tours available 3 pm Saturday and Wednesday

Melkweg (Map 4; ☎ 624 17 77, Lijnbaansgracht 234A) – world-renowned cultural centre, with anything from music and film to plays, dance and multimedia productions

Soeterijntheater (Map 7; ☎ 568 85 00, Linnaeusstraat 2) – theatre of the Tropenmuseum with plays, dance, film and anything else relating to non-Western culture

Stadsschouwburg (Map 4; ☎ 624 23 11, Leidseplein 26) – the city's most beautiful theatre built in 1894 and refurbished in the mid-1990s; features large-scale productions, operettas, summer English-language productions and performances by the stolid Toneelgroep Amsterdam

Universiteitstheater (Map 4; ☎ 623 01 27, Nieuwe Doelenstraat 16) – home to the Institute for Dramatic Art, with some performances in English

Vondelpark Theatre (☎ 673 14 99, Vondelpark) – large (1800-seat) open-air amphitheatre in the middle of the Vondelpark, with a wide range of performing arts in June, July and August

Westergasfabriek (Map 2; Haarlemmerweg 8–10) – former gas factory that hosts a wide range of theatre and music performances, events and festivals; for details contact the Amsterdam Uitburo

GAY & LESBIAN

Amsterdam's gay scene is the biggest in Europe, with close to 100 gay and lesbian bars, cafés, clubs, shops and hotels. Apart from the commercial venues listed below there's an active alternative circuit, for instance at the *COC (Map 4)*, which has a mixed club Friday night and a lesbian club Saturday night; and also at *De Trut (Map 1; no phone, Bilderdijkstraat 165E)*, a Sunday-night-only club (mixed lesbian and gay, queue well before the 11 pm opening time and be prepared for strict 'door police'). Unfortunately these clubs are so popular that they're becoming less 'alternative'. Queer club nights (with names like Sissy-Club, Planet Pussy and Lip Lickers) are held weekly at some of the larger nightclubs.

They generally don't last long, changing their name or theme every few months. Ask around or contact the Gay & Lesbian Switchboard (☎ 623 65 65) to find out about the latest 'in' places.

Amsterdam's lesbian scene is much quieter than the gay scene. Apart from the women's cafés listed earlier in this chapter, the following club nights may be worth investigating:

You II (Map 4; ☎ 421 09 00, Amstel 178) has a weekly women-only night on Thursday ('vulgar chique' nightclub ambience). *Getto (Map 4)* – see under Warmoesstraat – runs the hot 'Getto Girls' on Tuesday from 7 pm.

Desmet (Map 5) – see Cinemas earlier in this chapter – often has gay cinema on Saturday night or Sunday afternoon. For other movie options, inquire at gay venues or ring the Gay & Lesbian Switchboard.

The following centres of gay culture are always busy and a good way to start exploring the city:

Reguliersdwarsstraat (Map 4)

The street also known simply as the Straat, has some of Amsterdam's most famous gay establishments. It attracts hip and beautiful men who go to the bars and cafés to cruise and schmooze. Plan to spend at least a whole evening here in summer and bring plenty of money (you won't get a beer for under f4).

April (☎ 625 95 72, Reguliersdwarsstraat 37) – famous for its happy hour (6 to 7 pm Monday to Saturday, to 8 pm on Sunday) and the beautiful guys who patronise the bar

Downtown (☎ 622 99 58, Reguliersdwarsstraat 31) – daytime eatery; friendly staff, good coffee and cake and the best gay reading table in town

Exit (☎ 625 87 88, Reguliersdwarsstraat 42) – multistorey nightclub playing underground house with a selection of bars, dance floors and an always busy darkroom

Havana (☎ 620 67 88, Reguliersdwarsstraat 17) – camp Art-Deco bar with gorgeous bar staff (some of whom are drag queens) and thumping club music

Other Side (☎ 421 10 14, Reguliersdwarsstraat 6) – gay coffeeshop playing a mix of disco, funk and soul and selling hash, grass and energy drinks

Soho (☎ 626 15 73, Reguliersdwarsstraat 36) – currently 'the' bar on the Straat; decorated like

an old-world English library, it attracts young, friendly guys who enjoy drinking and flirting

Amstel & Rembrandtplein (Map 4)

This is real queen territory with a selection of interesting bars. Some are camp (singalongs to Dutch pop songs), some are cloney (lots of moustaches) and some are refined and quiet (attracting gay businessmen who pop in after work for a quick drink).

iT (☎ 625 01 11, Amstelstraat 24) – one of the most extravagant clubs in town features weekly gay nights

Monopole (☎ 624 64 51, Amstel 60) – a mixed gay crowd shakes their groove thing to old-school disco classics at this kitschly decorated brown café

Montmartre (☎ 620 76 22, Halve Maansteeg 17) – quite an experience: bar staff and patrons sing Dutch ballads and pop songs (think Abba) at the top of their voices; it's kind of like a camp, festive Eurovision song contest

De Steeg (☎ 620 01 71, Halve Maansteeg 10) – during the week young professionals congregate at this popular bar for after-work drinks; on the weekend it's just as busy as a venue for pre-club refreshments

Vivelavie (☎ 624 01 14, Amstelstraat 7) – this popular 'lipstick lesbian' café pumps on the weekend

Warmoesstraat (Map 4)

Kinky Amsterdam congregates in the red-light district at a variety of clubs catering to lovers of leather, rubber, piercings, slings, darkrooms and, of course, hard-core porn. Patrons are quite clear about what they want.

Argos (☎ 622 65 95, Warmoesstraat 95) – leather boys of all ages head here for the famous darkrooms, cabins and toys; open Sunday to Thursday from 10 pm to 3 am, to 4 am Friday and Saturday

Cockring (☎ 623 96 04, Warmoesstraat 96) – nightclub playing techno, hard house and trance; live strip shows and a cruisey, hot darkroom for sexy, young leather boys; open Sunday to Thursday 11 pm to 4 am and to 5 am Friday and Saturday

Cuckoo's Nest (☎ 627 17 52, Nieuwezijds Kolk 6) – busy club and bar with the largest 'playroom' in Europe, open daily from 1 pm to 1 am

ENTERTAINMENT

Getto (☎ 421 51 51, Warmoesstraat 51) – restaurant and bar, loved more for its fun nightly entertainment (tarot readers, DJs, bingo competitions) than the quality of its food

Queen's Head (☎ 420 24 75, Zeedijk 20) – old-world-style café run by an outrageous drag queen called Dusty, who used to call the bingo nights in Getto and is now famous through his starring role in a 'reality soap' about the Zeedijk; the fact that he combines drag with rubber, piercings and tattoos adds to his charm

Other Areas

The gay establishments tend to cluster around the above three areas, but there are a few lesbian-oriented ones elsewhere.

Saarein II (Map 4; ☎ 623 49 01, Elandsstraat 119) – refurbished lesbian bar and restaurant with a great reading table and pool table

Sarah's Grannies (Map 6; ☎ 624 01 45, Kerkstraat 176) – lesbian-friendly café serving snacks, salads and warm meals

De Spijker (Map 4; ☎ 620 59 19, Kerkstraat 42) – leather boys and clones feel right at home at this friendly bar; entertainment in the form of pool tables, videos and a very busy darkroom

Vandenberg (Map 2; ☎ 622 27 16, Lindengracht 95) – eetcafé popular among older lesbians

SPECTATOR SPORTS

See Activities in the Things to See & Do chapter for sports you can engage in as well as watch. If you only want to watch, there are few sporting events worth seeking out apart from soccer (of course), field hockey and the unique Dutch sport of korfball. For general information on sporting events, contact the Amsterdam Sport Service on ☎ 552 24 90.

Soccer (Football)

Local club Ajax is usually at or near the top of the European league. Other Dutch leaders are PSV (the Philips Sport Association) from Eindhoven and Feijenoord from Rotterdam, and if any of these clubs play against one another it's a big event. Dutch soccer is 'cool' and 'technical', characterised by keep-the-ball and surgical strikes. Local hooligans, however, are every bit as

hot-headed as their British counterparts but you should be quite safe if you buy seat tickets (as opposed to standing-room tickets).

Ajax plays in the new Arena Stadium (☎ 311 13 33; metro: Bijlmer), office address Haaksbergweg 59, which seats 52,000 spectators and has an Ajax museum with cups and other paraphernalia. It's a massive and massively expensive, high-tech complex with retractable roof, built over a highway. The turf refused to grow through lack of wind, but this was solved by putting huge blowers along the boundaries. Soccer games usually take place Saturday evening and Sunday afternoon during the playing season, which lasts from early September to early June (with a winter break from just before Christmas to the end of January).

Hockey

Dutch (field) hockey teams compete at world-championship level. In contrast to soccer, which is played by working-class boys in school yards, streets and parks, hockey is still a somewhat elitist sport played by either sex on expensive club fields. The season is more or less the same as that for soccer. A good contact for information and matches is Hockey Club Hurley (☎ 619 02 33), Nieuwe Kalfjeslaan 21 in the Amsterdamse Bos, with mixed training and games Monday and Tuesday evening from 9 pm (children Wednesday afternoon and Saturday morning).

Korfball

This sport elicits giggles from foreigners who don't understand how appealing the game can be. It's a cross between netball, volleyball and basketball, where mixed-sex teams toss a ball around and try to throw it into the opposing team's hoop which is 3.5m off the ground; players can only mark opponents of the same sex. There's a vivid local club scene. For information, contact the Amsterdam Sport Council (☎ 552 24 90) or try SVK Groen-Wit (☎ 646 15 15), Kinderdijkstraat 29.

ENTERTAINMENT

Shopping

With a few exceptions – dope, pornography, flower bulbs, rounds of cheese, obscure types of *genever* (Dutch gin) – there's nothing in Amsterdam that you won't find elsewhere, and fantastic bargains are rare. Where Amsterdam shines is in its speciality shops and markets. You might be able to find a glow-in-the-dark toothbrush or banana-flavoured condom back home, but Amsterdam has whole shops devoted to toothbrushes or condoms – or hammocks, mosquito nets and, of course, clogs, to name just a few of the eccentric goods on offer.

Worth chasing are pictorial art, music, funky clothes, diamonds, pastries/chocolates and collectors' books (but not current English-language books, which are prohibitively expensive). Potheads can purchase smoking paraphernalia at most corner tobacco shops, but should keep in mind that flights from Amsterdam attract more than their fair share of attention from customs officials elsewhere.

The most popular shopping streets are lowbrow Nieuwendijk and slightly less lowbrow Kalverstraat, with department stores, clothing boutiques and speciality shops that cater for large crowds on Saturday and Sunday (good days to avoid). Leidsestraat is more upmarket with less junk, though the goods are still rather mainstream. Well-heeled shoppers head for the expensive shops and boutiques along PC Hooftstraat, and antique and art buffs check Nieuwe Spiegelstraat and Spiegelgracht. The Jordaan neighbourhood is full of quirky shops and galleries, as are the radial streets in the canal belt, especially in the western section.

Souvenirs are sold everywhere, most of them tacky, but try a Delft-blue tulip vase or bulbs to plant back home (home legislation permitting). Metz & Co department store has interesting but pricey gifts.

As for markets, the Albert Cuyp is not to be missed, with its food and other goods from all corners of the globe. The floating flower market along Singel is unique, though photographers will be frustrated by the crowds and the fact that most of the market is in the shade. Waterlooplein flea market specialises in bric-a-brac, army clothes and music; other markets might be cheaper but don't stock as wide a selection.

Most stores are open seven days a week but many start late on Monday. Shopping hours are normally 1 to 6 pm on Monday, 10 am to 6 pm on Tuesday, Wednesday, Friday and Saturday, 10 am to 9 pm on Thursday and noon to 6 pm on Sunday, but there are many individual variations.

If you intend to do serious shopping (eg, diamonds) and live outside the EU, see Taxes & Refunds under Money in the Facts for the Visitor chapter about reclaiming the 19% value-added tax.

ART GALLERIES & ANTIQUE STORES

Amsterdam is full of art galleries, from tiny operations with one person's work, to huge, commercial, museum-like complexes. Most of the city's best antique stores are found in Nieuwe Spiegelstraat and the nearby side streets. Try the following:

Art Works (Map 4; ☎ 624 19 80) Herengracht 229–231 – a small gallery displaying paintings and sculptures by Dutch, Spanish, Belgian and Swiss artists

Arti et Amicitiae (Map 4; ☎ 626 08 39) Rokin 112 – well-established artists' club displaying contemporary art; open Tuesday to Sunday from noon to 6 pm

Aschenbach Gallery (☎ 685 35 80) Bilderdijkstraat 165C – large gallery focusing on contemporary figurative tendencies and photography

Astamangala (Map 6; ☎ 623 44 02) Kerkstraat 168 – ancient art and ethnographical objects from the Himalayan region; open Tuesday to Saturday from noon to 6 pm

Boekie Woekie (Map 4; ☎ 639 05 07) Berenstraat 16 – handmade books, postcards, monographs and *objets d'art*, made by local and international artists

Decorativa (Map 4; ☎ 420 50 66) Nieuwe Spiegelstraat 7 – a massive jumble of European antiques, collectables and weird vintage gifts

Eduard Kramer (Map 6; ☎ 623 08 32) Nieuwe Spiegelstraat 64 – specialising in antique Dutch wall and floor tiles and crammed to bursting with vintage homewares

EH Ariëns Kappers (Map 6; ☎ 623 53 56) Nieuwe Spiegelstraat 32 – prints, etchings, engravings, lithographs and maps from the 17th to 19th centuries, Japanese woodblock prints too; open Tuesday to Sunday from 11 am to 5 pm

Foundation for Indian Artists (Map 6; ☎ 623 15 47) Fokke Simonszstraat 10 – contemporary and mostly figurative art by Asian and Indian artists; open Wednesday to Saturday from 1 to 6 pm, and first Sunday of the month from 2 to 5 pm, closed in August

Gallery Nine (Map 4; ☎ 627 10 97) Keizersgracht 570 – monthly exhibits of abstract painting and sculpture by emerging and established Dutch and Belgian artists; open Wednesday to Sunday from 1 to 5 pm

Guido de Spa (Map 6; ☎ 622 15 28) Tweede Weteringdwarsstraat 34 – ceramic art, paintings, etchings and drawings; open Wednesday to Saturday (and first Sunday of the month) from 2 to 5 pm

Jaski (Map 6; ☎ 620 39 39) Nieuwe Spiegelstraat 27–29 – paintings, prints, ceramics and sculptures by the most famous members of the CoBrA movement

Josine Bokhoven (Map 4; ☎ 623 65 98) Prinsengracht 154, across the canal from the Anne Frankhuis – contemporary art including young artists; open Tuesday to Saturday (and first Sunday of the month) from 1 to 6.30 pm

Kunsthaar (Map 4; ☎ 625 99 12) Berenstraat 21 – contemporary Dutch art; collective exhibitions; open Tuesday to Friday from 10 am to 6 pm, Saturday from 9 am to 4 pm

Lieve Hemel (Map 6; ☎ 623 00 60) Nieuwe Spiegelstraat 3 – exemplary contemporary Dutch realist painting and sculpture

Montevideo (Map 4; ☎ 623 71 01) Keizersgracht 264 – institute for media art, videos etc

Nanky de Vreeze (Map 6; ☎ 627 38 08) Lange Leidsedwarsstraat 198–200 – large, impressive gallery with contemporary art; open Wednesday to Saturday (and first Sunday of the month) from noon to 6 pm

Open Space (Map 2; ☎ 420 09 58) Korte Prinsengracht 14 – open Wednesday to Saturday from 3 to 7 pm

Parade (Map 6; ☎ 427 46 46) Prinsengracht 799 – bimonthly exhibits of big-name American and German pop and postmodern artists and photographers; open Monday to Saturday from 11 am to 6 pm

Paul Andriesse (Map 4; ☎ 623 62 37) Prinsengracht 116 – contemporary art; open Tuesday to Friday from 11 am to 6 pm, Saturday from 2 pm and first Sunday of the month

Prestige Art Gallery (Map 4; ☎ 624 01 04) Reguliersbreestraat 46, near Rembrandtplein – specialist in 17th to 20th-century oil paintings and bronzes; open Monday to Saturday from 10 am to 5 pm

Reflex Modern Art Gallery (Map 6; ☎ 627 28 32) Weteringschans 79A, opposite the Rijksmuseum – prominent gallery with contemporary art, aimed at tourists

SAK (Stichting Amsterdamse Kunstenaars – Foundation of Amsterdam Artists; Map 4; ☎ 420 31 54) Keizersgracht 22, in De Zaaijer 'clandestine' church – large, impressive gallery with works by local artists; open all week from 10.30 am to 6.30 pm

Steltman (Map 4; ☎ 622 86 83) Spuistraat 330, off Spui Square – large gallery with unusual surrealist and romantic paintings, figurative modern art and design; open Tuesday to Saturday from 11 am to 6 pm

XY (Map 4; ☎ 625 02 82) Tweede Laurierdwarsstraat 42 – figurative, contemporary paintings on trendy themes; open Tuesday to Friday from noon to 5 pm, Saturday to 4 pm

BOOKS

Amsterdam is still a major printing centre in Europe. Unfortunately books are expensive whether they're imported or locally produced, and you may wish to steer clear of English-language titles if you're used to US or British prices. However, bibliophiles will delight in the large number of bookshops, both new and antiquarian, with knowledgeable and enthusiastic staff. The following are some of the better known outlets, but keep an eye out for obscure, second-hand shops where you might find some real bargains. See also the following Markets section for dedicated book markets.

English-Language

The American Book Center (Map 4; ☎ 625 55 37) Kalverstraat 185 – 10% discount with a valid student card; interesting sales; good travelguide section, cheaper than competitors; many US newspapers and magazines (Sunday edition of the *New York Times* for f30); an outlet of *Gary's Muffins* is in the basement

The English Bookshop (Map 4; ☎ 626 42 30) Lauriergracht 71 – interesting selection of English books; open Tuesday to Friday from 1 to 6 pm, Saturday from 11 am to 5 pm

Waterstone's (Map 4; ☎ 638 38 21) Kalverstraat 152 – specialist in English-language books; strong on travel guidebooks, maps and novels; translated Dutch literature on the 1st floor

Gay & Lesbian

Intermale (Map 4; ☎ 625 00 09) Spuistraat 251 – gay photo books, magazines and videos

Vrolijk (Map 4; ☎ 623 51 42) Paleisstraat 135 – most of the major gay and lesbian magazines worldwide

Vrouwen in Druk (Map 4; ☎ 624 50 03) Westermarkt 5 – women's books, new and second-hand (the name means 'Women in Print')

Xantippe Unlimited (Map 4; ☎ 623 58 54) Prinsengracht 290 – large selection of women's books, anything from classical fiction to modern research; gay books too

Health, Environment & Philosophy

Au Bout du Monde (Map 4; ☎ 625 13 97) Singel 313 – Eastern and Western philosophy, alternative medicine and other esoteric subject matter

Oininio (Map 2; ☎ 553 93 44) Prins Hendrikkade 20–21 – large selection of New-Age titles

Travel

à la Carte (Map 6; ☎ 625 06 79) Utrechtsestraat 110 – travel books, maps and globes

Amber (Map 4; ☎ 685 11 55) Da Costastraat 77 – behind the travel agency is a crammed bookshop that's a veritable Aladdin's Cave, with many hard-to-find (and some pretty obscure) travel guidebooks in Dutch, English, German and French

Evenaar Literaire Reisboekhandel (Map 4; ☎ 624 62 89) Singel 348 – travel literature

Jacob van Wijngaarden (Map 6; ☎ 612 19 01) Overtoom 97 – geographical bookshop with a large collection of travel guidebooks and maps

Pied à Terre (Map 4; ☎ 627 44 55) Singel 393 – specialist in hiking and cycling books, maps and travel guides

Other Bookshops

Antiquariaat Kok (Map 4; ☎ 623 11 91) Oude Hoogstraat 14–18 – wide range of antiquarian stock (literature, coffee-table books, old prints etc)

Architectura & Natura (Map 4; ☎ 623 61 86) Leliegracht 22 – architecture, landscape, coffee-table books on the ground floor, antiquarian art and architecture titles upstairs

Athenaeum (Map 4; ☎ 622 62 48) Spui 14–16 – vast assortment of unusual books for browsers; the separate newsagency has the city's largest selection of international newspapers and magazines

The Book Exchange (Map 4; ☎ 626 62 66) Kloveniersburgwal 58 – rabbit warren of second-hand books

Broekmans & Van Poppel (Map 6; ☎ 679 65 75) Van Baerlestraat 92–94 – the best address for sheet music (classical and popular)

The Frisian Embassy (Map 4; ☎ 422 27 41) Leliegracht 18 – not an embassy but a tiny bookshop and information centre for Friesland

Lambiek (Map 4; ☎ 626 75 43) Kerkstraat 78 – for serious collectors of comic books; doubles as an informal museum

Scheltema Holkema Vermeulen (Map 4; ☎ 523 14 11) Koningsplein 20 – the largest bookshop in town has recently expanded; a true department store with many foreign titles, a restaurant and thorough New-Age and multimedia sections

De Slegte (Map 4; ☎ 622 59 33) Kalverstraat 48 – specialist in second-hand or remaindered titles; a lot of dirt-cheap books on the ground floor but some gems upstairs

Stadsboekwinkel (Map 7; ☎ 551 17 33) Voormalige Stadstimmertuin 4–6, near Theater Carré – bookshop run by the city printer; books and other publications about Amsterdam, some in English

CAMPING & OUTDOOR

The Dutch enjoy outdoor pursuits and don't mind spending money on the right gear. Quality and prices tend to be high.

Bever Zwerfsport (Map 6; ☎ 689 46 39) Stadhouderskade 4, near Leidseplein – large range of camping and other outdoor gear

Carl Denig (Map 6; ☎ 626 24 36) Weteringschans 115, near the Rijksmuseum – probably Amsterdam's best in its field, though you pay for the quality; good selection of packs, tents and hiking/camping accessories

Demmenie (Map 4; ☎ 624 36 52) Marnixstraat 2 – professional outdoor gear for the serious enthusiast (mountaineering, tents, shoes, clothes etc)

Perry Sport (Map 6; ☎ 618 91 11) Overtoom 2 – cheaper than Bever Zwerfsport nearby, but quality could be less; camping goods kept downstairs

EDWARD AM SNIJDERS

Former warehouse on a canal

JULIET COOMBE

Souvenir dolls

JEREMY GRAY

One-man concert on the Prinsengracht

JULIET COOMBE

'A little cake wouldn't be too devilish, would it?'

DAVID STANLEY

Celebrating Koninginnedag (Queen's Day)

JULIET COOMBE

Statue outside the grand Hotel de l'Europe

JULIET COOMBE

Relax at a sunny café terrace and watch the world go by.

CHILDREN

There are lots of trendy kids clothing, toy and bookshops in the city. Particularly interesting are the stores selling wooden toys, doll's houses and puppets. Instead of a normal doll's house, why not purchase a wooden replica of a canal house? Most children's clothing stores sell miniature versions of current street fashion at close to adult prices. For less expensive kids' or baby wear, visit some of the markets which often sell clothes at remarkably low prices.

BamBam (Map 4; ☎ 624 52 15) Magna Plaza, Nieuwezijds Voorburgwal 182 – luxurious clothes and handmade baby furniture for pampered little princes and princesses

Bell Tree (Map 6; ☎ 625 88 30) Spiegelgracht 10, not far from the Rijksmuseum – toys for kids of all ages; good selection of technical toys for children aged eight to 14

Exota Kids (Map 4; ☎ 420 68 84) Nieuwe Leliestraat 32 – hip parents shop here to make sure that their children look just as chic as they do; Exota's own label, Petit Louie, is worn by Amsterdam's grooviest kids

De Kinderboekwinkel (Map 4; ☎ 622 77 41) Nieuwezijds Voorburgwal 344 – most of the books are in Dutch, but there's a large selection of picture books (especially by Dick Bruna) for preschoolers

Kitsch Kitchen Kids (Map 4; ☎ 622 82 61) Rozengracht 183 – colourful and crazy Mexican toys, dress-ups, furniture and birthday presents

Knuffels (Map 4; ☎ 427 38 62) Nieuwe Hoogstraat 11 – this entrancing shop delights adults and kids; it's full of colourful, fluffy soft toys, puppets, beautiful mobiles, teddies, jigsaw puzzles and more

Mechanisch Speelgoed (Map 2; ☎ 638 16 80) Westerstraat 67 – fun shop crammed full of nostalgic and wind-up toys; snowdomes, glowlamps, masks and finger puppets

Pinokkio (Map 4; ☎ 622 89 14) Magna Plaza, Nieuwezijds Voorburgwal 182 – wooden and educational toys, rocking horses, mobiles and of course, lots of Pinocchio dolls

Prenatal (Map 4; ☎ 626 63 92) Kalverstraat 40 – well-priced chain store selling trendy baby and kids' clothes, maternity wear, toys, prams, cots and more

De Speelmuis (Map 4; ☎ 638 53 42) Elandsgracht 58 – an outstanding array of doll's houses, miniature toys, hand puppets and jigsaw puzzles

Storm (Map 4; ☎ 624 10 74) Magna Plaza, Nieuwezijds Voorburgwal 182 – designer clothes (European and American) for hip preteens and teenagers; labels like Paul Smith, Kenzo Elle and Donna Karan dominate

CLOTHING

This is not the place to buy extravagant designer clothes. The Calvinist ethos frowns on conspicuous consumption and demands value for money, and as a consequence clothing is stylish but low-key and very reasonably priced. A stroll down Kalverstraat indicates the city's abundance of inexpensive chain stores. Amsterdam is in a league of its own, however, in funky and alternative apparel, often second-hand and sold at markets and in countless small boutiques. The choice seems endless – simply go for a walk in the Jordaan or along the radial streets in the canal belt. Otherwise, the following shops may be of interest:

Analik (Map 4; ☎ 422 05 61) Hartenstraat 36 – Analik, Amsterdam's pre-eminent young designer, creates feminine, modern pieces for smart young things

Awareness Winkel (Map 6; ☎ 638 10 59) Weteringschans 143, near the Rijksmuseum – environmentally friendly clothing; everything from hats to socks made from organically grown cotton

Cora Kemperman (Map 4; ☎ 625 12 84) Leidsestraat 72 – floaty, layered separates and dresses in raw silk, cotton and wool

Exota (Map 4; ☎ 620 91 02) Hartenstraat 10 – funky clothes emporium for men, women and kids; well-known labels (Lee, Kookai and French Connection) are mixed in with more alternative brands

Fun Fashion (Map 4; ☎ 420 50 96) Nieuwendijk 200 – street, surf and skate wear for guys; Carhartt, Stussy, Oakley and Birkenstock stockist

Hennes & Mauritz (Map 4; ☎ 624 06 24) Kalverstraat 125 – one of the better fashion chain stores with clothes for kids, teens, men and women; quality can be questionable but prices are remarkably low

Housewives on Fire (Map 4; ☎ 422 10 67) Spuistraat 130 – inexpensive club clothes, jewellery and a hairdressing salon

Lady Day (Map 4; ☎ 623 58 20) Hartenstraat 9 – premier location for unearthing spotless vintage clothes from Holland and around the world; the leather jackets and woollen sailors' coats are well priced

euro currency converter f1 = €0.45

Laundry Industry (Map 4; ☎ 420 25 54) Spui 1 – well-cut, well-designed clothes for hip, urban types

Mango (Map 4; ☎ 427 27 60) Kalvertoren shopping centre, Singel 457 – all the latest trends in street wear, club gear and office separates at reasonable prices

Van Ravenstein (Map 4; ☎ 639 00 67) Keizersgracht 359 – sleek men and women shop here for upmarket Belgian designers (Dries Van Noten, Ann Demeulemeester and Dirk Bikkembergs)

Reflections (Map 6; ☎ 664 00 40) PC Hooftstraat 66–68 – labels like Issey Miyake, Dolce e Gabbana and Comme des Garçons for the haute-couture crowd with unlimited funds

Shoebaloo (Map 4; ☎ 626 79 93) Koningsplein 7 – chic shoes, imports like Patrick Cox, Miu Miu and Prada Sport, and the less expensive house label

Zipper (Map 4; ☎ 627 03 53) Nieuwe Hoogstraat 8 – vintage clothes for funksters; good range of jeans and customised club gear

DEPARTMENT STORES

With the possible exception of Metz & Co and sections of the Bijenkorf, the department stores stick to safe, mainstream products.

Bijenkorf (Map 4; ☎ 621 80 80) Dam 1 – the city's most fashionable department store; there's a small restaurant or snack bar on each floor and the design-conscious will be more than pleased with the well-chosen clothing, toys, household accessories and books

Hema (Map 4; ☎ 638 99 63) Nieuwendijk 174, among other locations – the nation's equivalent of Woolworths or K-Mart has recently undergone a major facelift and now attracts as many design aficionados as bargain hunters; expect low prices, reliable quality and a wide range of products including good-value wines and delicatessen goods

Kalvertoren (Map 4) Singel 457 – opened in 1997, this popular, modern shopping centre contains a small Hema, Vroom & Dreesmann and fashion stores like Replay, Quicksilver, Levis, Timberland and Guess

Magna Plaza (Map 4; ☎ 626 91 99) Nieuwezijds Voorburgwal 182 – this grand 19th-century building used to be the city's main post office; now you'll find over 40 upmarket fashion, gift and jewellery stores and a good brasserie on the top floor

Maison de Bonneterie (Map 4; ☎ 531 34 00) Rokin 140 – exclusive and classic clothes for the whole family; men are particularly well catered for with labels like Ralph Lauren, Tommy Hilfiger and Armani; note the amazing chandeliers and beautiful glass cupola

Metz & Co (Map 4; ☎ 520 70 36) Keizersgracht 455, at Leidsestraat – luxury furnishings and homewares, upmarket designer clothes and gifts; lunch room with a splendid view on the top floor (see the Places to Eat chapter)

Vroom & Dreesmann (Map 4; ☎ 622 01 71) Kalverstraat 201 – large national chain with a wide range of products, slightly more upmarket than Hema; popular for clothing and cosmetics; what makes it worth a visit, though, is its fabulous cafeteria, La Place, which serves well-priced, healthy and freshly prepared salads, sandwiches, hot dishes and pastries

DIAMONDS

Amsterdam has been a major diamond centre since Sephardic Jews introduced the cutting industry in the 1580s (one of the few occupations open to them at the time). The 'Cullinan', the largest diamond ever found (3106 carats), was split into more than 100 stones here in 1908, after which the master cutter spent three months recovering from stress. The 'Kohinoor' or Mountain of Light was cut here too – a very large, oval diamond (108.8 carats), acquired by Queen Victoria, that now forms part of the British crown jewels.

WWII dealt a serious blow to the industry but there are about a dozen diamond factories in the city today, five of which offer guided tours – the Gassan tour is probably the most interesting. The tours are free (the theory being that you'll buy diamonds, though you don't have to) and are usually conducted seven days a week from 9 am to 5 pm, but ring ahead for details.

Diamonds aren't necessarily cheaper in Amsterdam than elsewhere but prices are fairly competitive. At least you will have seen how they're worked, and when you buy from a factory, you get an extensive description of the purchase so you know exactly what you're buying. The Diamond Stock Exchange (Diamantbeurs Amsterdam; ☎ 696 22 51) is in the Bijlmer at Hogehilweg 14, 1101 CD Amsterdam.

Amsterdam Diamond Center (Map 4; ☎ 624 57 87) Rokin 1

Coster Diamonds (Map 6; ☎ 676 22 22) Paulus Potterstraat 2–6

Gassan Diamonds (Map 5; ☎ 622 53 33) Nieuwe Uilenburgerstraat 173–175

Stoeltie Diamonds (Map 4; ☎ 623 76 01) Wagenstraat 13–17

Van Moppes & Zoon (Map 6; ☎ 676 12 42) Albert Cuypstraat 2–6

FOOD & DRINK

Dutch cuisine is nothing to write home about but some of the following shops are hard to resist:

Australian Homemade (Map 4) Leidsestraat 59 – apart from the Aboriginal designs squiggled all over these handmade chocolates, there is nothing particularly Australian about them; never mind, they're decidedly delicious; try the freshly made ice cream too

Bakkerij Paul Année (Map 4; ☎ 623 53 22) Runstraat 25 – a healthy organic bakery with delicious breads

De Belly (Map 4; ☎ 330 94 83) Nieuwe Leliestraat 174 – this organic supermarket in the Jordaan has a great bakery and a superior selection of gourmet items

De Bierkoning (Map 4; ☎ 625 23 36) Paleisstraat 125 – hundreds of different beers, glasses and other paraphernalia

Le Cellier (Map 4; ☎ 638 65 73) Spuistraat 116 – genevers, liqueurs, large selection of New World wines and over 75 types of beer

Eichholtz (Map 4; ☎ 622 03 05) Leidsestraat 48 – small deli bursting with everything homesick Brits and Americans yearn for, like Oreo cookies, Betty Crocker cake mix, Lea & Perrins sauce and Baxters tinned soup

Geels & Co (Map 4; ☎ 624 06 83) Warmoesstraat 67 – tea and coffee merchant; the shop is open normal hours, but have a look at the interesting little museum upstairs if you visit Tuesday, Friday or Saturday between 2 and 4 pm (4.30 pm Saturday)

De Kaaskamer (Map 4; ☎ 623 34 83) Runstraat 7 – hundreds of cheeses from all over Europe and Holland and deli items like paté, cured meats and baguettes; it does a roaring trade at lunchtime selling filled sandwiches

Meeuwig & Zn (Map 2; ☎ 626 52 86) Haarlemmerstraat 70 – over 50 types of olive oil from around the world; bottles of gourmet vinegar, mustard and chutney, and fresh olives too

Puccini Bomboni (Map 4; ☎ 427 83 41) Singel 184 – large, handmade chocolate bonbons with rich fillings (try the unforgettable spicy bonbon with peppers)

Simon Lévelt (Map 4; ☎ 624 08 23) Prinsengracht 180, opposite the Anne Frankhuis; and also Ferdinand Bolstraat 154 (Map 6; ☎ 400 40 60) – old-fashioned tea and coffee merchant

De Waterwinkel (Map 6; ☎ 675 59 32) Roelof Hartstraat 10 – more than 100 types of bottled water from all parts of the world

Wijnkoperij Otterman (Map 4; ☎ 625 50 88) Keizersgracht 300 – French wines with character; also wines without preservatives

MARKETS

No visit to Amsterdam is complete if you haven't experienced one or more of its lively markets. The following is merely a selection. For more information about some of these markets, see the relevant entries in the Things to See & Do chapter. Oh, and watch out for pickpockets.

Albert Cuypmarkt Albert Cuypstraat (Map 6) – general market with food, clothing, hardware etc, often very cheap; wide ethnic mix (Amsterdam's melting pot in action); daily except Sunday

Antiques market Noordermarkt in the Jordaan – antiques, fabrics, second-hand bric-a-brac etc; Monday morning

Antiques market Nieuwmarkt Square – many genuine articles; every Sunday from April to October

Antiques market (Map 4) Elandsgracht 109, in the Jordaan – indoor stalls in the De Looier complex; daily except Friday

Art markets on Thorbeckeplein and Spui Square – quiet markets with quality art, mostly modern pictorial, but too modest in scope to yield real finds; every Sunday between March and October from 10.30 am to 6 pm

Bloemenmarkt along Singel near Muntplein (Map 4) – floating flower market, colourful in the extreme; daily except Sunday

Boerenmarkt (Farmer's Market) on Noordermarkt in the Jordaan and on Nieuwmarkt Square – home-grown produce, organic foods, herbs etc; only on Saturday

Book market Oudemanhuispoort (the old arcade between Oudezijds Achterburgwal and Kloveniersburgwal; blink and you'll miss either entrance) – frequented by students from the surrounding university buildings; anything from a 19th-century copy of *Das Kapital* to a semantic analysis of Icelandic sagas; weekdays

Book market Spui Square – not very cheap but a good selection; only on Friday

Mosveldmarkt (Map 1) Mosveld, Amsterdam North; take bus No 34 or 35 from Centraal Station to the first stop after the IJ-Tunnel – typical Dutch market not intended for tourists; mostly food and clothing; Wednesday, Friday and Saturday

Plant market Amstelveld – all sorts of plants, pots and vases; every Monday during summer

Stamp and coin market Nieuwezijds Voorburgwal 276, in front of the Nova Hotel – stamps, coins, medals; Wednesday and Saturday from 10 am to 4 pm

Waterlooplein flea market Waterlooplein – curios, second-hand clothing, music, electronic stuff slightly on the blink, erotica, hardware etc; daily except Sunday

MUSIC

CD prices are steep, so Amsterdam is not the place to buy popular material. Collector's items are another story, thanks to the wide variety of shops with often interesting (not to say obscure) stock. Also, many shops and markets sell second-hand CDs that can be absolute bargains.

Blue Note (Map 4; ☎ 428 10 29) Gravenstraat 12 – jazz (Dutch, European and American), Japanese pressings and a smattering of acid jazz and related dance CDs

Broekmans & Van Poppel (Map 6; ☎ 675 16 53) Van Baerlestraat 92–94 – classical music

Concerto (Map 6; ☎ 623 52 28) Utrechtsestraat 52–60 – rambling shop spread over several buildings; the city's best selection of new and second-hand CDs and records, from classical, jazz and world music to techno, often cheap and always interesting; great facilities to listen before you buy

FAME Music (Map 4; ☎ 638 25 25) Kalverstraat 2–4, at Dam Square – the largest number of titles in Amsterdam, with broad collections of pop, jazz, classical, CD-ROMs and videos; also sells tickets to big dance, rock and pop concerts

Get Records (Map 6; ☎ 622 34 41) Utrechtsestraat 105 – eclectic range of rock, folk and blues

Kuijpers (Map 6; ☎ 679 46 34) Ferdinand Bolstraat 6 – chamber music, baroque

Musiques du Monde (Map 4; ☎ 624 13 54) Singel 281 – great source of world-music CDs (some second-hand), though they cost a few guilders more than elsewhere; specialist in Indian and Middle Eastern music; publishes the quarterly magazine *Wereldmuziek* (in Dutch, free subscription, or f27 outside the country)

Rush Hour Records (Map 4; ☎ 427 45 05) Spuistraat 98 – vinyl only, imported dance music (speed garage, hip-hop, house, big beat, Brazilian); you'll find Amsterdam's best DJs flicking through the racks of new releases

Soul Food (Map 4; ☎ 428 61 30) Nieuwe Nieuwstraat 27C – rap, R&B, house, garage, big beat, imports and six turntables for budding DJs to hone their skills

Tropenmuseum (Map 7; ☎ 568 82 00) Linnaeusstraat 2 – this museum has one of the most interesting selections of ethnic-music CDs for sale anywhere

Virgin Megastore (Map 4; ☎ 622 89 29) Magna Plaza, Nieuwezijds Voorburgwal 182, in the basement – top-40 hits, dance music and a good selection of magazines and merchandise like T-shirts and videos

SMART DRUG SHOPS

Smart drug shops began popping up all over the city five years ago and are now an established addition to the coffeeshop scene. They sell legal, organic hallucinogens like magic mushrooms, herbal joints, seeds (opium, marijuana, psychoactive), mood enhancers and aphrodisiacs. It's legal to sell magic mushrooms over the counter in Amsterdam because the Dutch Ministry of Health has found that they are not hazardous when used responsibly (heed their warning) but the same products are probably illegal to bring back home.

The stores listed here sell all manner of mood and mind-enhancing products as well as books, jewellery, trancey videos and bongs. Before you make a purchase, ask the staff to explain exactly what dosage to consume and what to expect from your trip.

Botanic Herbalist (☎ 470 88 89) Cornelius Trooststraat 37 – highly recommended by the trade for their potent psychoactive plants (especially the rare salvia) and huge range of hemp products

Chills & Thrills (Map 2; ☎ 638 00 15) Nieuwendijk 17 – the most commercial smart shop in the city is always packed full of tourists trying to hear each other over the thumping dance music; it sells herbal trips, mushrooms, psychoactive cacti, amino-acid/vitamin drinks, novelty bongs and spooky lifesize alien sculptures (f350); check the mini vaporiser: a smokefree way to consume grass; open daily from 11 am to 9 pm

Conscious Dreams (Map 4; ☎ 626 69 07) Kerkstraat 117 – Amsterdam's original smart shop still sells magic mushrooms and other natural products that enhance whatever might need enhancing; informative leaflets and enthusiastic staff explain everything; good selection of books on psychedelia and esoteria and club fliers (upcoming trance/ambient nights)

Kokopelli (Map 4; ☎ 421 70 00) Warmoesstraat 12 – Conscious Dreams' second store is a large, beautiful, chilled-out space smack bang in the middle of the red-light district; as well as selling mushrooms and smart drugs there's an art gallery, Internet facilities and a peaceful lounge area overlooking Damrak

The Magic Mushroom Gallery (Map 4; ☎ 427 57 65) Spuistraat 249 – fresh and dried magic mushrooms on sale (the owners recommend that first-timers try the Mexican ones for a relaxed, happy trip) as well as mushroom growing kits, herbal aphrodisiacs and trippy art hanging on the walls; be sure to visit the bathrooms to view more psychedelic art; open Sunday to Thursday from 11 am to 10 pm, and Friday and Saturday from 10 am

TRADITIONAL SOUVENIRS

Need a traditional reminder of your visit to Amsterdam? Best pick up a pair of clogs, some tulip bulbs or a Delft vase then.

Bloemenmarkt (Map 4) along Singel near Muntplein – floating flower market; the traders should be able to tell you if the flower bulbs you wish to purchase can be taken back home: Ireland and the UK allow an unlimited amount of bulbs to be brought back in, as do Canada and the USA (but you need a certificate for them); Japan permits up to 100 certified bulbs while Australia and New Zealand ban the importation of bulbs altogether

Galleria d'Arte Rinascimento (Map 4; ☎ 622 75 09) Prinsengracht 170 – Royal delftware, all manner of vases, platters, brooches and Christmas ornaments; interesting selection of 19th-century wall tiles and plaques as well

Heinen (Map 4; ☎ 627 82 99) Prinsengracht 440 – four floors of delftware; all the major factories are represented and all budgets are catered for (you can spend f9 on a spoon or f5000 on an antique vase)

De Klompenboer (Map 4; ☎ 623 06 32) St Anthoniesbreestraat 51 – Bruno, the eccentric owner of this cute clog shop gets his mum to hand-paint all the shoes (the cow print ones are pretty funky); brush up on the history of clogs at the tiny museum that has samples of miniature wooden shoes and a pair 700 years old; open daily from 10 am to 6 pm

SPECIALITY SHOPS

At a loss for souvenirs or gifts for yourself? Try some of the following:

Art Unlimited (Map 4; ☎ 624 84 19) Keizersgracht 510 – thousands of well-catalogued postcards with unusual and unexpected subject matter; beautiful art posters

Aurora Kontakt (Map 4; ☎ 623 59 89) Vijzelstraat 27, near Muntplein – huge assortment of electronic gizmos at competitive prices

Beaufort (Map 4; ☎ 625 91 31) Grimburgwal 11 – hand-crafted contemporary jewellery; the necklaces and rings are particularly alluring

Computercollectief (Map 6; ☎ 638 90 03) Amstel 312 – one of the best addresses in the country for computer software, books and magazines, at prices higher than in the USA

Condomerie Het Gulden Vlies (Map 4; ☎ 627 41 74) Warmoesstraat 141 – hundreds of different types of condoms; very well situated for its trade

Foto Professional (Map 4; ☎ 624 60 24) Nieuwendijk 113 – photographic gear and repairs, and the country's largest selection of second-hand cameras, lenses etc; you'll probably find what you need here

The Frozen Fountain (Map 4; ☎ 622 93 75) Prinsengracht 629, near the main public library – progressive furniture and other interior design; from f20 for small gifts up to f6000 for custom-made furniture

Hajenius (Map 4; ☎ 623 74 94) Rokin 92 – renowned for tobacco products and paraphernalia, including traditional leaf cigars (house brand) and clay pipes; beautiful Art-Deco interior

The Headshop (Map 4; ☎ 624 90 61) Kloveniersburgwal 39, on the corner of Nieuwe Hoogstraat – all kinds of drug devices and books on shamanism, psychedelia and spiritualism

3-D Hologrammen (Map 4; ☎ 624 72 25) Grimburgwal 2 – gallery and shop with an interesting collection of holographic pictures, jewellery, stickers etc

Kitsch Kitchen (Map 4; ☎ 428 49 69) Bloemdwarsstraat 21 – everything you need to transform your home into a colourful temple of kitsch; the tacky Mexican tablecloths and pink plastic chandeliers from India are big sellers

Maranón Hangmatten (Map 4; ☎ 420 71 21) Singel 488, at the floating flower market – Europe's largest selection of hammocks

Miffy Shop (☎ 671 97 07) Beethovenstraat 71 – Dutch illustrator Dick Bruna's most famous character, Miffy, is celebrated in books, toys and kids' merchandise

De Ode (☎ 419 08 82) Levantkade 51, on the KNSM Island – looking for a coffin with a difference? This shop, 'the ode' – which is also a play on *dode* (dead) – specialises in coffins and original funerals; buy a bookcase that converts to a coffin when you join the library in the sky, or a coffin on wheels with bicycle towbar so you can pedal your friend to his last bike rack, or a mega-rocket to launch grandpa's ashes from the beach (permit required)

Reina (Map 4; ☎ 428 23 90) Herenstraat 32A – dazzling little store aglow with Moroccan lanterns, Egyptian lamps and giftware from India and Tunisia

Santa Jet (Map 2; ☎ 427 20 70) Prinsenstraat 7 – Mexican shrines and religious icons, Day of the Dead paraphernalia, candles and love potions; the interior's vivid colours are worth a visit alone

De Witte Tanden Winkel (Map 4; ☎ 623 34 43) Runstraat 5 – large range of toothbrushes and other dental-hygiene products; free advice

THIRD WORLD & NEW AGE

This is one of the best cities for getting in touch with the Third World, nature and the inner you, often all at once.

Abal Wereldwinkel (Map 6; ☎ 664 10 83) Ceintuurbaan 238 – shop run by volunteers selling Third-World crafts, books, toys and food, with the profits going to the producers; some bargains

African Heritage (Map 4; ☎ 627 27 65) Zeedijk 59 – curios and clothing from Africa

Fair Trade Shop (Map 4; ☎ 625 22 45) Heiligeweg 45 – charitable shop featuring Third-World products including clothes, gifts and CDs; some interesting ceramics, sculptures and masks

Himalaya (Map 4; ☎ 626 08 99) Warmoesstraat 56 – a peaceful New-Age oasis in the middle of the red-light district; stock up on crystals, ambient CDs and books on the healing arts, and visit the lovely tearoom

Jacob Hooy & Co (Map 4; ☎ 624 30 41) Kloveniersburgwal 10 – this charming chemist shop has been selling medicinal herbs, homeopathic remedies and natural cosmetics since 1743

Oininio (Map 2; ☎ 553 93 34) Prins Hendrikkade 20–21 – wide range of ecologically aware products and New-Age gifts like aromatherapy oils, Tibetan healing bowls and didgeridoos; tarot, astrology, palm and numerology readings too; the Japanese tearoom on the 1st floor is a great place to chill out after all that shopping

Excursions

This is a small country, and you can visit many areas on day or overnight excursions from Amsterdam. All the major cities are less than 2½ hours away by train, even distant Maastricht (in the south-eastern province of Limburg) and Groningen (in the north-eastern province of Groningen). Many sights are concentrated in the west of the country, in the provinces of North and South Holland (Amsterdam itself is in the south of North Holland), and are less than an hour's drive or train ride away.

Getting Around the Country

See the earlier Getting There & Away and Getting Around chapters for general information about travelling by car or public transport. There's a dense network of freeways but in most cases the train is your best bet, and there are packages that combine train tickets and admission fees to numerous sights and events (see the following Rail Idee section).

Dutch trains are efficient, fast and comfortable, especially the new double-decker ones. Services along the major routes stop around midnight (often much earlier on minor routes), but there are night trains once an hour in both directions along the Utrecht-Amsterdam-Schiphol-Leiden-The Hague-Delft-Rotterdam route. Tickets for these cost the same as during the day or evening and can be bought at the counter (if it's open) or ticketing machines; if you don't buy a ticket beforehand, notify the conductor as you board the train, in which case you'll pay considerably more – almost double the normal fare!

Trains can be a *Stoptrein*, a faster *Sneltrein* (Fast Train, indicated with 'S'), or an even faster Intercity (IC), Intercity Plus (IC+) or EuroCity (EC) train. EuroCity trains travel between Amsterdam and Cologne nine times a day during the week, eight times a day on weekends, and only stop in Utrecht and Arnhem; they're quite fast (a 10-minute saving to Arnhem) but

you pay a f3 supplement at the counter or f7 on board the train. From Amsterdam, the high-speed *Thalys* only stops at Schiphol (from The Hague it only stops in Rotterdam) and requires a special ticket, available at the international ticket counters in Centraal Station.

The national train timetable book is available for f10.50 from train-station counters and newsagencies, but don't bother unless you're planning numerous trips to small destinations only serviced by local stop-trains. It includes a brief user's guide in English, German, French, Turkish and Arabic on pages 14–23. If you're online, check www.ns.nl; click on 'Reisplanners' (Travel Planners) in the top left-hand corner and choose the English-language option. There are frequent trains from Centraal Station to most corners of the country, and it's unlikely you'll have to wait long. Make a note of return trains listed on the timetable board at your destination.

All major train stations have luggage lockers and/or depots, and 100 stations throughout the country rent bicycles (with a discount in combination with a train ticket – see Bicycle Rental in the Getting Around chapter). You can bring your own bicycle on the train for a additional fee (f10 to f25) so long as the train has a separate luggage wagon (many of them do), but not on weekdays between 6.30 and 9 am or 4.30 and 6 pm (no hour restrictions in July and August). There are no restrictions or fees for collapsible bikes so long as they can reasonably be considered as hand luggage.

For train and ticketing information, ring the national public-transport number, ☎ 0900-92 92 (f0.75 a minute) weekdays from 6 am to midnight, weekends and public holidays from 7 am.

Tickets With a valid ticket you can get out anywhere along the direct route; in other words, with a ticket from Amsterdam to Rotterdam you can visit Haarlem, Leiden,

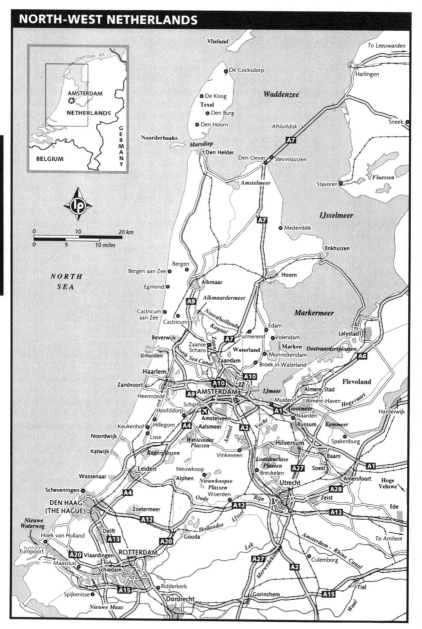

NORTH-WEST NETHERLANDS

Train Ticket Machines

More and more stations are relying on ticketing machines to cut personnel costs and queues at the few remaining counters, which is a bit of a problem for visitors because they're fairly complicated and instructions are in Dutch only. Check where you want to go on the alphabetical list of place names and enter the relevant code into the machine; then choose 1st/2nd class, *zonder/met korting* (without/with discount – eg, if you have a discount card, discussed in Tickets), and *vandaag geldig/zonder datum* (valid today/without date – if you choose the latter you can travel some other time but you'll have to stamp the ticket in one of the yellow stamping machines near the platforms when you do). The machine will then indicate how much it wants to be fed – coins only, though change is given.

The Hague and Delft along the way, but backtracking is not permitted. Return tickets are 10% to 15% cheaper than two one-ways but, like one-way tickets, are only valid on the same day. The only exception is a weekend return *(weekend-retour)*, which costs the same as a normal return and is valid from 7 pm Friday to 4 am Monday.

Children aged under four travel free if they don't take up a seat; those aged between four and 11 pay a so-called *Rail-runner* fare of f2.50 if accompanied by an adult (maximum of three kids, otherwise it's 40% discount on normal fare) or they get a 40% discount on the normal fare if travelling alone.

A *Dagkaart* (Day Card) for unlimited train travel throughout the country costs f81.75 (2nd class) or f122.75 (1st class), which is the same as you'll pay for a return ticket to any destination more than 233km away. Add f12 for a *Stad/Streek-Dagkaart* (City/Region Day Card) and you'll have use of trams, buses and metros as well.

A *Meerman's Kaart* (Multiple-Person Card) provides unlimited train travel for up to six people during the same periods as the *Voordeel-Urenkaart* discussed in the next paragraph; for two people this costs f112 (2nd class) or f174 (1st class).

If you plan to do a lot of travelling, consider investing f99 in a *Voordeel-Urenkaart* (Advantage Hours Card) valid for one year, which gives 40% discount on train travel on weekdays after 9 am, as well as all weekend, on public holidays and throughout July and August. The discount also applies to up to three people travelling with you on the same trip. As well, the card gives access to evening returns valid from 6 pm (but not on Fridays) that are up to 65% cheaper than normal returns. A similar version for those aged 60 and over gives an additional seven days' free travel a year. The card is available at train-station counters (passport photo required, plus driving licence or passport for the 60-plus version).

In July and August you can buy a *Zomertoer* (Summer Tour) ticket that allows three days' unlimited train travel within the country during any 10-day period for f99 (only 2nd class); two people travelling together pay f129. Stamp your ticket in the yellow machines at the stairways to the platforms. If you pay an extra f19 (f27 for two) the ticket becomes a *Zomertoer Plus* which is also valid for all trams, buses and metros during those three days.

A *Waddenbiljet* (Wadden Ticket) combines the train, ferry and bus tickets required for a visit to one of the Wadden Islands in the north of the country (Texel, Vlieland, Terschelling, Ameland or Schiermonnikoog), and so long as you don't take more than a day each way you can stay there for up to a year if you like. The ticket costs the same as two one-way train fares and a 40% discount applies if you hold a *Voordeel-Urenkaart*, though pensioners may be better off buying all tickets separately because of ferry discounts.

Rail Idee The NS offers numerous Rail Idee day trips throughout the country (and even to Antwerp, Brussels, Ghent or Bruges in Belgium, with the possibility to return the next day). These packages include a return 2nd-class ticket plus selected admissions, brochures, bicycle hire and even

EXCURSIONS

meals. The price is sometimes less than a return ticket by itself. These trips are not advertised to foreign tourists and the illustrated *Er-op-Uit!* booklet (f6.75) describing the trips is only in Dutch, but anyone can sign up. The booklet is available at train-station counters, where you can also book the actual trips.

The NS Reisburo (Travel Bureau; ☎ 0900-92 92 for domestic, ☎ 0900-92 96 for international) in Centraal Station might be able to help you choose the trip, but its main focus is organised tours and other packages offered by more than 30 companies. There's another NS Reisburo (☎ 427 05 41) at Rokin 44.

Train Taxi More than 100 train stations offer an excellent train taxi *(treintaxi)* service that takes you to/from the station within a limited area. This costs f7.50 per ride if you buy your special taxi ticket at a train-station counter or ticketing machine; buy another one for the return ride or else it's f9.50 from the driver. The service operates daily from 7 am (from 8 am Sunday and public holidays) till the last train, which varies per station.

These are special taxis (normal taxis don't take part in this scheme) and it's a shared service – the driver determines the route and the ride might take a bit longer than with a normal taxi, but it's usually much cheaper. Ask the counter operator or taxi driver for a pamphlet listing all participating stations and the relevant phone numbers for bookings.

Unfortunately some major stations (Amsterdam CS, The Hague CS or HS, Rotterdam CS) are excluded but Delft, Leiden Centraal and Utrecht CS are in the scheme – and what's more, the train taxis there operate all night because of night trains.

NORTH OF AMSTERDAM

The finger of land north of Amsterdam used to be known as West Friesland; today it's the northern tip of the province of North Holland, whose capital is Haarlem. Much of it is polder that has been claimed from the water in the past 400 years.

Waterland

Just north of Amsterdam is Waterland, a region of green farmland with dykes, ditches and some unique flora and fauna. It's an important bird-breeding area. The construction of the Noordhollands Kanaal in the 1820s cut the area in two. In the west near Landsmeer is the nature reserve and recreational area Het Twiske – see the introduction to Activities in the Things to See & Do chapter.

The eastern half of Waterland in particular is well worth exploring for its isolated farming communities that seem frozen in time. If you're looking for an interesting cycling trip on a pleasant summer's day, this is it (bring a picnic). From Amsterdam North, follow the sea dyke from Schellingwoude via Uitdam to Monnickendam. Backtrack a bit and cut through to Broek in Waterland, with its old wooden houses, and continue westwards to the Noordhollands Kanaal and the bird-breeding areas around Watergang. When you return to Amsterdam you'll suffer from culture shock.

IJsselmeer Towns

Several towns along the IJsselmeer have proud maritime histories and are well worth exploring.

The lively little port of **Hoorn**, which gave its name to Cape Horn at the southern tip of South America, was the capital of West Friesland and a mighty trading city (one of the six founding members of the United East India Company). Many of its 17th-century buildings are still intact, and its small harbour full of old wooden fishing boats and barges is as picturesque as they come. The ANWB/VVV office (☎ 0229-21 83 43) is at Veemarkt 4.

North-east of here, **Enkhuizen** was another founding member of the East India Company, and an important fishing and whaling port. There's some interesting architecture but the big attraction is the wonderful Zuiderzee Museum (☎ 0228-35 11 11) at Wierdijk 12–22, especially the outdoor section with a reconstructed village open in summer; the maritime exhibits in the former East India Company buildings are also worth a look. The VVV (☎ 0228-31 31 64) is at Tussen Twee Havens 1.

North-west of Enkhuizen is **Medemblik**, one of the oldest towns along the IJsselmeer, with a history going back to the early Middle Ages. Its Gothic cathedral and medieval castle are well worth visiting. The VVV (☎ 0227-54 28 52) is at Dam 2.

Closer to Amsterdam is **Edam**, a pretty town that was once a whaling port but is now known mainly for its cheeses. The cheese market is held Wednesday morning in July and August. The stained-glass windows in the 17th-century Grote Kerk are stunning. The VVV (☎ 0299-31 51 25) is at Damplein 1 in the centre of town.

South-east of Edam is **Volendam**, a former fishing port that reinvented itself as a tourist town when the Afsluitdijk killed the fishing industry. It's picturesque enough but the hordes of tourists spoil the fun – you'll encounter fewer of them when you explore some of the pretty streets behind the harbour. The VVV (☎ 0299-36 37 47) is at Zeestraat 37.

Monnickendam also attracts tourists and justifiably so: its meticulously restored 17th-century houses and old fishing cottages are picture-postcard material, and the whole setup is far less tacky than in Volendam. The tower of the former town hall has a beautiful carillon with mechanical knights. The VVV (☎ 0299-65 19 98) is at Zarken 2.

Marken was an isolated fishing community on an island that was connected to the mainland by a causeway in the 1950s. Tourists flock here in summer to photograph people in costume. The location is impressive and you can easily imagine how harsh it must have been here with frequent Zuiderzee storms. For more information, contact the VVV in Monnickendam or Volendam.

Getting There & Away A fun way to see some of these IJsselmeer towns is on a 'Historische Driehoek' (Historic Triangle) train/boat/train package included from April to October in the Rail Idee offerings. This involves a train from Amsterdam to Enkhuizen, a connecting boat to Medemblik,

a narrow-gauge steam train from Medemblik to Hoorn, and the train from Hoorn back to Amsterdam. You'll need to get an early start if you want time to look around the Zuiderzee Museum in Enkhuizen before catching the boat. The whole package is f53.50 per person.

Useful Connexxion buses leaving from the Open Havenfront in front of Centraal Station about every half-hour include No 111 to Marken, Nos 110 and 112 to Volendam and Edam, and No 114 to Hoorn. An excellent, inexpensive day excursion would be to take a morning bus from Amsterdam to Marken, which has pleasant trails along the shore. Hike around the island in a couple of leisurely hours, then take an excursion boat from Marken to Volendam (April to September only). Edam is only five minutes from Volendam by bus No 110. From Volendam or Edam, catch a bus back to Amsterdam with the possibility of a stop at Monnickendam.

If you use a strip ticket this would only cost six strips from Amsterdam to Marken and another seven from Volendam back to Amsterdam. In winter, or whenever the ferry isn't operating, you could backtrack from Marken to Monnickendam on bus No 111, then catch another bus up to Volendam from there. For the money, this is one of the best-value day trips in Europe.

The Afsluitdijk

The IJsselmeer (IJssel Lake) north-east of Amsterdam used to be known as the Zuiderzee before it was cut off from the open sea in 1932 by a large dyke, the 30km Afsluitdijk (Barrier Dyke). This impressive dam (it's not really a dyke because there's water on either side) connects the provinces of North Holland and Friesland (Fryslân).

Driving along the dyke's A7 motorway, you'll pass the **Stevinsluizen**, sluices named after the 17th-century engineer Henri Stevin, who first mooted the idea of reclaiming the Zuiderzee.

You can cross the dyke on the hourly Interliner bus No 350 from Alkmaar to Leeuwarden, but not by train. Singles/

euro currency converter f1 = €0.45

returns cost f30/51 and you can buy your ticket on the bus (strip cards aren't valid).

A second dyke from Enkhuizen slices this inland sea in half – the southern portion is officially known as the Markermeer. The original plan was to drain these seas and reclaim the land, as happened in the south-eastern portion of the IJsselmeer now known as Flevoland, but these schemes have been shelved for environmental reasons. On a nice day you'll see hundreds of yachts and traditional Zuiderzee fishing and cargo boats (see Sailing under Activities in the Things to See & Do chapter for boat rental details).

Wadden Islands

The country's five northern isles in the shallow Waddenzee stretch in an arc from Texel to Schiermonnikoog. They are important bird-breeding grounds and provide an escape for stressed southerners who want to touch base with nature. Ferries connect the islands to the mainland, and there are (mainly summer) hostels on all except Vlieland. Bicycles are a good way to get around and can be hired. Texel belongs to the province of North Holland and the language is Dutch; the other islands are Frisian.

Texel This is the largest and most populated island. Its 24km of beach can seem overrun all summer but even more so in June when the world's largest catamaran race is staged here. The biggest village is **Den Burg**, where you'll find the VVV (☎ 0222-31 47 41) at Emmalaan 66. For information on the ecology of the island and the Waddenzee in general, visit **EcoMare** (☎ 0222-31 77 41) at Ruijslaan 92 in De Koog – it's also a hospital for sick seals from the sometimes polluted Waddenzee.

You could visit Texel in a day from Amsterdam if you catch an early train but it's best to allow a day or two. Upon arrival, you'll get a good introduction to the island by taking bus No 29 to De Cocksdorp at the north end. Immediately change to bus No 27 from De Cocksdorp to De Koog on the west coast. Hike south along the beach a couple of kilometres, then cut inland to a lovely moor and forest with hiking trails.

Follow any of the signs pointing towards Den Burg and you'll find another bus stop eventually (allow a couple of hours for this hike).

For camping in isolation, head to **Loodsmansduin** (☎ 0222-31 92 03, Rommelpot 19), near Den Hoorn. **De Krim** camping (☎ 0222-39 01 11, Roogeslootweg 6) in Cocksdorp is open all year.

There are two NJHC hostels on opposite sides of Den Burg: the pleasant **Panorama** (☎ 0222-31 54 41, Schansweg 7) – take bus No 29; and **De Eyercoogh** (same phone number, Pontweg 106), 10 minutes' walk from town, or get bus No 28 from the ferry.

Hotel De Merel (☎ 0222-31 31 32, Warmoesstraat 22) has rooms for f65 per person. **'t Koogerend** (☎ 0222-31 33 01, Kogerstraat 94) charges f81/112 for singles/doubles.

Trains from Amsterdam to Den Helder (f22.50, 1½ hours) are met by a bus that whisks you to the awaiting hourly car ferry. The ferry trip takes 20 minutes, and costs f10/5 return for adults/children; cars/bicycles are charged f50/6.50.

Vlieland & Terschelling Both these islands are connected by ferry to the Frisian town of Harlingen. Vlieland is one of the two car-free isles, Terschelling is the group's longest. Vlieland is a popular family island and has one village, **Oost-Vlieland**; its western sister drowned in the 1700s. The VVV (☎ 0562-45 11 11) is on Havenweg 10.

Terschelling, 30km long, is known as a good-time isle, but it also has some stunning scenery and is great for cycling. Its main village is **West-Terschelling**, where the VVV (☎ 0562-44 30 00) is at Willem Barentsz-kade 19, opposite the ferry terminal.

Accommodation on Vlieland includes **De Stortemelk** camping ground (☎ 0562-45 12 25, Kampweg 1). The 'cheapest' hotel is **De Herbergh van Flielant** (☎ 0562-45 14 00, Dorpsstraat 105), with doubles for f110.

On Terschelling, **Dellewal** camping ground (☎ 0562-44 26 02) is next to the **NJHC hostel** (☎ 0562-44 23 38, Burgemeester van Heusdenweg 39). On the same road, **Dellewal Hotel** (☎ 0562-44 23 05, Burgemeester van Heusdenweg 42) charges f55 per person. In the town centre, **Hotel NAP** (☎ *0562-44 32 10, Torenstraat 50*) has impressive singles/doubles from f120/150. The very best restaurant on Terschelling (indeed on all the Wadden Islands) is **De Grië** (☎ *0562-44 84 99, Oosterend 43*). You'll pay around f80 for a meal but won't regret it.

Twice-hourly trains run from Leeuwarden to Harlingen (f8.25, 25 minutes) where three boats a day in summer (two in winter) make the 1¾-hour voyage to Vlieland. A return costs f34.85/17.45/17.45 for adults/children/bicycles. The trip to Terschelling takes the same time and costs the same – cars can be taken but that's expensive. There's also a faster ferry – three times a day to Terschelling and twice daily to Vlieland – that costs f8 extra each way and takes 45 minutes.

Ameland Ameland has no notable features except for its quaint villages and the number of tourists who explode onto the scene in summer. There are four villages; the main one, **Nes**, is home to the VVV (☎ 0519-54 65 46) at Rixt van Doniastraat 2.

At Nes, there's **Camping Duinoord** (☎ *0519-54 20 70, Jan van Eijckweg 4*). The **NJHC hostel** (☎ *0519-55 61 65, Oranjeweg 58*) near the lighthouse at Hollum – take bus No 130 from Nes. **Hotel de Jong** (☎ *0519-54 20 16*) across from the VVV in Nes has singles/doubles from f60/125. In the quieter village of Ballum, **Hotel Nobel** (☎ *0519-55 41 57, Kosterweg 16*) has rooms for f75/145.

From Leeuwarden, take bus No 60 to the port at Holwerd; from Groningen it's bus No 34. On weekdays there are six boats a day, weekends four. Returns cost f19.65/10.35/9.35 for adults/children/bicycles, and cars start at f133 (all prices are slightly cheaper in winter). The ferry trip takes 45 minutes.

Schiermonnikoog This is the smallest island (with a most tongue-tying name) and is off limits to cars. In the only village, about 3km from the ferry terminus, you'll find the VVV (☎ 0519-53 12 33) at Reeweg 5.

Accommodation options include *Seedune* camping (☎ *0519-53 13 98, Seeduneweg 1*), or you could stay at **Hotel Zonneweelde**

(☎ *0519-53 11 33, Langestreek 94*), with singles/doubles for f75/140.

There are four ferries on weekdays (two on weekends) from the village of Lauwersoog, between Leeuwarden and Groningen. To get there from Leeuwarden, take bus No 50; from Groningen, bus No 63. The voyage takes 45 minutes each way and return tickets cost f20.30/11/9.35 for adults/children/bikes (fares are a few guilders cheaper in winter).

NORTH-WEST & WEST OF AMSTERDAM
Alkmaar
This pleasant town with a picturesque old centre is famous for its **cheese market**, staged in the main market square (Waagplein) at 10 am every Friday in summer. Arrive early if you want to get more than a fleeting glimpse of the famous round cheeses being whisked away on sledges carried by porters with brightly coloured straw hats (the colours denote which guild they belong to). Other attractions include the **Waag** (Weigh House) with its cheese museum, and an interesting **beer museum** across the square. Nearby are the seaside resorts of **Bergen**, **Egmond** and **Castricum**, which require a bit of effort to reach but are far more pleasant than overdeveloped Zandvoort (see the later Zandvoort section). The VVV (☎ 072-511 42 84) in the Waag at Waagplein 3 provides information on the surrounding areas as well.

There are two trains an hour from Centraal Station (30 minutes) and at the other end it's a 10-minute walk to Waagplein.

Zaanse Schans
Several authentic working **windmills** stand along the Zaan River at Zaanse Schans just north of Zaandam, a bustling city northwest of Amsterdam. There are a few small **museums** among the old houses of the Zaanse Schans 'tourist village' but it costs nothing to stroll around and several attractions are free, such as the cheesemaker's shop (free samples!) and the wooden shoe factory with a contraption that copies clogs in a similar way to a locksmith's key machine. A tourist boat does 45-minute cruises

EXCURSIONS

on the Zaan several times a day (f9, children half-price) from April through September.

Zaanse Schans is a great picnic spot, so take a lunch and don't forget your camera! Also be sure to visit old **Zaandijk** directly across the Zaan from Zaanse Schans. It's far less visited by tourists and provides a more authentic appreciation of 'old Holland'.

In **Zaandam** itself, you could pay a quick visit to the small wooden cabin at Krimp 23, where Tsar Peter the Great of Russia stayed incognito for five months in 1697. He worked as a shipwright's apprentice on the nearby wharves, where he learnt much about shipbuilding, drinking and swearing in Dutch. Entry is f2.50/1.50 for adults/children. The Zaandam VVV (☎ 075-616 22 21 or ☎ 635 17 47) is at Gedempte Gracht 76.

Getting to Zaanse Schans by train is only three zones (four strips) and takes about half an hour. From Centraal Station, take the *Stoptrein* towards Alkmaar and get off at Koog Zaandijk – it's an eight-minute, well-signposted walk to the Zaanse Schans open-air museum.

To continue to Zaandam, cross the large bridge to the left of Zaanse Schans, take the first street on your right into Zaandijk and board the southbound bus No 89. Ask the driver to let you out at the large canal in the centre of town; Zaandam's pedestrian shopping mall is directly in front of the bus stop. All in all, in good weather it's a great afternoon out.

IJmuiden

The huge **North Sea locks** are one of the main attractions in this town at the mouth of the North Sea Canal – the largest is 400m long and 45m wide. Few people realise, however, that IJmuiden is also the largest fishing port in Western Europe, home to factory trawlers that stay out in the North Atlantic for weeks at a time. Several fish restaurants line the fishing harbour. The huge **beach** at low tide is a kite-flyer's delight, but the steel mills on the north side of the locks are less attractive. The VVV (☎ 0255-51 56 11) is at Plein 1945 (the name of the square) at No 105.

The easiest and most enjoyable way to get here by public transport is to take the

hydrofoil (☎ 639 22 47) from Pier 7 behind Centraal Station (hourly on the hour, half-hourly during peak times), which costs f14/8.25 return for adults/children. It skims along the North Sea Canal and 25 minutes later deposits you in Velsen, 3km short of IJmuiden itself, from where you catch Connexxion bus No 70 into town. It's a good idea to take a bicycle (an extra f7 return) because things are a bit spread out. Cycle from Velsen along the dyke towards the locks and go across the 'small' and 'middle' locks to the big lock on the far side; along the way you'll find an interesting information centre (open afternoons only).

You could also take a train to Haarlem and catch Connexxion bus No 70, 75 or 86 (25 minutes, six buses an hour Monday to Saturday, four an hour Sunday). Alternatively, take Connexxion bus No 82 from Amsterdam Sloterdijk station (25 minutes, two buses an hour weekdays, one an hour weekends). If you travel by road along the North Sea Canal, you'll have the surreal experience of passing huge, ocean-going ships that float well above road level.

Haarlem

The capital of the province of North Holland is a small but vibrant city with a beautiful centre similar to Amsterdam's. There are a couple of great museums that can easily be covered in a day if you don't plan to visit the nearby Keukenhof gardens as well (see the following South of Amsterdam section).

The VVV (☎ 0900-616 16 00) is at Stationsplein 1, to the right outside the impressive, semi-Art Nouveau **train station** (1908). From here it's a 10-minute walk southwards, straight down Kruisweg, to the city's pleasant central square at Grote Markt.

The **Frans Hals Museum** (☎ 023-511 57 75), another 10 minutes south of Grote Markt at Groot Heiligland 62, features many of the master's group portraits and works by other great artists – a must-see if you're interested in Dutch painting. It's open Monday to Saturday from 11 am to 5 pm, Sunday from 1 pm, and costs f7.50/3.50 for adults/children. The **Teylers Museum** (☎ 023-531 90 10), just east of

Grote Markt at Spaarne 16, is the oldest museum in the country (1778), with a curious collection including drawings by Michelangelo and Raphael. It's open Tuesday to Saturday from 10 am to 5 pm, Sunday from noon, and costs f7.50/3.50 for adults/children.

The impressive Gothic cathedral on Grote Markt, the **St Bavo**, also known as the Grote Kerk, is home to the stunning Müller organ – one of the most magnificent in the world – that was played by a 10-year-old Mozart. You can hear it roar on Tuesday at 8.15 pm (May to October) and also Thursday at 3 pm (July and August). The church is normally open to visitors Monday to Saturday from 10 am to 4 pm. Entry is f2.50/1.50.

Intercity trains run every 15 minutes to/from Centraal Station (f6.25, 15 minutes) and Leiden (f9, 30 minutes).

Zandvoort

The seaside resort of Zandvoort is 10 minutes by train from Haarlem. In summer it seems as if half of Amsterdam deposits itself here, and the only reason you might want to do likewise is that it's easy to get to – trains leave every 30 minutes from Centraal Station and a return trip costs about f15 (do not – repeat, not – try to get here by car on a sunny weekend day in summer). The famous Formula One road-racing track in the dunes still hosts motor-sports events, but lost its (and therefore the country's) round of the world championship in the 1970s when smug residents complained about noise.

A worthwhile day trip involves a return ticket to Zandvoort and stopping off in Haarlem en route. After lunch, continue to Zandvoort and stroll along the beach before returning to Amsterdam.

SOUTH OF AMSTERDAM

The compact Randstad (literally 'rim-city') is the circular urban agglomeration formed by Amsterdam, The Hague, Rotterdam and Utrecht, and smaller towns such as Haarlem, Leiden and Delft. It's the Netherlands' most densely populated region, with a 'green heart' of farmland and

lakes that begin immediately south of Amsterdam. The region's many sights are highlighted by the bulb fields, which explode in intoxicating colours between March and May.

Amstel & Vecht Rivers

A trip along the Amstel is a popular excursion for cyclists, and with good reason. The road southwards along the west bank soon leaves the city behind, and goes upriver through rural moors and polders. The town of **Ouderkerk aan de Amstel** is a few centuries older than Amsterdam and has several pleasant riverside cafés. Continue along the west or east bank to the township of **Nes aan de Amstel**, and then head eastwards along the Oude Waver River back to Ouderkerk along the Waver and Bullewijk Rivers. These peat-drainage rivers enclose an empty polder called **De Ronde Hoep** that attracts many birds, impervious to Amsterdam's skyscrapers looming in the distance. On this trip you'll experience the serenity of the flat Dutch landscape, with church steeples and the occasional windmill on the horizon, and you'll understand how Dutch artists learned to paint such dramatic skies.

South-east of Amsterdam, the winding Vecht River is another cyclists' paradise, and a popular touring route to Utrecht. Before the completion of the Amsterdam-Rhine Canal this was an important waterway but it's peaceful now. The scenery is not as starkly rural as along the Amstel – the small towns, woods and 17th and 18th-century country mansions provide plenty of variety. Brooklyn was named after the town of **Breukelen**.

You can take a day cruise by hydrofoil (☎ 639 22 47) to the Vecht once a week in summer from Pier 7 behind Centraal Station. It leaves at 10 am and returns at 5.30 pm, and costs f42.50/21.25 for adults/children.

Nieuwkoopse Plassen

The Nieuwkoop Lakes south of Amsterdam and west of the Vecht River are former peat lakes in an old polder area in the Randstad's 'green heart'. You can go

EXCURSIONS

windsurfing, sailing, rowing or canoeing, but the lakes are also a nature reserve with the world's largest colony of purple herons. In the town of **Nieuwkoop**, Tijsterman (☎ 0172-57 17 86), Dorpsstraat 118, rents boats, and the similarly named restaurant next door has a pleasant terrace and good *dagschotels* (dishes of the day) from f25.

From Centraal Station, take bus No 170 along the Amstel to Uithoorn and change to bus No 147 (50 minutes). By car, take the A2 towards Utrecht, turn off at Vinkeveen and follow the signs to Mijdrecht, De Hoef and Nieuwveen to Nieuwkoop.

Aalsmeer

This town south-west of Amsterdam hosts the world's biggest **flower auction** weekdays in Europe's largest commercial complex (600,000 sq metres, or 100 football fields). The experience will blow you away. Bidding starts early, so arrive between 7.30 and 9 am to catch the action from the viewing gallery. Selling is by Dutch auction, with a huge clock showing the high starting price dropping until someone takes up the offer. Admission costs f7.50 for those aged over 12 (free for those under). Take bus No 171 or 172 from Centraal Station.

Keukenhof & Bulb Fields

The Keukenhof is the world's largest flower garden, between the towns of Hillegom and **Lisse** south of Haarlem. It attracts a staggering 800,000 people for a mere eight weeks every year. Nature's talents are combined with artificial precision to create a garden where millions of tulips and daffodils bloom every year, perfectly in place and exactly on time. It's open from late March to May but dates vary slightly, so check with the Amsterdam VVV or the Keukenhof itself (☎ 0252-46 55 55). Admission costs f17.50/8.50 for adults/children. Take bus No 50 from Haarlem station to Lisse, then change to bus No 54.

The whole region between Hillegom and Katwijk (west of Leiden) is full of bulb fields – tulips, daffodils and hyacinths – that burst into bloom each spring and carpet the countryside in bright swathes of red, yellow or purple. The middle of April tends to be a good time for viewing, which is most enjoyably done by bicycle along the back roads (smell the scents). The train between Haarlem and Leiden passes through many of these fields as well.

The **Museum de Zwarte Tulp** (Black Tulip Museum; ☎ 0252-41 79 00), Grachtweg 2A in Lisse, displays everything you want to know about bulbs, including why there is no such thing as a black tulip. The Lisse VVV (☎ 0252-41 42 62) is at Grachtweg 53A.

Leiden

Leiden is a cheerful city with an aura of intellect generated by the 20,000 students who make up a sixth of the population. The university, the oldest in the country, was a present from William the Silent for withstanding a long Spanish siege in 1574. A third of the residents starved before the Spaniards retreated on 3 October, still the date of Leiden's biggest festival.

Most sights lie within a confusing network of central canals, about a 10-minute walk south-east of the train station. The VVV (☎ 0900-222 23 33) is at Stationsplein 210 in front of the station.

The **Rijksmuseum van Oudheden** (National Museum of Antiquities; ☎ 071-516 31 63) at Rapenburg 28 has a world-class collection and tops Leiden's list of 11 museums. Its striking entrance hall contains the Temple of Taffeh, a gift from Egypt for the Netherlands' help in saving ancient monuments from inundation when the Aswan High Dam was built. It's open Tuesday to Saturday from 10 am to 5 pm, Sunday from noon, and costs f7/6 for adults/children.

Another worthwhile museum is the **Rijksmuseum voor Volkenkunde** (National Museum for Ethnology; ☎ 071-516 88 00), near the station at Steenstraat 1, which focuses almost entirely on the former Dutch colonies and has a larger collection of Indonesian stuff than the Tropenmuseum in Amsterdam.

The **Hortus Botanicus** (☎ 071-527 72 49), Europe's oldest botanical garden (late 1500s), is at Rapenburg 73. It's open daily

The Hague's 'tits & penis'

Classic Dutch windmill

Reflective waters of a canal in Delft

Outside section of the Zuiderzee Museum, Enkhuizen

Hoorn harbour

Part of the Binnenhof complex, seat of government in The Hague

Ransdorp, Waterland

Harbour dyke at Marken

Police station, The Hague

Smell the grass: open-air abstract art, Scheveningen

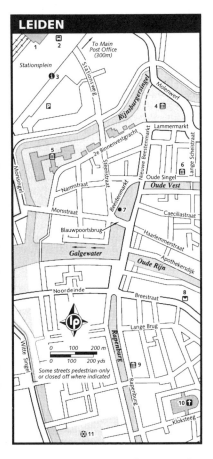

LEIDEN

1 Centraal Station
2 Bus Station
3 VVV Tourist Office
4 De Valk
5 Rijksmuseum voor Volkenkunde
6 Lakenhal Museum
7 Canal Cruises
8 Post Office
9 Rijksmuseum van Oudheden
10 Pieterskerk
11 Hortus Botanicus

EXCURSIONS

invention. It's open Tuesday to Saturday from 10 am to 5 pm, Sunday from 1 pm, and costs f5/3 for adults/children.

There are trains every 15 minutes to/from Amsterdam (f13, 35 minutes).

The Hague (Den Haag)

The Hague is the country's seat of government and residence of the royal family, though the capital city is Amsterdam. Officially it's known as 's-Gravenhage (the Count's Domain) because a count built a castle here in the 13th century, but the Dutch call it Den Haag. An interesting bit of trivia is that this third-largest city in the country, the capital of the province of South Holland, never received city rights and is still officially a village – the Dutch cities didn't want their seat of government to upstage them.

It has a refined air, created by the many stately mansions and palatial embassies that line its green boulevards north and northwest of the city centre, though there's a far poorer side to all this finery south of the centre. Much of the centre itself has been transformed into a concrete jungle and architectural showcase in the last 25 years and the construction-mania shows no signs of abating. There's a lot to see but it's all a bit scattered: prestigious art galleries, the biggest indoor jazz festival in the world in mid-July, and the miniature town of Madurodam.

Orientation & Information Trains stop at Station HS (Hollands Spoor), 20 minutes' walk south of the centre, or CS (Centraal Station), five minutes east of the centre;

from 9 am to 5 pm (Sunday from 10 am) but is closed Saturday in winter. Admission costs f5/2.50 for adults/children.

The 17th-century **Lakenhal** (Cloth Hall; ☎ 071-516 53 60), Oude Singel 28–32, houses an assortment of works by old masters, as well as period rooms and temporary exhibits. It's open weekdays from 10 am to 5 pm, weekends from noon, and costs f5/2.50 for adults/children.

De Valk (The Falcon; ☎ 071-516 53 53), Leiden's landmark windmill at Tweede Binnenvestgracht 1, is a museum that will blow away notions that windmills were a Dutch

euro currency converter f1 = €0.45

THE HAGUE (DEN HAAG)

1 Panorama Mesdag
2 Royal Palace
3 British Embassy
4 Lange Voorhout
   Palace Museum
5 French Embassy
6 US Embassy
7 Belgian Embassy
8 Main Post Office
9 Grote Kerk
10 Old Town Hall
11 Gevangenpoort
12 Binnenhof
13 Mauritshuis
14 VVV Tourist Office
15 Centraal Station (CS)
16 New Town Hall

head straight up Herengracht. The main VVV office (☎ 0900-340 35 05) is at Koningin Julianaplein 30 in front of CS; the other is in the seaside suburb of Scheveningen (same phone number), at Gevers Deynootweg 1134. Both are closed Sunday except in July and August when they're open from 11 am to 3 pm.

Things to See & Do The **Mauritshuis** (☎ 070-302 34 56), Korte Vijverberg 8, is a small but grand museum. It houses the superb royal collection of Dutch and Flemish masterpieces (several famous Vermeers, and a touch of the contemporary with Andy Warhol's *Queen Beatrix*) in an exquisite 17th-century mansion, open Tuesday to Saturday from 10 am to 5 pm, Sunday from 11 am; admission costs f12.50/6.50 for adults/children.

The parliamentary buildings around the adjoining **Binnenhof** (Inner Court) have long been the heart of Dutch politics,

though parliament now meets in a new building just outside the Binnenhof. Tours take in the 13th-century **Ridderzaal** (Knight's Hall) and leave from Binnenhof 8A daily, except Sunday, from 10 am to 4 pm (f6/5 for adults/children).

Outside the Binnenhof, the **Gevangenpoort** (Prison Gate; ☎ 070-346 08 61) at Buitenhof 33 has hourly tours showing how justice was dispensed in early times. It's open Tuesday to Friday from 11 am to 5 pm (last tour at 4 pm), weekends from noon, and costs f6/4 for adults/children. Nearby, the 1565 **old town hall** on Groenmarkt is a splendid example of Dutch-Renaissance architecture, but unfortunately you can only admire it from the outside. The huge **new town hall** on the corner of Grote Marktstraat and Spui is a much-criticised architects' delight. The same applies to the two new government buildings that dominate the city-centre sky, commonly referred to as the tits and the penis.

Admirers of De Stijl, and in particular of Piet Mondriaan, won't want to miss the Berlage-designed **Gemeentemuseum** (Municipal Museum; ☎ 070-338 11 11) at Stadhouderslaan 41. It was recently refurbished at great expense and houses a large collection of works by neo-plasticist and other artists from the late 19th century onwards, as well as extensive exhibits of applied arts, costumes and musical instruments. Mondriaan's unfinished *Victory Boogie Woogie* takes pride of place (as well it should since the museum paid f84 million for it); stare at it for a couple of minutes and you'll be gripped by the vibrancy of his ode to the USA. The museum is open Tuesday to Sunday from 11 am to 5 pm, and costs f10/5 for adults/children – take tram No 7 or 10 or bus No 4 or 14. The adjoining **Museon** (☎ 070-338 13 38) displays the world and its people for school kids, and next door is the **Omniversum** Imax theatre (☎ 070-354 54 54) with impressive documentaries of the earth (but Dutch commentary).

Another worthwhile art museum is the **Panorama Mesdag** (☎ 070-364 45 44) at Zeestraat 65, which, together with the nearby **Mesdag Museum** (☎ 070-362 14 34) at Laan van Meerdervoort 7F, displays works by the Hague School of artists who so influenced Mondriaan in his early years. The Panorama houses the impressive *Panorama Mesdag* (1881), a gigantic, 360° painting of Scheveningen viewed from a dune. It's open Monday to Saturday from 10 am to 5 pm, Sunday from noon (the Mesdag Museum only Tuesday to Sunday from noon to 5 pm).

The **Peace Palace** (☎ 070-302 41 37) at Carnegieplein 2 is home to the International Court of Justice. It can be visited weekdays from 10 am to 4 pm but only with a guided tour, which costs f5/3 for adults/children – inquire there or at the VVV. You can also attend public hearings but need to book seats in advance (naturally, security has to be strict with some of the issues under investigation). To get there, take tram No 7 or bus No 4 from CS.

Towards Scheveningen is **Madurodam** (☎ 070-355 39 00), George Maduroplein 1,

a miniature town containing everything that's quintessentially Netherlands. It's big with children and adults alike, and is open daily from 9 am to 10 pm (to 5 pm from October to March, and 8 pm March to June). Admission is f19.50/16 for adults/children. Take tram No 1 or 9, or bus No 22, from CS.

Scheveningen itself is an important fishing port and an overdeveloped seaside resort. There's plenty of beach, a fun-fair pier, a casino and the landmark Kurhaus hotel. It gets very crowded on summer weekends.

Saturday is a busy shopping day in The Hague as elsewhere in the country, especially in the morning, which is a good time to visit. The indoor general **market** south of Grote Marktstraat gets quite lively. The **Passage**, a glass-covered shopping arcade between Spuistraat, Buitenhof and Hofweg, is a stylish affair.

Getting There & Away Trains to/from Amsterdam (f16.75, 45 minutes), Delft (f4, five minutes), Leiden (f5.75, 10 minutes) and Rotterdam (f7.25, 15 minutes) travel via Station HS. The line that takes in Schiphol airport (f13, 40 minutes) via Leiden on its way to/from Amsterdam uses CS. It's a bit confusing because some trains to Schiphol branch off to Amsterdam Zuid WTC and don't go to Amsterdam Centraal Station – check before you board and change in Leiden if that's the case (you'll seldom wait more than 15 minutes). Utrecht trains (f16.75, 45 minutes) all use CS.

Delft

Historic Delft is well worth visiting for its 17th-century buildings and distinctive blue-and-white pottery – the famous delftware that 17th-century artisans copied from Chinese porcelain. Delft is home to the country's largest technical university, which helps explain the high proportion of young males.

The train and neighbouring bus station are a 10-minute stroll south of the central Markt. The VVV (☎ 015-212 61 00) is at Markt 83–85.

Things to See & Do Most visitors come here to buy delftware, and there are three

EXCURSIONS

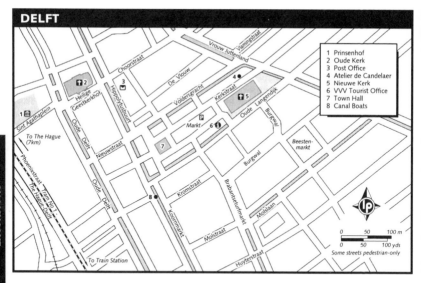

DELFT

1 Prinsenhof
2 Oude Kerk
3 Post Office
4 Atelier de Candelaer
5 Nieuwe Kerk
6 VVV Tourist Office
7 Town Hall
8 Canal Boats

factories where you can watch working artists. The most central and modest outfit is **Atelier de Candelaer** (☎ 015-213 18 48) at Kerkstraat 14. The other two factories sit poles apart outside the town centre. **De Delftse Pauw** (☎ 015-212 49 20) at Delftweg 133 is the smaller, employing 35 painters who work mainly from home (take tram No 1 to Pasgeld, walk up Broek-molenweg to the canal and turn left). It has daily tours but you won't see the painters on weekends. **De Porceleyne Fles** (☎ 015-256 92 14), south at Rotterdamseweg 196, is the only original factory operating since the 1650s, and is slick and pricey. Bus No 63 from the train station stops nearby, or it's a 25-minute walk from the town centre.

The 14th-century **Nieuwe Kerk** houses the crypt of the Dutch royal family and the mausoleum of William the Silent. It's open daily except Sunday, and costs f2.50/1 for adults/children. The Gothic **Oude Kerk**, with 140 years' seniority and a 2m tilt in its tower, is at Heilige Geestkerkhof. A combination ticket to both churches costs f4/1.50 for adults/children.

Opposite the Oude Kerk is the **Prinsenhof** at St Agathaplein 1, a collection of buildings where William the Silent held court until he was assassinated in 1584 – the bullet hole in the wall has been enlarged by visitors' fingers and is now covered by perspex. The buildings host displays of historical and contemporary art Tuesday to Saturday from 10 am to 5 pm, Sunday from 1 pm; admission is f5/2.75 for adults/children.

Getting There & Away Delft is 10 minutes by train to Rotterdam, less to The Hague. A pleasant alternative to/from The Hague is tram No 1, which leaves every 15 minutes from in front of Delft train station for the 30-minute trip.

Rotterdam

The catastrophic bombardment of the country's second-largest city on 14 May 1940 left it crippled then and somewhat soulless today. Its centre is modern, with mirror-window skyscrapers and some extraordinarily innovative buildings. The city prides itself on this experimental architecture as well as on its port, the largest by tonnage in the world. The Delta Works in the province of Zeeland south-west of the city, with massive causeways, bridges and mobile dams, were constructed after the disastrous floods of 1953; they represent Dutch water-engineering at its most grandiose.

Searching for a city 'centre' is fruitless: there is none. The sights are scattered over a large area, accessible by determined foot-slogging, metro or tram. They lie within a region bordered by the old town of Delf-shaven, the Meuse River (Maas in Dutch) and the Blaak district. The VVV (☎ 0900-403 40 65) is at Coolsingel 67.

Things to See & Do The city's major museum is the **Boijmans-van Beuningen** (☎ 010-441 94 00), a rich gallery of art from the 14th century to the present (Dutch, Flemish and Italian masters, Kandinsky, surrealists etc), at Museumpark 18–20. It's open Tuesday to Saturday from 10 am to 5 pm, Sunday from 11 am, and costs f7.50/4 for adults/children.

The 185m-high **Euromast** (☎ 010-436 48 11) pricks the skyline at Parkhaven 20, offering stunning views of the city and its harbour; admission is f14.50/9 for adults/children (tram No 6 or 9, or the metro to Dijkzigt). The **Kijk-Kubus**, a series of 'cube houses' with Escher-like design, offer a new angle to modern living. The display house is open daily from 11 am to 5 pm (from November to February it's open Friday to Sunday only). Adults/children pay f3.50/2.50 (metro: Blaak).

Rotterdam's old port (now closed off) is **Delfshaven**, where the Pilgrim Fathers set off for the New World in the *Speedwell*. They joined the *Mayflower* in Southampton but had to return there several times for repairs; eventually they gave the *Speedwell* up as unsafe and crowded on to the *Mayflower*. Before leaving Delfshaven they worshipped in the Oude Kerk at Aelbrechts-kolk 20 (metro: Delfshaven).

Spido (☎ 010-275 99 88), Leuvehoofd 1, runs daily 75-minute harbour cruises that cost f15.50/9 for adults/children, and day trips from f40 to the heart of the modern harbour at Europoort, or through the north-ern part of the Delta works (f45), taking in the windmills at Kinderdijk and the historic fortified town of Willemstad.

Getting There & Away There are trains every 15 minutes to/from Amsterdam (f22.50, one hour), Delft (f5.25, 10 min-utes), The Hague (f7.25, 15 minutes) and Utrecht (f14.75, 40 minutes). Half-hourly services run to/from Middelburg, the cap-ital of Zeeland (f32, 1½ hours), and Hook of Holland (f8.25, 30 minutes).

Utrecht

Utrecht is a historic city, the ecclesiastical centre of the Low Countries from the early Middle Ages. Today it's an antique frame surrounding an increasingly modern inter-ior, lorded over by the tower of the Dom (Cathedral), the country's tallest church tower. The 14th-century canals, once-bustling wharves and cellars now brim with chic shops, restaurants and cafés. The stu-dent population (Utrecht is home to the country's largest university) adds spice to a once largely church-oriented community.

The most appealing quarter lies between Oudegracht and Nieuwegracht and the streets around the Dom. None of this historic character is evident when arriving at the train station, which lies behind Hoog Catharijne, the Netherlands' largest indoor shopping centre and a modern-day monstrosity. The VVV (☎ 0900-414 14 14) is five minutes east of the station at Vredenburg 90.

Things to See & Do There are excellent views from the **Dom Tower** if you survive the 465 steps to the top. From April to Oc-tober, it's open weekdays from 10 am to 5 pm, weekends from noon; at other times of the year it's open only on weekends from noon to 5 pm. Entry costs f5.50/3.50 for adults/children.

There are 14 museums, most of them bizarre hideaways for paraphernalia – a laundry museum is one example. The **Gro-cery Museum** on Hoogt 6 is worth 10 minutes: the one-room collection sits above a sweet shop filled with the popular Dutch *drop* (salted or sweet liquorice). It's open Tuesday to Saturday from 12.30 to 4.30 pm, and entry is free.

The **Nationaal Museum Van Speelklok tot Pierement** (National Museum From

euro currency converter f1 = €0.45

Musical Clock to Street Organ; ☎ 030-231 27 89), Buurkerkhof 10, has a colourful collection of musical machines from the 18th century onwards, demonstrated with gusto on hourly tours. It's open Tuesday to Saturday from 10 am to 5 pm, Sunday from noon, and costs f9/6.50/5 for adults/students/children. **Het Catharijneconvent** (☎ 030-231 72 96) winds through a 15th-century convent at Nieuwegracht 63 and has the country's largest collection of medieval Dutch art. It's open Tuesday to Friday from 10 am to 5 pm, weekends from 11 am, and costs f7/5 for adults/students (children free).

Getting There & Away Utrecht is the national rail hub, and there are frequent trains to/from Amsterdam (f11, 30 minutes), Arnhem (f16.75, 40 minutes), Den Bosch (f13, 30 minutes), Maastricht (f40.75, two hours), Rotterdam (f14.75, 40 minutes) and The Hague (f16.75, 45 minutes).

EAST OF AMSTERDAM
Muiden

This historic town at the mouth of the Vecht River has a large yacht harbour, where you can rent sailing boats to tour the IJsselmeer (see Activities in the Things to See & Do chapter) or join an organised trip to the derelict fort on the island of Pampus. The VVV (☎ 0294-26 13 89), Kazernestraat 10, has details.

The main attraction in the town itself is **Muiderslot** (Muiden Castle; ☎ 0294-26 13 25), Herengracht 1, a 13th-century castle where the popular count of Holland was murdered by jealous colleagues in 1296. In the 17th century the multitalented PC Hooft entertained his male and female friends here; these gatherings of the century's greatest artists and scientists (including Vondel, Huygens, Grotius, Bredero and probably Descartes) became known as the Muiderkring (Muiden Circle). The period rooms dating from this time can be visited only on guided tours; ring to find out if you can join one in English (worth the effort).

Muiden is a pleasant bicycle trip from Amsterdam if the sun is out and the wind behaves itself. You can also take the twice-hourly

Connexxion bus No 136 from the terminus at Weesperplein metro stop (it travels past Hotel Arena and Amstelstation). For a pleasant walk on a sunny day, stay on this bus to the beach at Muiderberg (near the bridge to Flevoland polder) and walk back several kilometres along the dyke to Muiderslot.

Naarden

The fortifications and moat in the shape of a 12-pointed star around this little town were built in the late 17th century, partly in response to the Spaniards' total massacre of the inhabitants a century earlier. The perfectly preserved walls and bastions were still staffed by the army until the 1920s, and can be visited at the **Vestingmuseum** (Fortress Museum; ☎ 035-694 54 59), Westwalstraat 6. The VVV (☎ 035-694 28 36) is at Adriaan Dortsmanplein 1B.

The town has become a bit of a tourist attraction and is well worth exploring for its quaint little houses and impressive **Grote Kerk**, with stunning vault paintings and famous 'St Matthew Passion' performances over Easter. Czechs will be interested to know that the 17th-century educational reformer Jan Amos Komensky (Comenius) is buried here – the **Comenius Museum** (☎ 035-694 30 45) is at Kloosterstraat 33.

There are two trains an hour from Centraal Station to the station at Naarden-Bussum (more trains if you change at Weesp), but bus No 136 (see the previous Muiden section) also brings you here.

Hoge Veluwe & Arnhem

The Hoge Veluwe (High Veluwe, pronounced VAY-loo-wer), about an hour's drive east of Amsterdam, is the country's largest national park and home to the prestigious Kröller-Müller museum with its vast collection of Van Goghs and sculptures.

The town of Arnhem is south of here, the site of fierce fighting in 1944 between the Germans and Allied airborne troops during the failed Operation Market Garden. Today it's a peaceful town, the closest base to the park if you're travelling by public transport.

The Arnhem VVV (☎ 0900-202 40 75) is at Stationsplein 45, to the left out of the train station, but is closed Sunday. Buses to the various sights leave from the right as you exit the station.

Things to See & Do Arnhem is a pleasant town, worth a quick look. Its pedestrianised centre around the well-hidden Korenmarkt is a five-minute walk from the station – head down Utrechtsestraat, cross over Willemsplein and cut through Korenstraat.

The **Airborne Museum Hartenstein** (☎ 026-333 77 10), Utrechtseweg 232 in the western suburb of Oosterbeek, is housed in the villa where the Allies had their temporary headquarters. It displays the failed Allied operation and is open daily from 11 am to 5 pm, Sundays from noon (bus No 1).

The **Open-Air Museum** (☎ 026-357 61 11) at Schelmseweg 89 has a collection of rural buildings including farmhouses, workshops and windmills, and is more attractive than it sounds. It's open from 1 April to 1 November (bus No 3).

The **Hoge Veluwe** park itself, covering nearly 5500 hectares, is a strange mix of forests and woods, shifting sands and heathery moors that provide a sense of isolation found nowhere else on the Dutch mainland. Red deer, wild boar and mouflon (a Mediterranean sheep) roam here. The area is most impressive from mid-August to mid-September when ablaze with heather, or during the red deer's rutting season in September and October, and is best seen on foot or bicycle – 400 bicycles are available

free of charge from the visitors centre inside the park.

There are three entrances, but if you're using public transport the easiest route is on special bus No 12 that leaves from the VVV in Arnhem and goes to the visitors centre (☎ 0318-59 16 27). It runs at least three times a day from early April to 31 October. Alternatively, you could catch the hourly bus No 107 from Arnhem bus station to Otterlo. From there, you can either follow the signs to the entrance 1km away and then walk the remaining 4km to the visitors centre, or wait for the hourly bus No 110 to Hoenderloo which will drop you at the visitors centre. The park is open daily from 8 or 9 am to sunset and costs f7/3.50/8.50 for adults/children/cars. A Museumcard is not valid.

The **Kröller-Müller Museum** (☎ 0318-59 10 41), Houtkampweg 6, Otterlo, is near the Hoge Veluwe visitors centre. Its 278 Van Goghs are only a start: there are works by Picasso and Mondriaan, and out the back is Europe's largest sculpture garden, with works by Dubuffet, Rodin, Moore, Hepworth and Giacometti, among others. Admission is included in the park fee. It's open Tuesday to Sunday from 10 am to 5 pm.

Getting There & Away Trains to/from Amsterdam (f25.25, 65 minutes) and Rotterdam (f29.50, 75 minutes) go via Utrecht (f16.75, 40 minutes).

There are a couple of Rail Idee packages to the Hoge Veluwe but these aren't good value.

Language

Most English speakers use the term 'Dutch' to describe the language spoken in the Netherlands and 'Flemish' for that spoken in the northern half of Belgium. Both are in fact the same language, called Netherlandic *(Nederlands)*. The differences between Dutch and Flemish *(Vlaams)* are similar to those between British and North American English.

Dutch nouns come in one of three genders: masculine, feminine (both with *de* for 'the') and neuter (with *het*). Where English uses 'a' or 'an', Netherlandic uses *een*, regardless of gender.

There's also a polite and an informal version of the English 'you'. The polite is *u* (pronounced like the German 'ü'), the informal is *je*. As a general rule, people who are older than you should be addressed as *u*.

Pronunciation
Vowels

a	short, as the 'u' in 'cut'
a, aa	long, as the 'a' in 'father'
au, ou	pronounced somewhere between the 'ow' in 'how' and the 'ow' in 'glow'
e	short, as in 'bet', or as the 'er' in 'fern' (without pronouncing the 'r')
e, ee	long, as the 'ay' in 'day'
ei	as the 'ey' in 'they'
eu	a tricky one; try saying 'eh' with rounded lips and the tongue forward, then slide the tongue back and down to make an 'oo' sound; it's similar to the 'eu' in French *couleur*
i	short, as in 'it'
i, ie	long, as the 'ee' in 'meet'
ij	as the 'ey' in 'they'
o	short, as in 'pot'
o, oo	long, as in 'note'
oe	as the 'oo' in 'zoo'
u	short, similar to the 'u' in 'urn'
u, uu	long, as the 'u' in 'flute'
ui	a very tricky one; pronounced somewhere between au/ou and eu; it's similar to the 'eui' in French *fauteuil*, without the slide to the 'i'

What's in a Name?

Dutch, like German, strings words together, which can baffle a foreigner trying to decipher (let alone remember) street names. *Eerste Goudsbloemdwarsstraat* (First Marigold Transverse Street) is a good example! Chopping a seemingly endless name into its separate components might help a bit. The following terms appear frequently in street names and on signs:

baan – path, way
binnen – inside, inner
bloem – flower
brug – bridge
buiten – outside, outer
dijk – dyke
dwars – transverse
eiland – island
gracht – canal
groot – great, large
haven – harbour
hoek – corner
huis – house
kade – quay
kapel – chapel
kerk – church
klein – minor, small
laan – avenue
markt – market
molen – (wind)mill
nieuw – new
noord – north
oost – east
oud – old
plein – square
poort – city gate
sloot – ditch
sluis – sluice, lock
steeg – alley
straat – street
toren – tower
veld – field
(burg)wal – (fortified) embankment
weg – road
west – west
wijk – district
zuid – south

Consonants

ch, g	a strong guttural 'kh' sound as in Scottish *loch*
j	as the 'y' in 'yes'; sometimes as the 'j' in 'jam' or the 's' in 'pleasure'
r	a trilled sound made with the tip of the tongue
s	as the 's' in 'save'; sometimes as the 'z' in 'zoo'
v	similar to English 'f'
w	at the beginning of a word, a clipped sound almost like a 'v'; at the end of a word, like English 'w'

Greetings & Civilities

Hello.	*Dag/Hallo.*
Goodbye.	*Dag.*
See you soon.	*Tot ziens.*
Yes/No.	*Ja/Nee.*
Please.	*Alstublieft/Alsjeblieft.*
Thank you.	*Dank u/je (wel)* or *Bedankt.*
Excuse me.	*Pardon.*
How are you?	*Hoe gaat het met u/jou?*
I'm fine, thanks.	*Goed, bedankt.*
What's your name?	*Hoe heet u/je?*
My name is ...	*Ik heet ...*
Where are you from?	*Waar komt u/kom je vandaan?*
I'm from ...	*Ik kom uit ...*

Language Difficulties

Do you speak English?	*Spreekt u/Spreek je Engels?*
I don't understand.	*Ik begrijp het niet.*
Please write it down.	*Schrijf het alstublieft/ alsjeblieft op.*

Getting Around

What time does the ... leave/arrive?	*Hoe laat vertrekt/ arriveert de ...?*
bus	*bus*
train	*trein*
tram	*tram*

Where is the ... ?	*Waar is de/het ... ?*
bus stop	*de bushalte*
metro station	*het metrostation*
train station	*het (trein) station*
tram stop	*de tramhalte*

I'd like a one-way/ return ticket.	*Ik wil graag een enkele reis/een retour.*
I'd like to hire a car/bicycle.	*Ik wil graag een auto/ fiets huren.*

Directions

What street/road is this?	*Welke straat/weg is dit?*
How do I get to ...?	*Hoe kom ik bij ...?*
(Go) straight ahead.	*(Ga) rechtdoor.*
(Turn) left.	*(Ga naar) links.*
(Turn) right.	*(Ga naar) rechts.*
at the traffic lights	*bij het stoplicht*
at the next corner	*bij de volgende hoek*

Around Town

Where is the ...?	*Waar is de/het ...?*
bank	*de bank*
embassy	*de ambassade*
exchange office	*het wisselkantoor*
post office	*het postkantoor*
public toilet	*het openbaar toilet*
telephone centre	*het telefoonkantoor*
tourist office	*de VVV*

What time does it open/close?	*Hoe laat opent/sluit het?*

Accommodation

Do you have a room?	*Heeft u een kamer?*
How much is it per night/per person?	*Hoeveel is het per nacht/per persoon?*
Is breakfast included?	*Is ontbijt inbegrepen?*
May I see the room?	*Mag ik de kamer zien?*

camping ground	*camping*
guesthouse	*pension*
hotel	*hotel*
youth hostel	*jeugdherberg*

Food

I'm vegetarian.	*Ik ben vegetarisch.*

breakfast	*ontbijt*
lunch	*lunch/middageten*
dinner	*diner/avondeten*
restaurant	*restaurant*

Shopping

How much is it?	*Hoeveel is het?*
Can I look at it?	*Kan ik het zien?*
It's too expensive for me.	*Het is mij te duur.*

bookshop	*boekwinkel*
chemist/pharmacy	*drogist/apotheek*
clothing store	*kledingzaak*
laundry	*wasserette*
market	*markt*
supermarket	*supermarkt*
newsagency	*krantenwinkel*
stationers	*kantoorboekhandel*

Health

I need a doctor.	*Ik heb een dokter nodig.*
Where is the hospital?	*Waar is het ziekenhuis?*

I'm ...	*Ik ben ...*
asthmatic	*astmatisch*
diabetic	*suikerziek*
epileptic	*epileptisch*

antiseptic	*ontsmettingsmiddel*
aspirin	*aspirine*
condoms	*condooms*
constipation	*verstopping*
diarrhoea	*diarree*
nausea	*misselijkheid*
sunblock cream	*zonnebrandolie*
tampons	*tampons*

Time, Dates & Numbers

What time is it?	*Hoe laat is het?*
When?	*Wanneer?*
today	*vandaag*
tonight	*vanavond*

Emergencies

Call the police!	*Haal de politie!*
Call an ambulance!	*Haal een ziekenauto!*
Help!	*Help!*
I'm lost.	*Ik ben de weg kwijt.*

tomorrow	*morgen*
yesterday	*gisteren*

Monday	*maandag*
Tuesday	*dinsdag*
Wednesday	*woensdag*
Thursday	*donderdag*
Friday	*vrijdag*
Saturday	*zaterdag*
Sunday	*zondag*

1	*één*
2	*twee*
3	*drie*
4	*vier*
5	*vijf*
6	*zes*
7	*zeven*
8	*acht*
9	*negen*
10	*tien*
100	*honderd*
1000	*duizend*
10,000	*tienduizend*

one million	*een miljoen*

1st	*eerste*
2nd	*tweede*
3rd	*derde*
4th	*vierde*
5th	*vijfde*

Glossary

(See also the Language chapter for a list of terms commonly encountered in street names and sights.)

bruin café – brown café; traditional drinking establishment
café – pub, bar; also known as *kroeg*
coffeeshop – place to buy and consume marihuana products (as distinct from a *koffiehuis* or a tearoom)
CS – Centraal Station
dagschotel – dish of the day in restaurant
drop – salted or sweet liquorice
eetcafé – café serving meals
gasthuis – hospital or hospice
gemeente – municipality
genever – Dutch gin
GG&GD – Municipal Medical & Health Service
GVB – Gemeentevervoerbedrijf; the Municipal Transport Company
GWK – Grenswisselkantoren; official money exchange offices
hof – courtyard
hofje – almshouse

koffiehuis – espresso bar (as distinct from a *coffeeshop*)
koffieshop – see *coffeeshop*
koninklijk – royal
krakers – squatters
meer – lake
NAP – Normaal Amsterdams Peil; zero reference (sea level) for measuring elevation
NS – Nederlandse Spoorwegen; national railway company
polder – land reclaimed from the sea or lakes by building dykes and pumping the water out
Randstad – 'rim-city'; the circular urban agglomeration formed by Amsterdam, The Hague, Rotterdam and Utrecht, and smaller towns such as Haarlem, Leiden and Delft, surrounding a green 'heart'
Rijk – the State
spoor – train station platform
strippenkaart – strip ticket used on public transport
Vlaams – Flemish
VVV – Vereniging voor Vreemdelingenverkeer; tourist office
winkel – shop
zee – sea

Acknowledgments

Thanks

Many thanks to the travellers who used the 1st edition of this book and wrote to us with helpful hints, useful advice and interesting anecdotes. Your names follow:

A & B Lucas, Andris Blums, Anita Nemeth, Anuradha Nathan, Arthur Stanley, Audrey Leeson, Bo Li, Brie Jongewaard, Camilo Munoz, Carlos Checa Barambio, Cynthia Fenton, David Benjamin, David Cohen, Elise van Vliet, Elizabeth Hanna, Erna Mastenbroek, Ferry Grijpink, G G Howard, George W Long, Guus Bosman, H Tweedie, Herby Hulsebos, Ian Cragg, Ivan Dell'Era, Jan Bohuslav, Javier Cerdio, Jeff Skinner, Jenny Tap, Jitso Keizer, John Caswell, John Griffith, John Morcombe, Josh Polette, Joy Glazener, Joyce Chia, JT Borst-Fuerst, Kate Jackson, Kevin Murray, Kirsty Keter, Lucy James, Lynn Nicholas, Marjolein Hegge, Martha J Hardman, Martin Laderman, Marvin Badal, Mick Santoro, Micki Honkanen, Mirjam Skwortsow, Morag Bardey, N P Padalino, Naomi Tasker, Nicholas Reinhard, Nicola Yates-Bell, Noelle Zeilemaker, Orlaith Mannion, Owen Fairclough, Patrick Groenewegen, Patrizia Maier, Paul McGirr, Paul Willems, Peter Slater, Rachel Fitzpatrick, Rebecca O'Reilly, Reinout van Roekel, Richard Body, Richard Koris, Robert Henke, Rudi Serle, Sandip Srivastava, Sandra Morneau, Sheila Ditchburn, Simon Li, Sky Lew, Stephen Murphy, Steve Ewens, Steve Los, Susan Hughes

LONELY PLANET

Phrasebooks

L onely Planet phrasebooks are packed with essential words and phrases to help travellers communicate with the locals. With colour tabs for quick reference, an extensive vocabulary and use of script, these handy pocket-sized language guides cover day-to-day travel situations.

- handy pocket-sized books
- easy to understand Pronunciation chapter
- clear & comprehensive Grammar chapter
- romanisation alongside script to allow ease of pronunciation
- script throughout so users can point to phrases for every situation
- full of cultural information and tips for the traveller

'... vital for a real DIY spirit and attitude in language learning'
– Backpacker

'the phrasebooks have good cultural backgrounders and offer solid advice for challenging situations in remote locations'
– San Francisco Examiner

Arabic (Egyptian) • Arabic (Moroccan) • Australian *(Australian English, Aboriginal and Torres Strait languages)* • Baltic States *(Estonian, Latvian, Lithuanian)* • Bengali • Brazilian • British • Burmese • Cantonese • Central Asia (Uyghur, Uzbek, Kyrghiz, Kazak, Pashto, Tadjik • Central Europe *(Czech, French, German, Hungarian, Italian, Slovak)* • Eastern Europe *(Bulgarian, Czech, Hungarian, Polish, Romanian, Slovak)* • Ethiopian (Amharic) • Fijian • French • German • Greek • Hebrew • Hill Tribes • Hindi & Urdu • Indonesian • Italian • Japanese • Korean • Lao • Latin American Spanish • Malay • Mandarin • Mediterranean Europe *(Albanian, Croatian, Greek, Italian, Macedonian, Maltese, Serbian, Slovene)* • Mongolian • Nepali • Pidgin • Pilipino (Tagalog) • Portugese • Quechua • Russian • Scandinavian Europe *(Danish, Finnish, Icelandic, Norwegian, Swedish)* • South-East Asia *(Burmese, Indonesian, Khmer, Lao, Malay, Tagalog Pilipino, Thai, Vietnamese)* • South Pacific Languages • Spanish (Castilian) *(also includes Catalan, Galician and Basque)* • Sri Lanka • Swahili • Thai • Tibetan • Turkish • Ukrainian • USA *(US English, Vernacular, Native American languages, Hawaiian)* • Vietnamese • Western Europe *(Basque, Catalan, Dutch, French, German, Greek, Irish, Italian, Portuguese, Scottish Gaelic, Spanish (Castilian), Welsh)*

Lonely Planet Journeys

Journeys is a unique collection of travel writing – published by the company that understands travel better than anyone else. It is a series for anyone who has ever experienced – or dreamed of – the magical moment when they encountered a strange culture or saw a place for the first time. They are tales to read while you're planning a trip, while you're on the road or while you're in an armchair in front of a fire.

These outstanding titles explore our planet through the eyes of a diverse group of international writers. JOURNEYS books catch the spirit of a place, illuminate a culture, recount a crazy adventure or introduce a fascinating way of life. They always entertain, and always enrich the experience of travel.

MALI BLUES
Traveling to an African Beat
Lieve Joris (translated by Sam Garrett)
Drought, rebel uprisings, ethnic conflict: these are the predominant images of West Africa. But as Lieve Joris travels in Senegal, Mauritania and Mali, she meets survivors, fascinating individuals charting new ways of living between tradition and modernity. With her remarkable gift for drawing out people's stories, Joris brilliantly captures the rhythms of a world that refuses to give in.

THE GATES OF DAMASCUS
Lieve Joris (translated by Sam Garrett)
This best-selling book is a beautifully drawn portrait of day-to-day life in modern Syria. Through her intimate contact with local people, Lieve Joris draws us into the fascinating world that lies behind the gates of Damascus. Hala's husband is a political prisoner, jailed for his opposition to the Assad regime; through the author's friendship with Hala we see how Syrian politics impacts on the lives of ordinary people.

THE OLIVE GROVE
Travels in Greece
Katherine Kizilos
Katherine Kizilos travels to fabled islands, troubled border zones and her family's village deep in the mountains. She vividly evokes breathtaking landscapes, generous people and passionate politics, capturing the complexities of a country she loves.

'beautifully captures the real tensions of Greece' – *Sunday Times*

KINGDOM OF THE FILM STARS
Journey into Jordan
Annie Caulfield
Kingdom of the Film Stars is a travel book and a love story. With honesty and humour, Annie Caulfield writes of travelling in Jordan and falling in love with a Bedouin with film-star looks.

She offers fascinating insights into the country – from the tent life of traditional women to the hustle of downtown Amman – and unpicks tight-woven western myths about the Arab world.

LONELY PLANET

Guides by Region

L onely Planet is known worldwide for publishing practical, reliable and no-nonsense travel information in our guides and on our Web site. The Lonely Planet list covers just about every accessible part of the world. Currently there are thirteen series: travel guides, shoestring guides, walking guides, city guides, phrasebooks, audio packs, city maps, travel atlases, diving & snorkeling guides, restaurant guides, first-time travel guides, healthy travel and travel literature.

AFRICA Africa on a shoestring • Africa – the South • Arabic (Egyptian) phrasebook • Arabic (Moroccan) phrasebook • Cairo • Cape Town • Cape Town city map • Central Africa • East Africa • Egypt • Egypt travel atlas • Ethiopian (Amharic) phrasebook • The Gambia & Senegal • Healthy Travel Africa • Kenya • Kenya travel atlas • Malawi, Mozambique & Zambia • Morocco • North Africa • Read This First Africa • South Africa, Lesotho & Swaziland • South Africa, Lesotho & Swaziland travel atlas • Swahili phrasebook • Tanzania, Zanzibar & Pemba • Trekking in East Africa • Tunisia • West Africa • Zimbabwe, Botswana & Namibia • Zimbabwe, Botswana & Nambia Travel Atlas • World Food Morocco

Travel Literature: The Rainbird: A Central African Journey • Songs to an African Sunset: A Zimbabwean Story • Mali Blues: Traveling to an African Beat

AUSTRALIA & THE PACIFIC Auckland • Australia • Australian phrasebook • Bushwalking in Australia • Bushwalking in Papua New Guinea • Fiji • Fijian phrasebook • Healthy Travel Australia, NZ and the Pacific • Islands of Australia's Great Barrier Reef • Melbourne • Melbourne city map • Micronesia • New Caledonia • New South Wales & the ACT • New Zealand • Northern Territory • Outback Australia • Out To Eat – Melbourne • Out to Eat – Sydney • Papua New Guinea • Pidgin phrasebook • Queensland • Rarotonga & the Cook Islands • Samoa • Solomon Islands • South Australia • South Pacific • South Pacific Languages phrasebook • Sydney • Sydney city map • Sydney Condensed • Tahiti & French Polynesia • Tasmania • Tonga • Tramping in New Zealand • Vanuatu • Victoria • Western Australia

Travel Literature: Islands in the Clouds • Kiwi Tracks: A New Zealand Journey • Sean & David's Long Drive

CENTRAL AMERICA & THE CARIBBEAN Bahamas, Turks & Caicos • Bermuda • Central America on a shoestring • Costa Rica • Cuba • Dominican Republic & Haiti • Eastern Caribbean • Guatemala, Belize & Yucatán: La Ruta Maya • Jamaica • Mexico • Mexico City • Panama • Puerto Rico • Read This First Central & South America • World Food Mexico

Travel Literature: Green Dreams: Travels in Central America

EUROPE Amsterdam • Amsterdam city map • Andalucía • Austria • Baltic States phrasebook • Barcelona • Berlin • Berlin city map • Britain • British phrasebook • Brussels, Bruges & Antwerp • Budapest city map • Canary Islands • Central Europe • Central Europe phrasebook • Corfu & Ionians • Corsica • Crete • Crete Condensed • Croatia • Cyprus • Czech & Slovak Republics • Denmark • Dublin • Eastern Europe • Eastern Europe phrasebook • Edinburgh • Estonia, Latvia & Lithuania • Europe on a shoestring • Finland • Florence • France • French phrasebook • Germany • German phrasebook • Greece • Greek Islands • Greek phrasebook • Hungary • Iceland, Greenland & the Faroe Islands • Istanbul City Map • Ireland • Italian phrasebook • Italy • Krakow •Lisbon • London • London city map • London Condensed • Mediterranean Europe • Mediterranean Europe phrasebook • Munich • Norway • Paris • Paris city map • Paris Condensed • Poland • Portugal • Portugese phrasebook • Portugal travel atlas • Prague • Prague city map • Provence & the Côte d'Azur • Romania & Moldova • Rome • Russia, Ukraine & Belarus • Russian phrasebook • Scandinavian & Baltic Europe • Scandinavian Europe phrasebook • Scotland • Slovenia • Spain • Spanish phrasebook • St Petersburg • Switzerland • Trekking in Spain • Ukrainian phrasebook • Venice • Vienna • Walking in Britain • Walking in Ireland • Walking in Italy • Walking in Spain • Walking in Switzerland • Western Europe • Western Europe phrasebook • World Food Italy • World Food Spain

Travel Literature: The Olive Grove: Travels in Greece

INDIAN SUBCONTINENT Bangladesh • Bengali phrasebook • Bhutan • Delhi • Goa • Hindi & Urdu phrasebook • India • India & Bangladesh travel atlas • Indian Himalaya • Karakoram Highway • Kerala • Mumbai (Bombay) • Nepal • Nepali phrasebook • Pakistan • Rajasthan • Read This First: Asia & India • South India • Sri Lanka • Sri Lanka phrasebook • Trekking in the Indian Himalaya • Trekking in the Karakoram & Hindukush • Trekking in the Nepal Himalaya

Travel Literature: In Rajasthan • Shopping for Buddhas • The Age Of Kali

LONELY PLANET

Mail Order

Lonely Planet products are distributed worldwide. They are also available by mail order from Lonely Planet, so if you have difficulty finding a title please write to us. North and South American residents should write to 150 Linden St, Oakland, CA 94607, USA; European and African residents should write to 10a Spring Place, London NW5 3BH, UK; and residents of other countries to PO Box 617, Hawthorn, Victoria 3122, Australia.

ISLANDS OF THE INDIAN OCEAN Madagascar & Comoros • Maldives • Mauritius, Réunion & Seychelles

MIDDLE EAST & CENTRAL ASIA Arab Gulf States • Central Asia • Central Asia phrasebook • Dubai • Hebrew phrasebook • Iran • Israel & the Palestinian Territories • Israel & the Palestinian Territories travel atlas • Istanbul • Istanbul to Cairo • Jerusalem • Jerusalem City Map • Jordan & Syria • Jordan, Syria & Lebanon travel atlas • Lebanon • Middle East on a shoestring • Syria • Turkey • Turkey travel atlas • Turkish phrasebook • Yemen
Travel Literature: The Gates of Damascus • Kingdom of the Film Stars: Journey into Jordan • Black on Black: Iran Revisited

NORTH AMERICA Alaska • Backpacking in Alaska • Baja California • California & Nevada • California Condensed • Canada • Chicago • Chicago city map • Deep South • Florida • Hawaii • Honolulu • Las Vegas • Los Angeles • Miami • New England • New Orleans • New York City • New York city map • New York Condensed • New York, New Jersey & Pennsylvania • Oahu • Pacific Northwest USA • Puerto Rico • Rocky Mountain • San Francisco • San Francisco city map • Seattle • Southwest USA • Texas • USA • USA phrasebook • Vancouver • Washington, DC & the Capital Region • Washington DC city map
Travel Literature: Drive Thru America

NORTH-EAST ASIA Beijing • Cantonese phrasebook • China • Hong Kong • Hong Kong city map • Hong Kong, Macau & Guangzhou • Japan • Japanese phrasebook • Japanese audio pack • Korea • Korean phrasebook • Kyoto • Mandarin phrasebook • Mongolia • Mongolian phrasebook • North-East Asia on a shoestring • Seoul • South-West China • Taiwan • Tibet • Tibetan phrasebook • Tokyo
Travel Literature: Lost Japan • In Xanadu

SOUTH AMERICA Argentina, Uruguay & Paraguay • Bolivia • Brazil • Brazilian phrasebook • Buenos Aires • Chile & Easter Island • Chile & Easter Island travel atlas • Colombia • Ecuador & the Galapagos Islands • Healthy Travel Central & South America • Latin American Spanish phrasebook • Peru •Quechua phrasebook • Rio de Janeiro • Rio de Janeiro city map • South America on a shoestring • Trekking in the Patagonian Andes • Venezuela
Travel Literature: Full Circle: A South American Journey

SOUTH-EAST ASIA Bali & Lombok • Bangkok • Bangkok city map • Burmese phrasebook • Cambodia • Hanoi • Healthy Travel Asia & India • Hill Tribes phrasebook • Ho Chi Minh City • Indonesia • Indonesia's Eastern Islands • Indonesian phrasebook • Indonesian audio pack • Jakarta • Java • Laos • Lao phrasebook • Laos travel atlas • Malay phrasebook • Malaysia, Singapore & Brunei • Myanmar (Burma) • Philippines • Pilipino (Tagalog) phrasebook • Read This First Asia & India • Singapore • South-East Asia on a shoestring • South-East Asia phrasebook • Thailand • Thailand's Islands & Beaches • Thailand travel atlas • Thai phrasebook • Thai audio pack • Vietnam • Vietnamese phrasebook • Vietnam travel atlas • World Food Thailand • World Food Vietnam

ALSO AVAILABLE: Antarctica • The Arctic • Brief Encounters: Stories of Love, Sex & Travel • Chasing Rickshaws • Lonely Planet Unpacked • Not the Only Planet: Travel Stories from Science Fiction • Sacred India • Travel with Children • Traveller's Tales

Index

Text

Bold indicates maps.

Bold indicates maps.

Boxed Text

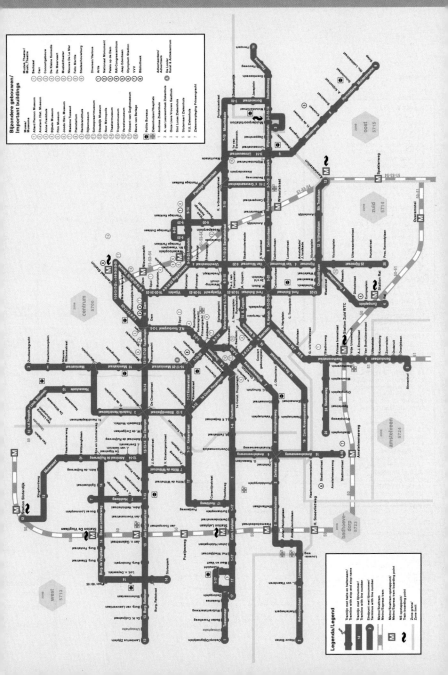

MAP 1 - GREATER AMSTERDAM

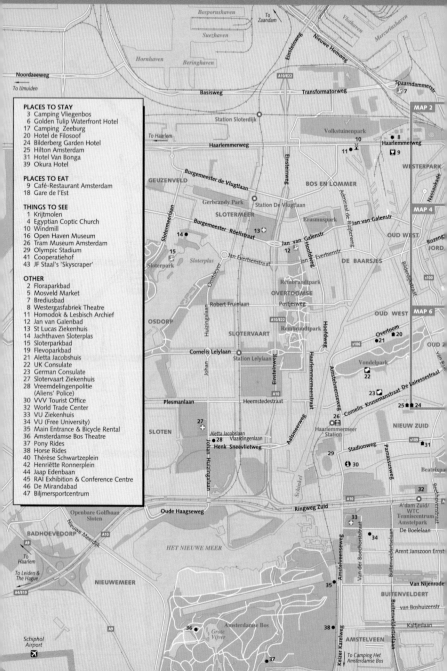

PLACES TO STAY
3 Camping Vliegenbos
6 Golden Tulip Waterfront Hotel
17 Camping Zeeburg
20 Hotel de Filosoof
24 Bilderberg Garden Hotel
25 Hilton Amsterdam
31 Hotel Van Bonga
39 Okura Hotel

PLACES TO EAT
9 Café-Restaurant Amsterdam
18 Gare de l'Est

THINGS TO SEE
1 Krijtmolen
4 Egyptian Coptic Church
10 Windmill
16 Open Haven Museum
26 Tram Museum Amsterdam
29 Olympic Stadium
41 Cooperatiehof
43 JF Staal's 'Skyscraper'

OTHER
2 Floraparkbad
5 Mosveld Market
7 Brediusbad
8 Westergasfabriek Theatre
11 Homodok & Lesbisch Archief
12 Jan van Galenbad
13 St Lucas Ziekenhuis
14 Jachthaven Sloterterplas
15 Sloterparkbad
19 Flevoparkbad
21 Aletta Jacobshuis
22 UK Consulate
23 German Consulate
27 Slotervaart Ziekenhuis
28 Vreemdelingenpolitie
   (Aliens' Police)
30 VVV Tourist Office
32 World Trade Center
33 VU Ziekenhuis
34 VU (Free University)
35 Main Entrance & Bicycle Rental
36 Amsterdamse Bos Theatre
37 Pony Rides
38 Horse Rides
40 Thérèse Schwartzeplein
42 Henriëtte Ronnerplein
44 Jaap Edenbaan
45 RAI Exhibition & Conference Centre
46 De Mirandabad
47 Biljmersportcentrum

MAP 1 - GREATER AMSTERDAM

MAP 2

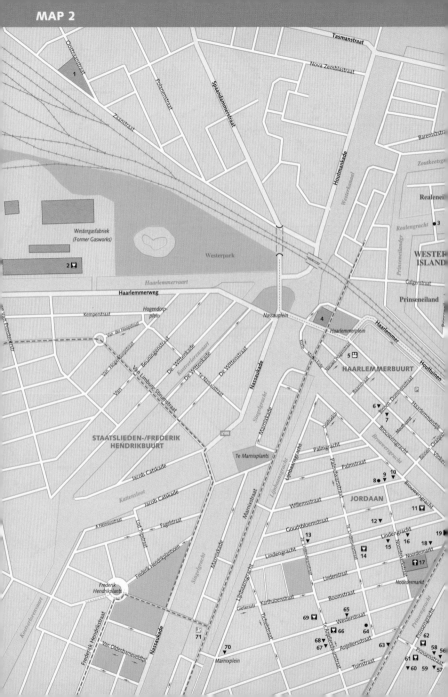

Tasmanstraat

Nova Zemblastraat

Oostzaanstraat

1

Zaanstraat

Polanenstraat

Spaandammerstraat

Houtmankade

Westerkanaal

Barentszstr

Zoutkeetsgr

Realenei

Westergasfabriek
(Former Gasworks)

2

Westerpark

Realengracht ● 3

Realengracht

Prinseneiland

WESTER
ISLAND

Galgenstraat

Haarlemmervaart

Prinseneiland

Haarlemmerweg

Nassauplein

Haarlemmer

Houttuinen

Kemperstraat

Hogendorp-
plein

Haarlemmerplein

4

Van der Hoopstraat

De Wittenkade

Nassaukade

Haarlemmerplein

Kleine Haarlemmer

Nieuwe Nassaus

5

HAARLEMMERBUURT

Van Hogendorpstraat

Van Beuningenstraat

Kostverlorenvaart

De Wittenkade

De Wittenstraat

Buiten-Dommersbuurt

Haarlemmerdijk

Quellijn

Van Limburg Stirumstraat

1e Nassaustraat

Singelgracht

Diaboli

Brouwergracht

Moddere

Brouwersgracht

Buiten-Vinkel

STAATSLIEDEN-/FREDERIK
HENDRIKBUURT

6 ▼
7

100

1e Marnixplants

Marnixkade

Palmgracht

Lijnbaansgracht

Palmdwarsstraat

Palmstraat

8● 9 ▼ 10
▼

Brouwersgracht

Jacob Catskade

Willemsstraat

JORDAAN

11

Kattensloot

Jacob Catskade

Marnixstraat

Goudsbloemstraat

12 ▼

19

A. Heinlinstraat

Fagelstraat

13
▼

Lindengracht

15

Lindengracht

16

18 ▼

1e Hondraat

Noorderdwarsstraat

Noordermarkt

14

17

Frederik Hendrikplantsoen

Singelgracht

Marnixkade

Lindenstraat

Lijnbaansgracht

Lindenstraat

Boomstraat

Noordermarkt

Frederik Hendrikplants

Gieters

Karthuizersstraat

Tichelstraat

65

Westerstraat

Prinsengracht

Frederik Hendrikstraat

71

69

68▼
67▼

66

64

62

58 56

Van Oldenbarneveldtpl

70

Marnixplein

Anjeliersstraat

63 ▼

61 ▼ ▼60

Prinsenstraat

59 57

Tuinstraat

MAP 2

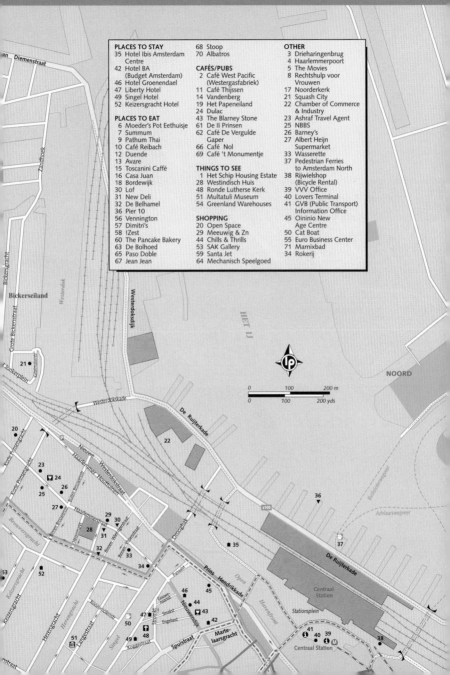

PLACES TO STAY
35 Hotel Ibis Amsterdam Centre
42 Hotel BA (Budget Amsterdam)
46 Hotel Groenendael
47 Liberty Hotel
49 Singel Hotel
52 Keizersgracht Hotel

PLACES TO EAT
6 Moeder's Pot Eethuisje
7 Summum
9 Pathum Thai
10 Café Reibach
12 Duende
13 Avare
15 Toscanini Caffè
16 Casa Juan
18 Bordewijk
30 Lof
31 New Deli
32 De Belhamel
36 Pier 10
56 Vennington
57 Dimitri's
58 IZest
60 The Pancake Bakery
63 De Bolhoed
65 Paso Doble
67 Jean Jean

68 Stoop
70 Albatros

CAFÉS/PUBS
2 Café West Pacific (Westergasfabriek)
11 Café Thijssen
14 Vandenberg
19 Het Papeneiland
24 Dulac
43 The Blarney Stone
61 De II Prinsen
62 Café De Vergulde Gaper
66 Café Nol
69 Café 't Monumentje

THINGS TO SEE
1 Het Schip Housing Estate
28 Westindisch Huis
48 Ronde Lutherse Kerk
51 Multatuli Museum
54 Greenland Warehouses

SHOPPING
20 Open Space
29 Meeuwig & Zn
44 Chills & Thrills
53 SAK Gallery
59 Santa Jet
64 Mechanisch Speelgoed

OTHER
3 Drieharingenbrug
4 Haarlemmerpoort
5 The Movies
8 Rechtshulp voor Vrouwen
17 Noorderkerk
21 Squash City
22 Chamber of Commerce & Industry
23 Ashraf Travel Agent
25 NBBS
26 Barney's
27 Albert Heijn Supermarket
33 Wasserette
37 Pedestrian Ferries to Amsterdam North
38 Rijwielshop (Bicycle Rental)
39 VVV Office
40 Lovers Terminal
41 GVB (Public Transport) Information Office
45 Oininio New Age Centre
50 Cat Boat
55 Euro Business Center
71 Marnixbad
34 Rokerij

MAP 3

Hagedoornweg

Nieuwe Leeuwarderweg

Johan van Hasseltweg

To Monnicke

Adelaarswe

Meeuwenpl

Van der Pekstraat

NOORD

IJ-tunnel

Adelaarsweg

Kanaal

Noordhollands

Adelaarsweg

To Cam
Vliegenbos

Buiksloterkanaal

Buiksloterweg

Haviksteen

Willemsluis

Meeuwenlaan

Gedempte Insteekhaven

IJ-Tunnel

Adelaarswegveer

HET IJ

0   100   200 m
0   100   200 yds

Java Eiland

Sumatrakade

Javakade

Bungy Jump
Holland

Ship Passenger
Terminal

IJ Haven

De Ruijterkade

Piet Heinkade

LEANNE LOGAN

GIANT
MOZART TULP
10 VOOR 20.=
20 VOOR 37.50
LEAVES 2.=
6 VOOR 10.=

TULPEN 2.=
6 VOOR 10.=

ANTHONY PIDGEON

LEANNE LOGAN

JULIET COOMBE

LEANNE LOGAN

Amsterdam's wonderful floral displays are not limited to tulips – or even to real flowers!

MAP 4

MAP 4

MAP 4

PLACES TO STAY
12 Hotel Toren
13 Canal House Hotel
29 Bob's Youth Hostel
30 Hotel Brian
36 Flying Pig Downtown Hostel
38 Victoria Hotel
42 Hotel Continental
45 Hotel Kabul
48 Golden Tulip Barbizon Palace
55 Hotel Crown
58 Centrumhotel
59 Stablemaster Hotel
63 Frisco Inn
64 Hotel Beursstraat
69 Hotel Winston
80 Swissôtel Amsterdam
97 Hotel van Onna
102 Christian Youth Hostel Eben Haëzer
109 Pulitzer Hotel
112 Hotel Nadia
113 Hotel Clemens
114 Hotel Pax
115 Hotel De Westertoren
118 Hotel Belga
146 Hotel Hoksbergen
147 Hotel Estheréa
163 RHO Hotel
164 Grand Hotel Krasnapolsky
175 Christian Youth Hostel 'The Shelter'
189 The Grand Westin Demeure
251 Hotel De l'Europe
255 Stadsdoelen Youth Hostel
258 Hotel Nes
259 Hotel Eureka
304 Waterfront Hotel
306 Hotel Agora
308 Ambassade Hotel
327 International Budget Hotel
344 Hotel Titus
345 Hotel Impala
346 Hotel Kooyk
347 Hotel King
365 Aerohotel
381 The Veteran
382 Hotel De Admiraal
385 Golden Tulip Schiller Hotel
387 City Hotel
394 Hotel Adolesce
395 Hotel Fantasia

PLACES TO EAT
1 Burger's Patio
7 Rozen & Tortillas
10 Spanjer en van Twist
11 Christophe
19 Foodism
22 Villa Zeezicht
26 La Strada
31 Keuken van 1870
37 Dorrius
57 Si-Chuan Kitchen
79 De Roode Leeuw
94 Restaurant Speciaal
95 De Vliegende Schotel
110 Koh-I-Noor
131 Rakang Thai
134 Nielsen
136 Hein
139 Turqoise
142 Caprese

145 Grekas
156 Supper Club
166 Sukasari
170 Hoi Tin
171 Hemelse Modder
172 Café Bern
179 Zosa
182 Oriental City
220 De Visscher
222 Haesje Claes
224 d'Vijff Vlieghen Restaurant
225 Kantjil en de Tijger
238 Caffe Esprit
245 Vlaams Friteshuis
254 Atrium
257 Eetcafé De Staalmeesters
260 Tom Yam
265 Puccini
270 Szmulewicz
278 Planet Hollywood
281 Memories of India
287 Rose's Cantina
289 Gary's Muffins
291 Gauchos
293 Sichuan Food
294 Le Pêcheur
295 Dynasty
297 Zet Isie
310 Goodies
314 Cilubang
316 Tout Court
323 Riaz
332 Pastini
333 Café Morlang
334 Café Walem
353 Indonesia
374 Pasta e Basta
376 Pygma-lion
388 Sluizer

CAFÉS/PUBS
2 De Tuin
3 Café 't Smalle
4 De Reiger
6 De Prins
9 De 2 Zwaantjes
35 In de Wildeman
43 Himalaya
51 Molly Malone's
56 Last Waterhole
68 Durty Nelly's
75 De Drie Fleschjes
125 Van Puffelen
129 Saarein II
144 Gollem
151 Bar Bep
152 Diep
167 Proeflokaal Wijnand Fockinck
174 Lokaal 't Loosje
177 Maximiliaan
210 Blincker
212 Café-Restaurant Kapitein Zeppo's
221 Pilsener Club (Engelse Reet)
226 Café Dante; Steltman Gallery
228 Hoppe
230 Luxembourg
235 d'Oude Herbergh
244 De Schutter
253 Café De Jaren
261 Café-Restaurant Dantzig
269 Vivelavie

271 Mulligans
272 Mediacafé De Kroon
275 Monopole
296 Downtown
301 Other Side
315 Café De Doffer
328 De Pieper
331 Café Het Molenpad
355 Eylders
356 Reynders
384 Café Schiller
386 Old Bell

ENTERTAINMENT
20 Grey Area
23 Café ter Kuile
27 Homegrown Fantasy
33 Cuckoo's Nest
34 Akhnaton
52 Queens Head
53 Casablanca
60 Getto
65 Cockring
66 Argos
101 Mazzo
106 Pi Kunst & Koffie
108 COC Amsterdam
127 Korsakoff
128 Maloe Melo
135 Felix Meritis Building
143 Kadinsky
153 Seymour Likely
168 Trance Buddha
176 Bethaniënklooster
184 Greenhouse
198 Bimhuis
211 Frascati Theatre
236 Dansen bij Jansen
243 Meander
252 Universiteitstheater
266 Sinners in Heaven
268 You II
273 Escape
274 Montmartre
276 De Kleine Komedie
277 De Steeg
280 Tuschinskitheater
286 Exit
288 Soho
292 April
298 Havana
305 Odeon
318 La Tertulia
322 De Trut
325 De Koe
341 Canecão
342 Bamboo Bar
348 Theater Bellevue
349 Bellevue/Calypso Cinema
350 Melkweg
351 Stadsschouwburg
352 Boom Chicago
354 Cinecenter
357 The Bulldog
359 De Uitkijk
361 De Spijker
367 Global Chillage
383 Heeren van Aemstel
391 iT
392 Soul Kitchen

MAP 4

THINGS TO SEE
16 House with the Heads
40 Seksmuseum Amsterdam
   (de Venustempel)
49 St Nicolaaskerk
50 Schreierstoren ('Wailing Tower')
61 Museum Amstelkring
62 Geels & Co
67 Oude Kerk
71 Effectenbeurs
81 Nieuwe Kerk
82 Royal Palace
85 Bartolotti House
86 White House & Theatermuseum
87 Homomonument
88 René Descartes' Residence
89 Greenpeace
90 Anne Frankhuis
91 Westerkerk Headquarters
123 Groote Keyser
158 Madame Tussaud Scenerama
161 Nationaal Monument
169 Erotic Museum
173 Waag & Cafe
180 Tattoo Museum
181 Hash & Marihuana Museum
191 Oostindisch Huis
193 Trippenhuis
196 Zuiderkerk
201 Mozes en Aäronkerk
203 Museum Het Rembrandthuis
205 Pintohuis
206 Pentagon Housing Estate
208 Huis aan de Drie Grachten
   (House on the Three Canals)
209 Universiteitsmuseum De
   Agnietenkapel
215 Allard Pierson Museum
217 Miracle Column
218 Amsterdams Historisch Museum
219 Civic Guard Gallery
231 Lutheran Church
234 University Library
237 Maagdenhuis
247 Rasphuis Gateway
262 Former Leeuwenburg Sewing-
   Machine Factory
283 Munttoren
285 Kattenkabinet
290 Bloemenmarkt (Flower Market)
307 Krÿtberg
309 Bijbels Museum
335 Metz
336 PC Hooft Store
340 Paleis van Justitie
370 Milk Factory
371 Keizersgrachtkerk
378 Goethe Institut
379 ABN-AMRO Bank Building
380 Geelvinck Hinlopen Huis
389 Museum Willet-Holthuysen
393 Amstelhof

SHOPPING
5 Exota Kids
8 Paul Andriesse Gallery
14 Architectura & Natura Bookshop
15 Frisian Embassy

17 Reina
21 Puccini Bomboni
24 Le Cellier
25 Rush Hour Records
28 Soul Food
41 Foto Professional
47 Kokopelli
54 African Heritage
70 Condomerie Het Gulden Vlies
74 Hema Department Store
76 Blue Note
77 Fun Fashion
78 Bijenkorf Department Store
84 Housewives on Fire
92 Josine Bokhoven
96 De Belly
98 Galleria d'Arte Rinascimento
99 Simon Lévelt
100 Kitsch Kitchen
103 Kitsch Kitchen Kids
107 XY Gallery
111 Vrouwen in Druk
117 Art Works
119 Lady Day
120 Exota
122 Analik
124 Montevideo
126 The English Bookshop
130 De Speelmuis
132 Xantippe Unlimited
133 Kunsthaar
137 Boekie Woekie
138 Wijnkoperij Otterman
140 Evenaar Literaire Reisboekhandel
141 Au Bout du Monde
148 Intermale
149 The Magic Mushroom Gallery
150 Musiques du Monde
154 De Bierkoning
155 Vrolijk
157 FAME Music
160 Amsterdam Diamond Center
178 Jacob Hooy & Co
186 Prenatal
187 De Slegte
190 Antiquariaat Kok
192 The Headshop
194 Knuffels
195 Zipper
197 De Klompenboer
207 The Book Exchange
213 Beaufort
214 3-D Hologrammen;
   Pannenkoekenhuis Upstairs
216 Hajenius
223 De Kinderboekuinkel
227 Athenaeum Bookshop &
   Newsagency
229 Pied à Terre
239 Hennes & Maritz
240 Laundry Industry
241 Arti et Amicitiae
242 Waterstone's
246 Fair Trade Shop
248 Maison de Bonneterie
249 American Book Center
250 Vroom & Dreesmann
   Department Store

267 Stoeltie Diamonds
279 Prestige Art Gallery
282 Aurora Kontakt
299 Maranón Hangmatten
300 Shoebaloo
302 Scheltema Holkema Vermeulen
311 Van Ravenstein
312 De Witte Tanden Winkel
313 De Kaaskamer
317 Bakkerij Paul Année
319 Antiques Market de Looier
324 Demmenie
330 The Frozen Fountain
337 Eichholtz
338 Cora Kemperman
339 Heinen
362 Australian Homemade
363 Art Unlimited
369 Lambiek
372 Gallery Nine
373 Conscious Dreams
375 Lieve Hemel
377 Decorativa

OTHER
18 Deco
32 Bureau voor Rechtshulp
39 Thomas Cook
44 Warmoesstraat Police Station
46 Happy Inn Laundry
72 Holland Rent-a-Bike
73 American Express
83 Albert Heijn Supermarket
93 Bike City
104 Moped Rental Service
105 MacBike
116 Main Post Office; NBBS
121 Gilde Amsterdam
159 Eurolines
162 Thomas Cook
165 Damstraat Rent-a-Bike
183 Wasserette Van den Broek
185 Budget Air
188 Flemish Cultural Centre (De
   Brakke Grond)
199 Albert Heijn Supermarket
200 MacBike
202 Holland Experience
204 Lock-Keeper's House
232 Kilroy Travel
233 The Mini Office
256 Municipal Medical & Health
   Services (GG & GD)
263 City Hall Information Centre
264 Post Office
284 VSB Bank
303 Albert Heijn Supermarket
320 Police Headquarters
321 Amber Reisbureau
326 Thermos Day Sauna
329 Centrale Bibliotheek (Main Public
   Library)
343 Police Station
358 VVV office
360 Mandate
364 The Clean Brothers
366 Thermos Night Sauna
368 Norwegian Consulate
390 Italian Consulate

MAP 5

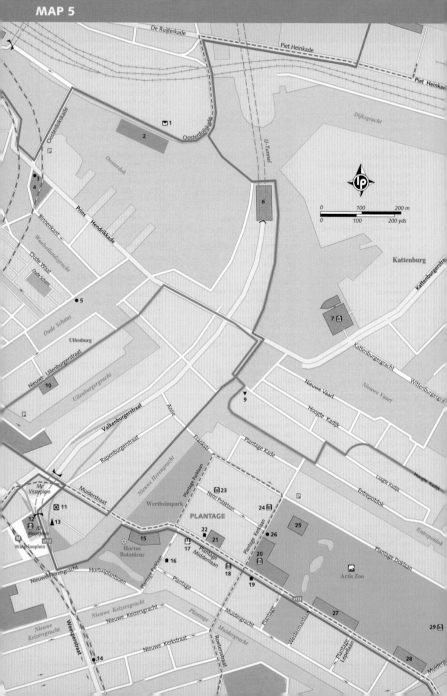

MAP 5

KNSM Eiland

't Heinkade

IJ Haven

Veemkade

Oostelijke Handelskade

PLACES TO STAY
2 Amstel Botel
16 Hotel Pension Hortus
19 Hotel Pension Kitty
22 Hotel Rembrandt

PLACES TO EAT
9 Koffiehuis van
 den Volksbond
33 Gare de l'Est

THINGS TO SEE
4 Scheepvaarthuis
5 Montelbaanstoren
6 newMetropolis Science
 & Technology Center

7 Scheepvaartmuseum
 (Shipping Museum)
8 Oosterkerk
11 Portuguese-Israelite Synagogue
12 Joods Historisch Museum
13 Dockworker Statue
18 Hollandsche Schouwburg
20 Artis Geological Museum
21 Moederhuis
23 Nationaal Vakbondsmuseum
24 Verzetsmuseum
 (Resistance Museum)
25 Planetarium
26 Entrance to Artis Zoo
27 Artis Library
28 Artis Aquarium

29 Artis Zoological Museum
30 Museumwerf 't Kromhout
31 Oranje-Nassau Kazerne
32 De Gooyer Windmill
 & Bierbrouwery 't IJ

OTHER
1 District Post Office
3 GVB Head Office Entrance
10 Gassan Diamond Factory
14 Foreign Investment Office
15 Association for Nature &
 Environmental Education;
 Nature & Environmental
 Education Centre
17 Desmet Cinema

Rietlandpark

Piet Heinkade

Piet Heintunnel

Kattenburg

Kattenburgervaart

EASTERN ISLANDS

Wittenburg

Wittenburgervaart

Oostenburg

Oostenburgervaart

Grote Wittenburgerstraat

Wittenburger

Oostenburger

Nieuwe Vaart

Czaar Pieterstr.

Panamalaan

33 ▼

Cruquiusweg

Cruquiusweg

30

Cruquiuskade

Entrepotdok

Zeeburgerstraat

Zeeburgerpad

32 ☒

Zeeburgerdijk

Singelgracht

31

Sarphatistraat

Alexanderkade

Zeeburgerdijk

Mauritskade

Dapperstraat

Pontanusstraat

Borneostraat

Celebesstraat

Artis Zoo

...dergracht

Dapperbuurt

MAP 6

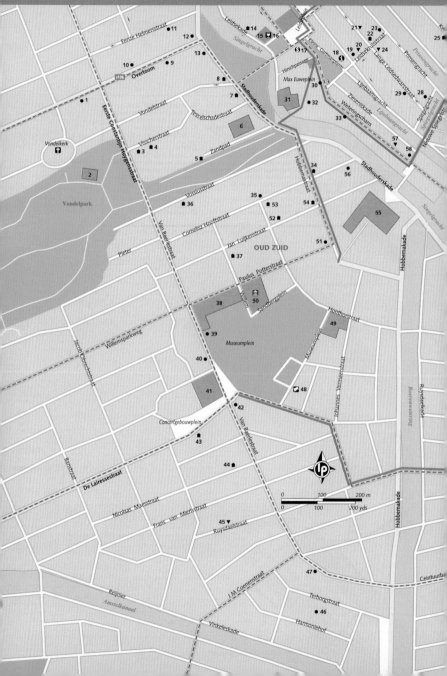

Leidsekade

Singelgracht

Eerste Helmersstraat 11

12

Leidsekade 14
15 16

Kleine Gartmanplants

21 23
22
19 20
18 Lange Leidsedwarsstraat 24
Leidsekruisstraat

Prinsengracht

25

13

10 9

Overtoom

8

Hirschpassage

17

Max Euweplein

30

Lijnbaansgracht

Eerste Constantijn Huygensstraat

1

Vondelstraat

Tesselschadestraat

7

Stadhouderskade

31

32

Ziezeniskade

Lijnbaansgracht

Weteringschans

33

57

29

28

Spiegelgracht

Nieuwe Spiegelstraat

58

Vondelkerk

Visscherstraat

6

3 4

Zandpad

5

34

56

Stadhouderskade

Singelgracht

2

Vondelpark

Vossiusstraat

36

35

53

54

55

Hobbemastraat

52

Van Baerlestraat

Cornelis Hooftstraat

Jan Luijkenstraat

51

OUD ZUID

Pieter

37

Paulus Potterstraat

38

Willem

50

Sandbergplein

Honthorststraat

49

Hobbemakade

Jacob Obrechtstraat

Willemsparkweg

39

Museumplein

40

Museumplein

Johannes Vermeerstraat

Ruysdaelkade

41

Van Baerlestraat

42

48

Concertgebouwplein

43

Banstraat

De Lairessestraat

44

0   100   200 m
0   100   200 yds

Nicolaas Maesstraat

Frans van Mierisstraat

45

Ruysdaelstraat

47

Ceintuurba

Reijnier

Amstelkanaal

J M Coenenstraat

Terborgstraat

46

Harmoniehof

Vinkeleskade

MAP 6

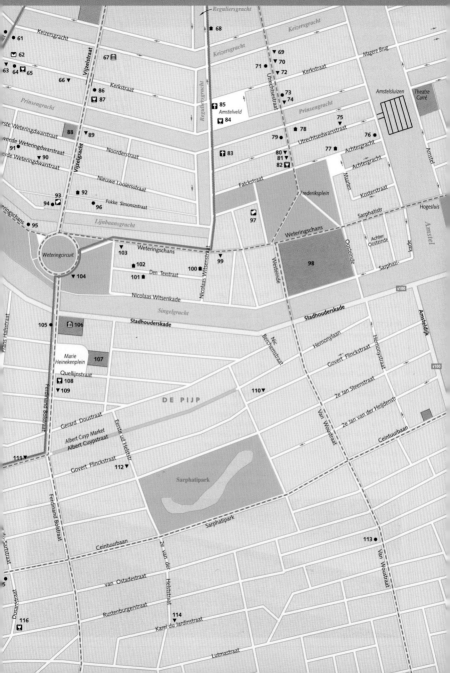

MAP 6

ELLIOT DANIEL

Deities, dildos and dope – you can get it all in Amsterdam

ELLIOT DANIEL

ELLIOT DANIEL

ANTHONY PIDGEON

MAP 7

MAP LEGEND

BOUNDARIES

International	————
State	– – –
Disputed	– – –
Fortified Wall	▪▪▪▪▪

REGIONAL ROUTES

Tollway, Freeway	════
Primary Road	————
Secondary Road	– – –
Minor Road	————

CITY ROUTES

Freeway		Unsealed Road	
Highway	Primary Road	One Way Street	
Road	Secondary Road	Pedestrian Street	
Street	Street	Stepped Street	
Lane	Lane	Tunnel	
On/Off Ramp		Footbridge	

TRANSPORT ROUTES & STATIONS

Train	—○—
Underground Train	—+—+—
Metro	—Ⓜ—
Tramway	—●—●—
Cable Car, Chairlift	⊢⊢⊢⊢
Ferry	– – ⛴ – –
Walking Trail	– – –
Walking Tour	~~~
Path	~~~
Pier or Jetty	▬▬▬

HYDROGRAPHY

River, Creek	
Canal	
Spring, Rapids	
Waterfalls	
Lake	
Dry Lake; Salt Lake	

AREA FEATURES

Building		Park, Gardens	
Market		Sports Ground	
Beach		Cemetery	
Campus			Plaza

POPULATION SYMBOLS

CAPITAL	National Capital	◎ CAPITAL	State Capital	● City	CITY
● Town	Town	● Village	Village		Urban Area

MAP SYMBOLS

■ Place to Stay		▼ Place to Eat	● Point of Interest

✈ Airport	⊕ Bank	⊕ Bus Terminal	⊕ Caravan Park	☼ Cave	✠ Church
🎬 Cinema	▣ Cycling	▣ Embassy	▣ Golf Course	✚ Hospital	⊡ Lookout
📖 Museum	🏞 National Park	P Parking	▣ Police Station	📮 Post Office	▣ Pub or Bar
⬥ Monument	☪ Mosque	▣ Shopping Centre	🛈 Tourist Information	▲ Temple	☎ Telephone
⊕ Synagogue	🏊 Swimming Pool	⬥ Winery	🦓 Zoo		

Note: not all symbols displayed above appear in this book

LONELY PLANET OFFICES

Australia
PO Box 617, Hawthorn, Victoria 3122
☎ 03 9819 1877 fax 03 9819 6459
email: talk2us@lonelyplanet.com.au

USA
150 Linden St, Oakland, CA 94607
☎ 510 893 8555 TOLL FREE: 800 275 8555
fax 510 893 8572
email: info@lonelyplanet.com

UK
10a Spring Place, London NW5 3BH
☎ 020 7428 4800 fax 020 7428 4828
email: go@lonelyplanet.co.uk

France
1 rue du Dahomey, 75011 Paris
☎ 01 55 25 33 00 fax 01 55 25 33 01
email: bip@lonelyplanet.fr
www.lonelyplanet.fr

World Wide Web: www.lonelyplanet.com or AOL keyword: lp

MAP 7

WATERGRAAFSMEER

Stadskwekerij
Frankendael

1 Theater Carré
2 Amstel Inter-Continental Hotel &
  La Rive Restaurant
3 NJHC (Youth Hostel Head Office)
4 Stadsboekwinkel
5 Liliane's Home
6 Kriterion Cinema
7 Hotel Arena
8 Muiderpoort
9 Tropenmuseum Theatre &
  Soeterijn Café-Restaurant
10 Onze Lieve Vrouwe Gasthuis
11 Muziekcentrum De IJsbreker
12 Café De IJsbreker
13 Kabouterhuis
14 Gemeentearchief
15 D-Reizen

15

Muiderpoort
Station

DAPPERBUURT

Dapperbuurt

Oosterpark